The Transition of the Patent System

This book investigates the institutionalized process, basic laws, and evolutionary trends of the patent system based on the analytical model of evolutionary theory and deploying a historical and comparative approach.

Unlike traditional scholarship that focuses solely on the analysis of legal texts, this book considers the patent system to be both a historical product and an evolving institution that requires a synchronic study of its institutionalization. The author traces the emergence and evolution of the patent system by examining the concept and derivative systems during the pre-industrial age, the medieval period, and the industrial age respectively, as well as the challenges it faces nowadays. By exploring the influencing factors and roles of technology, economy, culture, and power that have determined and shaped the patent system throughout history, the book provides insights into the impetus, principles, and mechanisms of its formation and evolution, shedding light on its future and advancement.

This title will greatly benefit students, researchers, legal professionals, and policymakers interested in intellectual property law and policy, particularly the patent system.

Yuan Feng is an associate professor at the East China University of Political Science and Law and a researcher at Renmin University of China. His research focuses on intellectual property law and communication law.

The Transition of the Patent System

Yuan Feng

Routledge
Taylor & Francis Group
LONDON AND NEW YORK

This book is funded by China Classics International.

First published in English 2025
by Routledge
4 Park Square, Milton Park, Abingdon, Oxon OX14 4RN

and by Routledge
605 Third Avenue, New York, NY 10158

Routledge is an imprint of the Taylor & Francis Group, an informa business

English Version by permission of China Renmin University Press.
Please note: some English-language quoted materials have been cited in their Chinese translations. In such cases, every effort has been made to quote the original English.

British Library Cataloguing-in-Publication Data
A catalogue record for this book is available from the British Library

Library of Congress Cataloging-in-Publication Data
Names: Yuan, Feng, 1990– author.
Title: The transition of the patent system / Yuan Feng.
Description: Abingdon, Oxon [UK] ; New York, NY : Routledge, 2023. |
Includes bibliographical references and index.
Identifiers: LCCN 2023027419 (print) | LCCN 2023027420 (ebook) |
ISBN 9781032605289 (hardback) | ISBN 9781032612034 (paperback) |
ISBN 9781003462453 (ebook)
Subjects: LCSH: Patent laws and legislation. |
Patent laws and legislation–History. | Intellectual property.
Classification: LCC K1505 .Y83 2023 (print) | LCC K1505 (ebook) |
DDC 346.04/86–dc23/eng/20230612
LC record available at https://lccn.loc.gov/2023027419
LC ebook record available at https://lccn.loc.gov/2023027420

ISBN: 978-1-032-60528-9 (hbk)
ISBN: 978-1-032-61203-4 (pbk)
ISBN: 978-1-003-46245-3 (ebk)

DOI: 10.4324/9781003462453

Typeset in Times New Roman
by Newgen Publishing UK

To Lin Dejin, my beloved great-grandmother

Contents

Introduction 1

1 Analysis of basic theories: Theoretical framework of the transition of the patent system 15

2 Pre-industrial age: Emergence and development of the patent privilege system 37

3 Industrial age: Formation and development of the private right system of patents 107

4 Post-industrial age: Internationalization and alienation of the private right system of patents 164

5 Technological age: Resurrection or decline of the private right system of patents 206

References *245*
Index *260*

Introduction

Background and significance of the research

The Intellectual Property Rights (IPR) institutions, including the patent system, are considered a product of reason and logic; therefore, research on IPR institutions often derives from the static meaning of legal texts based on logical deductions. A rational structure of institutions is the foundation of logical analysis and deductive reasoning and the shrine for ideal institutional systems. However, the institutional transition is not a spontaneous, idyllic evolution that fits a step-by-step logic; instead, it is a mixture of complexities, occasionality, and possibilities, consisting of stories within and beyond expectation. Many times, "realistic" research of history speaks louder than purely logical analysis and deductive reasoning. The value of historical research lies in demonstrating that the laws of IPR institutions today are not simply a matter of course, and their birth and development are complicated and full of alternatives. Therefore, an insight into this fact will improve the ability of critical, flexible, and innovative thinking.[1]

> The felt necessities of the time, the prevalent moral and political theories, intuitions of public policy, avowed or unconscious, even the prejudices which judges share with their fellow-men, have had a good deal more to do than the syllogism in determining the rules by which men should be governed. The law embodies the story of a nation's development through many centuries, and it cannot be dealt with as if it contained only the axioms and corollaries of a book of mathematics. 1

The logic of law is not equal to the law of logic; the law is a science of experience, which is not inborn but the collective result of various empirical factors.[2] In fact, as said by William Arnold in 1861, "History is the source of law; law is the source of history."[3] The famous Chief Justice of the United States Supreme Court, Oliver Wendell Holmes, Jr., once proposed an insightful interpretation: "A page of history is worth a volume of logic."[4] Based on similar opinions, this book believes that the patent system is a historical concept; it needs a story and a choice of post hoc interpretations. This book chooses a narrative or diachronic interpretation

DOI: 10.4324/9781003462453-1

method to study the patent system. "Incorporating institutions into history allows us to tell a much better story than we otherwise could."[5] The details are listed as follows.

First, the patent system is studied in this book as a historical and present existence. This book tries to explore the formation and development of the patent system from a historical perspective to improve the critique and knowledge of the system, principles, and laws of patents, which is especially of practical significance considering the absence of serious historical thinking in the patent system. The reasons are listed as follows.

1. As a new legal institution, the contemporary patent system is faced with unprecedented challenges and questions. As David Kairys and Susan K. Sell said, patent law before the twentieth century was a mysterious field that was far away from the center of legal research and only attracted attention from technical experts;[6] in the Post-industrial Era, IPR laws and policies, including the patent system, were suddenly viewed as closely related to free trade, the economic growth of a country, and international competition, stepping into the very frontier of legal research worldwide. The IPR laws became the focus of controversies all over the world. The national and international IPR's scope of protection was expanded, and a trend of alienation emerged. This trend was best evidenced by the irrational expansion of the private rights of patents, the intensification of the "patent privatization" phenomenon whereby patents are used by enterprises as a competition strategy, the internationalization of the private rights of patents, the developed countries' discourse power in the construction of the patent system, and the global "anti-patent movements."[7] Facing challenges and questions posed by the patent system, more and more people are questioning: what is the essence of the patent system? What is the origin of the transition of the patent system? What is the fundamental problem with the system, and what is its very motivation? Is the existence of the system still essential? Therefore, understanding the patent system anew from a historical perspective will be helpful to restore the truth and essence of the patent system and to reflect on and question its existence.
2. In terms of various questions and phenomena regarding the current patent system, scholars' explorations are often restricted to the transition of the patent system itself. Although they can provide miscellaneous explanations for the questions, historical factors are always neglected. In fact, it is barely possible, either logically or rationally, to provide a yes-or-no answer to these questions or even to obtain a reasonable explanation. The patent system is confronted with new challenges and questions like the right range of the patent system, the standard for balancing public interest, as well as the rapid change of technology (e.g., the Diamond v. Charabarty case (1980) and the Myriad case (2013) in the U.S.). In addition, legal concepts and principles about the patent system have been rewritten in history, and their original meaning has become lost, which makes some questions difficult to be logically reasonable. The patent system is not always the product of reason, because its evolution is full of contingencies

and gaming of interest. If the purport of the patent system is approached only by reading legal texts, it will be vulnerable to textualist thinking that is so narrow and restricted. This limits the thinking to the essence of patents, which explains why so many questions about the patent system remain unsettled to date. Therefore, in the modern research on the patent system, values are emptied, identification is hindered, and the only solution to many of its questions is to look to the past. Historical research possesses the most natural and direct power to explain; conclusions and judgments can be found in the facts of history. To the patent system, history means past facts and the beginning of a correct explanation of the present.[8]

3. From the historical perspective, the essence and evolutionary patterns of the patent system are explored by drawing conclusions from various historical details. Then, the veins of future development will be predicted and perceived, because "the more the past is neglected, the more control it is able to wield over the future."[9] North also told us that the importance of history lies in the fact that we can obtain benefits and learn lessons from the past and that the future and the present are connected to the past via the continuity of social institutions.[10]

Second, although the methods of historical research on the patent system could be multiple, there are many problems in the studies of previous scholars. On the one hand, there is no lack of different opinions in the historical studies of IPR institutions; however, the answers and explanations available are far from satisfactory. One of the most important reasons is their failure to provide a theoretical framework that can explain. An analytical framework and a scientific method are of great necessity to the long-term historical research. Otherwise, any historical research on IPR institutions will become nothing more than an accumulation of materials and will be unable to achieve its predominant purpose. In terms of historical research methods, Hu Shi concluded. First, "scientific methods" do exist in historical research. When it comes to the details, he concluded that the so-called scientific method is actually quite simple, for example, with respect to facts and proofs. In applications, it is merely bold assumptions and cautious confirmation.[11] "Bold assumptions" refer to the courage to suspect the clues and theories of historical transitions, because to suspect is the first step to think. "Cautious confirmation" refers to the confirmation of theories based on careful examination of materials.[12] Second, he proposed a set of research paradigms for the study of philosophical history, which is the specific interpretation of the scientific method he proposed, and it's suitable for historical research in various disciplines. In detail, this research paradigm contains three steps. The first step is to clarify changes and describe clues. The former refers to exploring the truth about the philosophical ideologists' behavioral styles, the origin of thoughts and doctrines, and identifying the clues regarding their transition and inheritance based on historical materials and facts. The latter refers to describing these clues with the right approaches, scientific methods, and precise thoughts by examining and sorting materials. The second step is to probe into the reasons, for example, to find out the reasons for the changes and inheritance of thoughts when the difference between temperament, times and situations, and the influence of thoughts and theories is taken into consideration. The third step is to judge. It is not a subjective judgment from the personal perspective of philosophical historians but the demonstration of "objective" values presented in every doctrine.[13]

On the other hand, current studies in China either take the form of an arrangement and research, which are restricted to the internal history of the patent system or merely focus on the static description of various historical facts. The problems with these studies include the lack of general and dynamic research or the confinement to the introduction of the historical background against which national and international patent systems were created. The analysis is not penetrating in that the fundamental reasons behind the evolution of the patent system are not sufficiently understood and examined, and the historical dimension is not thoroughly exploited. In fact, the mere discussion about the patent system itself will only lead the historical research to an impasse.[14] According to the theories of Marxist historical materialism, the development of laws is closely related to the development of social lives, such as the economic condition, social culture, and political relations.[15] Bodenheimer also told us, "Our historical experience has taught us that it is impossible to explain the institution of law in terms of any one single, absolute factor or cause. A number of social, economic, psychological, historical, and cultural components as well as a number of value judgments influence and condition the making and administration of the law."[16]

To sum up, this book believes the historical research of the patent system should concentrate on two points. First, a scientific and reasonable perspective or clue is necessary when we assess, describe, and learn from the institutional history. Second, one should focus on the transition of legal texts and pay attention to the macroscopic historical background of institutional formation and the social condition and motivational analysis of institutional transitions, which includes factors like technology, economy, culture, and authority. Therefore, this book uses a model of institutional transition from the fields of economy and sociology, conducting systematical and general research on the patterns in the historical evolution of the patent system from this perspective. On the one hand, the model of institutional evolution reveals its fundamental mechanisms, with a stronger explanatory power and wide-ranging feasibility. The theory of institutional evolution adopts a nondeterministic, nonlinear evolutionary thought, and its research focus lies not in the static existence but in the dynamic generation. The theory suggests drawing on the knowledge from biology and other natural and social sciences and uses metaphors to understand and handle dynamic, complicated socioeconomic systems. In line with the theory of institutional evolution, socioeconomic evolution is considered a Darwin process similar to biological evolution, which is increasingly preferred due to the emphasis on the features of the evolutionary process, such as complexity, contingency, and historical importance. The theory is suitable for the revolutionary progress of natural science and the development history of modern philosophy. What is more important is its strong power to integrate theories and explain reality. On the other hand, the model of evolutionary theory contains four factors, including technology, economy, culture, and authority, and provides a clue that is able to discover, sort, and analyze the evolutionary motivations and patterns in the patent system in the historical background. Therefore, this book explains the historical evolution of the patent system from the perspective of evolutionary theory and analyzes how the changes in technology, economy, culture, and power progressively promote the evolution of the patent system. It is based on economic and sociological theories and is able to fundamentally explain the evolutionary motivation of the patent system, bearing a strong power to explain.

Review of the literature

In current studies of the legal history of IPR, systematic research on the history of the patent system is the weak link. The weaknesses of the current literature are listed as follows. First, the emergence, construction, reformation, improvement, and internationalization of the patent system would be impossible without the joint efforts of different countries and regions (e.g., Venice, France, Germany, the United Kingdom, and the United States) in different historical periods. Therefore, it is necessary to conduct comparative studies with priority given to a particular field when the situations in different eras and regions are taken into full consideration. However, the current literature on patent history is fragmental and regional, and there are no systematic and holistic studies, not to mention the clarification of the patterns about the evolutionary motivation of the patent system. For example, Xu Haiyan's *A Study of China's Modern Patent System* (1859–1949)[17] is restricted to the history of the patent system between 1859 and 1949 in China. Zou Lin's *A Study of the Development of the British Patent System,*[18] Zong Hua's *The Battle for Patent Abolition in England in the 19th Century,*[19] Yang Lihua's *Studies on the History of Patent Law in the United States,*[20] Sun Xuhua's *The Historical Development of the U.S. Patent System,*[21] as well as Chen Hefang's *The History and Inspiration of the U.S. Patent System*[22] all focus on dynastic history of a country's patent system. Current studies excessively highlight studies on the British and American legal systems and ignore studies of the patent history in civil law countries. The prejudice on research horizons becomes the barrier to revealing the evolutionary patterns in the patent system using comprehensive comparison and analysis.

Second, current studies on patent history are insufficient when it comes to the history of patent privileges. Most scholars are familiar with and keen on studies about the *Statute of Monopolies* (1624) in England and tend to see the franchise rights in the fourteenth century in England as the origin of the patent system, even to consider the Statute as a unique origin of current patent laws.[23] There are few studies on the motivation and contents of the patent privilege institutions in Venice,[24] the very state where the modern patent system originated. In some Chinese literature, such as Zhang Xinfeng's *The Property Right Attributes of Patent Rights: A Study on the Path of Privatization of Technology,*[25] and Huang Haifeng's *The Discourse and Reality of Intellectual Property Rights: A Treatise on the History of Copyright, Patents, and Trademarks,*[26] the history of the patent privilege institution in Venice is merely mentioned, without detailed research. In addition, the patent privilege systems in France and Germany, although earlier than that in England, have not drawn enough attention from scholars. In foreign studies, Frank D. Prager's *A History of Intellectual Property from 1545 to 1787,*[27] Guilio Mandich's *Venetian Patents,*[28] and Maximilian Frumkin's *The Origin of Patents*[29] are all fragmental research on the legal texts and practice of patent privileges in Venice, France, and the United Kingdom. The studies of the internal evolutionary mechanisms of the patent privilege system are especially inadequate.

Third, most literature is merely research on the internal history of the patent system, and there is no research on the external history and macroscopic background (e.g., technology, economy, and culture). For example, Huang Haifeng's *The Discourse and Reality of Intellectual Property Rights: A Treatise on the History of Copyright, Patents, and Trademarks* provides historical details about the evolution of the IPR institutions; however, this research only examines and reconstructs the internal history of IPRs, and the external history is unattended. Similar problems can be found in national and international research. As Professor Oren Bracha said, other historians would be most interested in broadening the scope of the inquiry to issues of context and causation. From this perspective, the story of institutional transformation detailed previously would be put in its social context. Patents did not change from privileges into rights in a vacuum or through a purely "internal" process independent of other ideological, economic, political, and technological changes. However, such a contextual story does not necessarily have to be either a functionalist or a determinist one. The legal–institutional aspect upon which I have concentrated here should not be reduced to a mere "reflection" or to the "function" of other "real" social factors. In fact, the institutional story provided here gives reasons to assume neither that developments in the legal realm were always just reactive nor that the borderline between legal and other (e.g., ideological) factors can always be easily detected. A good contextual story would describe a complex web of causation in which all factors, including the legal–institutional ones, were active and reactive.[30]

Fourth, historical research on the patent system is conducted in the absence of a reasonable method or a formulating perspective. As a result, historical research on IPR institutions has become an effort to accumulate materials, and it can't show its academic significance. For instance, Li Zonghui has realized the importance of combining external and internal histories when studying IPR institutions. In his study, *The Intellectual Property from Historical Perspective*, he proposed that in the history of hundreds of years, the external and internal factors influencing the formation and development of the IPR institutions are so multidimensional that any discussion on a single aspect will be untenable. We must apply macro and microscopic analysis methods to history, based on materials of different qualities, quantities, directions, and levels, to reveal the positioning and features of the IPR institutions in the historical background in terms of historical periodization and thinking dimensions.[31]

This book tries to combine the internal history of IPR institutions and economic, technological, political, and cultural backgrounds to probe into the evolution of copyrights, patents, and trademarks. However, given the lack of a clear historical clue or model, this book shows an absence of organization in the discussion. It fails to precisely identify the evolutionary motivations behind the IPR institutions. Furthermore, in Professor Christopher and Professor Susan's study, *Intellectual Property Rights: A Critical History*, they try to use systematic theories of technology, culture, and (politics) to describe the entire history of IPR institutions, including the patent system; however, the systematic theories were only seen as a starting point in their research. It lacks both a theoretical explanation and a unified perspective and method to describe the history of IPR institutions. Most parts of this book are still the description of the practice and legal institutions of patents, which is totally disorganized and unconsolidated due to the excessively large range of history.[32]

In current literature, the perspective of evolutionary theories has not been used in the description of the historical evolution of the patent system. In the field of copyrights, Professor Paul David was the first to use the evolutionary theory in his research on the history of the copyright system. He studied the printing and publishing industries in the last five centuries. He believed that the development of technology, economy, and culture has led to a change in the concepts of copyright institutions. The gaming of interests is the main force shaping the institutions of copyright and printing and publishing industries, which gradually extend to fields like replication, audiovisual, and music in the era of the internet.[33] Nonetheless, the evolutionary theory model used in this study is too simple to give a convincing explanation, and the discussion on external histories like technology, economy, and culture is not adequate, nor is the combination of internal and external histories.

Research subjects and methods

Research subjects

In this book, the patent system is considered to be a historical and present existence. This book describes how the development of technology, economy, culture, and power promotes the evolution of the patent system in a historical background, based on the institutional evolution framework constructed in this book. The patent system mentioned in this book includes the patent privilege system, the patent private system, and related international conventions. The research subjects and scope cover the technological, economic, and cultural development history of countries like Venice, the United Kingdom, France, Germany, and the United States in the Pre-industrial Era, industrial eras, and Post-industrial Era, as well as texts, cases, and doctrines in the previous countries In addition, the research subjects of this book are all typical examples in a historical sense. Venice is where the patent privilege system first appeared, while France, Germany, and the United Kingdom inherited most of the regulations in the Venetian system. Although the patent system and rules in the United Kingdom have had a great influence on the construction of institutions in other countries, the private right of patents of the continental law system first appeared in France, and the private right of patents of the Anglo–American law system was first introduced in the United States. The TRIPS Agreement established the first binding mechanism of global IPR protection, which unifies the standards of IPR protection all over the world.

Research methods

Given the research subject and properties of this book, the research methods are listed as follows.

Model analysis method

This book uses a model of institutional evolution in sociology and economy and defines the theoretical framework for the study of the evolution of the patent system. In brief, the analytic framework of institutional evolution is: heterogeneous actors with self-interest motives generate new institutional concepts (mutation mechanisms) under the influence of material activities (technology, economy, and culture) → actors with various institutional concepts take the bargaining advantage (including economic and political strength as well as concept attraction) to compete for the power of institutional arrangements (the artificial selection mechanism) → winners in the battle of institutional power construct the institution, legislating, stabilizing, and replicating (replication mechanism) concepts that reflect their preferences.

Investigation of history and historical materials

This book is a research endeavor with a historical theme. It tends to combine the technical, economic, cultural, and political backgrounds and changes in the aspect of the internal history of the patent system. It conducts historical investigations of the interactions in all stages between technological, economic, cultural, and political changes on the one hand and the patent system on the other hand. To integrate investigations of technical changes into the evolutionary motivations of the patent system, studies on the history of technology and its developments are a must. That requires the emphasis on the investigations of historical materials (e.g., books, texts, and cases) at that time and applications of historical investigation methods. The methods used in this book include scenario analysis, text research, and the analysis of critical events. Scenario analysis refers to investigations of the given social environment, where given events happened, and the analysis of influences from various factors. The text research concentrates on expressions and figures in given texts and their influences on social practice. The analysis of critical events shows that this book doesn't attempt to make general descriptions of all events or figures during the evolution of the patent system. Instead, it devotes itself to revealing the behavioral methods and thinking logic motivating revolutions via observing critical historical events or figures and analyzing and commenting on social powers that have fostered the generation and development of the patent system in the previous centuries.

Comparative research

The comparative method used in this book contains a vertical comparison of one historical event or phenomenon in different eras and a horizontal comparison in different spaces; both highly generalized macroscopic comparisons of historical events and specific microscopic comparisons of certain events and phenomena based on given historical periods. Using comparative studies on technical, economic, and cultural events in different civilizations and countries in the Middle Ages, this book determines why the patent system failed to appear in the Middle Ages. In the pre-industrial age, the evolutionary motivations and patterns in the patent privilege system are explored using comparative research on historical facts like technology, economy, and the culture of Venice, France, Germany, and the United Kingdom, as well as the contents of their patent privilege system. In the industrial age, the evolutionary motivations and patterns of the private rights system of patents are revealed by the comparative research on historical facts of France, the United States, and Western European countries, as well as the content of their systems.

Structure and innovations

The patent system is a historical concept. This book uses the model of evolutionary theory to study the historical process, basic patterns, and mainstream trends in the transition of the patent system. This book tries to look beyond the patent system by delineating how changes in technical, economic, cultural, and authority factors promote the evolution of the patent system. Discovering the original appearance and essence of the patent system from historical details is helpful for reflecting on and questioning the existing value of the patent system, clarifying the motivation for the alienation of the patent system, and foreseeing the development themes of the patent system in the future.

The brief contents of the chapters in this book are listed below.

Chapter 1: "Analysis of basic theories: Theoretical framework of the transition of the patent system." After pinpointing that the transition process in the patent system among complicated historical clues would not be clarified without a scientific method and a theoretical framework, this chapter uses a model of institutional evolution based on the transition or evolution theories of sociology and economics and defines the main research framework and research clues in this book.

Chapter 2: "Pre-industrial Age: Origin and development of the patent privilege system." This chapter starts with an investigation of the social and historical situation of some civilizations in the Middle Ages. It concludes that the most fundamental reason why patent systems failed to develop in these civilizations is the lack of concepts like economic values and the applications of technologies, which are closely associated with the technical, economic, and cultural environment of civilizations. At the end of the Middle Ages, with the help of technical, economic, and cultural traditions in the guilds of Venice, institutional concepts of technical values and economic applications were germinated, and regulations that members of the guilds enjoy the benefits of the technology were also gradually formed. At the same time, the government of Venice paid increasing attention to the development of industry and commerce, taking all measures to foster the development of technology, industry, and commerce. The eventual compromise between the guild and the government led to the formation of the *Patent Privilege Law 1474* in Venice. However, the construction of the patent privilege system was still dominated by the Venetian government. With the development of technology, economy, and culture, conditions to construct the patent system were also fulfilled in France, Germany, and the United Kingdom, and the most critical motivation to introduce the patent privilege system in Venice was the mercantilism policies pursued by these governments. France, Germany, and the United Kingdom inherited most of the regulations from Venice. In the process of institutional transition and evolution, development paths are different, and the continuous gaming between private departments and the government exists in all these countries.

Chapter 3: "Industrial age: Formation and development of the private right system of patents." After defining the distinction between the standard of patent privileges and private rights paradigms, this chapter studies the history of France and the United States, investigating the evolutionary motivations of the private rights system of patents. In France, the development of handicrafts in the eighteenth century sowed the seed of industrial capitalism, and the concepts of technological monopoly appeared in emerging industrial capitalists. After the French Revolution, the patent privilege system was abolished. Claude and Bouveret, two representatives of industrial capitalists, tried to lobby and used the theories of Locke and Diderot to associate patents with natural rights and human rights, so the *Patent Private Right Act of 1790* was passed in France. In the United States, where the peasant economy was dominant and industrial technology, and the industrial economy fell behind at the beginning of its founding, Jefferson, on behalf of the interests of the peasant bourgeoisie, proposed thoughts of "an agriculture-based country" and "republicanism." He considered patents as monopolies and suggested strict restrictions on them, which exerted a profound influence on the formation of early patent systems. Each of the IPR clauses in *the U.S. Constitution*, the *Patent Act of 1790*, and the *Patent Act of 1793* was deeply affected by Jefferson. At the end of the eighteenth century, the patent system of the United States still took the form of a patent privilege pattern in which patents were granted at the discretion of governments based on standards of public interest. At the beginning of the nineteenth century, the development of industrial technology and economy strengthened the power of the industrial and commercial classes in the United States, and the ideological trends of individualism and liberalism also gradually flourished. The concept of the private rights of patents was conceived among inventors, lawyers, and emerging industrial and commercial classes and the private rights of patents were constantly claimed through patent applications and lawsuits. In addition, judges changed their mentality. These factors contributed to the formation of the patent private system, which was based on substantive examination and featured general patent entitlement standards in 1836. Finally, this chapter discusses the anti-patent campaign that broke out in Western Europe in the mid-nineteenth century and analyzes the reasons, development, and results of the campaign by reviewing technical, economic, cultural, and authority factors in that historical background.

Chapter 4: "Post-industrial Age: Internationalization and alienation of the private rights system of patents." In the Post-industrial Age, the complexity and diversity of technology helped forge a closer relationship between technology and the economy. Thanks to economic globalization, skill-intensive products are playing an important role in international trade. At the same time, neoliberal thought trends began to spring up in the Post-industrial Age, and large enterprises with the domination of economic developments have converted their concepts, interests, and proposals into policies and institutions via a variety of methods like allying and lobbying. On this occasion, the IPR institutions, including the patent system, tend to be international and even alienated. In terms of the internationalization of the patent system, this book reveals that the essence of the TRIPS Agreement is the interest product achieved by American enterprise groups via lobbying and designing skills using historical descriptions of the formation of the TRIPS Agreement. When it comes to the alienation of the patent system, this book believes the rent-seeking behaviors of these enterprises make the patent system gradually become the system that obstructs the diffusion of knowledge and new technology as well as occupying public interest. That patents become the competition strategy and tool of enterprises and that the one-size-fits-all patent system is unadopted to the development of technology industries are the most detailed expressions, and so are the irrational expansion of the private rights of patents and the explosive increase in patent applications and lawsuits.

Chapter 5: "The age of future technology: Resurrection or decline of the private rights system of patents." In the age of future technology, critical technical powers like big data, the Internet of Things, three-dimensional printing, and artificial intelligence will change the economy, culture, and authority in the future. Developments in technology will revolutionize the paradigm of technological innovations, and the sharing of economy, knowledge, and culture will be more popular. Large enterprises will decline, and middle and small-sized enterprises will rise. Therefore, nongovernment forces will be able to negotiate with governments and enterprises on equal terms and help build a far more reasonable patent privilege system. When technological innovations in future societies are no longer scarce, and the sharing economy and culture become a trend, the private rights system of patents will also lose its power. At the same time, this book explores fields like the fashion and database industries that have no room for IPR institutions at present. It demonstrates how enterprises and industries will evolve without the assurance of the patent system in the age of future technology.

This book has combined model analysis, the investigation of historical materials and history, and comparative research to study the historical process, basic patterns, and mainstream trends in the evolution of patent systems in the hope of achieving innovation as follows.

1. This book uses an institutional evolution model by seeking inspiration from the theories of institutional transition or evolution in sociology and economics.

The research on the evolutionary process of the patent system derives from this model, which assures that this book can follow a reasonable and clear historical vein.

2. The relationship between the patent system and technology, economy, culture, and authority is a "wasteland" in the theoretical research on the IPR. The patent system has usually been deemed as the product of the factors mentioned previously, and the research on their correlation is scarce. It seems as if something is in a black box: everyone knows that there is some subtle relationship between them, but no one can clearly describe the mechanism of these factors. Despite the discussions on some topics, current studies are restricted to the very surface in the absence of systematic and intensive deconstruction. Studies on the definition of their correlation and causality are especially farfetched and free from theoretical arguments. However, this book tries to investigate how changes in technical, economic, cultural, and political factors in various periods and regions promoted the evolution of the patent system.
3. This book is no longer confined to investigations of the change in the patent legal texts. The research on the patent system is conducted against a macroscopic historical background. It combines the internal and external histories (technology, culture, economy, and authority) of the patent system to make a profound analysis of the motivations behind the evolution of the patent system, which is beneficial for a better comprehension of the motivations and patterns in its evolution.
4. This book studies the patent privilege system of Venice, Germany, and France and fills the academic gap in studies of the patent system. It is the research on the patent system in the civil law system (France and Germany) that expands the perspective of comparative research to identify an institutional evolution pattern that is more universally applicable.
5. The IPR institutions have always been seen as the product of logic and reason, and this book will provide a brand-new perspective to reveal that the evolution of the patent system is full of complexity and contingency and releases the field of institutional imagination that has been long suppressed. The purpose of this book is to review past practices and search for thoughts of the historical figures that directed these events to realize the combination of horizons and comprehension of history. By reviewing past experiences, one can understand the thoughts of predecessors with sympathy and compassion.[34]
6. This book reveals varieties of alienation problems and their motivations in the current patent system. It clarifies that the changes in institutional concepts and authority subjects brought by the interactions between technology, economy, and culture are the important influencing factors of institutional evolution. These factors have provided reflections and prophecies for future development trends in the patent system. History can "accumulate heritages of predecessors and enlighten the descendants' wisdom" and amuse our imaginations, satisfy our avid or casual curiosities, test our memories, and contribute a convincible obscuration.[35]

Notes

1 Huang Haifeng. *The Discourse and Reality of Intellectual Property Rights: A History of Copyright, Patent and Trademark*. Wuhan: Huazhong University of Science and Technology Press, 2011:1.
2 Yu Jun. *The Evolution of Trademark Law*. Wuhan: Huazhong University of Science and Technology Press, 2011:15
3 James W. Thompson. *Economic and Social History of Europe in the Later Middle Ages (1300–1530)*. Translated by Xu Jialing, et al. Beijing: The Commercial Press, 1992:587.
4 *New York Trust Co. v. Eiser*, 256 U.S. 345, 349 (1921).
5 Douglass C. North. *Institutions, Institutional Change, and Economic Performance*. Translated by Hang Xing. Shanghai: Gezhi Publishing House, Shanghai Sanlian Bookstore, Shanghai People's Publishing House, 2014:156.
6 David Kairys. Eds. *The Politics of Law: A Progressive Critique*. Translated by Xin Chunying. Beijing: China University of Political Science and Law Beijing: China University of Political Science and Law Press, 2008:185; Susan K. Sell. *Private Power, Public Law: The Globalization of Intellectual Property Rights*. Translated by Dong Gang. Beijing: China People's University Press, 2008:178, 185.
7 In addition to the first Swedish Pirate Party based on original peer-to-peer (P2P) platforms, similar organizations have been constructed so far in France, Italy, Netherlands, Austria, Belgium, Germany, Poland, Norway, Spain, the United Kingdom, Russia, Peru, South Africa, the United States, Canada, Australia, and other countries. In 2006, global "pirate parties" founded the so-called "Global Association of Pirate Parties" in Europe.
8 Xiao Yudan. Copyright Cultural Transformation and Microhistorical Research Methods, *Northern Jurisprudence*, 2009 (4).
9 Brad Sherman, Lionel Bentley. *The Making of Modern Intellectual Property Law: The British Experience, 1760–1911*. Translated by Jin Haijun. Beijing: Peking University Press, 2006:2.
10 North. *Institutions, Institutional Change, and Economic Performance*, 123.
11 Hu Shi. *The Collected Works of Hu Shi*. Beijing: Peking University Press, 1998:105.
12 Hu Shi. *Collected Works of Hu Shi*, p. 519
13 Hu Shi. *Outline of the History of Chinese Philosophy*. Beijing: China Book Company, 2018:3–4.
14 Jin Haijun. *The Theory of Private Rights of Intellectual Property*. Beijing: China Renmin University Press, 2004:21.
15 Wang Weiguo. *The Principle of Fault Liability: The Third Emergence*. Beijing: China Legal Publishing House, 2000:2.
16 Edgar Bodenheimer. *Jurisprudence: The Philosophy and Method of the Law*. Translated by Deng Zhenglai. Beijing: China University of Political Science and Law Press, 1999:199.
17 Xu Haiyan. *A Study of China's Modern Patent System* (1859–1949). Beijing: Intellectual Property Press, 2010.
18 Zou Lin. *A Study of the Development of the British Patent System*. Xiangtan: Xiangtan University, 2011.
19 Zong Hua. *The Battle for Patent Abolition in England in the 19th Century*. Shanghai: East China University of Political Science and Law, 2014.
20 Yang Lihua. *Studies on the History of Patent Law in the United States*. Beijing: People's University of China Press, 2009.

21 Sun Xuhua. *The Historical Development of the U.S. Patent System*. Beijing: China University of Political Science and Law, 2007.
22 Chen Hefang. *The History and Inspiration of the U.S. Patent System*. Guangzhou: Jinan University, 2009
23 William C. Robinson. *The Law of Patents for Useful Inventions*, Vol. I. Boston, MA: Little, Brown, and Company, 1890:15.
24 Refers to the Republic of Venice in the Middle Ages.
25 Zhang Xinfeng. *The Property Right Attributes of Patent Rights – A Study on the Path of Privatization of Technology*. Wuhan: Huazhong University of Science and Technology Press, 2011.
26 Huang Haifeng. *Discourse and Reality of Intellectual Property Rights*.
27 Frank D. Prager. A History of Intellectual Property from 1545 to 1787, 26 *Journal of the Patent and Trademark Office Society*, 1944, pp. 711–758.
28 Guilio Mandich. Venetian Patents (1450–1550), 30 *Journal of the Patent and Trademark Office Society*, 1948, pp. 166–224.
29 M. Frumkin. The Origin of Patents, 27 *Journal of the Patent and Trademark Office Society*, 143, 1945, pp. 143–148.
30 Oren Bracha. *The Commodification of Patents 1600—1836: How Patents Became Rights and Why We Should Care. Loyola of Los Angeles Law Review*, 2004, pp. 240–241.
31 Li Zonghui. *The Intellectual Property System from Historical Perspective*. Beijing: Intellectual Property Press, 2015:4.
32 Christopher May, Susan K. Sell. *Intellectual Property Rights: A Critical History*. Boulder, CO: Lynne Rienner Publishers, 2006:17.
33 Paul A. David. *Techno-Institutional Co-evolution and the End of Copyright History*, available at www.epip.dk/papers/20041001/paris/slides/david-slides.pdf
34 Huang Haifeng. *Discourse and Reality of Intellectual Property Rights*, 3.
35 James Harwell Robinson. *The New History: Essays Illustrating the Modern Historical Outlook*. Translated by Qi Sihe. Beijing: People's University of China Press, 2011:9.

1 Analysis of basic theories

Theoretical framework of the transition of the patent system

The history of human society is the history of institutional recognition, selection, and evolution.[1] The evolution of institutions, which determines the way of social evolution in human history, is a complicated historical process. Its origin and motivation are the most interesting yet least explored part of economics and sociology and one of the hot topics over which the academic world has chronic debates. As Ratan said, the principle of the institutional transition always confuses economists and other sociologists interested in the history and institution of development.[2] Hu Shi believes that studying history needs bold assumptions and cautious confirmation.[3] "Bold assumptions" are made to illustrate clues and theories of the historical transition. One should dare to assume, for assuming is the first step of thinking. "Cautious confirmation" refers to the confirmation of the clue and theory based on the careful examination of historical materials.[4] So is the study of the history of complicated patent systems. A scientific and reasonable perspective is necessary to discuss and evaluate the history of the patent system and gain insights from it. Accordingly, based on theories of the transition and evolution of the relevant institutions in economics and sociology, this book uses a model of institutional evolution and, therefore, defines the basic theoretical framework for the study of the transition of the patent system.

A theoretical model of the institutional evolution

Since humans began to explore society, a specter has been haunting the social science field. Various titles are granted to this specter: the transition or evolution of institutions, rules, and regulations. Given its complexity and controversy, the transition or evolution of institutions has been one of the fundamental concerns of scholars of economics, history, politics, and sociology.[5] For instance, the three founders of sociology, Karl Marx, Max Weber, and Emile Durkheim, and the enlighteners of the old and neo-institutional school, Thorstein Bunde Veblen, John R. Commons, and Douglass C. North, were all dedicated to studying the patterns in institutional transition. This book has no intention to judge or analyze these theories but will select and use a scientific and reasonable model as a theoretical framework for discussion. This book believes a model is valueless and should

DOI: 10.4324/9781003462453-2

be abandoned once the model proves impractical. As long as its structure is well established, a model could offer scholars a template for analysis, set the theoretical basis for respective historical experiences, and fully reveal the essence of history – the unity of universality and individuality. The value of this model is the ability to enlighten rather than transmit information. Its concern is not to narrate events themselves but to teach people how to explore and understand facts better.[6]

Clarification of several basic concepts: Society, structure, and institution

Before relevant problems are analyzed, some basic concepts and consensuses must be clarified: society, structure, and institution.

First, when it comes to the concept of "society," this book adopts Giddens's definition. A society is a collection of individuals with systematical features, consisting of plural actors or participants (individuals and groups of individual members), structure (institutional system), and the physical environment. Given the dynamic dimensions of the social system, society cannot be interpreted as the simple addition of different individuals, and it possesses a structure that connects all individuals.[7] The physical environment refers to the natural world and human activities. Giddens and Bourdieu believe these environments essentially take the form of "time and space" or "places and moments."

Second is the concept of structure. Rules support society; relevant institutions form an institutional subsystem, and the entire institutional system that supports the society is the social "structure." Giddens holds that actors shape the structure, and the structure is the medium through which behavior acts, and it is also the consequence caused by behavior's repeated organization.[8] The structure is "virtual order" and exists only as "memory traces."[9] Therefore, the structure is a purely conceptualized concept, which is essentially an institutional system consisting of associated institutions that only exist in the social system of people. The institution means nothing for one person dwelling in the wild. Moreover, the structure isn't equal to the whole social system but a component that can glue individuals together.[10] Actor, structure (institutional system), and the physical environment are the building blocks of the social system. The actor is ontologically superior to the others because the actor and their activities have material input, while the structure is purely conceptualized. Considering that material forces are always ontologically superior to conceptual ones, so is an actor to the structure. However, according to systematical dynamics, structure and actor are mutually constructed. Once structure is created by the actor, it possesses its own life and shapes the actor and its activities directly or indirectly, publicly or secretly.[11] As Giddens said, structure is not to be equated with constraint but is always constraining and enabling.[12]

Third, as an essential element of structure, institution has a broad meaning in economics and sociology. This book adopts North's definition: institution is an artificial restriction on the activities and interaction of people. It constructs the motivation of the exchange in the political, social, or economic fields. It consists generally of formal (rules, laws, and constitutions) and informal constraints (behavioral regulations, conventions, and self-restricted disciplines).[13] Institution and organization are different. Organization is part of the actor and is commonly considered as the decision-making unit consisting of individuals who are bound by everyday purposes to reach specific goals, which include nations, political, economic, social, and educational groups.[14] The organization has material inputs; as a subelement of structure, the institution is the construction of concepts. Hence, organization is superior to institution and shapes it. As North said, "Institutions are the rules of the game, organizations are the players; it is the interaction between the two that shapes institutional change."[15] However, North only emphasized the institutional restriction but neglected its motivation. As Lin Yifu said, the institution itself can mitigate the uncertainty in the intercourse and interaction of people and decrease transaction costs. Hence, the institution has the function of security and economy.[16]

Finally, the institution is the epitome of social knowledge or is made of solidified concepts. Institution is essentially an epitome of concepts or regulated concepts. Concept is nothing but the product of our ideological activities. A concept can take various forms, such as beliefs, plans, perspectives, or scientific knowledge. Concepts related to institutions are the actor's concepts about the construction of institutional systems and the meaning of particular institutional arrangements.[17] Because different actors often hold different concepts, various concepts usually describe the expected form of future institutions. The essence of institutional transition is solidifying certain concepts into institutions. Therefore, institutional concepts are merely the prototype for creating a particular institution. Institution embodies concepts and can reversely shape the formation of concepts. Institution is not equivalent to concepts: only the "regulated" concepts belong to institution. In addition, that institution embodies concepts or regulated concepts doesn't mean that concepts are the cause and institutions are the consequences. That is a complicated evolutionary process, which will be discussed in detail later.

Evolution theory of institution: Background and significance

The evolution theory of institution refers to a science that applies a semantic system of biological metaphors, such as mutation, selection, and evolution and draws inspiration from the methodology of the evolution of creatures to study the patterns in economic growth and institutional transition. The generalized concept of social evolution could be traced back to ancient times and was proposed by scholars such as Alfred Marshall, Joseph Schumpeter, Karl Marx, Armen Alchian, Herbert Spencer, Carl Menger, Friedrich Hayek, Thorstein Veblen, and John Commons. In the 1980s, the theory stepped into a new stage with the emergence of Boulding, Nelson, and Winter. Then, a significantly promising research paradigm was developed, thanks to the collective effort of scholars such as Hodgson, Metcalfe, Dorsey, and Aoki Masahiko. Although the specific models they applied differed, their models all followed an analog principle of natural and socioeconomic evolution. The evolution theory of institution originated from the evolution theory of nature, especially the evolutionism of Lamarck and Darwin. Then, with the development of biology and social science, more and more scholars found the similarity between biology and other socioeconomic sciences. Therefore, the influence of evolutionism goes far beyond biology, arousing interest from anthropologists, sociologists, economists, and even politicians. The application of the concept "evolution" is expanded to the social science field, providing a theoretical perspective and analytic framework for research on the development patterns in social problems and economic phenomena. As Eisenhardt and Galunic pointed out, evolution takes the form of biological evolutions and exists in socioeconomic systems.[18] Winter also believes that the selection and evolution of nature should not be considered as concepts raised for certain purposes in biology and applied to certain economic purposes. Instead, they should be seen as the concept shared by biology, economics, and other social sciences.[19]

The evolution theory of institution has rich connotations in that the theory not only contains Darwin's principle of biological evolution but also absorbs nourishment from philosophy, physics, and economy. In terms of philosophy, it abandons the mechanical world outlook based on Newton's thoughts and applies the organic world outlook (i.e., believing that the fundamental feature of the world is an organic macrocosm that is in motion, in variation, nonlinear and nondeterministic; therefore, the holistic analysis method should be upheld). In terms of physics, it applies the thermodynamic system theory. In terms of economy, it sublates Simon's bounded rationality theory.[20] The evolution theory of institution has the following features: 1. The heterogeneity or diversity of individuals. The individuals assumed by the theory have bounded rationality and various interest preferences. 2. The mechanism of evolution. The system follows a specific evolutionary pattern; it possesses three factors similar to the three central concepts (heredity, mutation, and natural selection) in Darwin's theory of biological evolution. 3. The importance of history. The evolution theory attaches importance to two dimensions of history – process and time. Historical analysis has become an essential method in evolutionary analysis. Because the explanation of things involves the explanation of their origin and evolution, which is closely related to the peculiarity of history, the irreversibility of history explains the reason for path dependence.[21]

The evolution theory of institutions adopts a nonlinear and nondeterministic mindset of evolution, whose research focus doesn't lie in static existence but in dynamic formation. It advocates the absorption of abundant nourishment from biology and other natural and social sciences and the wide use of metaphors to comprehend and deal with dynamic, complicated socioeconomic systems. The evolution theory of institutions considered socioeconomic evolution a "Darwin process" akin to biological evolution, emphasizing the complexity, occasionality, and historical importance of the evolutionary process. Increasingly favored due to the features mentioned previously, the theory is more suitable for revolutionary developments in natural science and is in accord with the development process of modern philosophy. More importantly, it has a strong power to integrate theories and explain reality. First, since the discovery of DNA structure and the "punctuated equilibrium" proposed by Gould in 1953, scientific arguments have recognized evolutionism as scientific and enriched Darwinism, making it gradually permeate and influence the world outlook and thinking method of humans. Moreover, the development of quantum mechanics, chaos theory, and modern academic theories, including random processes, require humans to observe and understand the world from an evolutionary world outlook. Second, in modern Western philosophy, the irrational philosophy represented by Bergson begins to suspect rationality and recognize time, evolution, and creation. Western philosophy started to transform from rationalism to irrationalism. In scientific philosophy, at the same time, the historical–social school emphasized in the 1960s that science is a social-historical process instead of a logical process of rational natural development, which led to a revolution in scientific philosophy outlook.[22]

Evolution mechanism of institution

Biological evolution refers to "the survival of the fittest," in which organisms, species, adaptivity, genes, and mutations are intertwined in the mutual influence of creatures and their environments.[23] All evolutionary biological phenomena can be attributed to one of two processes: the acquisition and maintenance of adaptive characteristics or the origin and function of various characteristics of the creatures' organs. The primary mechanism to demonstrate the evolutionary process is the circulated effect of the mutation, selection, and replication mechanisms.[24] In analogy with the analytic method of Darwinism, the analytic framework of the evolution theory of the institution adopts its three fundamental biological metaphors: mutation, selection, and replication mechanisms. However, the evolution theory of institution is not a mechanical application of the evolution theory of nature. Its most significant distinction is that distinct from the passive adaptivity of creatures in biological evolution, only natural things can determine phenotypes. In institutional evolution, human intelligence determines the adaptivity of a particular institutional arrangement; for instance, the welfare effect of institutional arrangements is measured by human intelligence: the requirement for happiness and its welfare calculations determine whether a particular institutional arrangement can moderately improve welfare. As John Commons said, the artificial selection made by this happiness-seeking and self-interested behavior is the ultimate impetus and assurance of human progress. However, human progress is always long, challenging, and even bloody.

All social theories must accept some meta-facts on human society and its actors, which serve as the premise or logical starting point. The three meta-facts of the evolution theory of institution are listed as follows. First, the actors are self-interested or self-centralism; self-centralism is morally neutral due to evolution. It is also one of the most fundamental motivations of human behaviors; it is indispensable for survival. In addition, due to the bounded rationality of actors, their knowledge is always incomplete. Before a given institution is established, it's hard to determine whether that institution can improve individual and social welfare.[25] Second, given the scarcity of human force and material resources and the surplus of actors, heterogeneous actors with various preferences have to compete for resources, whose primary method is demonstrated in regulating one's rights and obligations by influencing the institutional arrangement to obtain and control existing human and material resources efficiently. As Commons said, the scarcity of resources provides a fundamental reason for the existence of institutions: the institution is almost of little use if there are sufficient resources.[26] Third, since humans evolved from apes, society and civilization have continuously advanced, which can be seen in such indices as population, average life expectancy, and gross domestic product per capita. However, human progress is full of obstacles and mistakes and can be repetitive (progression and regression) in a given space and time.[27]

Consequently, the evolution theory of institution considers endogenous factors (those from the actors themselves) as the origin of the institutional transition. As Boland said, explanations of the institutional transition must be based on endogenous rather than exogenous factors (factors external to the actors, such as wars and accidents).[28] The concept of actors is seen as genes, and institutional arrangements are phenotypes because concept genes are changeable in social evolution, and phenotypes are relatively stable. In addition, it is suitable for the individualistic fundament to see concepts as genes: concepts ultimately depend on individuals.[29] Due to the self-interest of heterogeneous actors and the diversity of knowledge (there are always multiple concepts in future institutional arrangements), the essence of institutional evolution is to select quite limited concepts from countless ones and convert them into institutions. The competition among concepts and the power to formulate institutions usually lies at the center of institutional evolution, which essentially follows the principle of "mutation – selection – heredity." In general, the process of institutional evolution contains three stages: 1. Heterogeneous actors generate new institutional concepts, 2. Actors use political or economic influences to contend for the power of designing and dictating given institutional arrangements. 3. Rules are formulated, justified, stabilized, and replicated. These three stages correspond to three stages in evolution: mutation, selection (to decrease mutations), and heredity (stabilization).[30]

Mutation mechanism: The conceptual formation of institutional arrangement

MATERIAL FORCE AND INSTITUTIONAL CONCEPTS

According to the institutional evolution theory, an actor has limited reason and knowledge and lacks the well-developed ability to process information. Concepts are the product of cognition and thinking activities of actors with limited reason. Institution-related concepts are actors' concepts about the construction of institutional systems and specific institutional arrangements. New institutional concepts are generated to provide artificial solutions or to create and introduce certain concepts to achieve tasks and expectations.[31] As the prototype for an institution, the institutional concepts could be more precise and concrete. Instead, most are initially vague, precisely as politicians tend to depict ambitious but vague prospects rather than concrete, detailed meanings. The construction of any institution is based on a primitive concept and serves this concept; institutions have materialized, enriched, and formulated concepts. The question is where this concept originates or how new concepts emerge.

Materialism theories believe material has an absolute superiority to the generation of concepts. The most typical case is Marx's theory, where he believed that material decides consciousness, and consciousness is only a simple, subjective reflection of the external material world.[32] However, according to the institutional evolution theory, concepts are rarely a simple reflection of the material world. Its generation is not random or blind. Instead, it is the reconstruction of actors who take the initiative to use human minds and material force.[33] The decisions of humans are based on a specific mental model, whose methods to process information depend "upon the brain's ability to learn by being programmed with one or more elaborately structured natural languages that can code for perceptual, attitudinal and moral (behavioral) as well as factual information."[34] As Merleau-Ponty and Adorno said, objects recognized and precepted by actors are not merely objects but new images created by the understanding and influence of the brain.[35]

The institutional evolution theory does not intend to negate the ontological superiority of material force in forming actors' concepts but to defy its absolute superiority. The formation of concepts is restricted to the material world to a great extent. Karl Popper and Donald Campbell proposed this in their "evolutionary epistemology." First, material input is ontologically superior. Second, concepts are restrained by materials; however, they are still the subjective construction of the brain. Third, human beings can change the material world and reshape the evolutionary environment of humans.[36] Therefore, what does the material world refer to? Lenin believed that material is the objective existence independent of the recognition and the influence of actors.[37] Marx believed that human society is a component of the material world, and it is impossible for human society to exist without the material, natural environment. Simultaneously, the activity in which humans obtain means of subsistence is material (practical).[38] Because the institutional concept is the social knowledge about the construction of institutions, it has little association with the natural environment and is essentially restrained by human practice. Because the subject, object, and method of practical activities are objective, the practice of humans is a material activity, which contains, to be more specific, economic activities (material production activities), creative activities of human technologies, and cultural activities (scientific and cultural practices).[39]

CONCEPTS OF TECHNOLOGY, ECONOMY, CULTURE, AND INSTITUTION

Although there are several definitions of technology in the academic world,[40] technology is essentially a practical activity in which humans use knowledge to achieve purpose and requirements. Technology has three meanings. First, technology is not knowledge but the product of its application. Knowledge is the occupation and maintenance of information, facts, and understandings to differentiate something from others. Knowledge is of great necessity for technologies; the creation of any technology is the application of knowledge accumulated by capturing or dominating phenomes. For instance, the invention of many electrical devices is derived from capturing or applying a series of phenomes. Static electricity, electromagnetic fields, electromagnetic induction, and electromagnetic radiation were discovered between 1750 and 1875. By capturing and taming these phenomes, quantities of practical knowledge were accumulated, and a series of facilities were created, including batteries, capacitors, inductors, telegrams, dynamos, telephones, and radios. Second, technology is aimed at functions; every technology serves some objective or function. Overall, the general function of technology is the artificial exchange of materials, energy, and information. For example, cutting metals on the lathe belong to material exchange, functioning heat engines and dynamos to energy exchange, storage devices, communication and decision-making to information exchange.[41] Third, technology should be a way of practice or a set of practical, operable commands. There is no restriction on its form: it can be either a device or a facility like a dynamo or be a way or process like the filtration of chemical substances.[42]

Economic activity mainly consists of the production, distribution, and consumption of goods and services to fulfill the requirements of a society. Cultural activity is the meaningful activity of symbol systems created by human history. Specifically, it includes thoughts, values, traditions, religions, conventions, and doctrines.[43] Max Weber called culture a web of meaning knitted by humans,[44] and Clifford Geertz called it a mechanism of symbol control.[45] The keynote they emphasized is the same: culture is the symbol world deliberately constructed by humans.[46] North pointed out that a concept is the reconstruction of material information, and the essential element of culture is language, with which culture encodes and deduces information transmitted to the brain. "The symbolic environment can affect how individual brains deploy their resources."[47] Therefore, the concept is constructed by exchanges in the web of symbols knitted by culture, and the actor changes the mental pattern of humans by the interaction between mental patterns and culture systems, then influencing the construction of concepts of the actor.[48]

The formation of the institutional concept is a complicated, dynamic, and systematic process, as well as a systematic process in which interactions among technological, economic, and cultural factors influence human minds. These activities keep changing, and these factors are relatively stable in a given time and space. When all factors achieve a state of coupling, the dynamic stability of the system can be maintained,[49] therefore spawning a new institutional concept. As revealed by system theory, a complicated system is internally a system of feedback and associations consisting of multiple subsystems. The speed and frequency of changes vary from one to another, and so does the time lag in the reaction to the state of other subsystems and the threshold value the reaction requires: some will react as soon as the other subsystems make a change; others will not react until changes in the other subsystems have accumulated and reached a certain extent.[50] Moreover, given the heterogeneity in the structure of human minds, different actors have different self-interested motives or interest objectives; therefore, the same environment of technology, economy, and culture will likely give birth to different institutional concepts.

RELATIONSHIP AMONG TECHNOLOGY, ECONOMY, AND CULTURE

There is an interactive relationship among technology, economy, and culture.

First, the economy and culture influence the transition path of technology. The study by technology historians Brian Arthur and Kevin Kelly indicates that the technological transition has its evolutionary pattern. For example, it will gradually evolve with the expansion of useful knowledge and "combinatorial evolution," demonstrating a tendency of increasing complication and self-generation.[51] The expert on technology history, Joel Mokyr, believes that technology evolves with the expansion of practical knowledge, which is increasingly accelerating. Before 1800, most technological advances sprang up naturally. Although new technologies emerged during industrial revolutions, their cognitive basis was relatively narrow, therefore fostering few (but not zero) continuous technological improvements. After 1800, the enormous expansion in cognitive basis marked a brand-new transformation or transition in patterns of useful knowledge that emerged in dynamic mechanisms, contributing to technological improvements.[52] However, the evolution of technologies is not purely based on internal logic or the pattern of the technology; it is a process full of heterogeneous factors, a web structure of multiple directions and dense distributions rather than a fixed, monodirectional process. Technology is the product of social construction, and the technological transition is heavily influenced by elements such as institution, economy, culture (value, religion, and outlook on technology), population, and the military. For instance, the famous American sociologist and science sociologist Merton applied the statistical methods of sociology, discovering that what promoted the development of science and technology in England in the seventeenth century was a series of social factors, including popularized interest in scientific vocations, Puritans' principles of rationalism and Benthamism, requirements of economic developments in industries such as mining and transporting, military technologies, new demands proposed by increasing population, convenient interactions among experts on technologies, belief in economy and technology and so on.[53] The American experts on technology history, George Basalla, Joel Mokyr, and sociologist Gilfillan, also believed that social factors affect the technological transition.[54] The most fundamental reason why technology has the feature of social construction is that technology is the activity created by humans to fulfill all their needs. In addition, these needs are multidimensional, including fame, survival, amusement, culture, war, and economy. The famous psychologist Maslow proposed in his book *A Theory of Human Motivation* that humans' needs can be classified into five types: physiological needs, safety needs, love and belonging, esteem, and self-actualization.[55] Everyone is situated in a social web structure, where social factors stimulate the diverse requirements of humans, prompting them to create.

Second, economic activity is influenced by technology and culture. The economic development follows several paths. First is the growth of investment, which is similar to the Solow Growth Phenomenon discovered by the economist Robert Solow. When capital accumulation grows faster than labor, the capital distributed by every worker will gradually increase, leading to economic growth and the growth of output per capita.[56] The classical economist David Ricardo also realized this point.[57] The second is commercial expansion. In microscopic economics, the standard cost in the middle processes shows that the increased exchange of goods, services, labor, or capital can benefit all parties. When two units are separated before commercial exchanges in products and services are achieved, the commercial benefit will increase both parties' income. Adam Smith proposed the phenomenon in 1776. He believed that trade profits derived from the division of labor, professionalization, labor skills (called "studying at work" or human capital), and the consequent increase in productivity. The division of labor intensified with the enlargement of the range of the service market. The finer the division was, the more every worker produced. The economic growth attributed to trade increase can be named Smith Growth.[58] Third, the effective distribution of production elements, including land, population, and other natural resources. There is an economic phenomenon called the "scale effect" that, by enlarging the scale of production elements, the increase in numbers can contribute to the enhancement in the productivity per capital in the economy, especially the expansion of the population, which can contribute to an increase in unit income.[59] Fourth, some economists also pointed out that cultural factors can improve economic growth. For example, one becomes more and more conscientious, cooperative, frugal, diligent, cautious, and has more trust in others. Some scholars mentioned that culture is the leading cause of the rise of the Western world. Traditions such as honesty, diligence, frugalness, and instructions to children are passed down from generation to generation. They can improve economic status and differ significantly in various societies.[60] Fifth are technological advances. The ways listed previously are all likely to bring short-term economic prosperity but will ultimately become the dilemma of a constant increase in rewards. Smith and Ricardo have already taken this into account. They believed that natural resources, including land resources, are scarce, and the input of labor and capital is also restricted, which will contribute to the constant decrease in the marginal return, profits, and capital accumulation, leading to the stagnation of economic development.[61] Nothing but technological advances are the most fundamental and durable impetus that can permanently eliminate the limit of prosperity.[62] Since the 1980s, new economists represented by Paul Romer, Robert Lucas, and Grossman have constructed new economic models, proposing that technology is endogenous in the economic system, and technology innovations are the fundamental element of economic development and the result of maximal profits pursued by manufacturers.

Technology influences economic growth as follows. First, technology can be repeatedly applied. New combinations of all elements improve the efficiency of current resources, alleviating scarcity and achieving scale of profits. Second, technological advances can improve productivity, achieve the optimal distribution of given elements, and increase external production. Third, technology will overflow; given the constant accumulation of technologies, different enterprises can learn technologies from each other. Fourth, since technology has become a sector of industrial research and development, it can be acquired by enterprises via investment and research, increasing the utilization efficiency of capital and the consequent accumulation of enterprise capital, finally achieving a virtuous cycle. Fifth, technological advances are materialized into "studying at work" and human capital, promoting economic growth. Workers' basic skills (human capital) are improved by "studying at work" or the enterprises' instructions and training, significantly increasing the productivity and production of the workers. Moreover, distinct from the wastage of material capital, "studying at work" and human capital can increase marginal incomes, constantly promoting economic growth.[63] However, the importance of technologies to economic growth is closely related to the paradigm of technological innovations and the levels of technological development in different historical stages. The technological innovations in early historical stages were all external to the enterprises, developed by individual inventors and technicians, and restricted by limited knowledge. Therefore, technological inventions were relatively "occasional" and scarce, and the application range and extent of the technologies were limited, and so was their impetus for economic growth. Economic developments were more likely to depend on commercial trade or production elements, such as land, population, labor, and capital. In the following historical stages, especially in the modern age, the accumulation and invention of technologies were gradually dominated by enterprises responsible for professional research and human capital investment. Technological inventions are controlled by enterprises, improving the applications, ranges, impetus on economic developments, and the speed of innovation of technologies.

Finally, technologies and economy influence the formation of culture. Different technologies and economies introduce different meanings, beliefs, and values into culture combined with a series of processes and elements, and the direction of changes is usually unpredictable. Combining technology, economy, meanings, beliefs, and values is thorough. For instance, when automobiles were not invented, traditional ideologies believed that only males could ride horses in public and females should stay where they should be. In addition, since the invention of automobiles during the industrial age, females were entitled to use automobiles, and their social roles and values began to transform. Therefore, more and more females used automobiles and even entered factories, and the movement of religious awakening, the emotions of aversion toward females, and attacks on homosexuals appeared under this background.[64] In addition, the United States in the eighteenth century was a country with a slow pace of technological development. It was dominated by an agricultural economy, where collectivism and republicanism were the mainstream ideologies. In contrast, the development of industrial technologies at the beginning of the nineteenth century brought prosperity in industry and commerce, as well as the rise of the thoughts of individual liberty and liberalism.

Mechanism of artificial selection: Competition for the power of institutional arrangements

Actors possessing or favoring some concepts about specific institutional transition are not necessarily the first to propose the institutional concepts, and the concepts can be purchased, absorbed, referenced, and even plagiarized from elsewhere. On most occasions, actors have no idea which concept can improve the welfare level, or more importantly, they have no faith that institutions enacted by others can improve their welfare level. Accordingly, the power to enact rules can only be determined via a single path: competition for the power of institutional arrangements.[65] The actors include individuals and organizations, such as governments and social and education groups. Generally speaking, the primary classification of actors is the government and private sector. Lin Yifu, a new institutional researcher, held that some politicians, political groups, or governors control the most significant government authority. Like any individual with limited reason, the government cares for its survival, economy, prestige, power, and historical status. The government has self-interested motives like the private sector.[66] The power to enact rules is contended by the government and private sectors via mobilizing material resources (e.g., financial resources) and political supports, the total amount of which determines, to a great extent, the result of the contention in the next stage.[67] Consequently, the actors often demand enough economic power or original charisma to participate in the institutional transition. In most cases, political and economic power is necessary for actors to join in the institutional construction, which is to be mobilized, deployed, maintained, and even improved by the actor during the process.

When contending the power of institutional arrangements, actors will probably see the contention as a zero-sum game, which is attributed to two reasons. First, if the actor succeeds in the contention of power, they will be entitled to enact rules at their will; if the actor fails, they will be imposed to obey the rules enacted by others. Second, a self-interested actor can hardly foresee how the rules enacted by others are, always concerned that their interests will suffer, although these rules will ultimately benefit them. Because actors consider the process of contending the power of institutional arrangements as a zero-sum game, their ultimate objective is to make all efforts to succeed in the contention, even resorting to violence, rather than achieve Pareto Optimality of collective welfare through cooperation, which could be seen almost everywhere in history.[68] In contending, actors usually use well-designed speeches, words, and political skills to make their proposed opinion more inviting and attractive. Actors are likely to convince other members to share the fundamental beliefs of society and economy, determine the knowledge they pursue, and improve the expansion of the legal frameworks of rights and obligations of the country.[69] Without complete information, audiences can hardly realize the influence of the institutional arrangements supported by a particular concept on their welfare. Consequently, on the same occasions, the actor with a stronger attraction to concepts is more likely to gain more support and take advantage in a power struggle. However, generally speaking, conceptual attraction is relatively inferior to the influence of economic and political power. Moreover, there are interesting games and power struggles for the power of institutional arrangements among private sectors and between private sectors and governments. When the private sector is spontaneously encouraged, organized, and performs to gain new economic interests. It obtains the power of institutional arrangements through economic power, political relations, or conceptual attractions, which means that the decision of the private sector dominates the process of institutional arrangement innovations; it is called the new institutional economy-induced institutional change. This is a bottom-up institutional arrangement where the private sector is the primary acting group, and the government is the secondary. In comparison, when the government obtains the power of institutional arrangements depending on its political power, and the institutional arrangements are actualized and improved by inference from the government and imposed by authorities, it is called compulsory institutional change, which is a top-down institutional arrangement where the government is the primary acting group.[70] Sometimes, a rational government will compulsorily demand the power of institutional arrangements due to public interests, such as the national economy or cultural development, to improve inland economic and cultural development or other public interests. However, the government is not always rational and will require power for its own interests; for example, the federal royal family would enact land regulations that exploit the subjects for royal or aristocratic interests. The relations between the government and the private sectors vary in forms: sometimes, they have no association with interests, and sometimes they are consistent. Applying their lobbying skills, private sectors manage to adjust national interests to their private interests, inviting the government into their alliance. Undoubtedly, support from the government is highly critical for private sectors to obtain the power of institutional arrangements.[71] However, if the two sides have a conflict of interests, they will have to obtain the power depending on their political and economic power or conceptual appeals, which is the same as the contention among private sectors.

Replication mechanism: Formulation of rules, legalization, stabilization, and replication

After resolving the contention over the power of institutional arrangements, the winner will have more power to turn the concepts reflecting their preferences into concrete institutions, therefore playing a dominating role in regulating the rules. When trying to enact the rules, the winner usually has three primary alternatives: promoting by force, absorbing some of the loser's opinions, or introducing the loser to the winner's camp. Although the three alternatives can independently or collectively function on different occasions, promoting by force is usually the first choice of the actor, because it is the most direct and fastest way to implement institutions that reflect the winner's preference and bring more benefits to them. Therefore, under most circumstances, the rule ultimately enacted is not the "public property" that can improve the welfare of society but the "private property" where winners reject losers. Even if some are likely to benefit society, it is nothing more than incidental or occasional exceptions instead of ordinary things.[72] Indeed, the winner may enact rules by cooperating with the loser in pursuit of more significant support to "stabilize" and "legalize" the rules that have finally been enacted. On this occasion, the process of enacting rules can be considered as the "bargaining" process. However, this kind of "bargaining" is made under an unfair circumstance, because both parties know that the distribution of bargaining power has been defined previously. The winner has absolute power in this context, and the cost of the failure of cooperation will be too great to withstand for the loser. Consequently, the rules enacted in this case still tend to reflect the preferences and benefits of the winner. In addition, on the occasion that different actors have similar bargaining power, the actors will also choose cooperation or negotiation, because the power distribution is not apparently out of balance. However, this situation is an exception rather than something that is expected during the institutional transition.[73]

After the final foundation of an institutional arrangement, its function or adaptability as a phonotype is to be tested in the social system. If the implementation of this arrangement can improve the welfare level of most people, or more importantly, the arrangers indoctrinate in advance an ideology that fully legalizes this arrangement, or no anti-ideology takes place and becomes strong enough to challenge this arrangement. It will be legalized, stabilized, and replicated.[74] After the completion of this stage, a single turn in institutional evolution is also complete. It is important to note that an institutional arrangement that fails to improve or even derogates social welfare (which has no legality) is likely to continue because it gains enough support from the political or economic powers. On this occasion, the seed of institutional transition has been sowed. Still, it will take quite a long time for changes to take place, because institutional transitions are not always facilitated to succeed (it requires political entrepreneurship and social activity that are efficient, have an advantage in power bargaining, and can overcome problems in collective campaigns). At the same time, people may get used to this institution, therefore losing the impetus of institutional transition, which is why there is path dependency in institutional transition.

In brief, the analytic framework of institutional evolution is as follows. Heterogeneous actors with self-interested motives generate new institutional concepts (mutation mechanism) under the influence of material activities (technology, economy, and culture); actors with different institutional concepts use their bargaining advantage (including economic and political powers and conceptual attraction) to contend with the power of institutional arrangements (artificial selection mechanism); the winner in the contention of institutional power constitutes the institution, legalizing, stabilizing, and replicating (replication mechanisms) concepts reflecting their preferences. Accordingly, what "leads to the coming of an era of concepts" and converts it into an institution? The most basic reasons are as follows. First, is the possibility that material activities (technology, economy, and culture) in the given time and space generate institutional concepts. Second is the process of power alternation and political games. According to Jack Levy, which concept can become an institution is fundamentally a political problem. The critical problem of institutional transition is how power subjects and political processes interact to shape institutional transition.[75]

Application of the evolution theory of institution to the patent system

This book defines the patent system as a historical and realistic existence to research, investigating the historical evolution of the patent system based on the theoretical framework constructed previously and searching for the motivations and obstacles behind it. The patent system is seen as the product of the coordination of technology, economy, culture, and politics. It integrates technological policies, economic systems, political tools, and legal rules. Therefore, the evolution of the patent system is inevitably a complicated historical process intertwined by technological, economic, cultural, and political factors instead of a spontaneous, idyllic evolution corresponding to progressive logic. In the Middle Ages, eighteenth and nineteenth centuries, technological, cultural, and economic environments were all different from those at present, and some differences were quite large. As Larry Kramer said, when we put down the material and utilitarian world today and come back to the world of the eighteenth and early nineteenth centuries, it is as if we were coming back to an alien world.[76] The recognition of concepts and institutions differs in time and space; therefore, we are required to give up today's prejudices and investigate institutional concepts in the corresponding technological, economic, and cultural environments.

From a macroscopic historical perspective, technological revolutions are usually the beginning of all civilizations. Humans have experienced three historical forms: pre-industrial society (before the 1760s), industrial society (1760s–1980s), and post-industrial society (1980s onwards), where the patent system experienced metamorphoses including privilege, private rights, and internationalization, gradually tending to be alienized. The evolutionary stages of the patent system seem to be fragmented and show different features; however, they are not completely separated but are associated to a certain extent. Karl Popper believes that history is subjective and likely to be explained in multiple ways; therefore, we can only see "the trend" rather than conclude a specific general principle in continuous historical events.[77] George Owen believes that history is not the combination of all factors but the record of human beings' purest and most basic motives.[78] This book investigates and studies the transition of the patent system from a historical perspective, with no intention to reveal the general pattern of its development. It tries to provide new perspectives and clues for explanations. In different historical stages, due to the different coupling among the levels of technological development, economic form, the combination of technology and economy, changes in the values and impetus of technology to the economy, and the cultural concepts of actors (including the outlook of technology, wealth and suitable, philosophical concepts, economic theory, and ideology), the motive, impetus of the construction, the form, and content of the patent system will be affected. Given the difference in the coupling extent of the technology, economy, and culture in different historical stages, institutional concepts will likely demonstrate different forms. Indeed, many conceptual forms of the actors may not be spontaneous but are borrowed from elsewhere according to their country's technological, economic, and cultural environment.

Nonetheless, the leading actor in the transition of the patent system is always the actor who has the advantage of the power and can take action according to the framework of the institutions. They have shaped the content of concrete institutions (including formal and informal) and the direction of institutional transition. The famous legal historian Stuart Banner pointed out in his *American Property* that although the concept of "what is property" in American society has constantly varied in the last two centuries, history has told us, "property has been an instrumental value, not an end in itself." "None of these changes happened by themselves, of course. People made them happen." "Over time, as new coalitions formed around particular goals, they pushed conventional understandings of property in one direction or another." "The actors driving these changes have unsurprisingly been the people to whom the gains would flow."[79] In addition, the patent system tells the same story. Due to different self-interested motives, different actors will generate or support different institutional concepts under the mutually associated influence of technology, economy, and culture, who apply their own political or economic powers to influence the institutional transition. When promoting revolutions, the actors will always depend on delicate expressions, claiming that their concepts are of general benefit or selecting concepts, contents, and the attraction of concepts that are beneficial to constructing their institutions to justify their institutional concepts. After gaining the power of institutional arrangements, either different actors achieve agreements on interest balance, or the winner turns institutional concepts reflecting their preferences into concrete laws and legalizes and stabilizes their concepts with further modifications. These institutions will influence the formation of institutional concepts of descendants, leading to path dependency in the patent system. Some scholars think merchants are the promotors of history in the evolutionary process of Intellectual Property (IPR) institutions, who shaped the appearance of the IPR institution.[80] This book believes that the opinion is biased. The leading actors in the transition of the patent system are the private sectors (including guilds, technicians, merchants, industrial and commercial classes, and enterprises, which take different forms in different historical stages) and the government. The patent is, on the one hand, the critical tool with which private sectors gain wealth in market competitions; on the other hand, it is the policy tool with which the government of a country controls technology and the economy. In the evolutionary process of history, they make games with each other based on respective objectives, sometimes achieving and sometimes breaking cooperation due to their interests and thus constructing and shaping the direction of the patent system. We will see that the patent system was initially the policy product of the country of developing industry and commerce, concentrating on the feasibility and public interest of technologies. As David Kairys and Susan Sell said, it was a mysterious field far from the center of the legal platform, only belonging to technical professionals.[81] Private sectors used various strategies to progressively personalize, materialize and internationalize it, attaching great importance to it from the government and the public.

Indeed, there is no denying that some accidents are likely to lead the patent system in quite a different direction, which may be eliminated or modified in history or influence the construction of the patent system forever. As Aoki Masahiko said, in the historical evolution, the shorter the time is, the more significant role conceptual factors play; the longer the time is, the more significant role non-conceptual or so-called objective factors play; in extremely long periods, however, the occasional factors are in dominance.[82] Professor Li Chen also pointed out that there are occasional elements in the evolution of legal institutions, and logic cannot explain all phenomena in history.[83] Therefore, the evolution of the patent system is everything but the modification of legal texts. The patent system is a historical concept, and its evolutionary process is uncertain. Although the evolutionary process of the patent system is usually progressive, as the process of the institutional transition is arduous (political entrepreneurship that is effective has an advantage in power bargaining and can overcome the problems of collective campaigns, and multiple factors like social activities and path dependency are a necessity), the transition of the patent system is also inevitable, as changes in human's practical activities like technology, economy, and culture always exist, and the pursuit of survival and welfare can never be satisfied. The gradual change in the patent system is the typical case. Still, sudden changes like gene mutations are also likely to occur because of the change in the actor's authority, unexpected events, or a series of changes over a relatively long period.

The patent system has finished the task of the era in the evolution of history. This book aims to reveal the history and beneficial structure of the patent system, especially opposing the opinion that the patent system is the product of nature, eternity, and absolute reason. History has provided a clue, and its response has a long-standing origin.

Notes

1 Douglass C. North. *Institutions, Institutional Change and Economic Performance*. Hang Xing. Shanghai: Gezhi Press, Shanghai Sanlian Bookstore, Shanghai People's Publishing House, 2014:20.
2 R. Coase, A. Alchian, D. North, et al. *Property Rights and Institutional Change: Collections of Translations of Property School and New Institutionalism School*. Liu Shouying, et al. Shanghai: Shanghai Sanlian Bookstore, 1994:329–338.
3 Hu Shi. *Hu Shi's Collected Works*. Beijing: Peking University Press, 1998:105.
4 Hu Shi. *Hu Shi's Collected* Works, 519.
5 Tang Shiping. *A General Theory of Institutional Change*. Beijing: Peking University Press, 2016:1–2.
6 David S. Landes. *The Unbound Prometheus: Technological Change and Industrial Development in Western Europe from 1750 to the Present*. Xie Huaizhu Trans. Beijing: Huaxia Publishing House, 2007:539.
7 Anthony Giddens. *The Constitution of Society: Outline of the Theory of Structuration*. Li Kang, et al. Trans. Beijing: China People's Renmin University Press, 2016:155–157.
8 Giddens. *Constitution of Society*, 15–16.
9 Tang Shiping. *General Theory of Institutional Change*, 15.
10 Tang Shiping. *General Theory of Institutional Change*, 15.
11 Giddens. *Constitution of Society*, 23–24.
12 Giddens. *Constitution of Society*, 23.
13 Hang Xing. *Institutions, Institutional Change and Economic Performance*, 3–7.
14 Hang Xing. *Institutions, Institutional Change and Economic Performance*, 3–7.
15 Douglass C. North. *Understanding the Process of Economic Change*. Zhong Zhengsheng, et al. Trans. Beijing: China Renmin University Press, 2013:55.
16 Coase, Alchin, North et al. *Property Rights and Institutional Change*, 264–265.
17 Tang Shiping. *General Theory of Institutional Change*, 13.
18 Kathleen M. Eisenhardt, D. Charles Galunic. Coevolving: At Last, a Way to Make Synergies Work, 78 *Harvard Business Review*, 2000, pp. 91–101.

19 Ren Li. *The Mechanism of Technological Progress in Economic Growth: A Study Based on Theory Change*. Shanghai: Shanghai Academy of Social Sciences Press, 2014:25.

20 Simon believed that economic analysis derives from practice and limited reason, instead of the assumption that a human has a complete ability to process information. The economy reason is a process rather than a substantive reason. Substantive reasons demand that given objects are automatically fulfilled under given circumstances, and process reasons don't require that every choice of the actor is completely correct, as long as the actor can adjust his behaviors based on experiences and improve the correctness of their decisions. For example, the accomplishment of process reason is totally dependent on its formation itself, and the reason is nothing but a constantly approaching process. Based on this, Simon proposed the satisfaction hypothesis: based on the concepts of limited reason and process reason, the basic acting pattern of people is to follow the satisfaction principle rather than to seek optimization. Herbert Simon. *The Cornerstone of Modern Decision Theory*. Yang Li, Xu Li. Beijing: Beijing Institute of Economics Press, 1989:53.

21 The path dependence is a system with a positive feedback mechanism. Random nonlinearities are likely to be influenced by external occasional events. Once this influence is adopted by the system, it will evolve in a given path, which is difficult to be replaced by other potentially even better paths. Therefore, path dependence explains how systems are locked in a path attributed to a certain historical event. Zhang Fujun. *Research on the Theory of Technology and Institutional Co-Evolution*. Beijing: Economic Science Press, 2013:25.

22 Yang Yonghua. *Technological Innovation Mechanisms and Policies in the Perspective of Evolutionary Economics*. Beijing: Social Science Literature Press, 2015:75–76.

23 The evolution is associated with the phenotypes of individuals as well as groups and species. Biological evolution refers that under the interaction between creatures and the environment, a series of irreversible changes occurred in their genetic systems, contributing to changes in the corresponding phenotypes. Under most circumstances, these changes render the entirety of creatures adaptive to the environment that they inhabit. In biological evolution, complexity and orderly increases are general cases. Qin Hai. *Institutions, Evolution and Path Dependence-A Theoretical Attempt at Institutional Analysis Synthesis*. Beijing: China Financial and Economic Press, 2004:78.

24 Liu Yejin. *Economic Evolution: Exploring the general evolutionary paradigm*. Beijing: China Social Science Press, 2015:87.

25 Tang Shiping. *General Theory of Institutional Change*, 57.

26 John R. Commons. *Institutional Economics*. Zhao Rui. Beijing: Huaxia Publishing House, 2017:342.

27 Commons. *Institutional Economics*, 342.

28 Lawrence A. Boland. A Critique of Friedman's Critics, 17 *Journal of Economic Literature*, 1979, pp. 503–522.

29 Genes are nucleotide sequences in a DNA molecule that contain specific information and are the minimum units of genetic materials. Through complicated biochemical processes, DNA sequences are translated into proteins or RNAs, and some of them also participate in the regulation of the translation process. Via accurate replications, genes can transmit genetic information to their descendants, expressing them into specific characters through a series of complicated biochemical processes, such as transcription and translation, which is called gene expression. Accordingly, the genetic constitution of a creature is the gene type, representing the sum of its genetic potentials. Obviously, it is only the specific characters demonstrated in the interaction with the environment that

make sense, and these characteristics of specific gene expressions are named the phenotype of gene types. Genes are various and variable, representing amounts of potential possibilities. Phenotypes that are expressed through a series of effects are more stable, and almost all characteristics of creatures are influenced by several or many genes.

30 Tang Shiping. *General Theory of Institutional Change*, 60.

31 Tang Jian. Systems, Time and Social Evolution-A Review of Tang, Shiping. (The Social Evolution of International Politics), *International Political Science*, 2015 (2).

32 Gao Fang, Gao Zhe, Zhang Shujie. *Selected Essays of Marx and Engels*. Beijing: Central Compilation Press, 2016:190–191.

33 Tang Shiping. The Foundational Paradigm of Social Science, *International Journal of Social Sciences*, 2010 (1).

34 North. *Institutions, Institutional Change, and Economic Performance*, 44.

35 Chen Huiping. Dialectical Development of Marxist Theory of Consciousness, *Journal of Shandong University of Science and Technology: Social Science Edition*, 2018 (1).

36 Karl Popper, *Objective Knowledge: An Evolutionary Approach*, Oxford: Claredon Press, 1979; Donald T. Campbell. Evolutionary Epistemology. *The Philosophy of Karl Popper*, 2 vols, ed. Paul Arthur Schilpp. La Salle, IL: Open Court, 1974.

37 Lenin. *Lenin's Selected Works: Volume 2*. The Bureau of Compilation of the Works of Marx, Engels and Lenin of the Central Committee of the Communist Party of China. Beijing: People's Publishing House, 2012:66, 89, 192–193.

38 The Writing Group of the *Concepts of the Basic Principles of Marxism*. Introduction to the basic principles of Marxism. Beijing: Higher Education Publishing House, 2018:29.

39 *Concepts of the Basic Principles of Marxism*, 57–58, 60.

40 Definitions of technology in today's academic world can be summarized into types as follows: 1. The essence of technology is objects, such as tools, machines, and consumer goods. 2. The essence of technology is knowledge, which reflects the preference of epistemology. 3. Technology is the tool, way, or process to achieve the objective. 4. The essence of technology is will, which is basically based on philosophical perspectives. 5. Technology can be divided into nature, social, and thinking technology.

41 Friedrich Rapp. *Contributions to a Philosophy of Technology: Studies in the Structure of Thinking in the Technological Sciences*. Liu Wu, et al. Changchun: Jilin University Press, 1988:17.

42 Brian Arthur. *The Nature of Technology: What It Is and How It Evolves*. Cao Dongming, Wang Jianyi, et al. Hangzhou: Zhejiang People's Publishing House, 2014:206–210.

43 Chris Freeman, Francesco Louçã. *As Time Goes By: From the Industrial Revolution to the Information Revolution*. Shen Hongliang, et al. Beijing: China Renmin University Press, 2007:130.

44 Clifford Geertz. *The Interpretation of Culture*. Han Li. Nanjing: Yilin Publishing House, 2008:5.

45 Geertz. *Interpretation of Culture*, 5.

46 Geertz. *Interpretation of Culture*, 5.

47 North. *Understanding the Process of Economic Change*, 31.

48 North. *Understanding the Process of Economic Change*, 31.

49 Coupling refers to the phenomenon that two or more systems or moving methods influence each other via a series of interactions to be mutually connected, which is also the dynamic relationship between mutual dependence, influence, and improvements due to the positive interactions among all subsystems. For instance, by binding a spring between two simple pendulums, they will fluctuate correspondingly and influence each other. This interaction is called simple pendulum coupling. Similarly, assuming that

the research object is the relationship between A and B, the phenomenon of the interaction and mutual influence between A and B through the respective coupling elements is defined as the A–B coupling.

50 Zhang Xukun. *Introduction to Institutional Evolutionary Analysis*. Hangzhou: Zhejiang University Press, 2007:42.

51 Arthur. *Nature of Technology*, 206–210; Kevin Kelly. *What Technology Wants*. Yan Lijuan. Beijing: Electronic Industry Press, 2016:110–115.

52 Mokyr. *Gift of Athena*, 20–21.

53 Robert King Merton. *Science, Technology, and Society in Seventeenth-Century England*. Fan Dainian. Beijing: The Commercial Press, 2000:36–259.

54 George Basalla, an American technology historian, uses Darwin's evolutionary theory to explain the transition of technologies. He considers artificial objects the basic unit of technology because their evolution is accumulative and continuous; that is, every artificial object is based on prototypical objects rather than unique and unprecedented. Elements, such as imagination, social, economic and cultural powers, diffusion of technologies, and science advances constantly encourage human innovations, ensuring the continuity and diversity of artificial objects. However, under the influence of economic, cultural, and military factors, the selection of a human renders some artificial objects to survive, while others are eliminated in the tide of history. (George Basalla. *The Evolution of Technology*. Zhou Guangfa. Shanghai: Fudan University Press, 2000:224–237). American sociologist Gilfillan took the invention of steamships as an example, expanding the analyzing framework of technology transition to nontechnological factors interacting with technological ones. He has proposed 38 social principles and environmental elements of invention, which include wealth, education, and population and industrialism. In his opinion, the transition of technologies is quite similar to Darwin's evolutionary process. (S. C. Gilfillan. *The Sociology of Invention*. Cambridge, MA: MIT Press, 1970:24). Joel Mokyr believed that society is the most critical part in the evolution of technology. He concluded the influence on technological evolution from such factors as institution and property, average life expectancy, nutrition, risk tolerance, geographic environment, path dependency, labor cost, religion, value standard, resistance against innovation, politics and government, war, open-minded attitude toward information, and population (Mokyr. *Gift of Athena*, 20–21.)

55 Maslow's Hierarchy of Needs was proposed by American psychologist Abraham Maslow in 1943 in his article *A Theory of Human Motivation*. The theory was classified needs into five types, listed from superior to inferior. The supreme needs are those for self-actualization, that is to achieve one's individual ideals and ambitions, to exert one's ability to the greatest extent, to reach the stage of self-actualization, to accept oneself and others, to improve one's ability to solve problems and self-discipline, to handle problems independently, to remain alone and undisturbed, to complete all things commensurate to one's ability. Therefore, one has to be competent to their job, which will be the greatest happiness. Maslow proposed that the path applied to fulfill the needs of self-actualization differs from person to person. The requirement of self-actualization aims at realizing one's potential, making one gradually closer to the ideal figure in one's expectations.

56 Joel Mokyr. *The Lever of Riches: Technological Creativity and Economic Progress*. Chen Xiaobai. Beijing: Huaxia Publishing House, 2008:5.

57 David Ricardo. *On the Principles of Political Economy and Taxation*. Guo Dali, Wang Yanan. Beijing: The Commercial Press, 1962:3.

58 Ren Li. *Mechanism of Technological Progress*, 25.

59 However, it is to be noticed, when other production elements have no or little increase, the constant increase in population will exert pressure on them, and the economy will convert from a gradual increase to a gradual decrease in rewards. Particularly, an excessive increase in the population will lead to tension in production and a decrease in average incomes. Consequently, a higher population increase is not always better in terms of economic growth. In fact, Malthus was the first to propose this opinion in his *Theory of Population*, even falling into the pessimism of economic growth.
60 Mokyr. *Gift of Athena*, 291.
61 Adam Smith. *The Wealth of Nations*. Yang Jingnian. Xi'an: Shaanxi People's Publishing House, 2006:25; Ricardo. *On the Principles of Political Economy and Taxation*, 3.
62 Mokyr. *Gift of Athena*, 291.
63 Ren Li. *Mechanism of Technological Progress*, 256.
64 William M. Dugger, Howard J. Sherman. *Reclaiming Evolution: A Dialogue between Marxism and Institutionalism on Social Change*. Zhang Lin, et al. Beijing: China Renmin University Press, 2007:60.
65 Tang Shiping. *General Theory of Institutional Change*, 63.
66 Coase, Alchin, North, et al. *Property Rights and Institutional Change*, 278.
67 Tang Shiping. *General Theory of Institutional Change*, 63.
68 Tang Shiping. *General Theory of Institutional Change*, 64.
69 Susan Strange. The Persistent Myth of "Lost" Hegemony, *International Organization*, 1987, 41 (4), pp. 551–574.
70 Coase, Alchin, North, et al. *Property Rights and Institutional Change*, 280.
71 Susan K. Sell. *Private Power, Public Law: The Globalization of Intellectual Property*. Dong Gang. Beijing: China Renmin University Press, 2008:183.
72 Christopher Clague. *Institutions and Economic Development: Growth and Governance in Less-Developed and Post-Socialist Countries*, Johns Hopkins University Press, 1997:23.
73 Tang Shiping. *General Theory of Institutional Change*, 65–66.
74 Tang Shiping. *General Theory of Institutional Change*, 66.
75 Tang Shiping. *General Theory of Institutional Change*, 67.
76 Larry D. Kramer. When Lawyers Do History, 72 *George Washington Law Review*, 2003, pp. 387–390.
77 Karl Popper. *The Poverty of Historicism*. Du Ruji, et al. Beijing: Huaxia Publishing House, 1997:95, 121.
78 James W. Thompson. *Economic and Social History of the Middle Ages*: 300–1300. Beijing: The Commercial Press, 1992: Preface, 1.
79 Stuart Banner. *American Property: A History of How, Why, and What We Own*. Chen Xiankai, Xu Ke. Beijing: China University of Political Science and Law Press, 2017:142, 32, 444, 445.
80 Huang Haifeng. *Discourse and Reality of Intellectual Property Rights: A History of Copyright, Patent and Trademark*. Wuhan: Huazhong University of Science and Technology Press, 2011:130, 131, 276.
81 David Kairys. *The Politics of Law: A Progressive Critique*. Xin Chunying. Beijing: China University of Political Science and Law Press, 2008:185; Sell. *Private Power, Public Law*.
82 Masahiko Aoki, Masakuan Okuno, et al. *Comparative Institutional Analysis of Economic Systems*. Wei, K. N., et al. Beijing: China Development Press, 1999:29. This emphasizes the function of occasionality in institutional evolution. In addition, Fogel points out that

the most meaningful part in the thesis, *The Evolution of the Public Selection System in England in the 17th Century*, published by North and others in 1989, is the function of occasionality in the institutional evolution. Robert Fogel and Douglas North. *Economic Theory: Frontiers of the New Institutional Economics*. Beijing: Economic Science Press, 2003:33.

83 Li Chen. A Historical Analysis of the Intellectual Property Paradigm, *Intellectual Property Rights*, 2004 (2).

2 Pre-industrial age

Emergence and development of the patent privilege system

The First Industrial Revolution, which was initiated in the United Kingdom in the 1760s, signaled the beginning of the Industrial Age. Since then, industrial technology and the economy have gradually developed and matured. The historical period preceding the First Industrial Revolution was called the Pre-industrial Age in this book. The patent system first appeared in the late period of the Middle Ages (the Middle Ages are usually divided into two periods: the early period (AD 476–AD 1150) and the late period (AD 1150–AD 1500)),[1] when human society remained in the Pre-industrial Age. As we know, advanced cultures and technology emerged somewhere in the Classical Times and the early period of the Middle Ages. For example, ancient Greece and Rome were centers of technological civilization during this historical period. However, the problem is why the patent system encouraging technological inventions failed to appear in these countries or religions. In the late period of the Middle Ages, when humans were still tortured by the unreconcilable Deity–Humanity relationship in their souls, how did Venice build such a pioneering institution like the patent privilege system? Most scholars show great interest in the study of Britain's *Statute of Monopolies 1624*. They usually think that the franchise rights in the fourteenth century in England marked the origin of the patent system, and they go further to consider the *Statute of Monopolies 1624* as the sole origin of current patent laws[2]. In fact, the patent privilege system in Britain originated in Venice, but there are scarce studies on the motivation and contents of the creation of the patent privilege system in Venice. Moreover, the patent privilege systems in France and Germany predate those in Britain, but current studies pay limited attention to this fact. What this chapter wants to do is to fill the gaps in those studies. Since the past is gone forever, we can unmask the truth about history only by dispelling misunderstandings.

The age predating the emergence of patent systems

Social panorama of the age predating the emergence of patent systems

The literature available indicates that Venice granted licenses for mechanical inventions as early as 1281–1296, took the initiative to grant a monopoly privilege

DOI: 10.4324/9781003462453-3

of a given term to inventors in 1416, and built a stable and well-organized patent privilege system in 1450–1550. In particular, the first patent law was enacted in Venice on 19 March 1474, which represented the start of the modern patent system. When the origin of the patent system is investigated, a question arises: why did the patent system first appear in Western Europe at the end of the Middle Ages? To put it another way, why did the patent system fail to emerge in the Classical Times and the early period of the Middle Ages? To find the right answers, it is necessary to look into the social history of these ancient civilizations. What will be examined in the following paragraphs are all economically and technologically developed civilizations that can serve as typical cases of their historical periods. This book tries to probe into the technology, economy, and culture of these civilizations to identify the fundamental cause for the absence of patent systems in these civilizations.

The ancient world

Two million years ago, when the human ancestor, *homo habilis*, managed to process the first stone tool earlier than all other primates, humans became the *homo sapiens* that could secure predominance over other animals. With technology, human beings ceased to worship the totems from nature and started to create their civilizations and history. At that time, human beings, out of instinct or for survival, garnered some basic technological principles and knowledge by observing and thinking in the face of nature. On this basis, human beings learned to use a variety of technologies: stone tools, fire-making, bows and arrows, ceramics, and bronzewares. In addition, some brilliant inventions appeared, like boomerangs and the tongue-and-groove jointed fish spears of the Inuit.[3] However, technological development in the prehistoric periods was prolonged and conservative. For example, artifacts like flint tools and earthen pots remained unchanged for several centuries.[4] The Paleolithic and Neolithic Ages were the childhoods of humans when their self-awareness was awakened. They believed some superior powers existed above them, so they cherished deep reverence for nature. Their knowledge about nature could help them have an empirical understanding of their powers, but it could not offer them a rational perspective on their abilities.[5] Accordingly, humans could hardly dominate and exploit nature, and what they could handle was only hunting, gathering, agriculture, and animal husbandry. Invention and creation at this stage were nothing but coincidences, and they were merely instinctive behaviors in their hunting-gathering practices. Big cities were never built, and large buildings like palaces or temples were not built either. No writing system was needed for recording purposes, and no advanced science or disciplines were formed. That was an age of savagery and ignorance.[6] Hereafter, in the Yellow River, Tigris River, and Indus River basins, large irrigation systems were built by exploiting the available water sources, and new intensive agricultures were developed. It was at this time that ancient civilizations emerged from ignorance. The establishment of slavery led to surplus labor in these countries, and science and technology in their infancy were generated to meet the daily needs of these farming and nomadic civilizations. For instance, the historical records reveal that ancient Egyptians and Babylonians already garnered some empirical knowledge and rules such as measurement, arithmetic, and eclipses.[7]

Ancient Egypt had the most advanced technology of this historical period, because Egyptians could use their knowledge to build large buildings like pyramids, temples, and palaces. Pyramids, as a symbol of their highly developed civilization, represented extraordinary technological accomplishments.[8] Ancient Egypt saw its first famous inventor, Imhotep, in 2650 BC.[9] However, in the age of ancient civilizations, those who pursued technological innovations out of personal interests were merely scarce exceptions because there was neither a technology-based division of labor nor any well-designed education plans. Most technological innovations accidentally emerged out of their long-term labor. Based on their instincts, they made or used simple implements, artifacts, and daily utensils that were fashioned from natural materials. The most advanced technologies were those used in large buildings financed by the government. Just like the activities that the ancestors were used to, technologies were mostly based on the human instinct for survival or in life, and they were not widely applied to various activities, including amusements. The ancients were not demanding of technologies, and simple technological creations could fulfill the requirements of farming civilization. Culturally, Babylonians believed that there were powerful spirits in nature and that constellations in heaven determined the fate of humans. Egyptians believed that constellations were consistent with the gods in their mythology. Due to this world outlook of enchanted divinity, the early technologies of humans were also an enchantment full of mystery and reverence, where humans, technology, and nature were perfectly coordinated. Humans were dimly aware that these technologies were necessary for survival; therefore, technologies were either cultural practices or idiosyncrasies in their eyes. There was no sign of technological privatization.[10]

Human technology dawned in Greece, the islands in the Aegean Sea. Between 600 BC and 300 BC, the Greek *polis* ushered into a golden age of science and technology. Favorable natural and geographical environments contributed to Greece's wealth and prosperity, and liberal and democratic city–state institutions enabled the Greeks to shine with the splendid glory of reason and technology. The Greeks said that all should be investigated and suspected. There should be no restriction to thoughts.[11] Therefore, basic science and engineering technologies embraced an unprecedented renaissance. Greek scholars charted constellations with great accuracy (Hipparchus), measured the size of the earth at an accuracy of 15% (Eratosthenes), initiated the heliocentric theory (Aristarchus), and developed geometry (Euclid). What deeply impresses us also includes the theory of figurate numbers of the Pythagorean School, the atom theory of Leucippus and Democritus, Archimedes' *On Floating Bodies* and the principle of levers, Apollonius' conic section, Hippocrates' medicine, and Hipparchus' astrology. There were three great scientists during this historical period. The first was the polymath of all ancient knowledge, Aristotle, whose books were the academic encyclopedia of the ancient world.[12] The second was Ctesibius, sometimes known as "Ancient Edison."[13] The third was the inventor Hero.[14] Moreover, many significant buildings stood in Greece, such as the Parthenon Temple and other magnificent stelas and sculptures, which involved the most excellent masons, carpenters, ceramists, and painters.[15] The age was later hailed as "the Greek Miracle."

After the fall of the Greek hegemony, the Romans built an empire whose rule reached every part of Europe. Romans were keen on political and power struggles, so they made outstanding achievements in political management but made few breakthroughs in research and invention.[16] They absorbed achievements like science, arts, and medicine from the Greeks.[17] The Romans left behind fewer memorable inventions than the Greeks, so their improvements in research and learning institutions were not really worth our reminiscence. But what we can't deny is that they made contributions to technologies, especially in agriculture and civil engineering.[18] Great scientists like architect and engineer Vitruvius, agricultural expert Varro, medical expert Galen, and astrologist Ptolemy also sprang up.

Ancient Greece and Rome were in the embryonic stage of technologies in Western Europe and the period of transition from primitive chance-typed technologies to craftsmen-driven ones. The social development during this historical period shows the following characteristics.

First, the economic development of ancient Greece and Rome was mainly dependent on agriculture. Xenophon of Athens said in *Oeconomicus* that agriculture was the fundament of the economic development in Greece. Whether agriculture could prosper determined the prospect of all other industries.[19] Although short-range commerce and trade appeared in Greece, the Greeks dismissed commerce as an inferior vocation unsuitable for *Polites*. Commerce, in their eyes, was aimed at making money by selling personal services or providing services for others. This practice defied the liberty of *Polites*.[20]

Second, technologies developed to a certain extent in ancient Greece and Rome, contributing to the division of labor and the appearance of craftsmen, a social class specialized in technological work. Technologies were passed down over generations of craftsmen and were occasionally improved. Craftsmen-driven technologies were closed up because it was impossible to separate them from craftsmen and production technologies from products. In other words, technologies remained empirical.[21] Although technology inventors did not have high status, guilds already emerged. Society was divided into two classes: slaves as laborers and freemen as rulers. Slaves initially mastered technologies, and then some freemen became interested in technologies and started to do technological work, but slaves created most inventions.[22] In the age of slavery, technologies were dismissed as something inferior, just like labor, which was the obligation of slaves. The labor force was so abundant and cheap[23] that there was little demand for improving labor efficiency or substituting natural force for the labor force. Inventors and businessmen had lower status and were ignored, so they failed to have independent and considerable influence.[24] "Ancient societies tended to look down on engineering as a subject not fit for gentlemen. This was notoriously true of Plato and Socrates, and according to Plutarch, even of Archimedes."[25] Plutarch said Greeks dismissed mechanical vocation and every technology as vulgar and ignoble. Aristotle believed that "no man can practice virtue who is living the life of a mechanic or laborer."[26] However, in the late Roman period, guilds appeared in *Polites* society.[27] Unlike the guild organizations in the Middle Ages, ancient guilds neither fulfilled the economic functions of protecting and teaching technologies and organizing and managing related technologies and industries nor had monopolies over trade and industries. They were nothing more than a social organization that provided public services.[28]

Third, Greece was the first country in the world to use scientific terms in literature and recognize and record scientific thoughts and their applications. The philosophers Plato and Aristotle are the best examples. In *Philebus*, Plato distinguished *techne* (technology) from political, human activities, and awareness and associated it with production activities that manipulated nonhuman material worlds, pointing out the clear distinction between theoretical and practical knowledge and qualitative and quantitative knowledge.[29] He proposed in *Utopia* that "*techne* is the form."[30] Aristotle absorbed Plato's theoretical thoughts, directly seeing technology as the practical activities of humans,[31] and he was the first to distinguish science from technology.[32] In the early fifth century BC or late sixth century BC, Xenophanes, a poet and philosopher of ancient Greece, pointed out that God exhibits his morals in some ways rather than through some things. With time passing, mortalities discover innovation through constant investigations.[33] After that, the opinion that humans obtained civilization through the gradual discovery of technologies frequently appeared in the books of Democritus (460 BC–370 BC), Lucretius, Theodoros, Vitruvio, and Seneca (all in the first century BC).[34] Protagoras (490 BC–421 BC), the representative of sophists in ancient Greece, even believed that the development of technology and art was the origin of human social civilizations. Moreover, many instructions and guides appeared for practical technologies and weapons, which reflected the strong interests of ancient Greeks and Romans in technologies.[35] Nonetheless, thoughts against technology were also found in some books. For example, Sophocles and Euripides said that people should appreciate nature.[36] After AD 200, books discussing technologies became fewer and fewer as people switched their interests to history, poetry, philosophy, and political affairs. According to some historians, the primary reason is that religions at that time proposed animism and anthropomorphism, which were the fatal enemies of technological revolutions.[37]

Last, the government did not realize the importance of technology to economic development. Technologies were generally encouraged when a need arose for public facilities and wars. For instance, the tyrant Dionysius of Syracuse in 399 BC attracted skilled workers from all over the Mediterranean Sea by recruitment, high salaries, or bonuses to work on military technologies, including giant warships and throwing or shooting weapons.[38] The attitude toward technologies varied in different governors. Some rewarded inventors due to their curiosity about and interest in technologies. For instance, the king of the Greek *polis* Sybaris in Sicily granted a 1-year protection term for new recipes of local cooks in 500 BC just because of his curiosity.[39] The governors of Rome were somewhat interested in technologies of public facilities and weapons, and successful inventors could apply for rewards from the emperors. At that time, inventor Sergius Ollata was rewarded for a central heating system. So was a Roman counselor and military commander, Marcus Vipsanius Agrippa, for designing new siege weapons and mangonels.[40]

When a mechanical engineer discovered a better way to carry heavy round pillars, Emperor Vespasian granted rewards but refused to apply this technology.[41] Some governors even punished innovators severely due to their excessive fear of new technologies. For example, Emperor Tiberius Caesar met the inventor of plastics (the unbreakable glass) and beheaded him to prevent him from saying, "gold would be as valueless as earth."[42]

Early Middle Ages

WESTERN EUROPE

Since the fall of the Roman Empire (AD 476), feudal separation spawned endless wars, and much classical literature was missing. In AD 529, Justinian I banned the School of Athens founded by Plato, which Hegel called the foundation of heretic philosophies. Since then, the dark and horrible rule of Christianity and religious trials enshrouded Europe. Europe was ushered into the long and dark Middle Ages when science and humanity were extremely oppressed. As Edward Gibbon said, the Middle Ages are the period where humans declined from the golden era and the age where barbarism and religions triumphed. Especially in the age between AD 500 and AD 800, the technology, economy, and culture in Europe were more primitive than in the Classical Times. Literacy was rare, and the upper class was addicted to chopping others into pieces by employing sophisticated fencing skills, even more addicted than the Romans. Technologies that were intertwined with witchcraft and alchemy prevailed. Roads, bridges, channels, ports, villas, and cities from the Roman Empire lay at waste. Life, property, and the operation of laws lost stability, and invasions from marauders, near or far, were commonplace.[43] No one cultivated the lands and maintained the channels in cities and the country, so acres of land became uninhabited due to the epidemics of dysentery.[44] However, there were still seeds of technological innovations in some corners of Europe. For example, heavy plows and a three-field system improved the efficiency of farming; waterwheels and dams facilitated the application of water energy; horseshoes, stirrups, and modern horse collars enabled horses to become the significant means of transportation in the Middle Ages; Scandinavians invented ships for short-range sailing around the eighth century.[45]

The main features of social development in Western Europe include slow technological development and restriction of technological applications to agriculture, water conservancy projects, transportation, and even alchemy and witchcraft. These technologies played no role in production and made little contribution to economic development. Moreover, the European economy, as a self-sufficient agricultural economy, was mainly dependent on natural resources and labor forces, so there was little demand for technologies. Christian theology had absolute authority in the ideological sphere. Disciplines like history, philosophy, and technology were all the handmaids of theology. The Christian Church, as the successor of Greek and Jewish conventions, had features of mysticism, asceticism, refusal of material life and wealth, and a thorough condemnation of labor and all worldly activities. As a dominant trend, it stressed self-discipline and yearned for the afterlife. God occupied a supreme position in the minds of West Europeans in the Middle Ages. Christians showed little interest in nature, belittled individual proposals and wealth, and believed spontaneous individual thoughts must yield to authority.[46] "There remains a strong current in popular Christianity that condemns certain acts of technological prowess as assaults on the divine order: if God had intended man to fly, he'd have given him wings."[47] Therefore, Christian thoughts affected people's outlook on technologies and wealth and politically manipulated regimes by affecting the will of decision makers in the upper class. Moreover, nature and God were incredibly divine concepts that people were compelled to look up to. Christian monks had high social status, and secular groups, including craftsmen, were humble. In the Middle Ages, kings, bishops, and other political dignitaries hired engineers and skilled technicians to build public facilities and take part in military production, such as building military facilities and catholic churches. Bonuses they could achieve were merely rewards for their labor rather than encouragement for their innovations and inventions.[48]

THE ISLAMIC WORLD

While European technologies developed slowly, technological development in two civilizations was quite brilliant. The first one was Islamic civilization.[49] The Islamic world in the Middle Ages was a highly mobile society where traveling was common. They were especially keen on acquiring knowledge and culture from other civilizations, whether present or past. Therefore, the Islamic world was the most prominent successor of Greek and Roman civilizations and the meeting ground for advanced thoughts from Middle Asia, India, Africa, and even China.[50] Islamic scholars formed a transnational group from Iberia to Middle Asia. In many important mosques, large libraries were possessed by rulers and even by individuals. There were at least hundreds of libraries in the Islamic world. Seventy libraries stood in Cordoba, one of which housed 400,000–500,000 volumes of books.[51] From AD 700 to AD 1200, the Islamic world learned more about all different parts of the known world than any other civilization.[52] Its ability to conserve, improve, and develop the technologies from other civilizations contributed to its leadership in technology.[53] In science, Muslims had great attainments in architecture, medicine, and astrology.[54] In technology, many inventions had a great influence, such as lateen, the tide waterwheel, and naphtha (the oil derivatives akin to kerosene). Muslims significantly improved spices, acid technology, and the quality of glass and ceramic products. Their water mills and clocks preceded the West for hundreds of years; their agricultural technologies (including farmland cultivation and sugar refinement, candy production, absorption of varieties of crops in Asia, and world-leading water conservancy projects) were advanced.[55] However, the Mongol invasion in the thirteenth century led to the decline of the technological civilization in the Islamic world.

The striking features of social development in the Islamic world were the use of technologies mainly in agriculture, water conservancy projects, and dairy products.

Although some simple industrial technologies had emerged, they were still in their infancy, so they could not be put into practice. Therefore, their contribution to industrial and economic development was limited. The economic development of the Islamic world was mainly dependent on the self-sufficient agricultural economy and short-range trade, with little demand for technologies. Moreover, the religion in the Islamic world restrained the development of the technological outlook, as in Europe in the Middle Ages.

CHINA

East of the Islamic civilization, the Tang and Song dynasties of China stood at the peak of global technology and economy from AD 618 to AD 1279. Especially in the Song Dynasty (AD 960–AD 1279), the large old empire climbed to the top of the world in economy and technology by absorbing the thoughts and cultures of the ancestors. As the famous historian Chen Yinke said, after the evolution of centuries, Chinese culture stood at its very peak in the Song Dynasty.[56] Technological attainments, as well as its development momentum or speed, were equal, even superior, to those in Europe in the Renaissance. Their features are detailed as follows.

First, in agriculture, significant improvements in rice cultivation revolutionized Chinese agriculture. Iron plows were improved; advanced agricultural implements, including seeders and weeding harrows, were introduced; new fertilizers like slurry and lime were popularized; chemical and biological medicines were used to control insects and pests. In addition, many books on agricultural technologies were published, such as the *Agricultural Book of Chen Fu* and *Poems and Painting on Farming and Weaving*. Water conservancy facilities were incredibly advanced and magnificent, but they were all controlled by the government.[57] Second, ceramic and weaving technologies were more developed than ever before. However, skilled ceramic workers and weavers were mainly hired by the government. The imperial family had its kilns and workshops, almost on an industrial scale, and hired thousands of workers to manufacture utensils and silk for daily use and luxurious decoration.[58] Third, frequent battles and wars generated a high demand for military technologies during the Song Dynasty. Therefore, military technologies were so advanced that cold and hot weapons, chariots, and battleships were all well-developed, and powder was invented.[59] Finally, some other achievements also evidenced the first-mover advantage and sophistication of Chinese technologies. For example, Bi Shen invented typography with ceramic movable types in AD 1045; Su Song built the famous water-operated planetarium in AD 1086, which symbolized China's highest achievements in time measurement; some daily articles such as matchsticks, umbrellas, toothbrushes, and pokers were all invented by Chinese.[60]

Social development during the Song Dynasty showed the following features. First, their technological development mainly happened in public sectors, such as agriculture, military, and water conservancy projects, and could be found in daily supplies. Some of the technologies were still in their infancy, so they were of no value to production and life.[61] Although handicraft technologies like printing, silk weaving, ceramic and paper-making were advanced, they were not applied to increase labor productivity. In fact, they were monopolized by the government to meet the imperial family's need for luxury and enjoyment and protect the vested interests of aristocracies. On the one hand, these technologies lacked endogenous force for further development and remained underexploited. On the other hand, the importance of technology in economic development was quite limited. Second, the economy during the Song Dynasty depended mainly on self-sufficient agriculture. The commodity economy was underdeveloped, and technologies played a minor role in production. Economic development depended on natural resources and a labor force with limited technological demand.[62] Third, Chinese culture was chronically influenced by Confucianism, Taoism, bureaucracy-centered thought, and the thought of stressing agriculture while restraining commerce. The formation and development of outlooks on wealth and technologies were restricted, and technicians and businessmen had lower social status. Confucianism emphasized "harmony between man and nature," reverence to heaven (nature), social and interpersonal relationships, tradition and past wisdom, but ignored practical skills and opposed innovation. Taoism was convinced that Tao and everything supplemented each other, and it encouraged "inaction," which is essentially an objection to scientific investigations. Due to bureaucracy-centered thoughts, most elites in China paid exclusive attention to imperial examinations, ignoring the acquisition and exploration of technological knowledge.[63] Given the traditional thought of stressing agriculture while restraining commerce, Chinese businessmen were dominated by bureaucratic structure, and commercial development was restricted. Technological talents like craftsmen failed to receive due attention. They had to master skills through apprenticeship and experience, and they had to earn money by employing skills. They had low social status. Last, the feudal government failed to realize the importance of technology to economic development. The development of technologies like agriculture, water conservancy projects, and weaving was largely restricted by the decisions of the bureaucratic structure and the emperors. Sagacious monarchs encouraged technological development, but once they perceived any reactionary elements in the technological development, they would issue edicts of banning and oppression. Technological innovations were usually dependent on the interest and the goodwill of the feudal government. The interest in changing the situation declined among most officials and the government. Therefore, these innovations could not last long. When the government lost interest in technological innovation, that would be the end of the miracle.[64]

Motivation for the absence of a patent system

Historical civilizations in the Middle Ages, including ancient Egypt, Greece, Rome, Western Europe, the Islamic world, and China, appear to be fragmental, but they share something among them. This can provide enlightenment for us when we try to figure out why a patent system that encourages invention and innovation did not emerge in the Middle Ages. According to this book, the most fundamental motivation is that these civilizations failed to formulate concepts of economic value and the application of technology. As William Blackstone said, the essential precondition of property is the existence of economic values, and anything with economic values is likely to be the object of property rights.[65] The object of the patent system is technology. Only when people are aware of the economic value possessed by technologies and when technological applications can generate tremendous economic advantages will people wonder who should gain profits from innovations and begin to think that these innovations should belong to someone instead of being simply granted to the public. Only when people have fully understood the utility and scarcity of scientific technologies will they endeavor to protect technologies by resorting to related rights. As Leona, a social constructivist, stated, legalization of knowledge would not be considered as a right relationship unless the pursuit of technology is driven by eagerness for wealth rather than knowledge, in an aim to increase economic benefits and production, and unless technology can improve efficiency and increase wealth.[66] Veblen mentioned in *The Place of Science in Modern Civilization* that people will not resort to rights until technology has developed to the point where people know how to make better use of technology and believe that technology can lift them out of economic disadvantages. Other things that may, in time, come to exceed these in usefulness are still useless and economically nonexistent in the early levels of culture because of what men in that time had not yet learned.[67] To us modern people, technology's utility and commercial values are out of the question: they can provide countless possibilities for human welfare, changing our lifestyles and bringing continuous "free lunches." It is totally reasonable to recognize and reward inventors. Hasty judgments about ancient society are made because we have imposed our values and concepts on societies with different civilization forms. As Stevenson said, we always think the problems of societies in the Middle Ages were the same as those that we are faced with; however, many problems and solutions at that time may be much more distinct in detail from those now.[68]

Some scholars who opposed the aforementioned opinions believed that people in the Middle Ages had already realized the economic value of technology. For instance, ancient Greeks and Romans kept their inventions secret, even until their bodies were in coffins.[69] Other scholars have pointed out that Greeks and Romans were likely to have concepts of Intellectual Property Rights (IPRs), because critiques on the theft of works and technologies were common in these worlds. The critique from the Roman architect Vitruvius was the best known of all. He thought that the past achievements and works with regard to building materials, the design of temples, public buildings, and water conservancy were so precious that plagiarism deserved harsh critiques.[70] This opinion is a one-sided interpretation of historical materials. First, technology in its early days took the form of artifacts. Craftsmen kept secrets and passed down the technology used to make artifacts, and they knew that they could earn money and make a living from artifacts. However, they could not clearly distinguish between the values of technology from those of artifacts. Technology was merely a tool in their eyes to produce artifacts, so technology existed only for this purpose. Technological benefits did not stand alone but were still a part of artifacts. Craftsmen failed to realize the economic value of technology.[71] Second, on the one hand, critiques of plagiarism in books and technology by scholars like Vitruvius were only a single spark in the culture. As described previously, most people still regarded technology as something humble, which was similar to labor, not to mention the protection of technology. On the other hand, Vitruvius' critique was made merely because he cherished the thoughts of the ancients and safeguarded their fame, but not because he realized that literal works and inventions were beneficial to economic development or, just like goods, they had market values.[72]

As a matter of fact, the recognition of the economic values in technology was a historical process that gradually formed under social conditions and was influenced by technological, economic, and cultural activities.

First, technological development was slow at a low level. It mainly happened in public sectors like the military and engineering. Because technology was not used in commercial activities, it failed to play an independent role in the economy. Technological development, as a cumulative process, can keep expanding its influence as people gain more and more useful information. Due to people's limited cognition, technology developed intermittently, and continuous and large-scale expansion, improvement, and application were rarely seen in technology. For instance, the division of labor in the technical field didn't appear in prehistoric ages and ancient Egypt. Technological activities showed no difference from other activities, and the main players in technology were the ordinary people involved in everyday activities. Technologies were occasionally discovered due to the need for survival, and people made inventions based on simple, instinctive knowledge. After ancient Greece and Rome, a variety of technologies developed to a certain extent, and the craftsmen, a class specialized in technological work, emerged. Their engagement in technological activities showed clear purposes, but they lacked the necessary knowledge and social status to conduct self-motivated technological research. Experience was their major approach to some practical skills. There was an inseparable tie between skill and craftsmen and between technology and products. Skills were inherited through apprenticeship, and technological creation was mysterious, occasional, and unlikely to be promoted and applied, not to mention to form a solid social production force. The interest of intellectuals after these ages lay occasionally in technologies and mainly in other fields. In addition, after the Middle Ages, technological inventions and achievements mainly happened in public sectors, including public facilities, agriculture, and the military, but they did not benefit commercial activities or the private sector. In other words, there was limited practical significance in them. Invented agricultural tools and daily utensils were restricted to the necessities of survival and life. The development of handicraft and industrial technologies was slow-paced and restricted. Despite the new inventions in the Middle Ages, many of them could have promoted great economic reforms but failed to be developed to reach the logical end or to exploit as many economic profits as possible. It may be due to people's lack of interest in technological problems at that time[73] or because technology, still in its infancy, had no value in production or application. Consequently, technology could not be used in commercial activities or production; therefore, it failed to occupy a critical place in productivity or play an important role in economic growth. Some of them may have temporarily fostered economic development. However, they would gradually stagnate before they could become a strong driver behind sustainable economic growth, and they could not be an inexhaustible source of chances for explosive economic development and a stable increase in productivity.[74]

Second, the economic form limited the demand for technology. The main economic form in the Middle Ages was a self-sufficient agricultural economy. Although some countries like ancient Greece and the Islamic world relied on commerce and trade, the restricted market range limited their scales. The agricultural economy, which is distinct from other processing or manufacturing industries, is more dependent on natural factors (e.g., climate, soil, temperature, humidity, and illumination). In fact, these factors still play an essential role in modern times when tractors, harvesters, threshers, and agricultural chemical fertilizers were widely used, not to mention the days when agricultural productivity was not developed enough. Favorable geographical conditions played a more significant part in the growth of crops than any agricultural technology in ancient times.[75] The dramatic increase in population density contributed to more demands for clothing and food and the input of agricultural labor forces. According to growth economics, nontechnological elements are a much more important contributor to the growth of the agricultural economy than technological ones. Given that the development of the agricultural economy mainly relied on natural resources (e.g., soil and climate) and labor forces, there was no social demand or endogenous force for technology.[76] An abundant labor force and simple technology and experience could fulfill their requirements, and undeveloped trade relations were unable to motivate the creation and promotion of new technology.[77] Consequently, the traditional agricultural economy could not nurture economic value and application of the concept of technology, which can only emerge in an environment where industry and commerce are advanced. This is because industrial and commercial economies cannot develop merely by virtue of simple labor forces or limited natural resources, and more advanced technological supplies are needed. Technological innovation is a strong impetus for industrial and commercial development, therefore inevitably encouraging people to emphasize and explore technology.

Third, the cultural environment restrained people's interest in technology creation, production, and development. On the one hand, standards of values and group evaluation in every society determine the relative prestige of activities or characters; prestige is not equal to wealth, and prestige also entails the military, arts, governmental management, power, sports, learning, and teaching. The higher the accumulation of productivity, products, and wealth in ranking, the more likely a society is to be affected by economic values processed by technology.[78] Among the great civilizations, Greeks appreciated sports and learning; Romans emphasized military and power above all others; Muslims focused on learning and literary review; ancient China paid attention to governmental management (bureaucratic organizations). All these societies appreciated wealth while believing sports, learning, the military, and power were equal, even superior to wealth. In other words, the mainstream values in societies of the Middle Ages didn't stress technology and wealth. On the other hand, some religions and ideologies greatly affected people's outlooks on wealth and technology. The beliefs of Babylonians and Romans, the animism and anthropomorphism of Greeks and Romans, Christianity's objection to material and technological progress in Western Europe, as well as Confucian and Taoist thoughts of stressing agriculture while restraining commerce in ancient China all had adverse effects on the creation of wealth and technology. Religions and ideologies led to the reverence of gods, fear of and opposition to technologies, refusal of material lives and wealth, and lower social status of technicians. Only in a civilization where technology and production are encouraged, and creators of technology get enough respect, does the concept that technology should be economically applied emerge.

However, the concept of economic values in technology emerged neither in the private sector nor in the governments, namely the subjects of authority. In ancient Greece and Rome, or ancient China, the social status of technicians and businessmen was too low to become a considerable political and economic force, and the government was the ultimate decision maker for the formation of institutions. Once governors failed to realize the economic value of technology, the pursuit of profits from technology alone could not generate institutions. And the governors who were afraid and ignorant of technology would never allow the creation of an institution that encouraged technological development. Governments in Greece, Rome, Western Europe, and ancient China always restricted the use of technology in public facilities and military fields and seldom used it in production. Although some governors might sometimes be curious about technology, they remained conservative and detested innovation. Some rulers in ancient Greece and Rome even feared technology. As Finely, an expert on technological history, said, simultaneously, the Ptolemies founded and financed the Museum at Alexandria, which was the main Western center of scientific research and invention for two centuries. Great things emerged from the museum, including military technology and ingenious mechanical toys. But no one, not even the Ptolemies themselves, who would have profited directly and handsomely thought to turn the energy and inventiveness of a Ctesibius to agricultural or industrial technology. The contrast with the Royal Society in England is inescapable.[79]

Emergence of the patent privilege system: patent privilege system in Venice

Before AD 500, there was a quiet salt-water lagoon and some small islands in the Gulf of Adriatic Sea in Northern Italy. Residents living at the coast of the Adriatic Sea fled there to seek asylum from the persecution by "God's Whip" Attila and Germans, and their arrival prospered on this barren island. Hereafter, these islands constituted a political group to defend against the Goths and the Roman Empire. This political group was the embryo of Venice, the Water City, which was crowned the "Pearl of Adriatic Sea."[80] The historical city has witnessed so many prosperities and glories. It was the center of early-time technology in Europe and an avant-garde of the Renaissance, and it had a prosperous marine trade and industry. All these contributed to its glory and prosperity. The creation of the patent privilege system in Venice was closely related to its technological, economic, and cultural activities. More importantly, the democratic government of Venice was the first to enact the policies of "stressing commerce" and "stressing industry."

Motivation for the creation of the patent privilege system in Venice

The premature development of industrial technology and the prosperity of the industrial and commercial economy in Venice

We all know the highly developed technology and great achievements of the Industrial Revolution in England in the seventeenth century, but few know that the center of technology in the Middle Ages originated in Italy, specifically in Venice. The thriving technology in this city had much to do with the technological improvement in Western Europe. Western Europe was essentially a technological community. Changes in any one part would often be felt by other parts.[81] Ancient Greeks and Romans originally kindled the spark of technology and then experienced the Middle Ages with slow technological development. At the end of the Dark Ages in the eighth to ninth centuries, the initial signs of technological innovation emerged in European society and finally developed into a prevailing trend of technological innovations.[82] Western Europe experienced rapid and sustained development of science and technology since the twelfth century, and this historical period even overshadowed the Black Death, a severe crisis in the population and economy. Around AD 1200, economies in Western Europe absorbed most of the advanced technologies from civilizations like ancient China and the Islamic world. A series of inventions between AD 1200 and AD 1500 made it possible for Europe to finally become the leader in technology. The reasons for the rise of technology in Europe are described as follows: technological innovation was personal; the political background of feudal competition was beneficial to competition and the transfer of technology; Europeans were good at absorbing technologies from other civilizations; new dogma beneficial to technological development appeared in Christian thoughts.[83] Technological achievements could be found in hydraulic and wind facilities, shipping, shipbuilding, weaving, metallurgy, clocks, chemistry, printing, and military.[84]

Venice was the world's biggest trade hub and interpreter of civilizations during the Middle Ages. Thanks to its ready access to the Adriatic Sea, Venice established and managed a large commercial network in the thirteenth and fourteenth centuries. It controlled almost all trade routes that delivered goods from the East through the Mediterranean Sea to Europe and established numerous overseas colonies. It monopolized trade between Europe and other known parts of the world, and Venetian businessmen could be seen in every corner of Europe.[85] Venice was close to the route in which foreign products and technology were introduced to Europe, and this geographic advantage enabled its easy contact with the best technology.[86] Moreover, because Venice was a marine city with scarce freshwater or farming land, Venetians had no agriculture, and all materials and resources to support their daily lives depended entirely on commerce, trade, and industry. Venice was the only country organized to make trade,[87] which had a higher demand for technological and industrial development. As mentioned in Diderot's *Encyclopedia*, varieties of craft technologies emerged as early as the fifteenth century, and the advanced and matured industrial technology made Venice become the leading industrial center in Europe.[88]

Venice's most potent industrial technologies were demonstrated mainly in four aspects. First, glass processing technology. Venice had the most advanced glass processing industry, and glass technicians there enjoyed a global reputation.[89] With the efforts of hundreds of technicians, Venice rapidly emerged as the center of the glass industry. Murano was particularly a legendary land in the glass industry.[90] Second, the shipbuilding and navigation industry. Shipbuilding and navigation were significant in the marine city of Venice. The Republic had consumed immense materials and financial resources since the thirteenth century and introduced technological talents to build battleships that escorted merchant vessels. It built the biggest and most famous "arsenal" in Europe.[91] The fleet they built was so tremendous that no Christian had ever seen a better one.[92] All these indicated that Venice was equipped with the most advanced shipbuilding technology in the world and the most astonishing marine power. Third, silk weaving technology. As mentioned previously, Venice was the most significant trade hub in Europe. Venetians learned the silk weaving technology from the East and introduced many Luka weavers and businessmen who mastered the best silk dyeing technology in Europe. These Luka weavers helped Venice continuously introduce silk weaving and dyeing technologies,[93] facilitating Venice's processing of the most advanced silk weaving technology. Fourth, the introduction and popularization of typography. After Bi Sheng invented typography, the expedition of the Mongolian army helped tighten the commercial and diplomatic ties between Europe and China. Meanwhile, woodblock printing technology appeared in Venice and some parts of Germany. However, its diffusion to other parts of Europe was so slow that the printing technology did not spread throughout Europe until the Renaissance.[94] The shrewd Venetians quickly learned this technology, popularizing it in Venice and developing the printing and publishing industry much earlier than people in other European countries.

Advanced industrial technology, developed commerce and trade, and a broad overseas market in Venice facilitated the development of industry and the prosperity of the industrial and commercial economy during the Middle Ages, pushing Venice to the top of the industrial centers in Europe. Its important industries included glass processing, shipbuilding, leather, and silk weaving, and the products were sold throughout Europe and Mediterranean countries.[95] The production of mirrors, soaps, and metal ornaments also happened in Venice.[96] In the fourteenth century, the organization and technology of the Luka weavers showed some capitalistic features, and they had relatively complicated production procedures, which was especially true of the leather weaving industry. Workshop owners provided production facilities, and workers sold their labor in exchange for wages. The economic structure of the Venetian industry was changed, and capitalistic sprouts appeared.[97]

In addition, early Venetian printers set up and managed companies in the form of early capitalism to avoid interference from guilds and restrictions from the Venetian government.[98] At the end of the fifteenth century, about 100 typographic workshops were established, and some two million books were published. The development of this technology helped the printing industry in Venice to outperform the industry in Germany (Gutenberg's homeland).[99] At the same time, advanced commerce, trade, and industry generated a sizable financial business.[100] It's almost safe to say that all residents in Venice gave businessmen credits, which were spontaneously provided and could be acquired almost everywhere, thus greatly facilitating the businessmen's accumulation of capital and access to credits. This laid a solid foundation for Venetian businessmen's investment in the handicraft industry.[101] Venice was undoubtedly the cradle and leader in terms of industrial and commercial development in Italy and Europe. In the fifteenth century, the annual financial income of Venice totaled

1.59 million Ducato. Therefore, Venice became the "richest country in Europe"[102] and was hailed as "the world's first economic center" in Europe after the renaissance of commerce and cities during the Middle Ages.[103] Therefore, compared with other European countries in the Middle Ages, Venice already witnessed the separation of labor from capital in the development of an industrial and commercial economy. Some wealthy businessmen or workshop owners hired craftsmen for production and gradually acquired management ability or advanced technology. They came to realize the importance of technology to the productivity of goods and the access to more profits. They started to emerge as a new force.[104]

Athena's gift[105]*: "Disenchantment" and "innovation" of the Renaissance*

In commercially developed cities in Italy, such as Florance and Venice, as new technologies created tremendous productivity and economic values and prosperous commerce and trade introduced new lifestyles, some advanced intellectuals in the emerging industrial-commercial class generated new concepts of value. At the same time, oppressive Christian beliefs and corrupt churches increasingly aroused public discontent. People no longer believed in theological thoughts of Christianity that denied worldly life and pursued the afterlife. However, they began to look back on the ancient times, hoping to absorb nutrition from writers, artists, and poets during the Classical Times. They reproduced, researched, and imitated the classical works of ancient Greece and Rome that existed before the rule of Christianity. The light of reason dispelled the shadow of the Middle Ages, thus fostering the rise of the Renaissance movement. The development of printing technology in Western Europe altered the way of storing, renewing, and disseminating knowledge, facilitating the development of the Renaissance. The rise of the Renaissance in Italy was 200–300 years earlier than in Western European countries; therefore, Western Europe was the first to enter the stage of modern society. The influence of the Renaissance movement on Venice can be concluded in detail as follows.

First, the ideological trend of humanism in the Renaissance enlightened people's new knowledge and emphasized that social economy and technological life should be combined. This swept away the people's ignorance of technology and encouraged and praised scientists and technicians. Technological talents were respected, and technology was stressed. Encouraged by the naturalism of ancient Greece,[106] humanists began to focus on science and actively promoted a classical rational spirit that highlighted the attitude toward science. These positive factors and technical crafts reinforced each other, thus generating the seeds of modern natural science. Then, Europeans began to observe and explore nature and paid great attention to experience and experiments. For instance, Bruno once called on humanists by saying they should absorb scientific knowledge from all sources to enrich their thoughts, lest they feel void and poor. In addition, as more and more technicians participated in practical technologies, technicians as a whole gradually earned a higher social status. Based on their practical experience and work results, they wrote books such as craftsman and mechanic Senini's *Art of Craft*, Billinguccio's *Technology of Thermal Processing*, Agricola's *Metallography*, Ramilli's *Wonderful Machines,* and Verentius' *New Machinery*. Moreover, engineers became pretty confident. Their notes that survived were all about fantasies about new power sources and machines. Some modern records also described how clockmakers made an agreement on necessary improvements and fulfilled tasks in some systematic way.[107] Some technology fantasy works also appeared.[108] Technological books could not necessarily grant people the ability to make new inventions but gave them an illusion: the resolution to most social problems could be found in new technologies, and the importance of technology and inventors gradually became apparent.

The speed of innovation astonished writers in the thirteenth and fourteenth centuries. Engineers and technicians were regarded as heroes and praised by influential writers and thinkers for their contribution to human welfare.[109] During the Renaissance, books that listed essential inventions and inventors were published for the first time. For example, Virgil's *On Inventors* was the first book of this sort, which described kinds of inventions, such as glass crafts, silk, printing, and shipbuilding, and extolled inventors.[110] Moreover, many books with elaborate illustrations were published, some of which were descriptive in essence, precisely demonstrating the technological practice and the manufacturing of artifacts in the mining industry and metallurgy. One such book was of significant influence because it collected thousands of images of machines derived from existing machines. The innovations described in these books were not created. However, the delicate and vivid painting styles showed that people had begun to use art to express their respect for inventors and curiosity about new inventions.[111] The words of Nicholas of Cusa indicate that the ceramics and spoon makers had a higher status than painters because the latter did nothing but imitate nature. The former created something that didn't exist in nature.[112]

Second, the Renaissance began to liberate people from the oppression of divinity in Christianity and helped them to a positive outlook on wealth and technology. People turned their eyes to nature and wealth, and the first sign of pragmatism ignited people's passion for wealth and productivity. In the Middle Ages, the oppression of Christianity resulted in the ignorance of wealth and sex as well as a lack of interest in exploring nature. However, with germination of the industry and development of the commercial economy, huge wealth flew into cities, and the desire for wealth began to explode. The pioneers of humanism went with the development trend, seeking a theoretical basis for possessing wealth and opposition to asceticism. Guided by these theories, wealth began to be the source of happiness, and the restriction of asceticism tended to loosen and collapse.[113] Under the influence of humanistic thoughts, Venice probably embraced pragmatism earlier than other European countries. Famous European historian Henry Pullan pointed out that Venice was a city of businessmen; developed industry and commerce and booming trade made the commercial concepts widely accepted there; pragmatic philosophy began to dominate this city, and profits and calculation occupied all their attention in life.[114] According to Joel Mokyr, an expert on technological history, although this pragmatism did not exert its full influence until the seventeenth century, especially in Francis Bacon's books, pragmatism was likely to secretly exist in Venice years before.[115] Professor Robertson held that economic rationalism already existed in ancient Greece due to the thriving trade and was likely to revive during the Renaissance in Italy when great importance was attached to commerce.[116] Once Venetians began to regard pragmatism and "profits first" as their primary value standard, they showed a stronger thirst for economic development and higher productivity. In the practical desires of commerce, we can see the basic impetus of its major outward movements.[117] As Max Weber said in *The Protestant Ethic and the Spirit of Capitalism*, ascetic and pragmatic characters of Calvinism contributed to and motivated the emergence and development of capitalism; Merton mentioned in *Science, Technology & Society in Seventeenth Century Britain* that pragmatic values of Puritanism fostered the recognition of science and thirst for economy among the people of England in the seventeenth century.[118]

Third, humanism began to defy the excessive emphasis on collectivism in the Middle Ages and championed the independent wills of individuals, and individualism began to gain traction. In the Middle Ages, Western Europe was a society that emphasized groups and communities, which was featured in the vassal system, common lands, guilds, and religions. Excessive emphasis on groups oppressed the individual spirit.[119] The Renaissance movement enlightened and awakened the individual spirit, and people were aware that individuals could shake off the chains of God and embrace freedom in the creation of technology and arts. They enjoyed free and independent personalities in handling their economic activities and affairs, free from the inferences of others. Individualism catalyzed the self-governance concept in civil society, introducing the basic principles of modern civil laws that met the needs of personal emancipation, such as equality of personality, autonomy of will, and contract freedom, to the economic lives of countries like Venice. The Lex Romana, which emphasized personal property and contracting rights, began to revive significantly under the influence of the Renaissance. As Bugbee said, the revival of the Lex Romana in Italy helped facilitate the formation of individual rights and the law system based on contract law in Italy.[120]

Conclusion

The coupling effect between technological, economic, and cultural environments in Venice created a favorable condition for the concept of the patent system. First, due to the rise of technology in Western Europe at the end of the Middle Ages, the unique geographical advantage and broad overseas trade market enabled Venice to access the most advanced technologies in the East and the West. Growing recognition of technology and limited natural resources fostered Venetians' interest in technological innovations. When technologies in all Western countries were still used in navigation, agriculture, and daily lives, smart Venetians began to use scientific principles to extract systematic knowledge from handicraft experience and apply their experience to primitive industrial sectors, such as glass processing, silk, shipbuilding, printing, and publishing, thus achieving great benefits. The technological development at this time was far more than meeting the needs for life and survival or the public sectors, but instead served the purpose of ensuring adequate material resources and seeking economic expansion. In Venice, the embryonic form of capitalism first appeared, and these emerging industrial and commercial classes began to apply technologies in production. Its advanced commerce and trade and the broad overseas market further stimulated demands for industrial products and handicraft technology. Commercial capital and financial credits provided capital for the industrial and commercial economy and technological creation. Therefore, given the positive interaction between industrial technology and practice, savvy Venetian businessmen realized the commercial value of technological innovations in efforts to solve the problem of inadequate resources. They started to stress the benefits of technology, which was the means of objective production. Second, the Renaissance movement played the following roles: 1. The humanistic thought in the Renaissance enlightened people's new knowledge. It proposed that the social economy and the practice of scientific lives should be combined. The new thought swept away the fear and ignorance of technology, offering a new perspective to the theories of science and technology and extolled and encouraged scientists and technicians so that technological talents were respected and technology emphasized. 2. The Renaissance liberated people from the oppression of divinity in Christianity and help people develop a positive outlook on wealth and technology. People were interested in nature and wealth, and the shoots of pragmatism sparked people's eagerness for wealth and productivity. 3. Humanism and the revival of Lex Romana in the Renaissance enabled people to emphasize the value of individualism. Indeed, the effect of all the previous factors was a complicated, slow-paced, and interactive process. However, when all conditions were made available in Venice, the concept of economic value and the application of technology first appeared in Venice. Venetians negated the excessive emphasis on collectivism during the Middle Ages. What's more, the independent wills of individuals were championed, which, in essence, promoted the formation of the institutional concept – that individuals should enjoy technological profits. However, this institutional concept could take diverse forms, such as foundations that encourage inventions, rewards for inventions, and franchises. As revealed in the following paragraphs, because the Venetian government and private sectors had respective self-interests at the beginning, they formed different institutional concepts.

Formation of the patent privilege system in Venice

Early concepts and regulations of technology protection in Venetian guilds

The commercial value of technologies was first discovered by the Venetian guilds, where the distinction between technologies and tangible objects was made, and technologies were named "intangible properties." Therefore, the earliest concepts of IPRs began to develop in Venetian guilds. In the eleventh and twelfth centuries, with the revival of the economy and technology in Western Europe, various guild organizations were founded in cities. However, they were too small and separate to influence the economy. It was not until the late thirteenth century that guild organizations began to prosper.[121] Especially in Venice, due to the city's expansion and economic development and the specialization of craftsmen, the government encouraged and supported the specialization of all sectors. Various guild organizations were founded and strengthened in Venice, making guilds dominate the central part of commerce and technology.[122] Guilds were groups of technology and industry employers who maintained a monopoly in respective sectors, many of whom were representatives of emerging capitalistic businessmen. Guild members possessed production tools, purchased resources, organized production, and sold products on their own.[123] The Venetian government gradually realized the importance of guilds and strengthened supervision. Guilds were closely related to the Venetian government: guilds depended on government regulations to protect their benefits, and the government depended on guilds to manage domestic technicians. Guilds were managed by a specific organ in the Venetian government. The organ selected suitable members as its officials, who were obliged to report the development status of guilds to this organ, and guild regulations should be reviewed and approved by this administrative organ. Therefore, guilds in Venice at that time had dual functions, including social groups of technicians and administrative management.[124] Nonetheless, guilds were not merely a tool used by the Venetian government to adjust and manage economic activities. Thanks to appealing processes inside the guilds, guild members were entitled to restrict administrative officials in the Venetian government. Therefore, in essence, they were beneficial independent groups.[125]

Intangible property values of technology were likely to appear in glass guilds in Venice. There were mainly three types of glass products, including glass balls (hollow vessels for daily use), mirrors, and lenses. The glass balls from Venice occupied a significant position in the Venetian glass industry in manufacturing and exporting.[126] Two reasons account for why Venetian glasses were of higher quality than those produced by other European countries. On the one hand, the developed port trade enabled Venice to obtain high-quality raw materials from the East. For example, the impurities in sodium were more readily identified than materials used by Northern European countries. On the other hand, advanced glass production crafts in Venice were world-famous, especially those on Mullane Island.[127] Glass technology brought Venice countless wealth and a reputation throughout Europe. It was the jewel of Europe and the object of jealousy. Many countries coveted the glass technology of Venice, sending many industry spies to steal glass-making methods from Venice. Even the French King Louis XIV hoped that the glass processing industry could be based on those in Mullane Island and entrusted a heavy task to his financial official

J. B. Colbert, who used to tempt glass-making masters in Venice with money but ended in failure.[128] The guild of glass-making gradually realized the commercial value of glass crafts. The awareness of collectivism was initially the mainstream, so the glass guild regarded the craft as the property of the guild. The guild, as a group, possessed the profit, and the members should not reveal their secrets. In fear that the technological properties of the glass guild would be leaked or transferred, the hirers of technicians in the guild began to demand that the government enact related regulations to protect their glass crafts. The Venetian glass products could be sold throughout Europe, and the export of the crafts was strictly prohibited. If the glass makers transmitted these crafts out of Venice, they would face severe punishment. For example, the glass-making guild and the Venetian government enacted specific regulations on the behavior of leaking glass crafts in 1271. Any worker with crafts of glass-making who fled from Venice without permission would be fined and no longer accepted by guild organizations.[129] The regulation became severer in 1281 where offenders would be sentenced to double fines. In 1291, the Venetian government and guild organization believed that the fine regulation made no sense and could not deter these offenders. Many glass technicians fled to other countries for benefits. Therefore, the former applied to Congress for more severe punishments and believed those who sold raw materials to leakers would be prohibited or dismissed, and if related guild members knew the source of the leaks, they would be obliged to inform the government, which the Congress finally passed.[130] In 1313, the Venetian glass guild and the government announced to Milan and Arito (famous commercial centers in Europe that the imperial court would judge any leakers and would be likely to be permanently dismissed by the guild).[131] In 1315, the Venetian glass guild and the government tried to use another way. They once again announced to the outside world via Milan and Arito that any leaker who returned to Venice within 2 months would be free from punishment; otherwise, they would be severely punished according to the regulations listed previously.[132]

A well-known story in Venice also reveals that Venice paid great attention to glass processing technology. Giorgio was an apprentice in a glass workshop of the famous Barovier family in Venice. He worked day to night, learning crafts and desiring to be excellent one day. Then, Giorgio stole Barovier's glass-making recipe and sold it to their competitors. As a result, Giorgio won a glass workshop that belonged to him and married the daughter of Barovier's competitor. Therefore, he became the ultimate winner. However, Giorgio soon realized that he had lost precious credit in the eyes of Venetians and was no longer respected or trusted by others. He could not immigrate to other countries to continue his career or work elsewhere on Mullane Island.[133]

Other guilds in Venice soon realized that other technologies had commercial value, and they demanded that the government enact related regulations to protect the collective properties of the guilds. For instance, the Venetian Congress enacted an act on 21 May 1297 that a recipe of medicines developed by a pharmacist according to the recipe he designed, if the best materials could be guaranteed to be used, belonged to the guild, and all guild members should hold the secret.[134] Therefore, before "Intellectual Property Rights" emerged as a professional term with specific content, it existed initially as the ownership of guilds to technologies. As technological knowledge became increasingly valuable, it also became the object of embezzlement or stealing. European countries have a separate, competitive country system. As the example of Giorgio showed, guild members would flee to other countries or regions with internal technologies or industries. Guild members excessively cherished their creations and were unsatisfied with the monopoly of the guild on the technologies created by themselves. These countries or regions promised high rewards to foreign technological talents to reduce the costs of importing products or developing economies. More importantly, there was a gradual emphasis on individual values due to the revival of Lex Romana and the Renaissance. Venetian guilds gradually realized the necessity of granting individual members profits on specific knowledge. Therefore, knowledge regarded as collective property before was considered to be possessed by internal guild members in the internal regulations of some guilds. The richer the experience of handling intangible technological properties in guilds was, the more concrete the regulations on similar problems were. For instance, the approval of intangible properties must be suitable for "unity of work," namely technicians or makers had to guarantee that the technology or product provided had unity of work. Otherwise, they would assume responsibility. A law of Venetian guilds in the fourteenth century regulated that if someone invented any "useful" mechanical device or method of silk making, they should not be applied by other members.[135] This standard was afterward absorbed in the *1474 Inventor Bylaws of Venice*, becoming one of the authorization standards of patents.[136]

The mercantilism policy and early practices of Venice

"VENICE MYTH" AND CAMERALISM POLICY

Although there are several doctrines about the origin of cities,[137] people have reached a consensus on one fact: modern cities first appeared in Italy.[138] At the end of the thirteenth century, the intensified overseas expansion of Venice facilitated many businessmen to accumulate wealth via overseas trade and became the emerging elite families. They were eager to gain political status and power; therefore, they directed the famous "closing the congress" event in the history of Venetian aristocratic politics. Since 1286, these emerging commercial aristocrats had constantly proposed bills to Congress to modify the qualification and procedure for the election of members of Congress, which was approved in February 1297. Therefore, a ten-man *Senato* of the republic, whose members were a closed elite class of commercial aristocrats represented by the governor (akin to today's president), was affirmed legally. The monarch of Venice, nominally the Emperor of the Holy Roman Empire, was actually a puppet.[139] The political system prevented the possibility that a dictatorship would appear on the grounds of an institution, becoming the political foundation of the republic's development in the next 500 years. It played a unique role in sustaining the persistent harmony and stability of the republic and shaping the "Venice myth."[140] The aristocratic class of Venice were typical commercial aristocrats whose pursuit of profits, resources, and spaces for self-sufficiency and survival was the original motivation for mastering and motivating the country machine of Venice. After setting up their status as governors, they devoted themselves to overseas expansion and commerce and trade activities instead of exiting from commercial activities like aristocrats in other Western European countries.[141]

The emphasis on commerce and the pursuit of economic profits by aristocrats directly influenced diplomacy and policies, and Venice and other commercially advanced cities were likely to be the origin of mercantilism policies. It is widely believed that mercantilism ideas were prevalent in Western Europe in the sixteenth–eighteenth centuries, accompanied by the rise of national states; however, during the age of the Renaissance, "cameralism" or state-governing methods popular in some city-states in Italy had traditional thoughts of "emphasis on commerce and industry," which was gradually spread to other countries (e.g., France, Britain, the United States, and Russia) and became fundamental breakouts in practice. According to studies by Christopher White and Nancy Spannaus, the core idea of the doctrine of "cameralists" was collective welfare, based on the following ideas: sovereignty must devote itself to educating and improving its populations via progress in science and technologies. Essentially, the economic tradition was built on production, considering people as producers with creativity and productivity rather than passive consumers receiving mechanical stimulations. As the foundation of the theory, collective welfare was positive about the role of a country. It believed the country's inference should mainly take the form of stimulating production, creating demands, and devoting itself to the progress of science and technology and improvements in population qualities. Generally speaking, the fundamental opinions of cameralists could be concluded as follows. First, man has productivity and creativity, and the will and wisdom of men constitute the source of wealth productivity. Second, the country should devote itself to improving public welfare, and the prosperity of the country depends on the policies on material and spiritual policies to improve its citizens. Third, the development of the crafts and manufacturing industry is essential to the development of agriculture, the increase in population, and the improvement in people's living standards. Fourth, education, infrastructure, and technological progress are significant to the prosperity of the manufacturing industry, improving population quality, and improving public welfare. The country is responsible for improving education, infrastructure, and technological progress. In conclusion, this tradition concentrated on domestic production and development, emphasizing the country's responsibility for its citizens, and its methods were organic and holistic.

In conclusion, Venice opened the trend of mercantilism in Western Europe, and the country was constituted of businessmen and entrepreneurs who paid great attention to mercantilism policies. It developed internal production (especially the manufacturing industry), improved population quality, prevented competition from entering the country (to protect domestic producers, markets, and employment), and exploited the positive functions of the government. It greatly emphasized the fundamental importance of the development of the manufacturing industry and technological progress to improve people's welfare. The industrial and commercial activities in Venice obtained great support and protection from the government. From the beginning, the Venetian government was either the spokesman or the arms and shields of businessmen.[142]

EARLY PRACTICES TO ENCOURAGE THE DEVELOPMENT OF INDUSTRY AND COMMERCE

The Venetian government implemented industrial and commercial policies. This actually showed that institutional concepts of economic value and the application of technology had already developed in the Venetian government, and these concepts assumed various forms, such as encouraging foreigners' entry into Venice, financial support, rewards for inventions, and patent privileges. The institutional concepts were all important means used by the Venetian government to encourage the development of industry and commerce. With the help of political powers, the government soon put these institutional concepts into practice, some of which even developed into written institutions. First, encouraging foreigners' entry into Venice was an institution designed to introduce technological talents. The Venetian government had invited foreigners to come and work in Venice long before,[143] just like the advanced Luka weavers mentioned previously. Around 1350, Venice passed a law that people residing in Venice for the required years could acquire the identity of permanent citizenship; however, the law was hindered by guilds, because the introduction of foreign talents would break the technological monopoly of local guilds. Second, the Venetian government created investment and reward institutions for technological inventions. For example, in 1332, the Venetian government provided a risk fund for Bartolomeo Verde because he promised the government that the windmill would be completed and start to function within 6 months, and he offered guarantees in advance. However, if he failed to complete this invention within the given period, he would have to refund and lose the offered guarantees. In the fifteenth century, the Venetian government subsidized lots of talents who claimed to have mastered mature or novel windmill technologies and some technologically creative talents who claimed to have mastered new or advanced machines. Perhaps there were more people who gained support from the government.[144] Third, the Venetian government provided rewards for useful inventions. For instance, to attract talent to the arsenal, its biggest and most important "arsenal" that produced weapons for the navy, Venice proposed high rewards and excellent welfare, including houses, to attract technological talents. Moreover, before the

1474 Inventor Bylaws were issued, the Venetian Congress enacted a comprehensive law on 18 January 1453 that involved all affairs about the finance and economy of Venice. As an extremely important provision set forth, if anyone proposed a method to make new inventions and this method proved to be practical, then whoever else used this method had to pay fees. The proposer was entitled to oversee the production of this invention and to obtain sufficient rewards given by congress. Although it was not a patent law, it was a law that granted special encouragement to the inventors of new things, who were entitled to obtain permission fees and sufficient rewards given by Congress. Historical materials indicated that this law has had certain effects since its enactment.[145] The last one was privilege. The Venetian government was likely to get enlightenment from the guilds' practice of granting technological benefits to the members, and it encouraged the development of crafts by granting privileges to the introducers of technologies or inventors of original technologies to develop industry and maintain leadership in the economy. At first, it was restricted to special fields like glass, medicine, or silk. Then, it became gradually open to all technological fields. For values, original privileges had no essential difference between introduced ones: the cognitive basis of Venetian technologies were all relatively narrow, the technologies mastered were limited, the transport at that time was undeveloped, and reserved technological literature was restricted. Therefore, original and introduced technologies were scarce resources. To develop the domestic economy, the Venetian government tried all means to acquire these technologies. It was called "the privilege" because in the guild system, whoever proposed new technologies first needed to obtain special permission or authorization from the government or royal family to break the monopoly of the guilds and to produce, sell, or apply new inventions, and this special permission or authorization was called a "privilege." Of note, various privileges were granted by the government or royal family, including land, freedom, and fame, which were always seen as gifts from the government or royal family. The privileges could be granted by signing a license with an official stamp called a "*litterae patentes*," which was the earliest form of patent. Because Venice's early patent system had no written legal regulations, it mainly depended on people's general practice, and its content became richer and richer in practice. The earliest privilege granting in Venice aimed at restricting the monopoly of the guilds and encouraging the development of industry. However, many privileges afterward had little relation to the guild system; for example, the granted privilege of facilities to maintain channels and provide food in Venice was related to public interests.[146]

The earliest type of patent privilege in practice was the franchise, which was to grant not a monopoly right of technology, but a permission qualification for producing some goods or participating in some industries. In this sense, franchise was akin to granting passports. As the historian Giulio Mandich revealed, the Venetian Congress granted franchises to produce various grinding millers during 1281–1296. Afterward, more diverse privileges appeared, which were essentially related to the constant requests of foreign technological immigrants, including promising to give innovators some benefits (rewards or tax exemption, building warehouses of the factory, and related materials)[147] via contracts, granting rights to prohibit others from using the facility without permission, requiring the right holder to grant licenses after others pay reasonable patent right taxes, and granting the inventor a monopoly right.[148] Types of privileges afterward were similar to a right to benefit rather than a franchise.

According to the literature, granting some technology-related benefits may have happened to the mining rights, which were introduced by businessmen to Venice from Germany. The mining right was primarily used in underground exploitation and mining activities, related to the exclusive management rights for a particular time to explore and exploit underground mineral resources, but excluded land ownership.[149] In the Middle Ages, the word "invention" in Latin had a similar meaning to today's "(accidental) discovery," such as the discovery of mineral resources, but it is meant differently from "invention" in today's patent laws. In the materials of Innsbruck, Austria, judgments in the Middle Ages often mentioned "Perkwerks Erfyndung," for example, inventing mineral resources. Because Celts[150] resided in the Alps, it had been the base for exploiting mineral ores. There was a convention in these mineral regions that the common law regulated; the first one to discover mineral resources had the right to exploit and the right to use wood and water. With increasing mineral resources being discovered in Saxton, Silesia, and Bohemia, the owners of the mineral regions began to use these unwritten common laws to protect themselves, which gradually became the basis of judgments in local courts. These laws were gradually elaborated: when ores on the ground were exhausted, further excavation and exploitation must be conducted. Because the exploiting and excavating facilities at that time were undeveloped, how to draw out the water from the mine would be a tremendous technological challenge. For instance, in the Fogel silver mine in Tailer, 600 people were hired to use buckets and ladders to remove the water from the mine. The earliest way to substitute human labor was to dig a drainage channel. Those who invested in the channel could obtain the agreed shares of the mine. The mine owner could not hire competitors to dig drainage channels without the investors' permission. They were obliged to maintain the drainage channel and expand it to meet the need for mining. It was also agreed that the law for "the first to discover the mine" was suitable for "the first to invent drainage facilities." Therefore, these inventors had the same privileges. Generally speaking, as long as the inventor of the drainage facilities put his thoughts into practice, he would obtain a fixed reward. If the facilities were expensive, he would also receive part of the deposits. Moreover, the inventor could obtain some rewards and some of the benefits from the mine over a given period, and the third man could not replicate or plagiarize this invention without special permission.

In the fourteenth and fifteenth centuries, the Venetian government absorbed and introduced many talents who were good at drainage facilities. On the one hand, the capacity of watermills should be expanded, the water in the drainage bunker should be drawn, and artificial canals should be dug out. On the other hand, the Venetian government planned to develop the mining industry within its territory. Those who could satisfy the government's needs asked the government to grant them privileges to prevent competition. In 1323, a master inventor and businessman in Germany, Johns Tusnikas, proposed his requirements according to the mining rights popular in Germany, as follows. If the contractor of the mine were granted the right to benefit from or monopolize new resources, he could fully satisfy the need for Venetian mines for drainage facilities. The Venetian government agreed to his requirements. If he managed to build a drainage model and prove his methods were feasible, he could receive rewards no higher than 80 Ducato and compensation decided by two other experts.[151]

We have no idea whether Johns managed to receive his rewards, but we know that more inventors and businessmen requested that Venice grant privileges based on the pattern of mining rights after that. This arrangement was then adopted in other activities. For example, Venice granted franchises to construct some crop mills so that the franchisees could receive fixed construction rewards. The Venetian government promised to give them at least several orders over a given period.[152] In addition, in 1409, Venice granted Henrikas von Haislingen in Germany the right to exploit a mining region and to use water and forest as he designed a new drainage facility. When granting rights, Venice indicated that this rule was based on the mining right, which was popular in German trades and guilds.[153] A lot of early patents in Venice were granted to mining technologies, including those in 1409, 1425, 1429, 1430, and 1443,[154] and the *Mining Law* granted by the Venetian Congress in 1488 has been reserved in the archives of Innsbruck, Austria. We find that this law largely plagiarized the *Mining Law* published by Tailors in Germany in 1408.[155] Then, due to constant requests by these businessmen and inventors, for example, on 20 February 1416, Venice granted Franciscus Petri, a Greek from Rhodes Island, a 50-year exclusive privilege to produce, modify, and rebuild machines built for this purpose after he introduced an advanced facility to mill silk from the Byzantine Empire into Venice. In 1443, Frenchman Antonio Marini applied for an exclusive 20-year monopoly to the Venetian government for a flour mill he invented that didn't use water.[156] This exclusive privilege granted to specific technologies and with a certain time limit was the prototype of the earliest patent system, called patent privilege. However, these exclusive privileges were merely occasional authorizations at the beginning; the authorization rules were not definite, and they belonged essentially to privileges granted by the government.

1474 *INVENTOR BYLAWS* OF VENICE: PRODUCT OF THE BALANCE OF INTERESTS

As mentioned previously, the Venetian government knew that the development of technology could be encouraged by introducing diverse institutions, and the patent privilege system was only one of the choices. Why would the Venetian government choose the patent privilege system as the primary measure to encourage patent technologies when the others vanished in history? Some scholars believe that the contingency of history may account for this. Venice encountered a financial crisis at the beginning of the fifteenth century, partly because of the wars to expand its territories in Italy and partly because of the threat from the Turkish. The Venetian government had to substitute monopoly for subvention.[157] Other scholars believe Venice chose the patent privilege as the primary way to attract talent because it found it more effective in practice and more readily accepted by history.[158] This book believes the selection and creation of the Venetian patent privilege system resulted from the constant game between the guilds and the government and was the product of their deliberate selection.

The guilds were the beneficial groups of local industries in Venice. To some extent, they were akin to large cartels in modern society, trying to set standards for all production and trade in a particular industry by enacting related laws with regard to the quality of ingredients and accessories of products, the scale, tool, procedure, specification and production, and trade rules.[159] From the benefits to internal members, the guilds constructed a monopoly situation in a given industry in the local market to prevent competition. However, they didn't expect the Venetian government to encourage the introduction of foreign technologies to develop industry and commerce. With the increase in people's demand for ordinary consumer goods, the guilds became increasingly restricted by competition from foreigners, and the introduction of new technologies broke the monopoly of the guilds. To handle the competition over new technologies and secure their monopoly over technologies, the guilds continuously persuaded the government to protect the inventions of the guild members according to the conventional procedures, which had the potency of customary law or common law in Venice rather than a gift. In some cases, during the early stages, Venetian guild members consistently applied for conventions to protect themselves.[160] In addition, they requested that the government build a suitable patent system for their interests. As mentioned previously, Venetian guilds and the government shared a close beneficial relationship, because the senate and the ten-man *Senato* could not manage all the detailed affairs in the country and had to rely on the guilds to manage their industries and economic affairs.[161] The guilds submitted their requirements to the Senate and the ten-man *Senato* directly or depended on their members in Congress, and they hoped the government could make a law that could protect their technological advantage (at least temporarily).[162]

The Venetian government had its own considerations. Venice established and managed a large commercial network. It controlled almost all trade routes through which goods were transported from the East via the Mediterranean Sea to Europe, established many overseas colonies, and developed its economy through comprehensive commerce and trade. However, compared with other commercial cities in Italy, Venice began to gradually lose its advantages, because this was not a sustainable development method. Venice's trade routes began to be controlled by the rising Turkish Empire, and the rise of Antwerp threatened Venice's position as a commerce and trade center. Although commercial capital remained more important than industrial capital until the eighteenth century, new industrial sectors occupied increasingly essential positions in the city economy since the fifteenth century. Therefore, it was suitable for the interest of the Venetian government to construct a domestic law that was beneficial to industrial development and encouraged competitive commercial practice. As revealed by historical materials, the *1453 Law of Rewarding Inventions* was issued during the fall of Constantinople and the rise of the Turkish Empire, and the *1474 Inventor Bylaws* were issued when Venice's trade routes were threatened by the Turkish Empire. That was not a coincidence of history.

Soon afterward, Venice witnessed the birth of the Venetian Senate's *1474 Inventor Bylaws*, the law most akin to modern patent law. This law was published in the "Greater Compendium" announcement of the Venetian Public Welfare Committee, which were all laws fundamental to Venetian people and had the properties of official bills or administrative orders.

In our city republic, there are people from distinct places and people who come here temporarily due to the fame and beauty of the city, and who have created delicate facilities with their talents. The law should protect the fruits they produced or invented, making others unable to easily imitate and produce similar products, to protect inventors' reputations and encourage them to devote themselves to technological innovations to improve the welfare of the whole society. Accordingly, the city congress has decided that anyone who has unprecedented, new, and novel inventions in this city should register in the General Bureau of the Office of Public Welfare in this city once the invention is complete and can be put into practice. Any third man must not produce the same or similar facilities without permission within ten years. If the regulations above are violated, the inventor is entitled to appeal to the Office in this city, and the offender will overtake the compensation for 100 Ducato and immediately destroy the imitated invention. The city's government can use this invention or facility based on its authority and judgment.

The *1474 Inventor Bylaws* were enacted 150 years earlier than the *Monopoly Act* in England. It was a comprehensive and elaborate patent law equipped with all the essential features of the modern patent system. The patent was considered a monopoly privilege to inventions; the main objective was to encourage the initiative of the inventor and to improve social welfare; the technology that was granted the patent right should be novel to Venice (only in this region because it encouraged introducing inventions); the inventions should be helpful (could be put into application and practice); the protection term was standardized (as long as 10 years); when the rights were offended, the patent owner could appeal for tort prohibition and compensation; the government was entitled to enforce permission if necessary.

Undoubtedly, this law was the product of the balance of interests between the guilds and the Venetian government. First, the law regulated the authorization standard of the novelty and utility of patents, and the utility standard was modeled on the internal regulations of the guilds. Second, the law highlighted the protection of public interest to improve social wealth and the Venetian government, based on its authority and judgment, could enforce permission to use other's inventions. Practice afterward indicated the preference for the public interest of the Venetian government. Third, the law was passed in an absolute vote of 116 versus 10 (four of which were abstention votes) and gained absolute support from the guilds. Although the law granted the inventor monopoly rights for the inventions and failed to dismiss the possibility that the introduction of inventions may harm the profits of the guilds, related materials demonstrated that the Senate promised to offer priority protection to local guild members and to introduce not so many foreign technicians as before.[163]

Contents and influence of the Venetian patent privilege system

AUTHORIZATION AND PRACTICE OF THE PATENT PRIVILEGE

As the *1474 Inventor Bylaws* of Venice were relatively simple, its concrete authorization standard and examination institutions were distributed in practice. Venice established a stable and well-organized patent privilege system during 1450–1550. Because the patent privilege system was a policy tool of Venice to encourage the development of domestic industry and economy, the Venetian government issued a substantive examination institution and specific authorization standard for the authorization of patents. Therefore, it could ensure that the government controlled and examined technology on most occasions. The applicant could file the applications to Congress or the Senate, sometimes to the Committee of Public Welfare, the Committee of Commerce, or the Continental Government. Except for the Congress's particular interest, ordinary applications were examined by the Senate, which would hire distinct local judges to examine inventions, conduct detailed investigations, and provide reports.[164] The governor would make the final decision at that time and publish it for the Senate through announcements (at that time, all laws were published on announcements; therefore, the issue of patents was similar to the issue of new laws). All authorizations were identified by the Senate based on particular cases, and distinct privileges would be granted according to the particular situation of every case, which gave the Venetian government great discretion when authorizing patents. The Venetian government could even repeal privileges granted based on the needs of the economy and public interests, which made the related privileges of the inventor quite unstable. As the number of patent applications was limited, the procedure for patent privilege was made through dialogue.[165] In the authorization procedure, if guilds found their monopoly interest harmed, they would be entitled to appeal for a hearing. For example, Francis was granted a patent for a certain kind of mirror, the guild appealed for a hearing, and the applicant needed to demonstrate to the guild how this invention worked. This showed that the granting of Venetian patent privilege was essentially based on the balance of interests.

As well as the applications, the applicant should describe the invention as clearly and precisely as possible, enabling others to distinguish it from previous technologies. Some other identification materials were also needed, such as the model or illustration of the invention, and there was no strict demand for the description or illustration patterns. Because technological development was restricted by time, almost all industrial inventions at that time belonged to mechanical technologies, the most significant part of which was the invention of hydraulic and wood-saving methods, including machines and methods such as the drainage system, bump, other machines specific to mining, smelters for metallurgy and refinement, salt-making, and ovens. In early practice, Venice was very eager for technologies and had no authorization standard as long as they were helpful. With the increase in patent applications, the Venetian government concluded the authorization standard based on the features of mechanical technologies at that time, for example, the novelty and utility regulated in the *1474 Inventor Bylaws* of Venice. However, the government did not thoroughly explain these standards, which contained great discretion. At the same time, to develop the domestic economy, the Venetian government paid little attention to concrete technological problems associated with the encouragement of technological creations and inventions as long as the products or technologies were not yet used in Venice. Those that were not too ordinary or too common were all likely to be authorized, regardless of the introduced or original inventions. Although the novelty was regulated in the *1474 Inventor Bylaws* of Venice, the Senate didn't demand the applicant provide direct proof of novelty. When another applicant applied for similar applications or when the committee had a dilemma on whether to grant authorization to the invention patent, the investigation on novelty would initiate. For example, in the sixteenth century, a patent on improved glass materials was finally repealed because the third man proved this invention lacked novelty.[166] However, although the novelty of an invention was suspected, the patent right was not necessarily denied. For instance, in 1513, Jakob was granted a patent for printing musical signs, and similar patents had already been granted to others.[167] Consequently, the novelty examination was not emphasized during the patent authorization process, and the most fundamental basis that Venice granted the patent privilege was its utility.

Generally speaking, utility also meant feasibility and the public interest. After being granted, the patent privilege had to be used within the stipulated period. Otherwise, it would be repealed. The feasibility required that the invention should be able to be used and used in the way corresponding to its applications. Indeed, if there were official reasons, such as financial difficulties or wars, the limit of practice could be postponed. The patent privilege system was originally the product of the government's mercantilism policies, and the government didn't care whether its institutional design could motivate technological inventions. However, it cared whether the applicant's invention was feasible, whether it could bring new economic resources to the country, and whether it could increase employment. As mentioned previously, a Frenchman, Antonio Marini, applied to the Venetian government for a 20-year exclusive monopoly right of a flour mill that didn't need water in 1443, and the precondition that the Senate granted the patent privilege of the flour mill was that the invention should be first put into practice in a town to ensure its utility. Finally, congress granted him a 20-year monopoly right, and during these years, only he could make and produce this machine, and he would be supported by the government in the form of sites and tax exemptions.[168] In another case, an engineer from Lombardy, Italy, applied for a patent for a boiler used for making dyes, and the Senate emphasized once again the utility of an invention. Specifically, his invention should first be tested in a town, overseen by the Committee of Public Welfare, and then the report should be submitted to the Senate. It should satisfy the requirements for utility that was beneficial to the public. As no one had used this method to make this kind of boiler within 10 years, the Senate finally passed this application.[169] In addition to this feasible direct demand, other indirect demands were included, such as revealing the secrets of crafts and training apprentices.[170]

The Venetian government greatly encouraged and emphasized the public interest in inventions. Venetian law's regulation for improving the welfare of society has demonstrated this point. In practice, although businessmen and inventors continuously emphasized the costs and energy they paid for creating inventions in the applications,[171] what the Venetian government cared about more was whether the invention of the patent applicant could be used in the interest of the public cause, especially Venice's economic development, such as reducing practical costs, exploiting nature more effectively, improving existing products, saving labor, and increasing the income of the country. If the examiner could be persuaded into believing the invention made a significant difference to the public interest, it would be more likely to be granted a patent. As Fernand Braudel stated, 90% of the authorized invention patents, whether important or not, aimed at solving city problems in Venice, and the tradeoff for social interest was of the greatest priority and importance according to the archives and registrations of the Venetian examination committee.[172] According to the degree of the utility of every case, the Venetian government granted distinct exclusive privileges besides restrictions on competitive activities of the third man, including rights to invent and produce newly introduced products, participation in newly introduced industries, an extension of time limit after improving the patent, the freedom of quality restriction of products. Even the protection time limit of the patent privilege owners was closely related to its degree of usage.[173] However, the Venetian government strictly prohibited registering or authorizing some inventions associated with the public interest in ordinary lives; for instance, the government prohibited others from monopolizing and selling glass used for glasses and reading.[174] During the examination, sometimes, the Senate found the applicant's invention unfinished. However, as long as the economic and social value of this invention was significant enough and able to achieve the result promised, it could still be granted a patent. For instance, in the red-black printing patent of Andrew Burgon in 1568, the Senate believed that although they failed to see any equipment or model, the patent could be granted as long as the applicant completed the result promised. The regulation of enforced permission and practice in the *1474 Inventor Bylaws* also demonstrated the emphasis on the public interest of the Venetian government. For example, in 1502, Aldus Manutius was granted the judgment issued by the highest 10-man committee of the Venetian government that ordered all residents in this city should respect his patent privilege and support his interest in Venice, the Florence Republic, and Lyons, France.[175]

In addition, although the Venetian government prohibited the transfer of some privileges, some of which demonstrated transferable property rights properties, fully demonstrating the property of tools in the patent privilege. For instance, after John, who was granted a patent authorization in 1470, passed away, the Venetian government pointed out clearly in his patent authorization file that this privilege had lost effect. Although his successors could continue their careers, they could no longer enjoy John's patent privileges.[176] In addition, in 1517, after a businessman who was once granted the patent privilege passed away, although his company survived, the patents he was granted became public property. Some practice also indicated that Venice admitted the patent privilege could be inherited by the successor or regarded as the object of the contract sale. For example, in 1531, one of Terracina's patents was transferred to his successor with the permission of the Venetian government; Aldus allowed others to use the patents he was granted.[177] Undoubtedly, although the privilege at that time was still a specially permitted authority from the government or royal family, it possessed the characteristics of properties to be transferred or inherited. In the feudal age, private rights were closely associated with public laws; therefore, there were few boundaries between definite franchises and the traditional rights of residents and subjects … .[178] These businessmen and craftsmen had realized that the patent privilege had the characteristics of property rights. However, they were still restricted to government control in practice.[179]

INFLUENCE OF VENETIAN PATENT PRIVILEGE SYSTEM

The patent privilege system was a mercantilism policy tool of the Venetian government to develop industry and economy, the focus of which was not to encourage inventions and creations but to encourage people to introduce new industries and technologies to create wealth for Venice. Venice was the first country to form and establish constant, stable rules and institutions for inventions and the earliest country that granted inventions monopoly privileges. The institutional framework it established became the basic legal framework of other countries and even modern ones.[180] In fact, the Venetian government granted many privileges related to printing technologies and the book trade, which gradually formed an independent copyright institution during the development. This indicated that the patent privilege was the origin of copyrights.[181] If Venice hadn't declined, the related rules and institutional system for modern copyright laws would have emerged in Venice and expanded to other countries.[182]

With the Red Sea blocked by the Portuguese and the opening of the Persian Gulf and the New Sea route, new sea routes that reached the East via the Cape of Good Hope were found. The trade center of Europe had switched from the former Mediterranean Sea to the Atlantic coasts, the rise of the Ottoman Empire dealt a heavy blow to Venice, and commerce and trade in Venice gradually declined since then. There were a lot of controversies about the actual function and influence of the Venetian patent privilege system among scholars. Some believed that, as Venice had constantly been at war since the fifteenth century to seize commercial domination in the Mediterranean Sea, the Venetian patent law was not effectively enacted in the country. The patent privilege system declined with the decline of Venice; therefore, it had a limited influence on the world. It could not be regarded as the origin of the modern patent system.[183] Other scholars held that the influence of this privilege system was relatively limited, mainly used to protect inventions and new trade activities in Venice.[184] However, according to related historical materials, in the

75 years before the issue of the patent law, Venice had granted 11 invention patents,[185] and after the patent law was issued, Venice was more popular with inventors and attracted many technological talents to Venice, and the number of patents granted in Venice increased significantly: 33 pieces during 1474–1500, 116

pieces during 1501–1550, and 423 pieces during 1551–1600.[186] The most critical was that the spark that Venice fired didn't extinguish with its decline. As the most vital trade center, Venice, in its prime, attracted Asian and European businessmen to this metropolis, and savvy Venetian businessmen secured their presence throughout Western Europe by virtue of their enormous commercial network. Open trade in Europe enabled the technological and patent monopoly system to spread to Italy and other European countries, such as Florence, Milan, Ferrara, France, Germany, Spain, Belgium, Holland, and England[187]. This could be evidenced by the granting of the patent privilege in these countries, because the earliest records of patents were all about technologies for glass-making, and this technology happened to be a distinctive technology in Venice.[188] Venice, like a main thread in the primitive patent system, connected other countries in one or several ways.[189] Other countries inherited the patent privilege system of Venice, and the spark of fire soon ignited the interest of Western Europe and even the world.

The development of the patent privilege system: Legislation and practices in Western European countries

France, Germany, and England were all technological and economic powers in Europe at that time, and they were similar to and associated with Venice in geography, economy, culture, and politics. The political atmosphere of liberal democracy and the stable, harmonious environment were respected and complimented by other Italian principalities and countries in the European continent.[190] It was hailed as modern Rome,[191] and any legislative innovation in Venice would be imitated and disseminated by other countries. Therefore, soon after the patent privilege system appeared in Venice, it was established in France, Germany, and England, respectively, which inherited the institutional framework of Venice. The patent privilege system appeared and developed earlier in France and Germany than in England, and a relatively systematic patent privilege system was established in the former. However, people did not focus their attention on the British patent privilege system until the outstanding achievements of the British Industrial Revolution. However, the British, German, and French governments established a patent privilege system to satisfy the need for policies to develop domestic commerce and industry. Their institutional construction was aimed at this purpose: the standard of utility was the primary standard to master technology. At the same time, the establishment and development of the patent privilege system were the product of the game between the government and private sectors. However, the government with the authority advantage occupied the dominant position.

The French patent privilege system

Motivations for the establishment of the French patent privilege system

In 1440, the nightmare of the Hundred Years' War finally ended, and absolute monarchism was officially established in France. Then, France gradually prospered thanks to the reconstruction efforts made by the kings over several generations.[192] In the sixteenth century, with the rise of the Renaissance movement, France entered the revival and development stage in technology, economy, and culture, like other Western European countries. First, the technologies of daily necessities, metallurgy, silk weaving, navigation, and shipbuilding were significantly improved during the sixteenth century.[193] Based on this, commerce and industry in France gradually developed. The development of daily technologies stimulated the change in the consumption structure in France: people in cities and in the country began to pursue fashion and purchase luxuries, which stimulated the distribution and improvement in the handicraft industry.[194] The weaving, steel, printing, and publishment industries were France's leading industries, and in these restricted industrial environments, capitalistic spirits emerged. During the reign of King Louis XIV, France, especially Lyons, was already the world's most significant center for the weaving industry.[195] In 1525, the annual iron production of Europe was 100,000 tons, and the production of France was 10,000 tons. In 1516, a gun production factory in Saint-Etienne, France, came into operation. Printing factories in Paris in the sixteenth century produced 25,000 editions of books (each edition printed 1,000 books on average), and in Lyon, this was 13,000 (Germany 45,000, England 10,000, and the Netherlands 8,000).[196] In the commercial field, marine insurance, double-entry bookkeeping, a public credit method, and a series of bank technologies were all introduced to France during the Renaissance. Therefore, the banking industry in France developed quite rapidly. During the sixteenth century, France had 206 businessmen-banker companies, 143 of which were in Lyon, which became the gathering place of Italians, Germans, and Swiss.[197] The development of the economy and technologies and the gradual elaboration and complication of industrial distribution led to the establishment of guilds in towns and cities. Second, the rise of the Renaissance ignited the enthusiasm for exchanging knowledge and technology. The attitude toward technology switched from "the substantial world" to the "world of experiments," and the bookshops were full of books introducing related scientific technologies, such as Jacques Besson's *General Introduction on Tools* and Rammcrli's *Various Artificial Machines*. The social status of technicians was also improved: a technician in the sixteenth century could claim without fear that machines were "the most esteemed in all crafts."[198] At that time, iron workers in France became the richest in the kingdom and did not need to pay any taxes, believing themselves to have privileges similar to French aristocrats, and they did have.[199]

Therefore, France gradually formed the conditions to build a patent system with the development of the economy, technology, and culture. Based on some separate historical records, in the beginning, the way it performed was a franchise. However, France finally introduced the concept of the Venetian privilege institution and made it the primary measure. This was due to the constant persuasion from the technicians and businessmen and because the French government implemented mercantilism policies to develop domestic industrial and commercial economies. Although absolute monarchism operated in France at that time, with the development of technology, industry and commerce, the French king adopted the mercantilism system once used in Venice, and the systematic mercantilism theory emerged in France far earlier than in other countries.[200] For foreign trade, the main objective of mercantilism policies was to encourage the domestic manufacturing industry and commerce so that exports from the country could surpass the imports and control them by monitoring domestic guild organizations. French guilds used to be a group without complete laws. With the development of technologies and economies, French guilds were established and developed. However, they began to be conservative and resist any kind of technological innovation. In the fifteenth century, King Louis XI began comprehensively supervising the guild by administrative and legislative means.[201] Louis believed, for the interest of the king or industry, that the king who enacted laws and regulations to guilds in all industries should not be bound by such laws and regulations, which was self-evident.[202] Moreover, because the French aristocrats failed in the political struggles with the king, the aristocrats were usually the supporters of the guilds. The development of the economy, technology, and culture made the French government more aware that technology was an essential force for industrial development in this country, and it could no longer ignore the technological monopoly of the guilds. In addition, since the mid-sixteenth century, persuaded by Edini Turquetti, inventor and representative of the emerging industrial and commercial class, France began introducing and performing a patent privilege system similar to Venice. The king attempted to support some innovations via patents and other methods to break the ossified guild monopoly, encourage inventions, and attract talent.[203] The trend of luxury was prevalent in the French royal family, and the need for craftsmen who were good at luxuries was quite enormous.[204] The French royal family established an official handicraft industry on a particular scale, such as felt factories in Paris and Beauvais,[205] where some luxuries and handicrafts of high quality were produced.[206] In 1610, when French King Henry IV passed away, there were 47 handicraft workshops in France, 40 of which he established.[207] Consequently, the French royal family hated to see that a particular industry was in the hands of a few, because that was to the government's disadvantage. The French government hoped to handle the barriers between the small industrial and commercial classes by controlling the patent privilege. Therefore, the patent privilege was essentially the policy tool where the royal family broke the monopoly of the guilds and supported, intervened, and controlled industrial and commercial economic activities based on the interest of the country and the monarchy.

The contents and evolution of the French patent privilege system

EARLY PRACTICES OF THE PATENT PRIVILEGE SYSTEM

At that time, the royal family granted the patent privilege; however, it needed to be discussed and registered by the Parisian Congress.[208] The ordinary pattern of the early French privilege system was similar to that in Venice: the government examined new inventions. The government usually chose to support the authorization of new inventions to break the monopoly of the guilds. In contrast, the guild chose to oppose them for the sake of the monopoly interest. Therefore, the authorization of French patent privileges was based on the compromise among the guilds, the government, and the inventor or introducer. There were various patent privileges: early privileges were mainly nonmonopoly. For example, the owner of French patent privileges had the privilege to use according to his invention and could prohibit others from imitating his inventions. The government offered him the privilege benefits, including credits, tax exemptions, and other assistance, and someone was even granted the warehouse due to new inventions.[209] For instance, in 1536, France occupied Piemonte, a region in Northwest Italy, where silk technology in Italy was highly developed. Edini Turquetti claimed to be the "inventor" of silk technologies and requested the French king to grant him the production privilege for this technology based on the practice of patent privilege, which had been adopted in Italy. France had coveted the advanced silk technology in Italy for a long time, and to attract these technological talents in North Italy, the French King Francis I granted Turquetti the privilege of silk production, which was the earliest patent privilege in France. However, Turquetti failed to obtain the monopoly privilege. He set up factories in Lyon, France, to produce silk with this silk technology and imparted the technologies to French workers who were obliged to hold the secrets. At the same time, the government of Lyon granted him and the foreign workers tax exemptions, loans, and other assistance, and he was entitled to impose privilege taxes on anyone who participated in silk production in Lyon afterward, the restriction of which lasted until his death.[210]

In 1551, the first monopoly patent in France was granted to another Italian, Theses Mutio, in Bolognia. The patent was for the production crafts of "Venetian-styled glass cups," and French King Henry II granted this Italian glass producer a monopoly right for 10 years.[211] The Parisian Congress modified it to 5 years when it was registered.[212] In the same year, French inventor Abel Fullon was granted the patent of the rangefinder with a 10-year time limit. At this time, French King Henry II believed that the inventor should fully expose his invention so that the public could benefit from it when the time limit passed. He demanded that Fullon prepare a patent specification, published in 1555, as the first patent specification in France.[213] In 1557, Henry II granted a patent right to Aldus Manutius, a publisher who designed a typeface called "Caractere civilite," which is no longer used today. Aldus Manutius was granted a Venetian patent in 1502, because he invented the new oblique typeface, italic, which is still used today.

During 1550–1600, France granted one patent every 2 years on average, and England granted one or more patents annually. French patents were fewer, possibly for the following reasons. On the one hand, the domestic situation in France was not entirely peaceful, and political and religious struggles led to an oppressed atmosphere; therefore, fewer inventors were willing to stay in a less tolerant country.[214] On the other hand, the guild rules that violated the national monopoly management institutions were strengthened. The Parisian Congress enhanced the interference in granting privileges to prevent the royal family from granting monopolies that should not have been made available otherwise. The congress was constituted mainly by some representatives of the aristocrats. Therefore, it tended to protect the benefit to the guilds and shorten or modify the patent privilege granted by the royal family; for instance, it modified the protection time limit of the patent privilege of Theses Mutio from 10 to 5 years, sometimes the patent of the royal family would be denied by the congress.

France did not grant patent privileges systematically until the late sixteenth and seventeenth centuries. On the one hand, this was likely because France witnessed the tangible results of Britain's granting of patent privileges and decided to imitate it. On the other hand, the French royal government accelerated industrial development out of the need for wars and economic development. France began to subsidize enterprises, modify *Suggestions on Commerce*, which was related to trade problems, technologies, innovations, and factories, to regulate economic behaviors, and introduce technological talents, including experts on mirrors, laceworks, and other luxuries from Italy, experts on mining, construction, and brick making from Sweden and Germany, and weaving experts from the Netherlands.[215] In fear that domestic technological experts would flee, France took strict measures. The technological talents who attempted to immigrate to foreign countries would likely lose their lives.[216] The patent was an essential tool for France to encourage industrial development. At this time, the granting of patent privilege gradually became normalized. At first, the privilege could only be granted in the presence of the king; therefore, the applicant had to grasp every chance for an application. After the Reformation, the applicant could apply for the patent to the French Royal Committee, but they needed to pay official and unofficial fees.[217] Before the committee decided whether to grant or not, expert opinions were required, which businessmen and craftsmen initially constituted. The Royal Committee made the primary decision and offered it to the French king for examination, who had the absolute right to the examination of patents. After the king agreed, he would issue a file through Congress that granted the exclusive privilege to the introducer or inventor of the new technology or machine. The third party could propose dissent to the Parisian Congress on the committee's decision. The description of the invention would be published after the operation of the invention so that the public could acquire the invention. Authorizing privileges was quite similar to today's patents: novelty, industrial utility, penalties on fakers, and the possibility to grant permission contracts.[218] However, like the Venetian government, because the authorization of the patent privilege was based on particular authorizations, these standards were quite vague, and industrial utility was the essential basis of the patent authorization by the French government. At the same time, the authorization of the patent privilege was accompanied by a strict operational obligation. Otherwise, the applicant would suffer from the sanction of losing the privilege. Therefore, the patent privilege granted at that time was limited. For instance, Pascal was granted the privilege of the abacus (1649), and Huygens was granted the privilege of clockworks (1657 and 1675).[219] Since the late sixteenth century, the authorization of some patent privileges possessed the characteristics of properties, such as inheritance and transference.[220]

In 1699, French King Louis XIV issued an act that empowered the Royal French Academy of Science to act as the expert counselor for patent examination. This could be seen as the earliest form of patent examination system.

However, this law was not compulsory. When the French royal family decided to grant a privilege, it would offer related privilege files to the Parisian Congress, which could consult the Academy about the utility and novelty of this invention, but the consultation was not strictly necessary. When the Academy examined this invention, the technological quality of the invention should have been the only subject to be examined. However, Congress paid more attention to the employment chances and tax value brought by this privilege, which indicated that the French government consistently considered the patent privilege as a policy tool to encourage industry and the economy. The economic benefits of the technology were always the most fundamental standard for building the patent privilege system.

1762 *ACT ON DERIVED RIGHTS OF THE PATENT*: THE VICTORY OF PHYSIOCRACY

Since 1740, the royal family began to emphasize the physiocratic power represented by Quesnay. The thoughts of these physiocrats were possibly earlier than the economic liberalism of Adam Smith. As the representatives of physiocracy, Quesnay and Boisguillebert proposed the concept of natural order, that social and economic life should conform to the natural law. Nature loves freedom, and nature always goes to freedom and completion. Therefore, they supported the free development of the economy and opposed interference by the country.[221] The mercantilism policy was considered as the chains that restricted the freedom of industry and commerce, and the position of agriculture was greatly underestimated. Consequently, they believed that mercantilism thought should be greatly oppressed[222] and that the agricultural economy should be improved and developed. They objected to the rigid guilds and suggested that the power of the French guilds should be oppressed and weakened. Because the patent privilege was seen as an essential way to develop an industrial and commercial economy, it was essentially a kind of monopoly and a barrier to liberal economic development. In the dogmatic policy system of physiocracy, the authorization of patents was proposed to be strictly restricted, especially during the patent examination: whether to grant the patent and the extent of protection (in terms of the geographic covering range and scale) was determined by the estimated economic value. In addition to the national privilege, local privileges were effective only in some regions and granted by the local authority. The patents could be repealed by the government, or simple patents could be replaced by more advanced technological ones invented by late competitors.[223] In 1762, the *Act on Derived Rights of the Patent* was officially issued as a strict regulation to authorize the patent privilege. The law reiterated the privileged property of the patent and that the patent privilege was to award the inventor's hard effort and grant him some rewards. It pointed out that failure to use a privilege was annoying because it restricted freedom but failed to bring the public any benefits that should be expected. Finally, the lack of publication of the privileges granted usually enabled the authorized to extend similar rights and hinder the work and labor of our citizens. Based on this, the law strictly restricted the time limit, transfer, and operation of the patent privilege, and the administration intervened in the patent authorization. According to the *1762 Act*, the protection term of the patent privilege was 15 years; the privilege could be transferred to the children or grandchildren when the inventor was alive, and it was not allowed to be transferred to others without royal permission. If the authorized person with the patent privilege passed away, their successor could not inherit this privilege. If the authorized person didn't or failed to operate the patent, this patent privilege would lose its potency unless the authorized person could propose a good cause.[224]

CONCLUSION

In the early practice of patent privileges in France, the power of the feudal monarchy was so strong that emerging industrial and commercial classes and craftsmen had little voice, and the aristocrats and guilds often intervened in the authorization of patents. However, the French government controlled the initiative in the patent privilege system. Then, as the government was influenced by the physiocracy thoughts, the dominant physiocrats as winners began to strictly restrict the patent privilege, which finally led to the issue of the 1762 *Act on Derived Rights of the Patent*. The patent privilege appeared as an institution for the first time, and it was always considered a tool of technological and economic policies governed by the government and local officials. On the one hand, in most cases, the French government would only grant the patent after conducting a careful examination and believing the authorization could improve new trade. The patent privilege was merely restricted to the range of 10 miles (approximately 16.1 km or maybe broader or narrower), which aimed at protecting existing trade or production.[225] On the other hand, there are two features of the French government's patent authorization. One was the passive authorization and strict restriction to the extension of the production scale and concentration of industrial capital, which slowed down the development of large industries. The other was about the particular authorization. Because the French royal family and higher status emphasized luxury and enjoyment and they had a more significant demand for handicraft products, the focus of authorization lay on handicraft technologies and inventions, emphasizing quality and beauty rather than quantity and benefit. This exerted a huge influence on the structure of the industries and economic development in France, making the handicraft industries in France, such as silk weaving, leather, glass, ceramics, and decorations, the best of the world.[226] The government determined the authorization standard based on particular cases, considering economic values like employment and taxes in the industrial utility as the fundamental basis of the authorization. The government could not efficiently judge the economic value of a technology, and the market was their best testing standard. However, it should be noted that France issued many other beneficial policies and measures in addition to the patent as supplements and substitutions to patents. For example, during the privilege, the inventor or introducer could enjoy unique treatments, such as the vocational title, pension (sometimes this could be extended to the spouse or children), loans (some were interest-free), one-time fund, production subvention, tax exemption, public purchase, and the possibility to use cheap labor in the hospital. After the French

Revolution, the complicated national policy of inventors and inventions was modified rather than canceled.

The German patent privilege system

Motivation for the establishment of the German patent privilege system

During the fifteenth and sixteenth centuries, Germany was a loose federation of feudal princes under the name of the "Holy Roman Empire," which was constituted by duchies, principalities, counties, feudalized bishops and monastery regions, and free cities resided in by tough citizens.[227] There were, at most, thousands of states in the country. However, the disassembly of politics didn't lead to social disintegration or economic decline. Instead, this highly separate situation made social and economic life at that time more active. First, because the metallurgy, steelmaking, and weaving technology in Germany were relatively advanced, and an outsourcing production line was widely applied,[228] the mining and handicraft industries in the German region were significantly improved in the fifteenth–seventeenth centuries.[229] In the early sixteenth century, the production of cast iron by the German Holy Roman Empire had occupied half of the total production of Europe, and the development of the flax and cotton weaving industries had surpassed traditional industrial development. The separate political situation generated a huge city population and many free cities, which established alliances to defend and benefit themselves, such as the Hansa, Rhine, and Schwaben Alliances. The establishment of these alliances significantly boosted the development of German commerce and trade.[230] Most of the time during the sixteenth century, the economic center of Europe was in the Mediterranean Sea. Based on the links with the Atlantic Ocean and the Mediterranean Sea and close market relationships with Italy, Germany occupied a central position in European economic development during the sixteenth century. In addition, Germany's financial development and capital accumulation had developed to a particular scale, and large companies and their commercial and financial activities had already gone far beyond Germany and entered other European countries.[231] Second, during the fifteenth and sixteenth centuries, the Renaissance movement began to increase in Germany. The Reformation movement, promoted by Martin Luther in AD 1517–AD 1546, had such a profound meaning that it broke the spiritual monopoly of the Catholic Church, liberating people's thoughts and developing humanism. Affected by these thought trends, German technicians like goldsmiths, metal processors, and carpenters became active in Augsburg, Nuremberg, Cologne, Vienna, Prague, Ulm, and other cities. Their works were highly praised throughout Europe, their social status was constantly improved, and they began to attract several sponsors.[232] The most famous one among which was the epoch-making great work *De re Metallica* (12 volumes), *De Natura Fossilium*, and *On Minerals* written by Georg Bauer in Saxony.

In this technological, economic, and cultural environment, Germany was equipped with the conditions to establish the patent privilege system. The earliest established institution was the franchise that combined German and Roman laws.

However, the German government finally introduced the concept of the Venetian patent privilege system, which was, on the one hand, because of the continuous persuasion from these powerful emerging industrial and commercial classes or technicians. On the other hand, the primary reason was the mercantilism policies of the German government to develop domestic industry and commerce. Since the Renaissance movement, the mercantilism ideas of countries like Venice have also influenced Germany. Since the sixteenth century, German monarchs have paid great attention to industrial and commercial development and regulated attractive, favorable industrial and commercial policies.[233] For instance, the legislation in Germany at that time liberated the tax and war obligations of the industrial and commercial classes. It granted them assistance payments to lower their production costs, making the price of raw materials they bought far lower than the average price in the market.[234] At the same time, similar to Venice and France, with the development of German economies and technologies, the power of the guilds became more extensive, monopolizing local industries and technologies and rejecting foreign ones. The monarchs of German states attempted to oppress the restrictions from the increasingly larger guilds to technologies and industries to develop domestic technologies and industrial and commercial economies. Due to the convenient and frequent commerce and trade between Germany and Italy, the practice of the Venetian patent privilege spread to Germany, and the domestic patent privilege system was gradually established in practice in Germany, which became one of the countries that were the earliest to grant patent rights in the European continent.[235]

The contents and evolution of the German patent privilege system

Existing materials indicated that the duchy governed by the Saxon Duke was the region with the most developed industry and commerce in Germany and the region that was the earliest to grant the patent privilege. It began to grant franchises for mine drainage facilities in 1378.[236] The authorization of franchises for mineral patents in early Germany was probably based on the combination of German and Roman laws, which was similar to the common law of the Anglo-Saxon ethnicity and was granted according to related principles established by the judge in practice.[237] In 1484, the businessman Blasius Dalmaticu requested to be authorized for the drainage facilities in his mine based on the monopoly privilege in Venetian law, and the Saxon government approved the authorization.[238] During 1500–1600, as more and more inventors and businessmen requested the granting of monopoly privileges, the Saxon government, which adopted mercantilism policies, began to introduce the Venetian pattern, combined with the social economic developing situation of this duchy, granting a number of monopoly patent privileges.[239] The acts of the Saxon Duke were imitated by other states and lords of the Holy Roman Empire, which also began to grant patent privileges.[240] For example, in 1545, Emperor of the Holy Roman Empire Charles V granted Hans Hedler a 12-year patent monopoly privilege for his water and windmilling facilities. According to current materials, the Saxon Duke granted 50 pieces of patent privileges during 1530–1630, and the Emperor of the Holy Roman Empire granted 100 pieces. The number of patent privileges would be incredible if those granted by local landlords like princes, dukes in other states and local territories, as well as by the Pope with religious and moral figures, were taken into account.[241] Although there were no definite laws to establish the validity of the patent privilege in Germany, the restriction from the customary laws had already been formed due to its numerous and continuous practice until 1600. Based on customary law, anyone could expect the benefit from the invention and demand that the royal family protect it, which could be proven in an application for the patent privilege in 1551 that highlighted, in this ancient empire with a long history, the invention of anything new (useful and beneficial) was always granted the privilege and abundant rewards by former monarchs.[242] It indicated that in Germany, similar to Venice, France, and England at that time, the patent privilege was definitely more than an ordinary privilege or practice and possessed a legal potency. In some patent authorizations in Germany, the patent privilege could be transferred to the successor or the third man of the applicant, which indicated that some businessmen at that time were aware of the property characteristics of the patent privilege. Regarding the granting procedure of the patent privilege, the German government established a substantial examination system on particular cases similar to the Venetian system. The applicant should propose an application, which was then offered to the Privilege Board in the Imperial Councillors' Chamber, constituted by legal experts. In the late sixteenth century, Germany began to emphasize technologies and inventions; therefore, some authority experts in related fields were usually invited to take charge, who were more open-minded and deeply interested in these complicated new things, and even some inventors who were granted the patent privilege were sometimes invited as experts. These legal experts examined the technologies and inventions proposed. If related technologies were highly complex, they would also ask for the opinions of technological experts. Then, the Privilege Board would offer an examination report to the king, and the king would sign and grant the patent.[243]

The German patent privilege had to satisfy some standards. First, the invention should be novel. However, distinct from France and Venice, because Germany was a country good at inventions, and its technological level was at a leading position in Europe, Germany emphasized relatively original inventions. Most patents were granted to original inventors, and few were granted to technological introductions or trade.[244] Due to the undeveloped transportation and communication technology at that time, the examination of the novelty by the German government was too strict to imagine. During the examination, these inventions should be startling enough to the Board with years of working experience. Otherwise, the Board was likely to initiate a novelty investigation.[245] Whether the creativity or advancement of the invention was the legal standard of the authorization of the patent privilege at that time remained unknown based on related privilege cases. However, some applicants would often claim in the application that their inventions were more technologically advanced than former examples. In practice, these inventions with technological advancement were consistently more likely to get authorization. Last, the most critical was that the inventions should be helpful. According to the customary law of the patent privilege, new machines or methods had to satisfy the "test standard," this new machine or method should be tested to observe whether it was feasible. Related models or samples needed to be offered to the Board. If the applicant lacked related models or samples, the Board would give the order to offer them. In addition, the Board mainly concentrated on examining the invention's value in the public interest. The examination element that the Board emphasized most was whether it was beneficial to improving employment, saving labor, or promoting the development of a particular industry, which the applicant also reiterated. The protection restriction of the patent privilege always depended on the degree of utility of each case, from 5 to 10 years, and 20 years was also probable.[246]

In the previous materials, there was a relatively developed patent privilege system during the sixteenth and seventeenth centuries in Germany, which was so distinct from other privileges that it possessed the potency of customary law despite being issued in the written form. This cognition was quite precious, because during and before the reign of Elizabeth I (1558–1603), there was no common law in the patent right in England. The cognition of the patent was merely a privilege granted by the royal family, nothing more than an administrative convention. Compared with England at the same time, Germany formed a patent privilege system earlier, and the system was more complete than the late British patent privilege system. The application fee was lower,[247] and its application mechanism could essentially prevent monopoly and abuse by the royal family. The early German patent privilege system was a complete institution with considerable fruits; however, it was destroyed by chaotic political struggles and wars, which destroyed it so thoroughly that it was almost completely forgotten. The political and economic environment in Germany was unbeneficial to innovational activities, and the narrow-sighted and conservative guilds gradually dominated the leading power in the domestic institutions, which continuously influenced the German government. Finally, they abolished the patent privilege system in Germany. Of course, the regulations of patent laws and common laws in Germany, the Netherlands, Belgium, and many European continental countries were all destroyed, and many legal frameworks and innovations were hardly discovered.[248] It was not until the Industrial Age that their patent systems began to emerge once again.

The British patent privilege system

Motivations for the establishment of the British patent privilege system

As a small country almost abandoned by Roman civilization on the coast of the Atlantic Ocean, England fell far behind other countries on the continent in terms of agriculture, industry, and trade. During the fifteenth and sixteenth centuries, England's technology, economy, and trade began to prosper, and so did the desire to establish the patent privilege system.

First, before the fifteenth century, there were traditional sectors like coal exploitation and mining in England. These sectors featured small-scale production and low-level technology. Then, England began to absorb investments from foreign capital and progressively introduced advanced industrial technologies and some emerging industrial sectors from other European countries. For example, England introduced the first paper-making factory, the first powdery factory, the first factory of coppers and aluminum sulfate, the first sugar refinement factory, and the first niter factory, and benefited a lot from this process. It was because British industry absorbed related foreign capital and technology that the emerging industries in England, like mining, smelting, weaponry, and shipbuilding, managed to develop gradually.[249] Since the 1470s, the "sheep eats people" enclosure movement was initiated in England. It caused numerous farmers to lose available land, therefore creating favorable conditions for developing agricultural capitalism in England and providing sufficient labor forces. With the opening of the new sea routes, the center of European trade switched from the Mediterranean Sea to the coast of the Atlantic Ocean. As a result, England developed from a frontier country to the economic trade center of Western European civilization. Since the sixteenth century, England began to expand its overseas markets in Asia, America, and Africa. The rapid expansion of overseas markets raised an ever-increasing demand for England's industrial products, and the overseas market became the big consumer of domestic industrial products.

> The Age of Tutors was an age of commerce, and it became more commercial with the progress of this century. Through the constant expansion of domestic and foreign markets, commerce and trade became England's most active economic activity in the Pre-industrial Age.[250]

While stimulating demands, the British Commercial Revolution generated and accumulated businessmen with enormous commercial capital, who put commercial capital into industrial production to achieve further profits and the conversion of capital.

Second, England's Renaissance and Reformation during the fifteenth and sixteenth centuries changed the outlook on technology and wealth. The humanistic spirit of the Renaissance encouraged people to attach great importance to natural substances. Technological innovations became increasingly critical, and the importance and status of technological talents like craftsmen were increasingly emphasized. At the same time, the House of Tutors began to launch a series of religious reformations to weaken the old aristocracy and strengthen its authoritarian governance. As Merton said, scientific technology was praised due to the social utilitarianism of "complementing God" by Purists, the diligent asceticism and the rational spirit of "God saves reason," which promoted the renovation of humanistic social science thoughts and the progress of scientific technologies.[251] Studies by John Wilkins and Max Weber all indicated that the dogma of Purists laid the moral foundation for the outlook on wealth, the pursuit of material benefits, and the accumulation of capital in England, which ultimately collapsed the traditional moral system in England, greatly motivated the British to accumulate wealth for the sake of expanding reproduction and promoted the emergence and development of British capitalism.[252]

In this technological, economic, and cultural environment, the conditions for establishing the patent system began to mature in the British government during the House of Tutors. In the early fourteenth and fifteenth centuries, the ruling class of England granted foreign technicians franchises to attract technological talents,[253] and the ruling class applied a way of secret agreements compromised by the royal family to attract foreign technological talents. For instance, armor makers in Germany, shipbuilders and glassmakers in Italy, and blacksmiths in France were attracted to go across the English Channel.[254] Like other European countries, the technology and products in England were controlled and monopolized by guilds, and the production and management of many emerging industrial and commercial classes were restricted by them. The guilds always persuaded the British government to introduce the monopoly patent privilege system that was similar to those in Venice and Germany.

For example, in 1537, Sir Antonio Guidotti, a British businessman living in Italy, wrote from Messina to Thomas Cromwell, the chief Minister of State of King Henry VIII, saying that he planned to deliver Italian silk to England and led businessmen to England to establish the Italian-styled silk production. He also mentioned that the patent privilege system was generally operated in Italy and the German Holy Roman Empire. For example, the Emperor granted the patent privilege to some Milanese and allowed them to participate in silk weaving in the territory. Therefore, he suggested that professional talents should be attracted to England by granting 20-year privileges to related silk-weaving technologies.[255] Whether Antonio Guidotti was granted this privilege remained unknown. As the influence of the Venetian patent privilege system grew, Thomas Cromwell realized the importance of the patent privilege system. As he said in 1549, he heard that in Venice and many other places, every talent who introduced new crafts and works was rewarded and cherished.

In addition, the patent privilege system was already implemented and granted in Germany at that time. The British businessman Gresham, as the commercial representative sent by the British to Antwerp, Germany, learned about the patent privilege granted by German Emperor Charles V in detail and developed a close relationship with the prominent German businessman Hochstetter, who had a number of patent privileges. After the accession of Elizabeth I (1558), with the rise of mercantilism thought, the British government began to encourage technological talents. It constantly granted a number of patent privileges by gaining inspiration from the Venetian and German patent privilege systems to use the monopoly patent of new technologies and industries as the main policy to stimulate the economy and increase income.[256]

The contents and evolution of the British patent privilege system

SUCCESSION OF BRITAIN TO THE VENETIAN PATENT PRIVILEGE SYSTEM

After the accession of Elizabeth I, several exclusive monopoly patent privileges were granted to develop domestic industry and commerce, which contained monopoly franchises and monopoly rights for inventions. For example, on 26 April 1552, the British king granted Henry Smith a 2-year monopoly privilege to produce Normandy glass. In 1559, the British king granted Jacobus Acontius, an engineer of fortifications from Trent, the patent privilege of new grinding mills.[257] In 1565, the British king granted Florentine Berty many monopoly patents. Many scholars believed that the authorization of patents by the British king was, at his will, nothing but an abuse without any standards. However, this was not the case. Although there was no specific legislation in England at that time, the practice of the patent privilege in England was largely modeled on the Venetian system.

First, the authorization of the patents in England was based on a substantial examination of particular cases. The applicant offered an application, and the Privy Council first examined the patent on behalf of the royal family and then submitted it to the royal family for the final decision. The authorization standard in the particular examination by the Council and the royal family included novelty and utility, and the latter was the most important. The invention should be helpful and bring benefits to the public. In other words, it should bring some unique benefits to England and the king. The benefits could take the form of reducing labor forces, assisting rotten cities, providing a required commodity that was better than import ones in price and quality, strengthening the defense of the territory, improving the employment of miners or sailors, or bringing a new export trade.[258] With the generalization of the practice, stating the public benefits brought by the invention in the application gradually became a convention. For example, in the 1622 "Dudley Case," the applicant reiterated that his iron invention could improve the public benefit and save the consumption of iron and wood.[259] Because the privilege was judged based on particular cases, the authorization of these privileges, in some cases, might be consistent, and they were granted the exclusive privilege for a certain time limit. However, every privilege was distinct. The content of the privilege granted differed in every invention, and the economic activity of every privilege was distinct. Sometimes, there were geographic restrictions. In other words, the privilege was effective only in a particular region in England. Sometimes, there were exemptions from other guilds or restrictive powers, for example, to perform specific jobs with reasonable salaries. Some privileges even had the property of the private right so that they could be sold or transferred.[260] The exclusive restriction of every privilege was also distinct. For instance, the restriction of the patent granted in 1571 was 6 years, and in 1577 the restriction was 30 years.[261]

Second, the patents granted in England had "operation terms," which inherited the feasibility of patents granted in Venice. The early patent authorization in England aimed at promoting the development and introduction of technology, requiring the authorized person to put the patent into commercial practice within a given restriction and the promise to sell at the given quality and price. Otherwise, the authorization would be repealed. For example, in 1563, Peter and George invented a new oven and were granted a 10-year patent privilege by the British government. According to the government's regulation, if the price of the authorized invention sold by the owner of the patent right was too high or if it failed to be put into practice within 2 months, the patent would lose its potency. To satisfy the requirements of England, Smalt's patent should meet quality standards, and he should promise that the salt produced within 7 years should be as cheap as other marine products.[262] Early patent authorizations should be subject to quality examinations by the administrative organs, because only providing products of good quality and at reasonable prices for the market could benefit the domestic economy, and the patent from the offenders would lose its potency. It could be proven that the invention did satisfy the promised practice by either examination ex-ante or requirements ex-post.[263]

Finally, since the patent was applied by Homes and Frampton in 1575, the Council introduced the repealing cause in the Venetian patent authorization, which gradually became generalized and began to substitute the operation terms. It was progressively elaborated in practice in England. If the patent granted proved to be inconvenient or prejudicial, the royal family and the Council were entitled to repeal it. The causes for repealing contained problems of the novelty and priority of the invention itself, failure to introduce this invention in a reasonable time in operation, or other problems like abuse of patents.[264] In the late seventeenth century, this term became a fixed feature of all inventions, which was reserved until the modern age. The inconvenience was the cause they used most frequently, and the Council could discuss the inconvenience of the patent within the repealing restriction before or after the authorization. For instance, in 1660, Traswell's patent was dissented, because Traswell was not the inventor, and his invention was regarded as unable to be fully understood or too difficult to put into practice. Similarly, Rersbey and Strickland's patent in 1665 was dissented, because the applicants had no empirical experience in the arts or publishment. Garill's method patent for casting gold coins and silver bricks was repealed because it was likely to harm trade and deprive thousands of workers of their posts and lives. It was likely to worsen the making of counterfeit coins and threaten social stability. The repealing procedure set by the Council was aimed at particular patents according to specific policies. Its patent examination involved explaining and applying the standard of authorization and considering various public interests, such as interest relations, policies, social costs, and probable benefits brought by the authorization. The consideration of abstract interests made the patent authorization at that time so unstable that the patent privilege was called a patent transaction or contract. The patent was seen as a transaction between the royal family (on behalf of the public interest) and the owner of the patent right. The owner had no right to get the patent; instead, they could only offer unique benefits to the public and request the king to grant the privilege. The king, based on an arbitrary power to grant the privilege, decided whcther the particular benefit brought by the invention of the applicant was suitable for the public interest and granted them the corresponding right and restriction. Even if the privilege were granted, it could be repealed based on public policy considerations.[265]

In addition, unlike France, the authorization in England stressed economic benefits. It didn't intervene in concrete production methods. The control in emerging industries was not as comprehensive as in France – important emerging industries like coal exploitation and metallurgy escaped from the control of the government, which was beneficial to the extension and concentration of the production scale as well as the primitive accumulation and development of significant industrial capital. By the seventeenth century, many large enterprises in England began to increase. In British industries, the weaving industry, as the traditional national industry, developed rapidly, and some new heavy industries rose rapidly. Heavy industries like coal mining, iron smelting, and shipbuilding enjoyed significant development. The coal production in England and Wales totaled 210,000 tons during 1551–1560 and increased to 2,982,000 tons during 1681–1690, implying a growth of about 14 times. Iron production totaled 5,000 tons in the 1550s and expanded to 24,000 tons in the mid-seventeenth century, representing a five-time increase. The total tonnage of trade ships in England was 5,000 tons in 1570 and increased in 1640 to 150,000 tons, up 30 times.[266]

POWER STRUGGLE AND THE OVERPRAISED *THE STATUTE OF MONOPOLIES 1623*

Because the utility standard and repealing procedure for British patents had an overwhelming discretion, the British royal family began to grant several monopoly privileges based on preferences and the financial requirements of the royal family (the patent owner of the exclusive authorization should pay a specific tax to the royal family at fixed intervals, which was one of the critical financial sources of the royal family at that time), or requirements to award subordinates and trusted relatives. Indeed, it was also closely related to the requests and lobbies from some industrial and commercial classes who applied for the patent, because the exclusive monopoly privilege could bring them abundant benefits.[267] The purpose and methods of the British royal family to grant a patent were various, such as increasing the retail price of products related to the patent, granting monopoly privilege of trade, and granting monopoly rights to those who didn't invent or introduce new products. According to the statistics, during 1561–1603, 55 pieces of monopoly privileges were granted in England, 21 of which were granted to foreigners. During the reign of James I, the abuse of the patent right was unbridled, and daily necessities like oil, salt, sauce, and vinegar were regarded as the objects of the patent authorization. The abuse of patent privileges by the royal family directly led to a disrupted market order and an unreasonable increase in the price of products. Even Hume complained that these monopolies were excessive.

The abuse of patent privileges led to dissatisfaction among Congress, justice, commercial groups, and the public; therefore, censure and resistance to restrict this royal privilege surged ahead. However, what was more critical was the different forms of power struggles behind it. Although England was a monarchy, it always possessed the "liberal tradition,"[268] which was distinct from absolute feudalism in France and Germany. The polity of England was a mixed polity,[269] where the king had no absolute monopoly power, and royalty, the congress, and the judicial organ counterbalanced each other. They always confronted the challenge from aristocratic and civilian powers.[270] With the development of British capitalism, the power of the industrial and commercial classes that mastered capital and technology became more substantial, and royal privilege was not the power they relied on but the barrier to their further development. Since the late sixteenth century, the congress and common court, on behalf of the emerging industrial and commercial classes, have heatedly fought against the royal aristocrats on behalf of feudal royalty. They proposed the supremacy of law as the principle of common law, suggesting that royalty should be restricted by law and obey the boundaries defined by the public interest and the liberty of citizens, criticizing the hazards of monopoly and the authoritarian royal family, believing any monopoly, except those granted to new inventions beneficial to the public interest, was illegal and should be abolished. The manuscript explaining common law proposed by the House of Commons in 1601 became the most potent antimonopoly act. However, people, including Francis Bacon, argued for the legality and reasonability of monopoly on behalf of the Queen; royal family supporters were still overwhelmed. Queen Elizabeth I had to make a speech that indicated the monopolies would no longer be abused and publicly approved the examination of the legality of the patent by the court, and Congress canceled the act.[271]

However, it only postponed the conflict. The "Dacey Case" in 1602 granted the common court the opportunity to make judicial examinations of royal authorizations.[272] The "Ipswich Weaver Case" in 1615 enabled the court to restrict the abuse of granting patent rights by the royal family by judicial examination. It facilitated people to think about considerations of public policies like the meaning and social costs of setting the patent system. The patent authorization of the British king should be restricted, and only those good monopolies beneficial to the public interest should be allowed and authorized.[273] As King James I continued to abuse the patent privilege, in 1621, Congress enacted a law to restrict the patent privilege. In 1623, the British Congress finally approved the *Statute of Monopolies,* which was famous in patent history and restricted the monopoly and patent authorization of the royal family. It defined that the first and true inventor of a new product could be granted the monopoly of a royal patent for no more than 14 years.[274] The Statute was seen as the Magna Carta of the rights of inventors. Some domestic and foreign scholars praised it as the origin of modern patent laws.[275]

However, generally speaking, the influence and meaning of the Statute were so limited that Christine called the overpraise of this law a mystery in history.[276] First, the Statute was similar in language to a declaration, which was not aimed at encouraging creations, inventions, and technological innovations but restricting the abuse of patent privileges of the royal family. The Statute regulated that ordinary courts could examine the authorization of the monopoly granted by the Queen to restrict irresponsible arbitrary authorizations, the principles and contents of which were already proposed in previous acts and legal cases. The Statute neither set new restrictions for the royal family nor regulated new rights for the public. Second, the Statute merely restricted the monopoly privilege to those for new inventions. Other types of monopoly privileges, such as management qualifications of industry and franchises granted to city companies and enterprises, were excluded. However, the patent was seen as a gift from the royal family, and the right to grant patents was still in the grip of the king. The Statute did not change the privileged property of the patent; the Statute was merely an administrative act. Finally, the novelty standard of granting patents and the protection term of the patent proposed in the Statute was nothing new. In fact, these provisions were already proposed in Venice, France, and Germany. Above all, the Statute only offered some restrictive frameworks instead of a unified standard for patent authorization, and the patent authorization remained the special authorization based on particular cases. In terms of practice in the seventeenth century, the British patent system was an informal administrative work to a great extent,[277] and the Council and royal family still made discretions based on the utility standard before repealing patents according to the repealing terms. The Statute failed to prevent the royal family from abusing patent privileges, which was even more serious over a period of time than ever before.[278]

Enlightenment of the history

The transition history of the patent system in the Pre-industrial Age could offer some enlightenment as follows.

First, the concept of economic value and the application of technology was the foundation for the formation of the patent system. During the early period of the ancient world and during the Middle Ages, due to the limited cognition of technological knowledge and slow technological development, the technological development in Western Europe or several Asian civilizations mainly happened in the public sectors such as military and engineering, or technology only served the needs of survival or subsistence. Technology played no role in the economy as an independent production force. The economy mainly took the form of an agricultural economy, which had limited needs for technology, and the value of technology and its effect on the economy were limited. The cultural environment, including values, wealth outlook, and religions, restricted people's interest in technology and production. The concept of economic value and the application of technology failed to appear in the private sector and the government.

Second, the technological, economic, and cultural environments in Venice, France, Germany, and England created the conditions for establishing the patent system at the end of the Middle Ages. Although specific environments may not be identical, these countries share some features. 1. Industry began to develop when practical knowledge was enriched, and technology was no longer limited to the public sector or basic survival and living necessities. Although industrial technology was not well-developed and was restricted to traditional industrial sectors like shipbuilding, glass processing, weaving, printing, and publishing, technology became an essential production force in the economy. As a means of objective production, the benefits of technologies began to be emphasized. 2. The industrial and commercial economies of all countries began to develop. The opening of foreign markets and the increase of commerce and trade provided broad markets for these industrial products, which stimulated the requirements for industrial products and technologies. The commercial capital and financial credits offered capital for the industrial and commercial economy and technological innovations. 3. The Renaissance movement and Reformation relieved people of the oppression of the Christian deity, helped people develop a positive outlook on wealth and technology and encouraged people to take a great interest in technological creation, wealth production, and individual values. Thanks to its unique economic, technological, and cultural traditions, Venice was the first to form the concept of the patent system. Due to the mercantilism policies adopted to develop industrial and commercial economies and promote competition, the governments of different countries put this institutional concept into practice. These governments increasingly advocated cooperation with businessmen or technicians to introduce technologies and develop the economy. As revealed by Frumkin, an empirical study demonstrated that the emergence and development of the patent privilege in some continental countries during the Middle Ages was closely related to its economic, technological, and cultural activities. The writer compared the transition of the patent system with the rise and fall of these activities, and his conclusion was that the patent system was formed in the context of the country's economic, technological, and cultural development and would become less important as these activities declined.[279]

Third, the game of interest was central to the formation and evolution of the patent privilege system. The Venetian guilds had different purposes of benefit from the government – the guilds aimed to oppose foreign competition, while Venice hoped to develop industry and commerce. They formed distinct institutional concepts; however, their ultimate compromise on benefits led to the issuance of the *1474 Inventor Bylaws*; therefore, the patent privilege system gradually became the Venetian government's primary approach to encourage technological development. This was also the case in France, Germany, and England. During the formation and transition of institutions, the constant game between the private sector (including the emerging industrial and commercial class, technicians, and guilds) and government happened in all these countries, although they followed different paths. The emerging industrial and commercial class and technicians hoped to extend the range and type of the patent privilege. At the same time, the guilds attempted to prevent new technologies and industrial competition brought by the former. The government granted patents to develop the industrial and commercial classes or to satisfy the financial requirements of the royal family. In France, there was a game between the political powers in favor of mercantilism and physiocracy, respectively. The latter persuaded the government to issue the 1762 *Act on Derived Rights of the Patent* to develop a liberal economy and restrict the patent monopoly. In Germany, the government was persuaded by the emerging industrial and commercial class and technicians to establish the patent privilege system and develop the domestic industrial and commercial economy. Then, due to the turbulence caused by wars, the guild powers took the initiative to abolish most patent systems in the country. In England, the royal family's abuse of power stirred up discontentment in the emerging industrial and commercial classes. Since the late sixteenth century, the congress and common court, on behalf of the emerging industrial and commercial classes, launched a fierce attack against the royal aristocrats on behalf of feudal kindship. Their fight finally contributed to the enactment of *The Statute of Monopolies* (1624).

Fourth, during the Pre-industrial Age, the feudal government was the most vital subject of authority in Venice, France, Germany, and England; therefore, it played a dominant role in building the patent privilege system. For instance, the Venetian government ensured that it could control and examine technology with particular examinations and practical authorization standards. The government was concerned with the feasibility and public interest rather than the novelty of technology. Based on this, the government had great discretion over the control and examination of patents. It could repeal patents to serve the public interests, which was the core of the patent privilege system. Then, France, Germany, and England inherited most provisions of the patent privilege system in Venice.

Fifth, accidents affected the transition of the patent system. Based on its premature technological, economic, and cultural environments, the Venetian government established a stable and well-organized patent system. It formed an independent copyright system in the practice of patent privilege. If Venice had not declined, the rules and institutional systems of modern copyright laws would have come into existence in Venice. However, with the Red Sea blocked by the Portuguese, the opening of the new sea routes, and the shocks from the Ottoman Empire to Venice, Venice began to decline, and so did its patent privilege and copyright systems, which gradually vanished in history. That was also true in Germany. A well-established system with abundant rewards was built earlier than that in England; however, it was destroyed during political struggles and wars. Finally, people were almost oblivious to the system. This pushed the transition of the patent system toward France and England.

Notes

1 Joel Mokyr. *The Lever of Riches: Technological Creativity and Economic Progress*. Chen Xiaobai. Beijing: Huaxia Publishing House, 2008:34.
2 Frank D. Prager. A History of Intellectual Property from 1545 to 1787, 26 *Journal of the Patent and Trademark Office Society*, 1944, p. 40.
3 Wang Hongsheng. *World History of Science and Technology*. Beijing: Renmin University of China Press, 2008:12.
4 Wang Hongsheng. *World History of Science and Technology*, 12.
5 Almost at the same time, when humans managed to use empirical observations or legends to handle simple phenomena and mysterious, unpredictable changes that they failed to understand or control, the seed of science began to grow. During the childhood of humans, when their self-awareness was awakened, limited technological ability led to limited dominance and applications of the natural environment. Death and mysterious natural phenomena contributed to the vague reverence and mystery for the world, leading to the generation of witchcraft and religions.

When the attempt of directly dominating the nature by witchcraft failed, human beings prayed to gods for this ability via worship and orison. When human beings realized that this made no difference and the rule of the nature remained unchanged, they stepped into the gate of science.

6 James E. McClellan, Harold Dorn. *Science and Technology in World History: An Introduction*. Wang Mingyang. Shanghai: Shanghai Science and Technology Education Press, 2007:42.

7 William Cecil Dampier-Whetham. *A History of Science and Its Relation with Philosophy and Religion*. Li Heng. Guilin: Guangxi Normal University Press, 2001:2.

8 Within four generations in 113 years (2834 BC–2722 BC), six Pharaohs built 13 pyramids altogether. During the rule of Ramses II, people could use technology to carry a 1,000-ton statue. McClellan, Dorn. *Science and Technology*, 58–62.

9 It was said Imhotep was a genius like Da Vinci, and also a flamen, scholar, sculptor, carpenter, poet, and doctor. As a slightly exaggerated polymath, he was highly praised by writers in ancient Greece and Rome thousands of years later. He was the designer of the first pyramid, solving the problem of carrying 50-ton granite blocks. Suzanne Scotchmer. *Innovation and Incentives*. Liu Yong. Shanghai: Gezhi Publishing House, 2010:4.

10 Zhang Xinfeng. *The Property Right Attributes of Patents-A Study on the Path of Privatization of Technology*. Wuhan: Huazhong University of Science and Technology Press, 2011:119.

11 Edith Hamilton. *The Greek Way*. Xu Qiping. Hangzhou: Zhejiang People's Publishing House, 1988:20.

12 He studied and improved almost all academic knowledge. Certainly, the most famous one was his contributions to technology. For example, *Physics* discussed the law of the motion of celestial bodies and nature; *Meteorology* studied the primitive concepts of chemistry, and the *History of Animals* discussed biological theories, including the division of animals and dissection.

13 His inventions involve an improved water pump, the first metal spring, the first air-operated pipe organ, the first keyboard, and an improved hourglass watch. He also built an ejector operated by compressed air but failed, because no one could manufacture and assemble enough components.

14 In addition to many published books on mathematics and physics, he invented improved gears, a measuring instrument, an air-operated fountain and a famous engine motivated by a steam jet. Scotchmer. *Innovation and Incentives*, 5–6.

15 J. J. Pollitt. *Art and Experience in Classical Greece*. New York: Cambridge University Press, 1972:64–70.

16 Wang Hongsheng. *World History of Science and Technology*, 12, 53.

17 Dampier-Whetham. *History of Science*, 69.

18 In agriculture, advanced irrigation systems, iron plows with wheels, improved hoes, rakes, spades and threshing tools, and the two fields system represented the most advanced agricultural technologies. In civil engineering, the Romans, practically minded, were keen on civil engineering technologies like roads, canals, baths, and arenas. Buildings and constructions were almost everywhere in the country. The road system during the Roman Age extended in all directions, with a length of 80,000 km. Lime concrete was invented, supporting magnificent buildings like the Great Arena and the Pantheon. Wang Hongsheng. *World History of Science and Technology*, 54.

19 Xenophon. *Oeconomicus: The Income of Athens*. Zhang Bojian, et al. Beijing: The Commercial Press, 1981:17.

20 Li Shangjun. Labor and Ancient Greek Society, *Journal of Shanghai Normal University* (Philosophy and Social Sciences), 2013(6).

21 Huang Xinrong. *Modern Western Philosophy of Technology*. Nanchang: Jiangxi People's Publishing House, 2011:9.

22 Mokyr. *Lever of Riches*, 217.

23 Jean-Yves Goffi. *Philosophy of Technology*. Dong Maoyong. Beijing: The Commercial Press, 2000:48.
24 Rudolf Krasser. *German Patent and Utility Model Law, European and International Patent Law*. Shan Xiaoguang, Zhang Taoliu, et al. Beijing: Intellectual Property Press, 2016:100.
25 Scotchmer. *Innovation and Incentives*, 7.
26 Mokyr. *Lever of Riches*, 219.
27 There were some guild organizations at the beginning of ancient Greece and Rome, but they were merely exceptions. It was not until the Age of Augustus (28 BC–AD 14) that guild organizations were widely distributed throughout the Empire.
28 They were originally free organizations consisting of menial craftsmen, laborers, and slaves, and then some ordinary freemen and even women joined these organizations. Their initial objective was to organize some sacrifices for collective religions, to offer funeral services for the poor, or to hold some social feasts. Then, people organized themselves for political purposes. Guild organizations with political objectives were often oppressed by the government; however, as long as they were not regarded as a hazard to social order, they could acquire permission from the government. Around the third century, Alexander of Rome began to control guild organizations in administrative ways and enacted many rules to oversee them. The guilds were transformed into one of the administrative departments of the government. Complicated and heavy burdens led to the departure of many members. For example, Augustus once oppressed and regulated some guild organizations with political objectives. Francesco M, De Robertis. *Il diritto associative Romano dai collegi della repubblica alle corporazioni del basso impero*. Italy: Bari, 1938:3–240; L. Ross Taylor. *Party Politics in the Age of Caesar*. University of California Press: Berkeley and Los Angeles, 1949:44; Susan Treggiari. *Roman Freedmen During the Late Republic*. Oxford: Oxford University Press, 1969:167–168.
29 In *Philebus,* Plato divided all knowledge into two types: knowledge about education and nurture and knowledge about manufacture. The latter was further divided into two subtypes: empirical knowledge developed from thoughts and instincts based on practice and experience, such as music, medicine, and agriculture; and operative knowledge about applying numbers, measurement, and weight consciously, such as carpentry and architecture. The latter has greater accuracy, and that is the primitive "techne." Carl Mitcham. *Thinking Through Technology: The Path Between Engineering and Philosophy*. Chen Fan, Qin Shusheng. Shenyang: Liaoning People's Publishing House, 2008:150.
30 He said, "The craftsman who makes a bed or a table stares at the idea or form, respectively making the table or bed we use" (Plato. *Utopia*. Beijing: Commercial Press, 1986:388). He pointed out in *Timaeus* that craftsmen make applications as the copy of ideas. Although Plato believed that gods created the idea of an artificial object, which is the authentic existence, and craftsmen "can only make things similar to, but distinct from authentic editions." Nonetheless, Plato granted a concept that was easily, at least in instinct, connected with modern technologies as the product of reason or manufacturing products efficiently with mathematic analysis.
31 He regarded technologies as "the wisdom of manufacture," clearly proposing the opinion that "technology is manufacture." He believed, literally speaking, "techne" is a custom of real awareness related to manufacture, whose true meaning is an ability to manufacture that was dependent on correct awareness or inference of the object to be manufactured. Therefore, Aristotle connected "techne" with "logos," which was the prototype of the word "technology," because "technology" in modern English originated from "technologia" in ancient Greek, which was the combination of techne and logos. He

also believed, "Without characters related to manufacture, technologies are unlikely to exist; without technology, nor are these characters. Therefore, technology is equivalent to characters that are suitable for logos and related to true manufacture. All technologies lead to the generation of some objects." Aristotle. *Nicomachean Ethics*. Liao Shenbai. Beijing: The Commercial Press, 2003:171.

32 He believed that technologies are featured with productivity and occasionality contrary to necessity, while science is the discipline of necessity. As pointed out in *Nicomachean Ethics*, "things where technologies can exist have no relation to things that are determined to be produced and things produced due to nature. To a certain extent, technologies and fortune are related to the same things." Obviously, although Aristotle regarded technologies as a kind of reasonable activity, it is a low-level reason, completely distinct from theoretical reason.

33 D. J. Conacher. *Aeschylus' 'Prometheus Bound': A Literary Commentary*. Toronto: University of Toronto Press, 1980:8.

34 Pamela O. Long. Invention, Authorship, "Intellectual Property," and the Origin of Patents: Notes toward a Conceptual History, *Technology and Culture*, 1991, 32 (4), pp. 846–884.

35 Long. Invention, Authorship, "Intellectual Property", pp. 846–884.

36 Mokyr. *Lever of Riches*, 217.

37 Animism and anthropomorphism believed that because every river, tree, and land resided with the gods, the environment was, therefore, changeable, unpredictable, and uncontrollable. Any attempt to change the environment and nature was likely to incur horrible anger from Zeus and local inferior gods. Mokyr. *Lever of Riches*, 221.

38 Scotchmer. *Innovation and Incentives*, 6.

39 In Sybaris, Greece, in 500 BC, the people there were keen on luxury. They regulated that if a cook or candy-maker invented a kind of delicious candy or dish, others could not make the same one within 1 year, so the inventor could obtain all profits brought by the invention within this year. Krasser. *German Patent and Utility Model Law*, 68.

40 Scotchmer. *Innovation and Incentives*, 6.

41 Mokyr. *Lever of Riches*, 7.

42 It was said that in Rome in AD 30, a craftsman invented an unbreakable glass cup. Tiberius Caesar, the emperor at that time, asked the craftsman to exhibit his invention and threw the cup onto the stone-paved ground. When the craftsman picked up the cup, it was slightly sunk like a bronze cup, and the craftsman restored it with a hammer. The emperor was quite astonished. The craftsman might have believed that he would be famous, especially when the emperor asked him, "Is there anyone else that knows the method to make such a cup?". When he answered "no," he was ordered to be beheaded. People could not understand why Tiberius made such an order, and the unbreakable glass cup remained unseen. There is no doubt that Tiberius's behavior played a negative role in the development of human civilization. It was said by others that the craftsman was an architect envied by the emperor, and was ordered to remove his name from all public records after the execution.

43 Mokyr. *Lever of Riches*, 34.

44 Dampier-Whetham. *History of Science*, 84.

45 Dampier-Whetham. *History of Science*, 35–43.

46 Abraham Wolf. *A History of Science, Technology, and Philosophy in the 16th and 17th Centuries*. Zhou Changzhong. Beijing: The Commercial Press, 1984:5–6.

47 David S. Landes. *The Unbound Prometheus: Technological Change and Industrial Development in Western Europe from 1750 to the Present*. Xie Huaizhu. Beijing: Huaxia Publishing House, 2007:23.

48 Toby Huff. *Why Modern Science Was Born in the West.* Yu Xia. Beijing: Peking University Press, 2010:56.

49 At that time, Spain, North Africa, and the Middle East were governed by Islamic civilizations, An ancient civilization that was based on the basic thoughts and principles of the *Koran* and *Hadith*, as a combination of Arabian, Persian, and Turkish cultures.

50 Mokyr. *Lever of Riches*, 43.

51 McClellan, Dorn. *Science and Technology*, 148.

52 McClellan, Dorn. *Science and Technology*, 43.

53 McClellan, Dorn. *Science and Technology*, 143.

54 For example, scientific books of mathematician al-Khwārizmī, medical scientist ibn-Sīna and Green, and chemist Gebel were transported to Europe, some of which were used for 500 years.

55 McClellan, Dorn. *Science and Technology*, 44–47.

56 Toby Huff. *The Rise of Early Modern Science.* Yu Xia. Beijing: Peking University Press, 2010:226.

57 The Government controlled powerful water conservancy projects, mastering water conservancy technologies, such as complicated gates, pumps, and noria. Until the twelfth century, navigable canals and waterways in China reached around 50,000 km. It is estimated that the number of water conservancy projects increased seven times from the tenth to the fifteenth century, and the population at most doubled at the same time.

58 Until the twelfth century, ceramic-making technology was developed enough to make delicate utensils. China created spinning wheels in 1035, which was ahead of the West for centuries, and the skilled technicians in China were able to use water power proficiently. The crafts of silk production were quite complete. An entire set of highly efficient technological processes was already perfected, from cultivating mulberry, bathing silkworms, reeling silk, winding silk, warp and weft to weaving. "Silk workshops in Chengdu Region in North Song Dynasty consumed 115,000 liang (traditional weight unit in China, approximately equal to 50 g, different in dynasties) of silk, 211,000 jin (traditional weight unit in China, approximately equal to 500 g) of dyes, 1,500 pieces of silk per year. Luo Ruilin, Liu Baimao. *The History of Chinese Silk.* Beijing: Beijing Textile Industry Press, 1986:113.

59 Emperors in the Song Dynasty focused on martial technologies, even establishing arsenals to produce weapons. Weapon workshops at that time included "North and South workshops," "Institute for Bows and Crossbows," and the "Guild of Bows and Arrows." According to records in the *History of Song Dynasty*, "When it comes to the production of weapons and armors, there are North and South workshops, Institute for bows and crossbows. Workshops in all provinces hire technicians and impose on regular products." In 1073 (the sixth year of Xining), Emperor Shen of Song adopted the proposal of Wang Wu and set up the bureau of military weapons, which set up workshops and gathered skilled technicians in the country. Since then, the weapons have become increasingly excellent. For example, the revolving scenic lantern invented during the Song Dynasty was a technological device at festivals. It was operated by heated gas, with scenes in the lantern revolving. Although it actualized the transformation from heat energy to mechanical energy, this technology was far away from practical production and applications.

60 Mokyr. *Lever of Riches*, 243.

61 Zhang Gongyao. *The History and Philosophy of Science and Technology.* Changsha: Central South University Press, 2007:57.

62 Zhang Gongyao. *History and Philosophy of Science and Technology*, 59.

63 McClellan, Dorn. *Science and Technology*, 189.

64 Mokyr. *Lever of Riches*, 264.
65 William Blackstone. *Commentaries on The Laws of England, 16th Edn.*, 1825:490–501.
66 Joel Mokyr. *The Gift of Athena: Historical Origins of the Knowledge Economy*. Duan Yibing, and Tang Le. Beijing: Science Beijing: Science Publishing House, 2011:233.
67 Thorstein Veblen. *The Place of Science in Modern Civilization*. Zhang Lin, Zhang Tianlong. Beijing: The Commercial Press, 2012:313.
68 James Westfall Thompson. *Economic and Social History in the Later Middle Ages (1300–1530)*. Xu Jialing, et al. Beijing: The Commercial Press, 1992:507.
69 Long. Invention, Authorship, "Intellectual Property", pp. 846–884.
70 Long. Invention, Authorship, "Intellectual Property", pp. 846–884.
71 Long. Invention, Authorship, "Intellectual Property", pp. 846–884.
72 Long. Invention, Authorship, "Intellectual Property", pp. 846–884.
73 Mokyr. *Lever of Riches*, 33.
74 Louis Uchitelle. In a Productivity Surge, No Proof of A "New economy", *New York Times*, 2008-10-8.
75 Zhang Gongyao. *History and Philosophy of Science and Technology*, 57.
76 Sheng Guorong. Science, Technology and Society: The Historical Evolution of the Relationship between the Three, *Journal of Northeastern University* (Social Sciences), 2006 (3).
77 E. A. Bogatayh, B. H. Levchenko. *The Origin and Class Essence of the Bourgeois Patent System. Chinese and Foreign Law*, 1979 (6).
78 Mokyr. *Lever of Riches*, 80.
79 Moses I. Finley. *The Ancient Economy*. University of California Press, 1999:148.
80 Beijing Continental Bridge Times Publications Co. *Italian Past*. Chongqing: Chongqing Publishing House, 2007:3.
81 Eric Jones. *The European Miracle: Environments, Economies, and Geopolitics in the History of Europe and Asia*. Chen Xiaobai. Beijing: Huaxia Publishing House, 2015:38.
82 Mokyr. *Lever of Riches*, 80.
83 The reasons why European technology rose at the end of the Middle Ages are listed as follows. 1. Technological innovations in Europe were made by private individuals, and in China or other civilizations, they were made by public officials and the government, and the latter ones were unlikely to last a long time (McClellan, Dorn. *Science and Technology*, 100). 2. Europe was fragmented and competitive during the Middle Ages, instead of being governed by a large empire, which was beneficial to the competition and transfer of technological thoughts. Cultural and religious links and competitions among European countries provided a foundation for the emigration of technical talents, leading to the sequent and interlaced diffusion of technologies in Europe (Jones. *The European Miracle*, 38–40). 3. Europeans were good at absorbing advanced technologies from other civilizations. Europe introduced a set of valuable, even fundamental technologies from the Eastern world: windmills from Persia, silkworm-feeding, silk-making, paper-making, iron-melting, powdery, cannons, paper money, printing from China and Arabic numbers, crops, and sugarcane (Wang Hongsheng. *World History of Science and Technology*, 85). 4. Some "heretic" ideas appeared in Christian thoughts, some new ideas began to "challenge the authority of God," and some started to begin to realize the value of technology. (Landes. *Unbound Prometheus*, 24). This belief was accepted by the public: a human is a colleague of God and in his work, so it is correct that technological products should be proven by the destiny of humans. Some religious

monk groups played an important role in education, agriculture, land reclamation, and craft technologies, and the Benedictines were the most famous among them.

84 Many facilities that used natural force like water or wind began to be put into practice, such as windwheels and canal locks. When it comes to transportation, Europeans applied a so-called caique building technology; 1,000-ton ships appeared in 1400. Europeans developed better navigation tools than ever before: compasses, sea maps, and navigation compasses were put into application during the thirteenth century; Ptolemy's *Geography* was translated into Latin and transferred to Europe in 1409, which led to the peak in the Renaissance of geography in Western Europe. When it comes to the textile industry, many new inventions sprang up. For instance, spinning wheels were invented in the twelfth century; silk throwing was mastered by Europeans during the thirteenth century; and the Saxon spinning wheel appeared during the fifteenth century, all of which greatly improved the efficiency and productivity of weaving. In terms of metallurgy, a water-operated blast furnace was invented; in noniron metallurgy, the craft of separating silver from copper ores with the help of lead was one of the greatest inventions. In terms of printing, Gutenberg's typography spread and was applied throughout Europe since its invention. There were 380 operating printing machines in Europe until 1480, and more books were printed in the
50 years after the invention than during the previous centuries. In the clock industry, the mechanical clock was regarded as the symbol of technological progress as well as the deep reason for it, for it constructed the order and organization of people's lives and production, creating a set of shared objective information, and allowed a precise measurement for productivity. In the martial industry, powdery and early firearms in China were introduced into Europe, and they invented new types of weapons like new cannons and muskets on this basis, governing and dominating Islamic and European countries at their will. In chemistry, the invention of many chemicals granted great convenience to people's lives. It changed their daily lives, such as glasses, colored windows, dyes, leather, oil painting, and medicines (Mokyr. *Lever of Riches*, 50, 51, 52, 53, 55).

85 Venice constructed and managed a large commercial network, making trade with countries in Western Europe, the Balkan Peninsula, Syria, Egypt, Crete, and Sicily. They entered Crem and built trade stations in the Don estuary (Shang Jie. *Medieval Century: A Study of Aristocratic Politics in Late Modern Early Venice*. Wuhan: Wuhan University Press, 2013:27).

86 Jie. *Medieval Century*, 27.

87 Venice grasped enormous profits from it. It was estimated that the business ships of Venice bought wood and ores to the mainland of Western Europe, carrying these resources to the Levent and North Africa, and selling luxuries like spices and silks from the East back to Venice, which could sometimes bring a profit of at most 1,200%. Roger Crowley. *City of Fortune: How Venice Ruled the Seas*. Lu Dapeng, Zhang Cheng. Beijing: Social Sciences Academic Press, 2015:15.

88 Fernand Braudel. *Civilization and Capitalism, 15th-18th Century*. Gu Liang, Shi Kangqiang. Beijing: SDX Joint Publishing Company, 1992:142.

89 The history of glass-making dates back to the thirteenth century. In 1204, during the Fourth Crusade, the Byzantine Empire was occupied, and many Byzantian glass technicians fled to Venice, bringing the technology of glass making. Then, Venetian businessmen brought potassium from Syria, which significantly influenced the craft of glass making.

90 Braudel. *Civilization and Capitalism*, 145.

91 There was a huge artificial water pool connected with canals with open water, where workers, including carpenters, sailmakers, caulkers, and ship designers, were hired to build solid and practical ships in efficient assembly lines of the factory, which included round bottom ships for short-range, heavy-burdened transportation, and long-shaped sailboats for war or ocean trade. Shang Jie. *A Study of Venetian Aristocracy in the Late Medieval and Early Modern Period*. Wuhan: Wuhan University Press, 2013:28.

92 San Nuto, a Venetian aristocrat, introduced this "arsenal" in his anthem for Venice.

> There is no doubt that it is the best scenario that you can ever imagine. It covers an area of 20 stadis (ca. 60 acres), located in District of San Martino Church, surrounded by beautiful city walls. Large galleys used for battleships are built here day and night .... About 1000 workers are working here every day, and you can find all technicians about shipbuilding here. The arsenal is surrounded by water, ships can enter the water directly after completion, leaving the arsenal and entering the great canal ...

Crowley. *City of Fortune*, 59.

93 Thompson. *Economic and Social History*, 343.

94 Thomas Francis Carter. *The Invention of Printing in China and Its Spread Westward*. Wu Zeyan. Beijing: The Commercial Press, 1957:109.

95 Huang Renyu. *Capitalism and the Twenty-first Century*. Beijing: SDX joint publishing company, 1997:179, 197.

96 Jiang Zhe'an. On the Causes of Economic Prosperity in Medieval Venice, *Journal of Anhui University*, 1998 (4).

97 Thompson. *Economic and Social History,* 342, 343.

98 Prager, History of Intellectual Property, pp. 711–758.

99 Prager, History of Intellectual Property, pp. 711–758.

100 The bank system was the first to appear. The "Deposit bank is not a new institution. It may exist as early as in the Roman age, but its renaissance should be dated back to the end of the 12th century and the 13th century." On this occasion, the first national bank in history was born in Venice. The word "bank" came from the Venetian word "Bankorott." The Ducato gold coin, cast by Venice in 1284, was the common currency in Europe. Second, the insurance industry appeared as a new financial institution. "Insurance emerged at this very time. As was expected, it was related to marine trade; its earliest founder was an Italian ... . The first known insurance credit could be dated back to 1287." Finally, a series of drafts and long-time credit institutions appeared. The "double-entry bookkeeping" was invented by Luca Pacioli in Venice. Since the late twelfth and early thirteenth centuries, especially during the fourteenth century, Venice had been equipped with all tools for economic activities: market, shop, warehouse, Lasantha trade fair, mint, governor's palace, arsenal, bank, and custom. Venetians accepted "the legality of credit business" based on "rules of businessmen."

101 Braudel. *Civilization and Capitalism*, 131–134.

102 According to Braudel's statistics, the financial income of Venice and its municipal districts in 1423 was some 750,000 Ducato, with an average income of 50–100 Ducato, which was almost equal to the national income of Spain, close to the income of Britain, and far much higher than other cities in Italy like Florence, Milan, and Genova. It was restricted to the financial income of Venice city and its surrounding islands. If one adds the income of its territories on the mainland (464,000 Ducato) and overseas territories (376,000 Ducato) to the income of administrative authority (75,000 Ducato), the total annual financial income of Venice will rise to 1.59 million Ducato, becoming "the richest country in Europe." What's more, the wealth of Venice was also demonstrated

in its population and city construction. In the late thirteenth century, Venice becomes a famous metropolis in Europe, with a population of more than 100,000, only lower than Milan (ca. 200,000), equal to Florence and Genova, much higher than other Italian cities (ca. 20,000–50,000). By the fifteenth century, as one of the most famous international metropolises, it had processed 200,000 commercial residents. Braudel. *Civilization and Capitalism*, 120–121.

103 Braudel. *Civilization and Capitalism*, 86–141.

104 E. E. Rich, C. H. Wilson, eds. *The Cambridge Economic History of Europe: Volume 5, The Economic Organization of Early Modern Europe*. Wang Chunfa, et al. Beijing: Economic Science Press, 2002:414.

105 There was a story about King Carcropus in classical Greek mythology. When he built a new city in Acropolis in Atika, he promised that whichever god granted the new city the best gift, he would name it after that gift. Poseidon, the god of ocean beat away stones, making a clear stream flowing across the city. Carcropus tasted the water, finding it salty. Athena, the goddess of knowledge and wisdom, granted him a more valuable gift: the olive tree, which symbolizes peace, wealth, and hope. The story hereafter was likely to be history rather than myth.

106 Naturalism embodied the renaissance of the atheistic classical academy and was encouraged by this renaissance. Its spirit was quite distinct from the supernaturalistic spirit that pervaded the rational atmosphere during the Middle Ages. It was not the result of the countermarch from reason but a greater rational step toward the reason that was more liberal, more complete, and beyond any restrictions. Wolf. *History of Science, Technology, and Philosophy*, 7.

107 Xu Liang. *Philosophy of Technology*. Shanghai: Fudan University Press, 2004:8.

108 For example, during the thirteenth century, Roger Bacon predicted that large battleships without oars would travel across rivers and oceans; vehicles without pulling animals would run throughout the land, while aircraft distinct from flying birds would soar in the sky; people would use diving bells to explore the mystery of the seabed (George Basalla. *The Evolution of Technology*. Shanghai: Fudan University Press, 2000:83). *The Greatest Show on Machines* was a relatively popular book at that time, because the technologies they demonstrated existed for amusing and instructing the readers and the public. Akin to today's science fiction films, people were curious about and ignorant of technology, so many of them expressed their technological imaginations in the form of literature. Professional articles that described strange machines appeared at that time; however, these machines went far beyond the capacity of technology. Therefore, these articles failed to provide technological details about these machines. One of the books that appeared at first was Konrad Kyeser's *Bellifortis* (1405), which was famous for war machines full of fantasies. In *Warriors*, similar to other books of this type, the machines or equipment described were unlikely to be created. Basalla. *Evolution of Technology*, 73–75, 79.

109 Basalla. *Evolution of Technology*, 141.

110 Basalla. *Evolution of Technology*, 142.

111 Li Zonghui. *The Intellectual Property System in Historical Perspective*. Beijing: Intellectual Property Press, 2015:42.

112 Nicholas of Cusa, Opera omnia, ed. L. Bauer, 1937, pp. 95–98.

113 Denys Hay. *The Italian Renaissance in its Historical Background*. Li Yucheng. Beijing: SDX joint publishing company, 1988:129.

114 Henri Pirenne. *Economic and Social History of Medieval Europe*. Le Wen. Shanghai: Shanghai People's Publishing House, 2001:18.

115 Mokyr. *Lever of Riches*, 195.
116 Robert King Merton. *Science, Technology, and Society in Seventeenth Century England*. Fan Dainian. Beijing: The Commercial Press, 2000:119.
117 Thompson. *Economic and Social History*, 15.
118 Merton. *Science, Technology, and Society*, 119.
119 Zhao Wenhong. *The Development of the Private Property Rights System: A Study of the Origins of the Western Market Economy and Capitalism*. Beijing: China Social Science Press, 1998:33.
120 In the system of Lex Romana, civil rights referred to the privileges owned by Roman citizens, including public and private rights. Public rights referred to political ones, while the core of private rights was property rights. Lex Romana put great emphasis on personal properties and rights to make contracts. Bugbee B. W. *Genesis of American Patent and Copyright Law*. Washington: Public Affairs Press, 1967:241.
121 M. M. Postan, E. E. Rich, and Edward Miller, eds. *The Cambridge Economic History of Europe: Vol. 3. Economic Organization and Policies in the Middle Ages*. Beijing: Economic Science Press, 2002:195–196.
122 William James Ashley. *An Introduction on English Economic History and Theory: The Middle Ages*, Vol. 2. London, UK: Longmans, 1914:67–123.
123 Ashley. *Introduction on English Economic History and Theory*, 131.
124 Richard Mackenney. *Tradesmen and Traders: The World of the Guilds in Venice and Europe*, c.1250–c.1650. Totowa, N.J.: Barnes & Noble Books, 1987:9, 43; G. Monticolo, E. Besta. *Icapitolari delle Arti Veneziane sottoposte alla Giustizia e poi alla Giustizia Vecchia dale original MCCCXXX,* 3 vols. Rome: Fonti per la storia d'Italia, 1896–1914:26–28.
125 Mackenney. *Tradesmen and Traders*, 21–28.
126 Thompson. *Economic and Social History*, 338–339.
127 R. J. Charleston, L. M. Angus-Butterworth. Glass. In *A History of Technology*, Vol. 3. Ocford, UK: Clarendon Press, 1958: 206–244.
128 Beijing Continental Bridge Times Publications Co. *Italian Past*, 13.
129 G. Monticolo, E. Besta. *I capitolari delle arti veneziane*, I IV, Roma, III, Capitulum Canpanarii et Laviçariorum, 1896:107–121.
130 Long. Invention, Authorship, "Intellectual Property", pp. 846–884.
131 Long. Invention, Authorship, "Intellectual Property", pp. 846–884.
132 Long. Invention, Authorship, "Intellectual Property", pp. 846–884.
133 Valerio Lintner. *A Traveller's History of Italy*. Guo Shangxing, Liu Yajie, et al. Shanghai: Shanghai Jiao Tong University Press, 2009:50–51.
134 Guilio Mandich. Venetian Origins of Inventors' Rights, 42 *Journal of the Patents and Trademark Office Society*, 1960, pp. 378–382.
135 Mandich. Venetian Origins of Inventors' Rights, pp. 378–382.
136 Frank D. Prager. The Early Growth and Influence of Intellectual Property, 34 *Journal of the Patents and Trademark Office Society*, 1952, p. 81.
137 Doctrines about the origin of cities include communes, manors, markets, right of exoneration, guards, local institutions in the Carolingian Dynasty, and German Guilds. James Westfall Thompson. *Economic and Social History of the Middle Ages: 300–1300*. Geng Yanru. Beijing: The Commercial Press, 1984:409–413.
138 During the late Middle Ages, the commercial economy had developed rapidly, and its republican and aristocratic had come into being. From the eleventh to the early twelfth century, the commercial millionaires in city centers in North Italy generally experienced a "commune revolution." With the revival of the commodity economy in

Western Europe during the late Middle Ages, cities in Middle and North Italy, which were actually independent or obtained legal autonomy rights from the Emperor of the Holy Roman Empire or Pope, gradually founded autonomous commune governments to manage the cities.

139 The bill restricted the membership of the congress to aristocrats who have presented the congress in the past 4 years and canceled the election procedure for membership of the congress. Aristocrats and members who were not listed would no longer have membership of the Congress as well as their aristocratic identification. The membership of the congress was directly related to the aristocratic identification, which symbolized the formal formation of the Venetian aristocracy in law and the formal foundation of the closed aristocratic system of the Venetian Republic. Jie. *A Study of Venetian*, 49.

140 The "Venice myth" was an idealized appreciation and expression of the Venetian Republic and its social lives by historians. In the "myth," Venice was described as an ideal republic that was a strong marine empire and a city republic independent from other powers and maintained chronicle social stability and harmony.

141 Jie. *A Study of Venetian*, 35.

142 Huang Renyu. *Capitalism and the Twenty-first Century*, 52.

143 Prager, History of Intellectual Property, pp. 711–758.

144 Prager, History of Intellectual Property, pp. 711–758.

145 Mandich. Venetian Origins of Inventors' Rights, pp. 378–382.

146 Prager, History of Intellectual Property, pp. 711–758.

147 Guilio Mandich. Venetian Patents (1450–1550), 30 *Journal of the Patents and Trademark Office Society*, 1948, p. 150.

148 John Martin. Venetian Narrative Painting in the Age of Carpaccio, 95 *Journal of the Patents and Trademark Office Society*, 1990, pp. 1238–1239.

149 Erich Kaufer. *The Economics of the Patent System*. Ke Ruihao. Beijing: Peking University Press, 2005:15–17.

150 Celts was a general term given to various ethnicities who were active in Middle Europe in 2000 BC and had common cultural and language characteristics. They were a loose ethnic group associated with a common language and cultural traditions belonging to the ancient ethnic group. They lived initially in the hinterland in Middle Europe, north of the Alps, and were mainly distributed in Gaul, North Italy (Cisalpine Gaul), Spain, Britain, and Ireland. This ethnicity is not completely equal to modern nations, which are formed by ancient ethnic groups via chronicle evolution and constant disassembly, combination, and recombination. Today, Celt mainly refers to ethnic groups in the British Isles and Bretagne in France, who have common points in language and culture to ancient Celts and usually refers to Irish.

151 Kaufer. *Economics of the Patent System*, 19.

152 Mokyr. *Lever of Riches*, 85.

153 Mandich. Venetian Patents, pp. 166–224.

154 Mandich. Venetian Patents, pp. 166–224.

155 Kaufer. *Economics of the Patent System*, 5.

156 Mandich. Venetian Origins of Inventors' Right, p. 50.

157 Mandich. Venetian Patents, p. 7.

158 Mandich. Venetian Origins of Inventors' Right, p. 52.

159 Dai Xuanyu. The Development and Evolution of Guild Organizations in Western Europe, *Journal of North Central University* (Social Sciences), 2011 (2).

160 At that time, Venice had neither constitution nor definite legislative, judicial, and administrative organs, and depended mainly on conventions and traditions to be the

most important rules to guide people's behaviors. Christopher May. The Venetian Moment: New Technologies, Legal Innovation and the Institutional Origins of Intellectual Property, *Prometheus*, 2002, pp. 159–179.

161 May. Venetian Moment, pp. 159–179.

162 May. Venetian Moment, pp. 159–179.

163 May. Venetian Moment, p. 167.

164 Mandich. Venetian Patents, pp. 166–224.

165 Prager, History of Intellectual Property, pp. 711–758.

166 Prager, History of Intellectual Property, pp. 711–758.

167 Prager, History of Intellectual Property, pp. 711–758.

168 Mandich. Venetian, pp. 166–224.

169 Mandich. Venetian, pp. 166–224.

170 Ramon A. Klitzke. Historical Background of the English Patent Law, 41 *Journal of the Patent and Trademark Office Society*, November, 1959, p. 638.

171 Mandich. Venetian Origins of Inventors' Rights, pp. 378–382.

172 Fernand Braudel. *The Structures of Everyday Life: The Limits of the Possible*, London: Collins, 1981:433–444.

173 In terms of the protection term in the patent right, despite the standardization of the *1474 Inventor Bylaws*, practical authorization was usually based on specific cases, which mainly depended on the degree of utility to the public. The applicant usually demanded a 50-year protection restriction; however, the protection term granted by the senate was always shorter than the period of application, and it seldom granted the 10-year restriction based on the *1474 Inventor Bylaws*. Related materials indicated the 50-year protection restriction was often granted during 1474–1500, while the 25-year restriction and even the 5-year restriction in two cases were usually granted during1500–1550.

174 Prager. History of Intellectual Property, pp. 711–758.

175 Mandich. Venetian Patents, pp. 166–224.

176 Mandich. Venetian Patents, p. 207.

177 Mandich. Venetian Patents, pp. 166–224.

178 Charles Howard McIlwain. *Constitutionalism: Ancient and Modern*. Zhai Xiaobo. Guiyang: Guizhou People's Publishing House, 2004:201.

179 Krasser. *German Patent and Utility Model Law*, 123.

180 Christopher May. The Hypocrisy of Forgetfulness: The Contemporary Significance of Early Innovations in Intellectual Property, 14 *Review of International Political Economy*, 2007, pp. 1–25.

181 As early as 1443, 1460, and 1472, Venice granted patent privileges to creators of the art diversities. For instance, Venetian historian Mark Antonio Saberick was granted the privilege with his book *Decades in Venice*, which was the first privilege granted to writers instead of printers or booksellers; in 1498, Nicolo Flastos was granted the patent due to "combining Greek letter typeface with accents." Then, Daniel Banburg was granted similar patents because of Hebrew typefaces with vowel marks. In 1516, Hugo was granted a patent for printing wood paintings with the method of contrast between light and dark. Antonio Gadano was granted the patent due to "new ways of printing songs." In 1516 and 1551, Rocco Bonisero was granted a patent due to a series of improvements in the printing system. In ca. 1500, art patents were granted to new and old books. People were gradually becoming aware that its necessary condition was "to have innovations that could be used by scholars." In 1517, a general copyright law was issued (although still called a patent at that time). Its demands on new books were

the same as the demands on a new invention in the *1474 Inventor Bylaws* and stipulated that the books of the patent right owner could not be replicated without permission.

182 At the early stage, most copyrights for books were granted to publishers instead of writers, but the writers requested no rights to supervise; instead, they were quite satisfied with this indirect protection. Then, in 1533 and 1537, Venice issued laws about book patents, and the protection of copyright was finally shaped in the 1544 *Venetian Typeface Law*, which was so groundbreaking that it supported writers, resisted publishers, and placed the successor of the writer on the same stage as the writer.

183 Zou Lin. *A Study on the History of the Development of the Patent System in the United Kingdom*. Xiangtan: Xiangtan University, 2011.

184 Pia Weiss. *Patent Policy: Legal-Economic Effects in a National and International Framework*. London and New York: Routledge, 2010:10.

185 Walterscheid E.·C. The Early Evolution of the United States Patent Law: Antecedents (Part 1), 76 *Journal of the Patent and Trademark Office Society*, 1994, p. 697.

186 Krasser, *German Patent and Utility Model Law*, 141.

187 Stephan R. Epstein. Property Rights to Technical Knowledge in Premodern Europe, 1300–1800, 94 *American Economic Review*, 2004, pp. 382–387.

188 Ulf Anderfelt. *International Patent-Legislation and Developing Countries*. Germany: Springer Science & Business Media, 2013:6; Christine MacLeod. *Inventing the Industrial Revolution: The English Patent System 1660–1800*. Cambridge, UK: Cambridge University Press, 1988:11.

189 These privileges included the privilege of introducing silk production (from Florence) in Milan, introducing gold foils production (from Venice), and silk cotton production (from Genova) in Ferrara. Among the nine earliest patent privileges granted in Belgium, six were granted to Italians. The first recorded patent privilege in France was when the French King Francis I occupied Piemonte in Northwest Italy in 1536 and granted local people a privilege to produce silk. The Netherlands (today's Holland) began to grant many patent privileges in the late sixteenth century, and most of those granted were Italians; for example, a Venetian glass technician was granted a patent privilege in Antwerp in 1541. M. Frumkin. Early History of Patents for Invention, *Transactions of the Newcomen Society*, 1947, 26, pp. 47–56.

190 Robert Finlay. *Politics in Renaissance Venice*. New Brunswick, NJ: Rutgers University Press, 1980:27–37.

191 Z. S. Fink. Venice and English Political Thought in the Seventeenth Century, *Modern Philology*, November 1940, 38, pp. 155–172.

192 Chen Wenhai. *History of France*. Beijing: People's Publishing House, 2014:114.

193 In terms of daily technologies, "Boxes were changed with closets; in the windows, window glass replaced cloth, semi-transparent paper or heavy and expensive stained glass. Glasses became more and more popular. Forks were used to have suppers in rich families, clocks, even watches were already placed, carriages with a flexible former part and suspensions were also used." (Georges Duby, ed. *History of France*. Lv Yimin. Beijing: The Commercial Press, 2010:612–613.) In terms of weaving technologies, France attracted a number of silk-weaving technicians from Venice, Genova, and Florence, leading to the rapid development of weaving technologies in France. (Thompson. *Economic and Social*, 641–642.) In terms of printing technologies, in 1470, a Frenchman and three Germans introduced the new printing technology into Paris. In 1473, printing craftsmen in Liege and Nuremberg began to use this technology in Lyon. The printing technology rapidly spread throughout the country from Paris and Lyon. In terms of navy technologies, the French Navy absorbed new foreign

technologies from Venice and adopted solar declination charts, Polaris charts, and rangefinders. It could build large trade ships, and the technology of floor sail was gradually promoted (Thompson. *Economic and Social History*, 501.).

194 "Various, highly professionalized industry workers, such as jewelry craftsmen, embroider workers, lacework makers, lacework overgilders, tassel makers, wood sculptors, have gradually appeared." Chen Chen. The Development of Luxury Goods Consumption in France from sixteenth to eighteenth Century and Its Impact on French Economy and Culture. *Journal of Northwestern Polytechnical University (Philosophy and Social Sciences)*, 1989 (3).

195 Thompson. *Economic and Social*, 641.

196 Wenhai. *History of France*, 614.

197 Wenhai. *History of France*, 615–616.

198 Duby. *History of France*, 613.

199 Duby. *History of France*, 614.

200 Rich, Wilson. *Cambridge Economic History*, 435.

201 Only in June 1467, he issued acts to shoemakers, fullers, ballmakers, glovemakers, tailors, and maillot makers. The legislative activity reached its peak with the act of managing the procession of woolens in the whole country in 1479. "On all occasions people could ever imagine, enforced orders of royal officials could be heard: such as modifying or approving regulations and laws, deciding labor time and holidays, even discussing the use of trademarks. regulation production procedures or deciding quality standards." Thompson. *Economic and Social History of the Middle Ages*, 639–640.

202 Thompson. *Economic and Social History of the Middle Ages*, 640–641.

203 Prager. History of Intellectual Property, p. 722.

204 Krasser. *German Patent and Utility Model Law*, 124.

205 Rich, Wilson. *Cambridge Economic History*, 435–436.

206 Wang Yuanming. A Comparative Study of the Industrial Policies of the British and French Governments in the Sixteenth and Seventeenth Centuries, *Journal of Hangzhou University* (Philosophy and Social Sciences), 1992 (1).

207 Braudel. *Civilization and Capitalism,* 351.

208 The Parisian Congress was controlled by monks and aristocrats and had performed a number of legislative, administrative, and judicial powers since the thirteenth century. Laws and orders of the king and other legal behaviors should be registered by the Parisian Congress to obtain potency. However, since the fifteenth century, the supporters of absolute monarchism began to turn the Congress into a pure rubber stamp exercise. They sometimes used the method by expelling or locking up the whole Congress. However, the theory that the patent needed to be registered in congress triumphed at last. Prager, History of Intellectual Property, p. 731.

209 Wang Yuanming. Comparative Study of the Industrial Policies.

210 Prager. History of Intellectual Property, p. 751.

211 Prager. History of Intellectual Property, pp. 751–752.

212 Prager. History of Intellectual Property, p. 724.

213 William James Ashley. *An Introduction To English Economic History And Theory: The Middle Ages*, Vol. 2. New York, Longmans, Green & Co, 1923:102–113.

214 Prager. History of Intellectual Property, p. 715.

215 Rich, Wilson. *Cambridge Economic History*, 435–436.

216 Rich, Wilson. *Cambridge Economic History*, 436.

217 Robert M. Sherwood. *Intellectual Property and Economic Development*. Boulder, CO: Westview Press, 1990:250.

218 Krasser. *German Patent and Utility Model Law*, 231.
219 Krasser. *German Patent and Utility Model Law*, 256.
220 Sherwood. *Intellectual Property and Economic Development*, 250.
221 Zhao Wenhong. *Development of Private Property Rights*, 315.
222 Tetsuo Tomita. *Intellectual Property Rights in Market Competition*. Liao Zhengheng, et al. Beijing: The Commercial Press, 2000:72.
223 Krasser. *German Patent and Utility Model Law*, 51.
224 Prager. History of Intellectual Property, p. 93.
225 Kaufer. *Economics of the Patent System*, 10.
226 Wang Yuanming. Comparative Study of the Industrial Policies.
227 In the Middle Ages, the political pattern in Germany was the exclusive "*Kurfürst*" institution. The Emperor was selected from seven lords, and the capital moved from one city where the lord lived to another. In Germany, all regions were likely to be in the center region as the capital of the country, and lords could be selected from the locals. Thompson. *Economic and Social History*, 173.
228 Distinct from guilds in the Middle Ages, the outsourcing system made a specialized distinction in production and let it operate separately. The primary producers worked for a contractor and sold the products to them. Workers established links to the external market via relationships with the entrepreneur, which greatly improved industrial production. Shen Han. The Place of Germany in the History of the Occurrence of Capitalism in the 15th–16th Centuries, *Guizhou Social Science*, 2016 (1).
229 For example, in 1500, the German Holy Roman Empire produced half of the cast iron in Europe; the flax weaving industry surpassed traditional industrial regions and developed into the Rhineland, Westphalia, Saxony, and Silesia. The cotton weaving industry infiltrated the South German empire cities, where linen and cotton yarn blend coarse twill was developed.
230 Thompson. *Economic and Social History*, 198–217.
231 They offered loans to monarchs and the Pope, becoming international financiers. German capitalists had acted worldwide, such as investing in colonies via the links to Antwerp in production or in commerce and trade. Shen Han. Place of Germany.
232 Robert Cole. *A Traveller's History of Germany*. Ouyang Lin, et al. Shanghai: Shanghai Jiaotong University Press, 2012:65–66.
233 Rich, Wilson. *Cambridge Economic History*, 437.
234 Shen Han. Place of Germany.
235 MacLeod. *Inventing the Industrial Revolution*, 201.
236 Hansjoerg Pohlmann. The Inventor's Right in Early German Law, 43 *Journal of the Patents and Trademark Office Society*, 1961, p. 125.
237 May. Hypocrisy of Forgetfulness, pp. 1–25.
238 Maximilian Frumkin. The Origin of Patents, 27 *Journal of the Patents and Trademark Office Society*, 1945, pp. 143–148.
239 Frumkin. Origin of Patents, pp. 121–139.
240 Frumkin. Origin of Patents, pp. 121–139.
241 Borghi Maurizio. *Writing Practices in the Privilege- and Intellectual Property Systems*, available at: http://ssrn.com/abstract=1031639.
242 G. Doorman. *Patents for Inventions in the Netherlands During the 16th, 17th and 18th Centuries: With Notes on the Historical Development of Technics*. The Hague: Martinus Nijhoff, 1942:151.
243 Pohlmann. The Inventor' Right in Early German Law, pp. 121–139.

244 Pohlmann. Inventor' Right in Early German Law, pp. 121–139.

245 For example, according to a patent application on 3 September 1575, the applicant believed the invention of mint production could bring "less waste." However, others believed "many others already knew this invention and produced it; therefore, it should be rejected." The Board asked for a novelty examination of it. The king of Saxony should approve this invention, and the expert should make written explanations to prove that this invention had successful feasibility in practice and importance.

246 Doorman. *Patents for Inventions*, 15.

247 In Britain at that time, the application fee for the patent privilege was so high that it surpassed the salary and living level of the technicians. Moreover, the British authorization organ usually imposed a series of extra fees on the applicant, which seriously influenced the initiative of the applicant. In contrast, the application fee in Germany was quite low, nothing more than a small sum of money and without any other fees or taxes.

248 May. Hypocrisy of Forgetfulness, pp. 1–25.

249 Liu Cheng, Liu Jinyuan, Wu Qinghong. *Britain-From World Domination to Return to Europe*. Xi'an: Sanqin Publishing House, 2005:33.

250 Zhang Weiliang. *The Historical Process of Commercialization in British Society: 1500–1750*. Beijing: People's Publishing House, 2004:35

251 Robert King Merton. *Science, Technology, and Society in Seventeenth Century England*. Beijing: The Commercial Press, 2000:111.

252 Weiliang. *Historical Process of Commercialization*, 95.

253 For example, in 1324, King Edward II invited skilled German miners to England and granted them franchises. In 1327, Edward III claimed to grant fullers, weavers, dyers, and other cloth makers franchises to encourage cloth production. In 1331, the royal family granted a franchise that could bring new industries to England to John Kempe and his company from Florence, which were entitled to participate in work such as cloth weaving, dyeing, and bleaching in England and obliged to train apprentices. The franchise was also regulated that whoever was willing to come to England and participate in production would also be granted the franchise by the king. In 1336, two weavers from Brabant were also granted similar franchises and resided in York. In 1368, the king granted a clockmaker from Delft three patents. These authorizations were all particular and restricted in the qualification of management rather than real monopoly privileges, and England didn't establish a systematic institution.

254 Paul A. David. The Intellectual Property Institutions and the Panda's Thumb: Patents, Copyrights, and Trade Secrets in Economic Theory and History. Gu Yanfang. *Technology and Law*, 1998 (4).

255 Frumkin. Early History of Patents for Invention, p. 51.

256 Leften Stavrianos. *A Global History: From Prehistory to the 21st Century*. Wu Xiangying. Beijing: Peking University Press, 2005:512.

257 Erich Hassinger. *Studien zu James Acontius*. Berlin: Berlin-Grunewald, Verlag für staatswissenschaften und geschichte, g.m.b.h., 1934, pp. 1–20.

258 E. W. Hulme. On the Consideration of the Patent Grant, Past and Present, *Law Quarterly Review*, 1897, 13, pp. 313–315.

259 Thomas Webster. *Reports and Notes of Cases on Letters Patent for Inventions*, Vol. 1. London: T. Blenkarn, 1844:14.

260 Hulme. On the Consideration of the Patent Grant, pp. 313–315.

261 Hulme. On the Consideration of the Patent Grant, pp. 313–315.

262 Webster. *Reports and Notes of Cases on Letters Patent for Inventions*, 11.

263 Hulme. On the Consideration of the Patent Grant, p. 145.
264 Oren Bracha. The Commodification of Patents 1600–1836: How Patent Became Rights and Why We Should Care, *Loyola of Los Angeles Law Review*, 2004, p. 177.
265 Hulme. On the Consideration of the Patent Grant, p. 145.
266 Wang Yuanming. Comparative Study of the Industrial Policies.
267 Huang Haifeng. *The Discourse and Reality of Intellectual Property Rights: A History of Copyright, Patent and Trademark*. Wuhan: Huazhong University of Science and Technology Press, 2011:130–131.
268 In England, laws that regulated common lawsuits were usually unwritten conventions or precedents, and a series of written laws were only enacted when royalty was involved. After the Norman Conquest, Henry I established feudal rights owned by the king in the legal form of the *Coronation Charter*, where the rights of feudal aristocrats were acknowledged, and the opinion that the king should obey the law was shown. Other British kings, after that, imitated and issued various "charters" or orders to list things the king could and could not do. The famous *Charter of Liberties*, which was signed by aristocrats and civilians to fight against tyranny, clearly stated that the liberty of people should be protected, and the king should obey the law and not impose taxes at his will.
269 Scott Gordon. *Controlling the State: Constitutionalism from Ancient Athens to Today*. Ying Qinian. Nanjing: Jiangsu People's Publishing House, 2001:100.
270 In this country, "the king, aristocrats, and the wealthy middle class made distinct alliances in distinct ages. In the reign of Edward IV and Louis XI, the king and middle classes united together to fight against aristocrats; in the reign of Louis XIV, king and aristocrats against the middle class." *The Oxford Terms* (1258) in the reign of Henry III suggested the appearance of the "congress" with the function of "supervising the state, considering the common need of the country and the king." Then, Congress controlled the legislative and tax imposing power, becoming an important power to restrict the royalty in economies. The struggle of famous Grand Justice Kerk against James I established the principle that the common law was superior to royalty, which led to the independence of judicial power.
271 Yang Lihua. *Studies on the History of U.S. Patent Law*. Beijing: Renmin University of China Press, 2009:21.
272 Dacey had the patent for importing, producing, and selling pokers, and the London businessman Ellen was charged to the court due to the offense of the patent. This case experienced three debates, which could be seen as a comprehensive examination of the reasonability of the patent monopoly and royal privilege.
273 William S. Holdsworth. *A History of English Law, 3rd ed.*, Vol. 4. London: Methuen, 1945:347.
274 The regulations in the Statute about patent protections were. 1. The authorization of the patent right was a royal bounty granted by the king. 2. The object allowed to be granted a patent should be a new manufacturer. In the territory of the British king, when the patent authorization was granted, if no one else was using this product, then this product was novel. 3. The object that the patent protected included two types: working of the new manufacture and making of the new manufacture. 4. If the owner of the patent violated the law, or the price of products rose because of the enjoyment of the patent privilege, so that the country suffered losses, this patent was to be repealed. 5. Only the first true inventor could be the owner of the patent right. 6. The protection restriction of a patent was 14 years.

275 Yang Lihua. From "Privilege" to "Property Right": An Exploration of the Origin of Patent Right, *Journal of Xiangtan University* (Philosophy and Social Sciences), 2009 (1).
276 Bracha. Commodification of Patents, p. 177.
277 Robert P. Merges, et al., *Intellectual Property in the New Technological Age*. Qi Yun. Beijing: China University of Political Science and Law Press, 2003:250.
278 Bracha. Commodification of Patents, p. 177.
279 Anderfelt. *International Patent-legislation and Developing Countries*, p. 125.

3 Industrial age

Formation and development of the private right system of patents

From the sixteenth to the eighteenth century, the Venetian patent privilege burgeoned and developed in Western European countries, and the patent privilege system gradually became the measure taken by these countries to develop technology and economy at that time. However, things will change when the time changes. Since the 1760s, European countries represented by Britain led the First Industrial Revolution, which spread to every corner of the world and assumed various forms. Comprehensive technological revolutions began to happen one after another. Machines replaced human labor, inanimate forces replaced human and animal forces, and humankind witnessed for the first time the historical breakthrough in which agriculture and handicrafts surrendered their economic dominance to industry and machine production.[1] The Industrial Revolution symbolized a critical turning point in the history of humans, and the great revolution of technology soon motivated great revolutions in the economy, culture, and politics. In the days of great industrial changes, the patent system was converted from privileges to private rights, therefore completing the transformation from a traditional patent system to a modern patent system. England was usually regarded as the cradle of the modern private rights of the Intellectual Property Rights (IPRs) by many scholars. However, France was the first country in the civil law system to introduce the modern private right of patents. At the same time, the United States was the first country in the common law system to introduce the modern private right of patents. Then, during the industrial and capitalist revolutions, why did the patent privilege have a different fate from other abolished privileges? How was the patent privilege converted into a private right? What was the motivation for the evolution of the private rights of patents? These are the questions that this chapter will try to answer.

Standard for distinguishing the paradigm of patent privilege from the paradigm of the private right of patents

The term "paradigm" was introduced by American scientific philosopher Thomas Samuel Kuhn to define all the traditions, basic methods, and basic regulations commonly followed by scientific groups in science.[2] The term gradually became

DOI: 10.4324/9781003462453-4

a generalized philosophical concept used in various academic areas. It refers to the sum of traditions, basic methods, and basic regulations commonly followed in a discipline and field in the given social reality.[3] When the social reality of an old paradigm in a discipline or field changes and the old paradigm cannot describe and interpret new phenomena and development, a new paradigm will appear, and a "paradigm shift" will happen. There is no exception in the patent system. As we know, the tradition of technology, economy, culture, and politics in the Pre-industrial Age chronically followed a privileged paradigm. Once these social motivations have changed and reached a critical point, the paradigm shift will happen. This is how the paradigm of the private right of patents came into existence.

As mentioned previously, although the paradigm of patent privilege somewhat changed in different countries and during different historical periods, the essence of this paradigm almost remained intact. First, a patent was seen as a "gift" granted by the government to the inventor or a particular benefit given by the state, so no one could intervene in it. The patent privilege was a policy tool used by the government to develop industry and commerce and attract new trade. A patent was seen by either the inventor or the government as a temporary grace or honor granted by the state to the inventor based on the considerations of unique benefits. Every patent was granted and published by the government in the form of decrees. The government had dominant control over the authorization of patents, which sometimes seemed so arbitrary that patents could be granted or repealed due to noncompliance with the authorization standard or for the sake of public interest. Second, there was no single standard for the authorization of patents, and each patent privilege was unique. The government judged every invention based on industrial and commercial policies or the public interest (usually the standard of "utility"), which depended much on discretion. The royal family or competent organ was responsible for formulating and implementing the standard. No matter how novel or creative an invention was, its authorization could never be absolutely guaranteed, and no institution or organization (the court or others) could declare and enforce the royal family or competent organ to grant this patent.

The modern patent system is built on the paradigm of the private right of patents, which will never change regardless of any improvement in the related laws of the patent system. It has the following features. First, the patent law is a unified law of universal application,[4] which means the concepts, content of the right, and procedure in the patent law are expressly provided by the universally applicable laws. The patent is neither granted by the government based on industrial and commercial policies or discretion nor by a particular decree issued by the legislative organ for a particular patent. The patent is given because everyone has the right to be given a patent based on their inventions. The contents of the right are the same for all inventors; however, the right is acknowledged and specified in written form by patent law. Patent law is a construct whose top concern is the protection of an inventor's benefits. Second, the standardization and legalization of the potential for protecting inventions. The object of the patent right is the result of intangible scientific inventions. Laws have to be expectable and prospective enough to establish a logically self-consistent system,[5] so the authorization standard of inventions should be abstracted and generalized. Once the protected object is generalized as a metaphysical "abstraction," the observation and measurement will cease to be accurate. Therefore, the unified standards to grant a patent should be explicitly defined and applied in legal form. The standards must be reviewed by a particular evaluation body according to the related laws and regulations rather than based on their personal judgments. Once these standards are satisfied, the evaluation body will be obliged to grant the patent to the inventor. Third, the boundary of intangible properties is defined in the form of a specification so that abstract, intangible technologies can be treated like tangible lands. In addition, the patent is registered and managed to ensure its feasibility through the creditability of public organizations. Finally, the patent right of the inventor is guaranteed and operated. Suppose the evaluation body believes that an invention does not measure up to the standard or refuses to grant the patent for other reasons. In this case, the applicant can either complain to the higher authorities, which is one way to guarantee the patent right or file a lawsuit with the court, whose role is to interpret and apply the standard for granting the patent. Suppose the court finds that the invention satisfies the standard. In this case, the court is obliged to order the evaluation body to grant the patent, which is another way to guarantee patent rights.

In conclusion, the modern paradigm of the private right of patents results from the rationalization movement that is built on the pattern of the real right. The private right is essentially a legal tool to clarify the interest relationship among people, and the interest relationship is usually complicated and involves high coordination costs. In comparison, the standardization pattern of the real right emphasizes people's control over objects, which reduces the cost of the third man to acquire information and helps actualize the materialization of abstract properties in a calculable method.[6] The rightful owner obtains an occupation similar to that of objects with occupation certificates, which ensures control over abstract properties. After clarifying the standard for distinguishing the paradigm of patent privilege from the paradigm of private rights, the time of establishing the private paradigm in the civil and common law systems will be clarified in the following parts, and the evolutionary motivations behind them will be investigated.

Origin of the private right of patents in the civil law system

In the eighteenth century, France was far less developed industrially than Britain. However, the private right of patents first appeared in France, gradually grew stronger, and finally became mature in the context of the French Revolution. The emergence of French private rights was attributed to its technological, economic, and cultural environments. However, this was a bumpy process under the influence of competing forces. This historical phase is rarely mentioned or has sunk into oblivion.

Motivations for the formation of the concept of the French private right system of patents in the eighteenth century

Development of the technology, economy, and industrial and commercial capitalism in France

In the eighteenth century, technological creation entered a new stage, where technological innovations didn't merely depend on the chance discovery of poorly educated technicians. Advanced inventors who specialized in invention and creation began to appear. These inventors either bore all invention-related costs and risks and sold their inventions for profit or depended on the financial support and reward from the businessmen and offered the inventions to them as a commodity.[7] According to the history of invention written by Darmsteller and Boardmund, the number of inventors was 170 during 1700–1750 and 340 during 1750–1800.[8] It is easy to find that the number of inventors was not very large, and most inventions still depended on technicians. During this stage, science and technology began to combine, and science began to serve as the source of knowledge for technical inventions. These highly creative people began to communicate among themselves. Technicians, inventors, chemists, physicians, and natural philosophers respected and shared with each other, and they formed a circle of communication, science associations, academies, and lectures increased constantly.[9]

The French always had a keen interest in science and technology, and the French royal family offered generous support for technological development to foster industrial and commercial policies. Since the days of Louis XIV and his minister Jean-Baptiste Colbert, the monarchy regime established a national network of organizations to support and improve scientific revolutions. The French Academy of Science, the Royal Observatory of Paris, and the Royal Garden provided salaries for scientists, established laboratories, published their works, and sponsored defense meetings. In the Industrial Revolution, which started in the mid-eighteenth century, various inventions and machines rapidly spread in France and other European countries. The French had a growing enthusiasm for technological inventions. As written by French mathematician Jean le Rond d'Alembert, technology makes people's thoughts active and explode, which naturally flows everywhere like a burst river. Until the end of the eighteenth century, French physicians, mathematicians, astrologists, and naturalists occupied leading positions in exploring frontier problems of scientific development. For example, in the early eighteenth century, Charles-Francois du Fay proposed the theory of positive and negative electrodes of an object. In 1775, Charles Augustin de Coulomb invented the electrometer and discovered the Coulomb Law on the mutual action between magnetic poles.

Jean le Rond d'Alembert published *Traité de Dynamique* in 1743. In 1789, Antoine-Laurent de Lavoisier, the "Father of modern chemistry," published *Traité élémentaire de chimie*.[10]

From the seventeenth to mid-eighteenth century, most of France was still local and agricultural. The vast majority of people worked in the handicraft industry (e.g., in 1870, French farmers made up as much as 50.6% of the labor force). New industrial technologies still spread and developed in a slow and unbalanced fashion.[11] Therefore, industrial and commercial capitalism in France developed quite slowly and was seriously restricted in many aspects by the feudal production relationship.[12] The rigid guild system, which was concerned about all the trivial details, became the barrier to the healthy development of capitalism. When the French king introduced the mercantilism policy, he encouraged the development of capitalism. However, he tightly controlled industrial development and especially restricted the expansion of production and concentration of industrial capital, therefore slowing down the development of large industries. In the early eighteenth century, the national commercial policy still showed the feature of mercantilism. However, when the physiocratic power emerged after the mid-eighteenth century, commercial policy was heavily influenced. Then, until the French Revolution at the end of the eighteenth century, the national commercial policy of France alternated between protectionism and free trade. However, regardless of the national commercial policy, France's commercial capital accumulated vast deposits in the sixteenth–eighteenth centuries. Family handicrafts and handicraft factories with the system of large industry already appeared, and those who occupied major positions were commercial capitalists. France was traditionally a power in the handicraft industry, with highly developed handicraft workshops specialized in silk, leather, glass, ceramics, and decorations. The French handicraft industry enjoyed a great reputation in upper society across Europe and created huge amounts of wealth for the country.[13] The foundation of modern industry in France was established in 1740–1775. The Industrial Revolution of France in the late eighteenth century mainly depended on commercial capital.[14] Very concentrated commerce gradually emerged in the industrial centers of France, such as Sedan, Rem, and Lyon. At the same time, the businessmen with a dominant influence gradually turned into the organizers of production, and the establishment of handicraft factories, supported by the commercial capital of the businessmen, was the first sign of French industrial capitalism. The capitalists who realized and emphasized the technology-related benefits gradually made improvements in production tools and used new inventions such as Buffon's high-heat furnace, Legendre's function, Hérault's wool fabric dyeing method, and Maag's improvement for silk weaving. French capitalists took every chance to use all British inventions during the Industrial Revolution.[15] For instance, the British flying shuttle was introduced in 1747, the cotton gin in 1771, and the water weaver in 1779.[16] Some factories even began to use steam-powered and British-type industrial facilities.[17] In fact, during the first 80 years of the eighteenth century, the industrial production of France was equal to that of Britain, maintaining a growth rate of 1%, and its production of handicrafts was even higher than that of Britain's.[18]

Despite the luxurious lives of the French royal family, the peasantry also hindered domestic industrial development and social revolution.[19] However, some ambitious businessmen and entrepreneurs emerged in France, where the capitalist mode of production assumed an embryonic form. Technology brought them abundant profits, strengthened the economic and political power of capitalism, and progressively stimulated their desire for technology. Technology became an effective tool in their hands to occupy the market and participate in the competition. As Lewis Mumford said, "But, more than an instrument of practical adjustment, the machine was, from 1750 on, a goal of desire." In a world of flux and disorder and precarious adjustment, the machine at least was seized upon as a finality.[20] Therefore, thanks to positive factors such as the improvement in production technology, the accumulation of commercial and usury capitals, the appearance of free laborers, and the booming international market, France followed in the steps of Britain to usher in the era of the Industrial Revolution[21] in the late eighteenth and early nineteenth centuries and kept expanding in terms of industrial production. France's industrial output value was second to that of Britain, the top industrial power then.

The Enlightenment and Diderot's Lettre sur le Commerce de la Librairie

THE ENLIGHTENMENT

Britain is the homeland of utilitarianism, and France is the homeland of rationalism. In the eighteenth century, France ushered in a new era of world history when a massive movement that championed enlightenment and reason unfolded.[22] The Renaissance saved humans from deities and asceticism. Then, the Enlightenment liberated humans from religious dogma and blind beliefs, which fully cultivated human intelligence and wisdom and lit up the future realm of freedom with the light of reason. Condorcet, the famous Enlightenment philosopher, appealed when mentioning the sacred mission of the Enlightenment: people should claim in every minute that the independence of reason and the freedom to write was the right and emancipation of humans, and he called upon them to roar the shout of fight: reason, tolerance, and humanity.[23]

On the one hand, the Enlightenment thinkers disseminated the thoughts of reason and science by substituting the rational principle for traditional authorities and principles and regarding reason as a benchmark used to judge all existing things.[24] On the other hand, they had a deeper understanding of what science and technology really meant. For example, the *Encyclopédie*, translated by Diderot in 1745, symbolized the highest achievement of the Enlightenment scholars in natural science and the spectacular result of the scientific spirit.[25] The book aimed to clarify the development process of human thoughts since ancient times and the classification of all scientific disciplines. The book objected to feudal governance and monarchy despotism, advocated science and technology, fostered industrial production, and attempted to transform human society based on rationalism. The Enlightenment was also a revolutionary force that fought the theocracy of the Church and feudalism. In essence, it criticized the religious, cultural, and ideological system of feudal society and tried to establish a new cultural and ideological system of a capitalist society. The champions of the Enlightenment were against the Church and feudal superstition and wanted to substitute human analysis and argumentation for the blind belief in God. The Enlightenment thinkers opposed feudal privilege with natural rights, rejecting the divine right of kings and claiming that people should have equal, inherent rights to pursue freedom and happiness. In addition, Jean-Jacques Rousseau's argument on human rights reached an extremely high level in the Enlightenment movement. In the *Social Contract*, he proposed the thought of popular sovereignty in which everyone should make a social contract within his right to represent the public will. The personal rights of liberty and equality were ensured through this public will, for instance, the law.[26]

DIDEROT'S *LETTRE SUR LE COMMERCE DE LA LIBRAIRIE*

In the Enlightenment movement, an event could affect the fate of the IPR in France. Similar to Britain's publishing industry at that time, the publication of any books in France had to be examined and approved by the royal family. After a series of political events broke out, the French feudal regime was extremely strict with the censorship and publication of books. For instance, Article I in the *Announcement for Publishers* issued in April 1757 in France stated: "Whoever writes or is instructed by others to write or to print any book that challenges the religion, instigates civil disobedience, attacks the authority, disturbs the national order, and gets published without permission, will be sentenced to death." Although France granted the writer copyright privileges, publications would often be restricted for the sake of political censorship.[27] The blasting fuse of the whole event was the Event of La Fontaine. La Fontaine was a famous poet in France who was granted a copyright privilege by the French Congress for his poem *Fables*. After his death, Congress granted the copyright privilege of La Fontaine's poems to his two female successors. Then, a bookman in Paris bought this copyright privilege and prepared to publish this poem. However, in 1761, the State Committee, an authority responsible for prepublication censorship in France, decided that the bookman was not entitled to publish this poem. This event aroused dissatisfaction among bookmen in Paris, who believed the legality of the copyright privilege was deprived by the authority for no reason. They were afraid that the arbitrary procedure of the French royal family would make the privilege valueless, finally leading to the abolition of all privileges.[28] To clarify the issue and complain to the chief of the Bureau of Publication and the public and to defend the benefits of bookmen, the chairman of the Association of Bookmen in Paris, Le Breton, invited Denis Diderot, the most famous Enlightenment thinker in France, to explain the legality of the patent privilege.

As one of the most excellent leaders of the Encyclopédiste and the Enlightenment movement, Denis Diderot detested the feudal privilege system. However, he defended and protected the system, including the copyright and patent privilege in the *Lettre sur le Commerce de la Librairie* published in 1763. Diderot wanted to call for "press liberty," while the bookmen thought more about their profits. After the book was completed, the book title was altered to *Lettre Historique & Politique Adressée à un Magistrat sur le Commerce de la Librairie, son état Ancien & Actuel, ses Règlements, ses Privilèges, les Permissions Tacites, les Censeurs, Les Colporteurs, le Passage des Ponts & Autres Objets Relatifs à la Police Littéraire*, and some parts of the book were deleted or revised.

Diderot's mixed feelings were embodied in this article. On the one hand, Diderot pointed out that the *Encyclopédie* was rejected by the commercial and production franchises, because these privileges hindered the free development of the economic laws. However, he had to try all means to demonstrate the legality of the publishing privileges for the liberty of publication. He talked about the embarrassing contradiction. This is a strange paradox. Experiences and common sense believe that all monopolies harm commercial development. All people believed that only the franchise could save the book trade. However, no matter how certain they were, they should not be scared. On the other hand, even though he knew that he served the benefit of those bookmen, he was very eager for the liberty of publication. In fact, he attempted to establish the right of writers stably to protect their benefits. To achieve this objective, he first considered the privilege as property instead of a gift granted by royalty. To eliminate some privileges that always accompanied it, especially the exclusive right to publish a certain book, which was always taken for granted, would make people regard the privilege certificate of the press as a grace that could be granted or repealed at will. People would forget that it was nothing but the guarantee of true ownership, which was illegal once the law was violated. He investigated the history of the privilege of French publishers and proved that the privilege was legitimate. He reiterated the opinion in the article written for the publishers: the literature property was converted into a contract. Because the literature property could be freely acquired or purchased, it was something of the same nature as land or immovable properties. "Let me ask you, monsieur, once someone has bought a house, he will enjoy all exclusive powers of it, won't he?"[29] This property could not be deprived, because it could neither be transferred against the will of its owner nor be shared with others. However, this property right was distinct from other exclusive rights, because it could not give the publisher the power to publish all books, even all books with the given theme, but it could give him the right to publish a given book. It could be only related to one manuscript, one legally transferred property. The manuscript should be legally acquired, and its right to be published only belonged to one purchaser. The power will harm the owner's power regardless of being transferred completely or partly, but owning this power cannot prevent others from writing–or publishing books with the same title.[30] When calling for exclusive fixed privileges for the publisher, Diderot attempted to make every writer aware of his ownership of the work. Since a writer would seldom publish his work (reserving the account book of income and expenses, asking and answering, communicating, receiving and delivering ... It is the followers of Homer or Plato!), he had to use the industry of bookmen. However, the contract between them, to be specific, was the witness of the writer to his work (the most precious part, the part that will never be effaced). The copyright privilege was a monopoly right. It appeared incompatible with common law. However, because the first one to acquire it participated in risky and progressive labor, their access to the copyright privilege should be deemed legal. Therefore, even if the copyright seemed to be against common law, it was not right to say that the copyright had exceeded the limit. Since the term of the monopoly was defined, it became more reasonable. The owner of the worker was no one but the writer himself.[31] He would say it once again: either the writer was the owner of his work, or no one owned his wealth. The bookman and writer owned the work. Therefore, it was the ownership of the writer that defined the legality of the privilege. In return, it was the stubborn privilege that served as indirect evidence for the writer's right.[32]

Diderot's opinion was influenced by Locke's natural rights and constructively applied the natural rights to intangible things like works. This was obviously applicable to the patent privilege as well. This manuscript was opened to the public in 1767 and 1789 when the feudal dynasty in France had seen its last days. His work, as the weapon to fight against the feudal dynasty, could especially encourage the public.[33] Diderot had not intended to fight for copyright or patent justice. He only wanted to use it as a tool to fight for the freedom of speech. However, beyond his expectations, his opinion was finally used by others to fuel the enthusiasm for the emerging industrial and commercial class, becoming the weapon to argue for their interest and the important basis on which the new regime reserved the patent and copyright system. In other words, without this defense, the French copyright and patent rights system would no longer exist.[34]

Conclusion

Since the mid-eighteenth century, science and technology in France developed to a new level. With the accumulation of commercial capital in France, the establishment of handicraft factories, supported by the commercial capital of businessmen, was the first sign of modern industrial capitalism in France. These industrial capitalists who realized and emphasized the technology-related benefits gradually made improvements in production tools and regarded some new inventions and technologies as an effective approach to competition. At the same time, the Enlightenment movement provided the theoretical basis for constructing the private right of patents by capitalism. The influence of the Enlightenment movement was first featured in its high praise for rationalism. On the one hand, it fueled the enthusiasm for scientific research and promoted the rapid development of technology. On the other hand, it provided the theoretical basis for the construction of the private right of patents by capitalism. The central position of rationalism in the thought of the Enlightenment movement was undoubted. Based on this, Enlightenment thinkers proclaimed the spirit of the natural law, emphasizing the consistency of justice, righteousness, and reason. This laid a solid theoretical foundation for constructing the property rights system in the private law that was free from intervention by despotic powers. The influence of the Enlightenment movement on the IPR system was also embodied in its publicity and promotion of capitalist political concepts, such as liberty, equality, natural rights, democracy, and justice. According to the ideological system of natural law, the Enlightenment movement considered a free and equal person as the foundation of national political organizations. It emphasized that liberty, life, property, security, and others were inalienable human rights, and no law could deprive people of these rights.[35] Diderot's *Lettre sur le Commerce de la Librairie* was a brilliant chapter in the Enlightenment movement and was also the turning point in the development history of IPRs in France. In this article, the opinion of natural rights was first used in intangible things like work. The work was seen as the writer's property, and the copyright was seen as his just right. In this technical, economic, and cultural environment, French citizens, especially those ambitious industrial capitalists, formed a new concept of the patent system, for instance, the private right of patents, which was put into legislation by Claude and Boufflers.

Association of Scientific Inventions, Boufflers, and the **Patent Act 1790** *in France*

In 1789, French citizens, under the influence of the British and American revolutions, knew their role and ability in social governance. At the same time, they adopted the political–economic doctrines of Montesquieu, Rousseau, Thünen, and Adam Smith, so they noticed the problems in parliamentary politics and economic liberty.[36] On 14 July 1789, the Parisians occupied the Bastille and ended the old regime. The feudalism, guilds, and mercantilism system vanished. The French Revolution was a revolution dominated by capitalists, who desired the industrial and agricultural liberty called by economists, which referred to the complete exemption from the strict supervision of the state on industries and commerce.[37] In 1789, any form of monopoly was detested, because monopoly was regarded as something closely related to the feudal despotic economic policies. Therefore, the privilege system, including invention privileges and other trade monopoly privileges, was abolished. However, the consistency and compromises between the capitalist government and the industrial capitalists enabled the French patent system to be established in a new form.

First, the newly established capitalist government in France gave much prominence to scientific and cultural careers and took all measures to encourage domestic industrial and commercial policies. They abolished a series of trade monopoly privileges and established various industrial laws, which cleared barriers to the development of domestic industries and commerce.[38] In addition, influenced by the British Industrial Revolution, they were deeply aware of the importance of technology to industrial economic development. During the French Revolution, the inventors and scientists eclipsed the bankers, great merchants, and entrepreneurs in terms of number and importance.[39] Moreover, due to the wars and abolishing the patent privilege, many French technicians fled to foreign countries.[40] The new government was very worried about the prospects for domestic industry. Therefore, it awarded 2 million Livres to those important scientific inventions on 22 August 1790.[41]

Second, some associations of scientific inventions in France continuously lobbied. They were mainly composed of industrial and commercial capitalists, inventors, scientists, and technicians, the most typical of which was the Association of "Inventions and Discoveries" (also called the Association of Scientific Inventions). Its chairman was Claude, the representative of the emerging industrial and commercial capitalists. He managed a large nitrate factory in Northern France. He made contact with and sponsored many famous scientific inventors at that time, such as Séguier, Poutal, and Lavoisier,[42] and deeply understood the meaning and effect of technology on the production profit of entrepreneurs. He also understood that the patent monopoly right was beneficial to maintaining their status of technology monopoly and to bringing new economic benefits. As the representative of the Association of Scientific Inventions, he lobbied to support a new patent system in France. In 1790, on behalf of the Association, he offered a petition to establish a new patent system to the Committee of Agriculture and Trade of France. The members of the Committee appointed Boufflers, the Governor of Senegal who once served as a judge, to draft the new patent law. Boufflers was probably persuaded by Claude to accept this appointment.[43]

Finally, it was quite important for the political strategy used by Boufflers when he drafted the patent system. Boufflers said frankly that there were three essential motives for drafting the patent law: 1) to encourage the emerging industrial and commercial class to improve production and to maintain their benefits; 2) to worry about the infiltration of the British industrial economy into France; and 3) to retain the industrial workers who prepared to flee at that time.[44] According to Boufflers's expression, he represented the benefit of the industrial and commercial classes. He was concerned about how to encourage the capitalist class to improve production and to lift France's industry and commerce out of its backward situation. Still, he knew that the French always respected technology and inventors. The spirit of that time was to support liberty and equality and to oppose any form of privilege or monopoly, and the patent privilege system could not be saved without an acceptable theory.[45] Such an idea enlightened Boufflers: the inventor has an inherent natural property right to their inventions, and whoever uses this invention without permission will harm their innate right. Boufflers smartly borrowed the argumentation for the copyright privilege in Diderot's *Lettre sur le Commerce de la Librairie* and Locke's theory of natural rights, and as he pointed out, if something were the innate property of an individual, it would be his thought. Boufflers and his friends emphasized the protection of the concept of the patent right of the inventor and deliberately misinterpreted the theory of the artificial invention property right to a part of human rights. Similar to the vocational liberty granted during the Revolution, this property could also be regarded as an overflow of human rights. Boufflers clearly knew what was behind its name. As a privilege, the patent of the invention would be rejected by the Constituent Assembly, and even if accepted, it would be spurned by the people; however, as a natural property right and human right, it would be accepted and respected, which was called the industrial property right by Boufflers. In addition, he absorbed Rousseau's social contract theory when writing the draft, and he pointed out that once the inventor disclosed his invention to the public as the obligation of the contract, society should grant him corresponding benefits.[46] The evaluation of the popular way of thought proved to be correct. However, Fritz Machlup pointed out in frustration: As monopoly privileges, the patents for inventions would be rejected by the Assembly or, if accepted, would be disdained by the people; as natural property rights, they would be accepted and respected. This appraisal of popular ways of thinking was certainly correct. For more than 70 years, scholars seriously debated the notion of property in ideas, a notion first proposed, to put it bluntly, as a political ruse.[47] After that, Boufflers also admitted that these theories were deliberately designed excuses.[48]

When he handled the institutional design for the draft of the patent, Boufflers centered on these theories. First, he defined the authorization standard of novelty and utility for inventions. Second, he abandoned the examination system inherited from Venice and established the registration system that made no official examination in advance of the novelty or utility. Once these examinations were performed, people would be likely to think about the restriction of guilds and administrative organs on industrial and commercial workers, which were overcome. In addition, as was revealed by the theory of natural rights, once the invention was completed, the inventor had rights to inventions similar to the property right without performing any forms. Hence, the authorization can only ensure the possession of this right. Consequently, the examination of novelty or utility would be unnecessary. Whether the invention satisfied the authorization qualification would be decided and judged by a judge when any controversy arose.[49] In Boufflers' opinion, the government was not responsible for the examination, because it would grant the government excessive discretion, and the administrative organ had no ability to judge the utility of new things; only the public was qualified for it. In addition, Boufflers designed a regulation to protect domestic industry and commerce. Foreign inventions were allowed to be introduced, and introduced inventions had the same status as original ones. However, if the patent that was already registered in France was registered in other countries, the patent in question would be regarded as abandoned. This regulation was designed mainly to attract the industrial and commercial class and technicians in Britain to invest and create in France and to prohibit French ones from bringing domestic technology to Britain.[50]

In the Constituent Assembly in December 1790, Boufflers published this draft. However, his draft aroused rejection from many people present, who considered the patent system a useless, monopoly privilege system.[51] Once again, Claude and his Association played a role. They lobbied around. On the one hand, they claimed that it was because of the protection of patents that Britain gained technological development, and the patent law was beneficial to the industrial economy of France. On the other hand, they kept emphasizing that the patent law was the guarantee to the natural rights and human rights of patent owners and the protection of inventions was just and necessary.[52] Boufflers also used his network in Congress and the court to finally approve the act[53]. The act was the famous *Patent Act of 1790* in French history.[54]

Undoubtedly, the *Patent Act of 1790* conformed to the paradigm of the private right of patents mentioned previously. The act was the embryo of the modern private rights system of patents in France. It was the world's first law that claimed in written form the patent was the natural right of inventors, treated the natural rights as human rights, and made it sacred and reasonable. France also became the first country to establish a registration system worldwide. The pattern of private rights in France rapidly spread to other countries, which made a great difference and became the blueprint for regulating patent laws in other countries, including Belgium, Costa Rica, Cuba, the Dominique Republic, Greece, Haidi,

Italy, Luxemburg, Morocco, Paraguay, Poland, Romania, Spain, Syria Republic, Lebanon, and Turkey.[55]

However, the private rights system of patents in France was merely a tool in the hands of the emerging industrial and commercial classes like Claude to maintain their technological monopoly and develop production. It was also the tool used by the new government to encourage the development of industry and commerce. The theory of the private right of patents failed to solve problems such as the protection term of a private right of patents, the relationship between the patent system and technological stimulations, and economic development. After the *Patent Act of 1790* was enacted in France, the patent system didn't motivate the development of the industrial economy. Instead, it brought many problems, and the criticisms and dissatisfaction never stopped.[56] As Zorina Khan said, the expert on the history of patent laws, the patent right declared during the French Revolution had only the meaning of declaration. It improved the renting activity, which was unbeneficial to competition.[57] Only during the fifth year of enacting the *Patent Act 1790* did the French regret protecting the inventions as a natural and human right.[58] In the 1795 French Constitution, the French believed that the inventor should gain the protection of compensation or exclusive rights, which indicated that the recognition of the patent in France returned to the stage of privileges. Moreover, in the new version of French patent law in 1844, the theory of natural rights of patents was no longer mentioned. The drafter showed that he attempted to eliminate the metaphysical design of natural rights and concentrated more on the practical application of patents.[59] The French first established the theory of the natural rights of IPRs and began to doubt themselves, which indicated that the so-called natural rights theory was merely the tool of those with vested interests. All these controversies implied the great discussion of the following patent abolishment movement.

Origin of the private right of patents in the common law system

There are always controversies on the origin of the private right of patents in the common law system. Britain is believed to be the cradle of the modern private right of patents. Still, this book believes that, as revealed in related historical records, the formal establishment of the British private rights pattern was later than that in the United States. In addition, the private right of patents in America was not established within a short period. We will witness the formation of the concept of the modern private right of patents in America, which was closely related to its transformation from an agricultural to an industrial culture and the game between different powers.

Misunderstanding in the history: Controversy over the origin of the private right of patents in the common law system

Two different opinions

There are great controversies on the standard and term for the formal establishment of the modern private right of patents in the current theoretical circles. There are mainly two opinions. First, the private right of patents was formally established in Britain. The motive and first objective of granting the *1624 Statute of Monopolies* was to prohibit the royal family from granting privilege monopolies, to liberate the management liberty right and ownership from arbitrary behaviors of the royal family, to make the monopoly of the king obey the examination of the Congress, and to set the existing property right under the protection of the court, which laid the foundation for the generation of modern private rights. Berman believes that only in the late seventeenth century was the patent right not first regarded as a monopoly granted by the king but a legal property right of the inventor. After the British Glorious Revolution, patent rights were normally granted to new inventions.[60] By the end of the eighteenth century, the patent system was gradually improved after other property rights were made available and the examination and registration system as technology was created. It was the jurisdiction of common courts and the patent specification system that facilitated the patent system to gradually liberate itself from the dominance of the government. The power of royalty began to fade, and it was considered the exclusive property right of businessmen.[61]

The main causes are detailed as follows. First, the jurisdiction of patents was converted from the Privy Council to the common courts. Because the authorization of patents was performed by royalty, any violation of the patent was regarded as a challenge to the royalty. Therefore, the royal court via the Privy Council was responsible for implementing patents and dissolving conflicts. As the consultation Committee of the British king, the king directly controlled the Privy Council, and its decisions tended to be for the royalty. Article II in the *Statute of Monopolies 1624* required that any problem with the jurisdiction should be judged by the regulations of common law to restrict the jurisdiction of the Privy Council. However, Article XI of this law regulated that the previous regulation was not suitable for authorizing invention patents. Therefore, the Privy Council never gave up its jurisdiction over patents.[62] According to the textual research by Hulme, the expert on the history of patents, the Privy Council actively abandoned the jurisdiction of patents until the Baker case in 1752.[63] Second, the establishment of the patent specification. In the patent system, the specification served as the boundary of rights. The patent specifications emerged during the early seventeenth century,[64] some of which were due to willingness, others due to the royal family's requirements to ensure that skilled workers could understand and use their invention with the help of the specification. After the eighteenth century, publishing the content of the invention patent gradually became one of the requirements in the practice of the patent.[65] In the case of "Liardet v. Johnson" in 1778 and the case of "Boulton & Watt v. Bul" in 1795, the judge declared that the patent specification was the price that the inventor had to pay to obtain an exclusive interest for a certain time.[66] The jurisdiction of the patent was converted from the Privy Council to the common courts. The latter didn't aim at operating and implementing the royalty but centering the policy considerations and concentrating on protecting the exclusive benefits of the businessmen, which created the condition for the patent to get rid of the control by royalty and enter civil society.[67] The institutionalization of the patent specification at the end of the eighteenth century guaranteed the technical schemes of intangible objects in written form. The inventor could define the boundary of the patent to make it suitable for the object of the patent. Therefore, the private rights of patents managed to be formed.[68]

According to the second opinion, the ultimate transformation from the privilege to the private right happened in the United States, especially symbolized in the IPR terms in the U.S. Constitution of 1787 and the *Patent Act 1790*. The United States granted the first patent in 1641, and the patent system was widely operated in all states after independence. In more than 100 years, by the design in which patents were granted to boost the development of industry and commerce and enhance public interests, the patent system was already widely accepted by citizens. However, before the federal *Constitution* was enacted, there was no common law that granted the inventor natural rights, whether in Massachusetts or other states; the authorization of patents in states still inherited the privilege pattern from Britain, and the legislation had apparent disadvantages. Because the patent was only effective in the state authorized, people in other states could freely use this technology, and there was no unified standard in all states, so conflicts became quite common.[69] After the Independence War, the "patent clause" was officially included in the U.S. Constitution of 1787, where the United States declared in the form of a constitution that the patent had become a property right protected by the constitution.[70] Other scholars also believe the *Patent Act 1790* specified that the examination standard of patents was novelty (not known or used before), utility, and important enough (the Patent Committee asked for enough improvements). It clarified the obligation for the applicant to submit the patent specification: a written specification, together with the illustration or model of the object concerned. The specifications should be so detailed that skilled technicians in this industry can produce and use this invention. The Act also provided that the examination organ of patents was the State Department, the applicant offered the patent application to the Secretary of State, and the Patent Committee constituted of dignitaries in the government, including the Secretary of State, Minister of Justice, and Minister of War, was responsible for the examination of patents. Therefore, after the enactment of the *Patent Act 1790*, the United States finally transformed from patent privilege to private rights.[71]

Scholars were divided in their opinions about the establishment of the Anglo–American private rights system of patents, because their argument was based on the patent history in different countries. The establishment of the British private rights system of patents was featured in the jurisdiction of the common court and the common practice of the patent specification institution. At the same time, the American system was symbolized by the "exclusive right" admitted in the patent clause of the U.S. Constitution of 1787 and the enactment of the *Patent Act 1790*. A specialized patent examination organ was established, and the elements of utility, novelty, and patent specification were clarified in the legislation. In the following section, we will investigate historical records to define the concrete time of the formation of private rights of patents in Britain and the United States and further research the agent of its formation based on investigating history at that time.

Investigation and clarification

The enactment of the *Statute of Monopolies 1624* in England didn't convert the patent from the privilege paradigm to the private right. First, this law framework defined an external limit for the authorization of patents: the privilege of monopoly trade beyond this limit could not be granted, and those within the limit could still be granted. However, within this limit, the power to grant the patent was still controlled by the royal family, which could still make particular authorizations based on the discretion beneficial to the public interest. Second, the standard of the patent depends on adjustment and adaptation in specific cases. Although royalty granted patent privileges based on the standard beneficial to the public interest, many privileges were actually granted based on considerations of special policies. The general patent standard regulated by this Statute originated from the consideration of special policies, which had great discretion and was not a feasible standard that was universally applied to all cases. The only change was that the standard was not operated by the former authorization organ but by other organs like the common courts.

Some changes happened in the practice of the British patent privilege during the seventeenth and eighteenth centuries. As various industrial and commercial monopolies boomed in the seventeenth century, the practice of patent authorization began to vanish. The fact that the monopoly patents were no longer important implied that the people began to lose interest in this form of governmental authorization, because the examination of patents by the British government was still based on the complete and strict consideration of the public interest, especially in cases directly and essentially related to the national interest. However, the government began to apply normal and standard procedures rather than conduct special investigations and examinations of these inventions. This led to the gap between the "textual law" and "law in practice." The textual law was not modified in more than 100 years, and the practice of patent authorization began to alter and get rid of the framework of the patent privilege. The procedure of patent application in Britain was regulated by the Civil Servants' law in 1535, which was strictly criticized for the excessive application fees and complicated application conditions. Unless the patent had great public interest, the examination of most patents was formalistic. The only substantial examination was the report from the judicial officer, and the Minister of Justice should examine the operation of the Statute. In regular cases, the officer rarely examined the novelty of the applicant and the public interest brought by the patent. However, this bureaucratic practice gradually turned into the customary law of the government, which was called "laissez-faire" by Christine MacLeod. The applicant would usually use all means to remove the procedure barriers to obtain the patent with a little examination by government officials. Although no one was entitled to impose this right, the patent would usually be implemented based on a standardized procedure of governmental investigation without particularity. The government's laissez-faire attitude facilitated the privilege of transforming to standardization, which was an unconscious transition.

However, to consider this transition as a witness of the conversion from privilege to the private legal right of Britain during the eighteenth century[72] was suspected to be exaggerated. First, the practice of authorization was pretty vague. Since the end of the seventeenth century, invention patents were usually granted without substantial investigations. Only when significant and special benefits, such as the national tax or the benefit to the army, were involved would the government officials examine the patent more seriously. More importantly, as long as no stakeholders opposed the authorization, the passive examination procedure of examiners would occupy most of the time. When someone opposed the patent privilege, the examiners would make a further investigation. Moreover, the Council would examine before or after the authorization, as mentioned previously, which was a special examination based on particular cases. When the Council found related patents "inconvenient" or harmful, it might not grant or even repeal the patent.

Influenced by E.W. Hulmes' opinion, many scholars believed that there was a long-term struggle between the common court and the Privy Council until 1753,[73] which led to the consideration of the Privy Council's jurisdiction in an aspect of the constitution and the Congress abandoning its jurisdiction to patent cases.[74] However, the materials revealed in Britain indicated that this argument was completely wrong. First, the relationship between the Privy Council and the common court was far more complicated than ordinary people could imagine, and the Privy Council finally surrendered after the continuous struggle against the common court. Some cases indicated that there were struggles between the Privy Council and the common court

(e.g., the case in 1624) but on most occasions, the relationship between these courts was harmonious, even cooperative. For instance, in the patent application cases in 1677 and 1680, the Privy Council advised the parties to apply their patent to the common court.[75] Second, the jurisdiction of patents and the subjective authorization by the Privy Council wasn't suddenly suspended in the mid-eighteenth century. Although Hulme believed the incident in 1753 led to the transfer of the patent jurisdiction of the Privy Council, he admitted in the article that the Privy Council was still responsible for the patent lawsuits.[76] It was indicated in related research that several patent conflicts were judged by the Privy Council, at least until 1794.[77] Even after that, the group for the practice of patent law was not worried about the transition of the Privy Council's jurisdiction to the common court. By 1902, the Privy Council officially claimed the repealing of related patents.[78] In the treatise about patent law published in 1847, W.M. Hindmarch wrote arguments about the repealing of patents by the Queen or Privy Council in his articles, and he particularly described the patent privilege. The authorization of patents was a grace of the British King, and the king could attach any condition to it. The king might consider whether this authorization was too rash and whether it might bring problems or social costs to the public.[79] The jurisdiction of the Privy Council to patents was gradually lost, and it was likely to last until the nineteenth century with a long time of vagueness. By the mid-nineteenth century, the jurisdiction of patents of the Privy Council was nothing but nominal.[80]

However, at the end of the eighteenth century, the British public began to discuss the property of the patents, and some distinct voices appeared at that time. The patent was regarded as the "right" or "property," and the term "obtain the property" began to be used. For example, in 1791, an anonymous publication defined the patent as a transmission from royal privilege to private property rights.[81] Some inventors or scholars began to prove the right property of the patent from the perspective of the natural rights theory or positivism. The former could be classified into two schools. One school was totally against the patent privilege paradigm, proposing that the patent itself should be a natural right, and it was discovered rather than created by the state, which was contrary to the opinion that the patent was derived from the grace of the British king.[82] For instance, in 1797, Joseph Bramah wrote to the grand justice in the common court, proposing that the invention was ... the product of individual thought and understanding ... it was the natural right of everyone ... unrelated to national policies.[83] The other school didn't intend to attack the legal framework for the pattern of patent privilege. In fact, the reason why they considered the patent as a natural right was that they were dissatisfied with the policy consideration that the patent authorization was based on particular cases, and they didn't oppose the authorization by the British king.[84] Some of them even believed that before the authorization, the patent should be considered based on an empirical investigation of whether it could be granted, whether it should take so many costs and whether authorization by the queen was required. They believed that the patent was the right regulated by the state, and its range and content should be clearly defined by the law to achieve public interests. They highly praised the private rights paradigm of patents, as it didn't require special considerations on particular cases but a generalized patent standard. Some more advanced theories even attempted to make systematic and complete arguments that the sovereign organ should not make policy considerations based on particular cases of patent authorization.[85] Adam Smith also stood at the very edge of the theory. Although he failed to clarify what he discussed was the patent privilege system at that time or a new patent right, he clearly pointed out it was the market rather than the government that compensated the inventor. If the invention were useful enough, he could benefit from the market; in contrast, if the invention was valueless, he wouldn't get any benefits from it. The fine itself could hardly make such precise distribution based on the value of the invention.[86] The reason why the government tended to use the patent instead of other methods to encourage and compensate for the invention was that the government didn't need to bear too much cost. Adam Smith understood the advantage of saving costs in the government's granting of patents and found that the government should not exercise excessive discretion in terms of evaluating the utility and value of the patent; instead, it should be left to the market.[87]

People did not discuss the legitimacy of the right property of the patent until the end of the eighteenth century; however, that was not the whole story. Actually, the legal framework of the patent privilege pattern was still solid, and the opinion that supported this pattern still played a dominant role. The group for legal practice was the group that held this pattern most firmly. For instance, Chancellor Thurlow declared clearly in his legal opinion: "If the British king refused to grant a patent, I, as well as anyone else, couldn't argue, as the patent itself was completely based on the grace of our great royal family, and nothing was more glorious than that."[88] As was said in this opinion, no one attempted to argue in the court that he had the right to be granted the patent or that the court could impose his patent within the protection term.[89] In addition, during the early nineteenth century, almost all frontier research findings about the patent considered the patent as the grace of the royal family. They believed that the content of the patent privilege was defined by the royal family based on particular cases.[90] For instance, Richard Godson pointed out in a groundbreaking thesis titled *No Right to Request the Patent,* published in 1823:

> No term or law regulates that the patent is a right. This benefit, which brings great motivation to the industry and brings us enormous wealth, is still the free grace of our king. It comes from the king, as the *Act of Subsidizing Arts and Science* is issued by him under our humble request, and his extension of this protection to inventors is the greatest grace to us.[91]

In addition, in 1846, Hindmarch discussed in his thesis:

> The inventor never has the right to ask for the privatization of the patent. They have merely the right to use the patent, which must be requested to be granted by the British king, and it is nothing but a kind of grace.[92]

Therefore, the theses at that time didn't indicate that the patent privilege was already nominal. Instead, it was still greatly supported by scholars at that time.

At the end of the eighteenth century, some concepts of the patent began to significantly diverge from the original, which was related to the concept of the patent, the legal requirements of the specification, and the probability of getting the reward from the licensees in the patent trade, but those would exert no influence on the paradigm of the patent privilege at that time. At the beginning of Collier's thesis in 1803, he mentioned that the patent "property" was the award of the creativity of everyone; however, when discussing the practical principles of the patent, he returned to the traditional patent privilege pattern. He insisted on the authorization pattern of considering particular cases, believing the patent was granted based on the grace of the royal family. The patent was granted by the king as judge of the commerce to those he considered qualified.[93] Accordingly, by the end of the eighteenth century, Britain was still far from completely converting privilege to private rights. The controversy over whether the patent had been completely converted was due to the discussion of the right property of the patent and excessive exaggerations by some lawyers. Although the practice of the patent examination, including the examiner, and the relationship between the Council and the patent led to vagueness and promoted the authorization toward standardization, the subjective judgment on particular cases was never abandoned. Despite the changes in the legal principles and thought, the institution of the patent privilege pattern remained solid. It was not until the enactment of the 1852 British patent law that Britain began to abandon the privilege pattern and adopt the private right pattern. The 1852 British patent law transferred the power to sign the application from the king to the Patent Committee. However, it still had many problems, the most outstanding of which was that the patent was still regarded as a privilege. The novelty examination and substantial examination institution were established in 1902,[94] which symbolized the formal establishment of the British private right of patents.

When it came to the United States, since the seventeenth century, large merchants, lawyers, and Puritans began to have organized activities in North American colonies. They constituted 13 colonies in pursuit of American wealth or fled religious oppression in Britain after applying for the privilege of the British king. Compared with European countries, the colonies in North America had abundant natural resources but a scarce labor force. The dominant economic sector was agriculture, especially the production of industrial crops such as sugarcane, vegetables, and wheat; the technical development fell far behind. North America was a long way from developed European countries, with a weak industrial and commercial basis, a small market, and an undeveloped economy. To promote the domestic economy, the North American colonies rapidly overcame the undeveloped economic form of simple and extensive fishing, hunting, and planting by tapping into abundant resources, developing the economy based on private ownership and oriented by the market; the constantly increasing commercial awareness led to the emergence of the capitalist market.[95] At the same time, the colonies took various measures, including governmental allowance, subsidies, awards, and granting limited monopoly patents to newly developed technologies and industries, to promote economic development and encourage research and introduction of new technologies.[96] Therefore, similar to Europe in the Middle Ages, the patent privilege system was only one of the various encouraging measures used in some regions in the American colonies to promote economic development. The patent system in the British North American colonies was derived from Britain and deeply influenced by the British system, which has the following features.

First, the authorization organ in the colonies was basically consistent with the organ in Britain.[97] Second, in terms of concepts and concrete operation, the colonies were deeply influenced by the British patent privilege pattern. The colonies generally believed that the authorization organ, the Congress of the colony, could freely judge it based on particular cases. The patent system usually included the operation term that required the operation of the patent within the given time. For example, Massachusetts' *Body of Liberties* in 1641 regulated granting the patent to new inventions beneficial to the state, and Connecticut regulated in 1672 that the monopoly was only granted to inventions that were considered "beneficial to the state." This indicated that the invention fact alone was not necessarily bringing the coherent, exclusive monopoly right of the inventor. Some privileges had the obligation to limit and restrict the quality or price of the product; others required the patent granted to instruct some apprentices.[98]

During the seventeenth and eighteenth centuries, the patent privilege system was mainly implemented in Massachusetts, Connecticut, and other places in the North

American colonies. In most colonies, including regions with developed industries, including Pennsylvania, the patent system was not implemented, because there was no large industrial foundation or market to put the patent technology into practice. Therefore, it was unnecessary to spend time, energy, and costs to pursue the exclusive authorization of patents. The competition between businessmen and craftsmen in the colonies was far less severe than in Britain. In the court of Britain and all colonies, no materials about the patent lawsuit in the colony that demonstrated the existence value of the patent, such as contending the belongings of the patent right and prosecuting patent infringement, was found,[99] which indicated that the patent in the colonies had limited value and social influence. Accordingly, the patent system was a local and temporary measure. From the American Independence War in the eighteenth century to the end of the eighteenth century, despite several patent laws being issued, the elements of technology, economy, culture, and authority in the United States were not enough to satisfy the social conditions to establish intellectual property and private rights. The American patent laws and practices indicated that it maintained the pattern of patent privilege and failed to completely achieve the conversion of the private right pattern,[100] which will be analyzed in detail in the following section.

The American patent privilege system from the Independence War to the end of the eighteenth century

Motivations for the transition of the concept of the American patent privilege system at the end of the eighteenth century

DIVERGENCE OF THE TECHNOLOGY, ECONOMY, AND CAPITALIST STRUCTURE

After independence, science and education in the United States fell behind, and scientific development was quite slow. Inventors and scientists with achievements were quite limited until the end of the eighteenth century. Some old ideas had a negative influence on scientific research and were hindered by narrow-sighted local awareness and religious prejudice. For instance, Louis Gallas and others insisted that various species in the world were not the result of chronic evolution but were created by God at the very beginning.[101] The craft technology in the United States fell far behind the developed countries in Europe; Britain experienced the Industrial Revolution, while France and Germany closely followed it. The main content of the American technological inventions was mechanical products, which mainly depended on the practical experience and accumulation of the engineer, especially intelligence and skills in mechanics. There were some self-educated amateurs of scientific technology, such as Franklin in colonial times and Samuel Fitch, who invented the first steamboat in 1786, but these excellent inventors were limited. In general, the development of production technology in the United States was still minor. Due to the lack of technical talents and limited level of scientific knowledge, the only effective method that the United States could adopt was to introduce advanced technologies that the European countries had already gained. If the level of production technology in the United States somehow improved, it was the result of imitating Europe,[102] and it mainly depended on introducing advanced technologies from European countries to develop its own industry and agriculture. For example, Oliver Evans established the first automatic flour factory in 1785 by introducing British technologies, Eli Whitney invented the cotton gin by learning from foreign technologies, and the set of weaving facilities in the first cotton weaving factory established in Rhode Island was introduced in 1789 when Samuel Slater immigrated into the United States, who was called the "Father of the American Manufacture Industry" by President Jefferson.[103]

Most states of the United States, after their independence, mainly depended on the agricultural economy, which was similar to what happened during colonial times. There were only four cities with more than 10,000 residents, and the proportion of land-holding farmers, slaves, and craftsmen was relatively higher. Most Americans made their living by agriculture; the residence, clothing, and agricultural production methods were primitive, and so was the manufacturing industry. Farmers were all self-sufficient: they made soaps, candles, blankets, and furniture by themselves.[104] In the South, the plantation economy mainly relied on plantations of rice and cotton, which developed the economy and relied on the increase in the land, slave, and commodity market. There were still some industries and commerce in the United States (including commerce, financial organizations, manufacturing industries, and transportation).[105] During the Independence War, some weaving industries and metallurgy developed, and a series of armories were established in Massachusetts and other regions. In the weaving industry, a weaving factory hiring 500 workers emerged; there were 41 workshops in New Jersey; the North American Bank was established in 1780, and financial organizations, such as the New York Bank and the Boston Bank, were established in 1784.[106] With the increase in the influence of the British Industrial Revolution during the mid-eighteenth century, some commercial capitalists were increasingly attracted by industry, and a group of intelligent commercial capitalists noticed the critical meaning of technological innovation and its potential economic effects. Boston businessmen paid significant attention to technology, encouraged invention with outstanding awards, and established technical schools to train weaving workers.[107] In the 1780s, commercial capitalists who accumulated much capital from the market attempted to invest some of their money into research on new weaving machines and establish some factories. They set up weaving factories in Beverly, Rensselaer, Newport, Philadelphia, and other cities; however, these factories were closed very soon due to the lack of advanced technology and management experience.[108] Although the industrial and commercial class, represented by Hamilton, the Minister of Finance, proposed to develop the manufacturing industry, the United States was still in the early primitive stage of capitalism, seriously lacking technology and capital. Therefore, the enormous development of industry and commerce could hardly be realized.[109] At the end of the eighteenth century, the capitalist class of the United States was gradually differentiated into two classifications: the industrial and commercial capitalist class in the North and the plantation capitalist class in the South, and the struggle and conflict between them became apparent. At the end of the eighteenth century, the North was relatively weaker, and the South was dominant.

"AGRARIAN STATE" AND THE "REPUBLICAN" THOUGHT

In the eighteenth century, French Enlightenment thought was also popular throughout the United States. On the eve of the American Revolution, a great number of political philosophers made a great contribution to it; the most excellent among these were Benjamin Fullan Cline, Thomas Jefferson, Hamilton, James Madison, and John Adams. The basic principles and concepts of the foundation of the revolution and construction of the United States mostly did not originate from them but from advanced thinkers in Britain and France, such as Locke, Rousseau, and Montesquieu; however, they combined these principles and concepts with the historical tradition and actual conditions in North America to research, develop, and promote. In addition, they tried all means to put them into practice and obtained brilliant achievements, which greatly influenced the thoughts of early Americans. Among them, the thoughts of Jeffersons as the founding figure in the United States played a dominant role and influenced the construction of the early patent system in the United States.

Jefferson was born into a family with a plantation in the country, and he had a naturally good impression of agriculture. Because he worked in France for a long time, he adopted the Enlightenment thought in France and promoted natural human rights. Influenced by the French physiocratic doctrine of Boisguilbert and Quesnay and Adam Smith's liberal economic theory, he proposed that economic life should obey the natural law; as nature always developed into liberty and completion, he proposed the liberal economy and opposed interference from the state. In Europe, he witnessed the gap between wealth and social conflicts that was aroused by the emergence of capitalist industry and commerce. Therefore, he was worried that the government constituted by industrial and commercial classes would harm the general public's rights, especially the benefits of farmers. Therefore, he thought that only in the agrarian society could equality be ensured. Jefferson's thought on state construction promotes physiocracy that a liberal democratic society should be constituted by farmers and craftsmen. "Those who labour in the earth are the chosen people of God, if ever he had a chosen people, whose breasts he has made his peculiar deposit for substantial and genuine virtue." In contrast, the industrial workers had no material conditions to actualize their labor force.

> It is the mark set on those, who not looking up to heaven, to their own soil and industry, as does the husbandman, for their subsistence, depend for it on the casualties and caprice of customers. Dependance begets subservience and venality, suffocates the germ of virtue, and prepares fit tools for the designs of ambition ...[110] This, the natural progress and consequence of the arts, has sometimes perhaps been retarded by accidental circumstances.[111]

He even pointed out that

> While we have land to labour then, let us never wish to see our citizens occupied at a work-bench, or twirling a distaff. Carpenters, masons, smiths, are wanting in husbandry: but, for the general operations of manufacture, let our work-shops remain in Europe...[112]

Apparently, these thoughts aimed at maintaining and extending the benefits of owners of the "land resource – slave labor force" intensive slavery plantations in the South.

In addition, leaders like Jefferson always insisted on "the republican thought" that governmental power was the right of the people. They hoped that the newly elected government could exhibit no prejudice and maintain justice when handling various conflicts between benefits in the country concerning the public interest and social rights,[113] which was reflected in their outlook on rights. As Jefferson said, the Creator infused some moral principles in the heart of humans as the natural law to guide group and individual behaviors of humans.[114] In the Declaration of Independence, published in 1776, Jefferson believed that "we hold these truths to be self-evident, that all men are created equal, that they are endowed by their Creator with certain unalienable rights, that they are among these are life, liberty and the pursuit of happiness..." He deliberately omitted property from the natural rights. He substituted the pursuit of happiness for the pursuit of property, which indicates Jefferson considered property rights to be social rights rather than natural rights.[115] In the newly constituted Federal Government of the United States, distinct from the "Federal Party" that promoted strengthening the authority of the federal government and emphasizing the protection of the benefits of the industrial and commercial class, the "Republican Party" constituted by Jefferson and Madison emphasized the protection of the large peasant class, worrying that an excessive powerful central government would offend the right and liberty of people, opposing despotism and monopoly.

CONCLUSION

In the time from independence to the end of the eighteenth century, the scientific development of the United States was quite slow due to low-leveled scientific knowledge and the lack of technical talent. At the same time, the United States was a country dominated by the peasant economy. The severe lack of technology and capital hindered the development of industry and commerce, and the agricultural economy mainly relied on natural resources like the labor force and the land rather than technology. Therefore, an abundant labor force, simple technology, and experience were enough to satisfy its needs. Therefore, technology played no apparent role in productivity, and its influence on the growth of the economy was quite limited. Moreover, Jefferson and other representative figures, on behalf of the benefits of the plantation capitalists in the South, significantly promoted the thought of "the agrarian state" to develop a liberal agricultural economy rather than an industrial and commercial economy and to oppose the mercantilism policy. They promoted republican thought, emphasizing the protection of public interests, considering the property right as a social right instead of a natural right, and opposing despotism and monopoly. Therefore, under these technical, economic, and cultural conditions, Jefferson generated the institutional concept that the patent was a monopoly and should be strictly restricted. He always believed the patent was a restriction on individual thoughts and liberty. He reiterated in letters written to Madison that the patent monopoly destroyed the structure of society and represented the clear interference by the government in an individual's affairs. He thought the government should not restrict but help citizens to achieve their pursuit of individual liberty and thought.[116] The letter written to McPherson in 1813 could demonstrate his opinions on patents best. He thought the invention, as the spiritual concept of the product of individual brains, could not be regarded as the object of property rights in essence. Society could grant people an exclusive right to benefit from it to encourage them to create beneficial and useful ideas, but this right should not be compulsory. Whether to grant and how to grant should be based on the will and convenience of society.[117]

Jefferson's influence on the early patent system in the United States

THE INTELLECTUAL RIGHTS CLAUSE IN THE CONSTITUTION OF 1787

Madison and Jefferson had a profound influence on shaping the early patent system; the latter was especially praised as the "Father of the American patent law."[118] In 1787, Jefferson failed to attend the Constitutional Convention due to a diplomatic mission to France. Madison and others absorbed the patent privilege pattern of the colony into the constitution,[119] such as today's intellectual rights clause. When Madison sent this draft to Jefferson, he was astonished because he disliked this term very much and distrusted whether the patent system could bring beneficial effects to society. Actually, he always attempted to remove the term to grant exclusive rights in the Constitution. When writing to Madison in December 1787, he pointed out that the monopoly should be restricted ... clearly and without the help of quibbling. When he found out the 1787 Constitution was approved, he continued expressing his opinions about the monopoly in the letter to Madison in July 1788. He pointed out that in terms of the intellectual rights clause, he thought it better to abolish monopoly than to do nothing. At this point, Madison didn't completely agree with Jefferson's opinion. He thought it tolerable to grant monopoly privileges with a given restriction to patents and copyrights, because it could bring some advantages to society. However, he frequently used terms like "a necessary evil" and "limited, artificial monopoly" in his reply.[120] Jefferson thought it inappropriate to introduce the patent system at this time; he was always convinced that the future of the United States was agriculture rather than industry, and the republican thought of cherishing public social benefits made him naturally oppose monopoly.[121] However, Jefferson had to accept the situation was already defined. He reminded Madison in his letter in 1789 that the term in the *Statute of Monopolies 1624* of Britain should be learned from in the constitution and that the patent and privilege should be defined as the monopoly with a given restriction. Madison agreed with his opinion; however, he believed that this term would violate the philosophical framework of the Constitution.[122]

Accordingly, in terms of the legislation background at that time, Jefferson or Madison regarded the patent as a monopoly privilege. No evidence proved that the United States completely abandoned the privilege pattern and created a "modern patent system" at that time. Early patent applicants and Congress didn't regard this term as completely deviating from the patent practice at that time. After the performance of the U.S. Constitution, Congress received many patent applications. Many applicants quoted the patent clause, but their applications followed the former privilege pattern. They clearly demonstrated the special social welfare brought by the invention in the application and requested Congress to make particular examinations on their inventions and grant exclusive privileges. In terms of the applicant, the only function of the patent clause was to convert the familiar pattern where the privilege was granted by states into the pattern granted by the federation.[123] Congress had no intention to pursue further breakthroughs; it didn't refuse these individuals' patent applications. Instead, it examined these patents on behalf of the public interest. Congress had attempted to grant authorization to every patent, but it was only abandoned to establish a generalized patent law.[124] The citizens throughout the country usually considered the patent as a monopoly to restrict people's liberty and a policy taken by the government to develop the economy and public interest, and they held a naturally negative attitude toward it.[125]

PATENT ACT 1790 AND PRACTICE

In March 1790, Jefferson returned from France and was nominated the Secretary of State when Congress discussed enacting the *1790 Patent Act*. According to related materials, Jefferson significantly influenced the enactment of the *Patent Act 1790*, which was likely to be enacted according to his project.[126] In 1790, the American patent law was officially issued via a complicated legislation process. In some respects, it achieved great breakthroughs; for example, it created a unified patent system, including a Patent Committee consisting of three dignitaries in the government, which granted patents to inventions "useful and important enough." In terms of the form, it was distinct from the patent privilege granted by the British Council in the name of the king and the specific legislation authorization on particular cases performed by legislatures in the states and the North American colonies. It even defined some standards of authorization, including novelty, patent specifications, unified time restrictions, and standardized administrative procedures of application and authorization, which were all great progress in the institutionalization and standardization of the patent. However, from the perspective of the framework and practice of the *Patent Act 1790*, the patent privilege system was still applied in the United States at that time.

First, the *Patent Act 1790* regulated that the Patent Committee should be constituted of three dignitaries in the government, for instance, the Secretary of State Jefferson, the Minister of Justice, and the Minister of War, who had full discretion over the authorization of patents. The Office of the State Council led by Jefferson was responsible for administrative affairs like the application, registration, copying, and writ making. Jefferson was the Secretary of State in the first Federal Government of the United States. Therefore, he became the first principal of patents. On condition of lacking concrete authorization rules, the Patent Committee members headed by the Secretary of State were the regulator and operator of the patent authorization rules, for example, the judge and the sportsman. Although patent law regulated some standards, they were merely external restrictions rather than concrete rules for judgments. How could an invention be judged "useful and important enough"? Who was the "first true inventor"? Which inventions could be granted the patent, or which conditions should an invention satisfy to be granted a patent? Lacking concrete rules, they had full discretion over the authorization of patents. Their authorization and examination of patents were political decisions based on whether the invention was suitable for public requirements, and the public interest was their basic standard. As dignitaries in the administrative system, they had important official affairs to handle, and patent authorization was only a part-time job in addition to their formal affairs; therefore, their time to handle patents was quite limited.[127] They had to process a great number of patent applications within a limited time. Once the application was rejected, the legislation at that time lacked the procession mechanism of patent lawsuits, so the applicant had no way to impose their so-called rights.[128] Due to Jefferson's cautious and conservative policy on patents, he wouldn't simply grant the patent due to busy affairs. The Patent Committee headed by him took a considerably strict standard on patent examinations, aiming at the authorization needed to improve the development of public interest, which was excessively emphasized by the committee rather than protecting individual benefits. Therefore, the authorization was too slow, and there were too many restrictions on inventors. According to the report of Remsen, the General Secretary of the Council, on the operation of patents in 1790, the Committee organized a meeting on the last Saturday of every month. Before the meeting, the messenger of the Council was responsible for notifying every member of the Committee of items to be discussed at the meeting. During the meeting, the members examined every application received in the last month, considered it for a month, and left it to be discussed at the next meeting.[129] To multiple patent applications proposed by several applicants on the same invention, like the steamboat patent, the Committee would deny the exclusive right pursued by the former inventor because (both as inventors) one could not be granted superior to another.

Second, from the applications of inventors at that time, their application pattern was still based on the traditional one. The applicant proposed the will to obtain the right in the specification rather than securing coherent natural rights.[130] No direct evidence could prove that the applicant considered the patent a right, not to mention that someone appealed to the court to impose operating their patent. For instance, William Pollard applied for a patent for his improved cotton weaving machine in 1790. He spent a large part of the application describing and explaining how big the social benefits brought by his invention were to the United States, like the increase in productivity. He promised to accept the price control by the Committee on his products. In addition, John Fitch applied for a patent for the steamboat he invented in 1790. He sufficiently proved the considerable public interest brought by his steamboat, which had large immediate effects and brought great changes to the United States and even the world in the future. It could save the labor force of people, horses, and travelers and was safer, faster, and more convenient.[131] It could be seen that John Fitch's application followed the traditional application pattern in the North American colonies, which attracted the sovereign organ to authorize it by describing the concrete public interest of the invention.[132] Their application also reflected that the Committee was only responsible for examining the public interest achieved by the invention and freely judging whether to grant the patent right.[133]

Therefore, the *Patent Act 1790* was not the traditional, case-oriented, particular, or special patent authorization legislation but generalized patent legislation oriented on all patent applications. However, its foundation was the traditional patent system in which the authority organ made particular authorization based on public policies, which had no substantial difference from the patent privilege pattern in Britain in the Middle Ages, in the North American colonies, or during the time of the federation. Still, the authorization organ was converted from the British king or the legislature to the administrative dignitaries defined in legislation. In other words, the *Patent Act 1790* established a generalized privilege, which was the middle product between the former patent privilege pattern and the modern standardized patent pattern. It began to explore the standardization of the substance and procedure in patent authorization. It attempted to construct a unified patent right; however, it failed to overcome the patent privilege pattern.[134]

PATENT ACT 1793 AND PRACTICE

Due to the slow-paced progress in patent authorization in the *Patent Act 1790*, the Patent Committee members were exhausted, and the inventors were generally dissatisfied. On this background, the *Patent Act 1793* was enacted and began to be implemented. Jeffersons suggested a revision of the *Patent Law* to Congress on 7 February 1791. He offered a revised draft proposing to cancel all examinations, the Council of State was only responsible for registration, and the potency of the patent was to be judged by the court. Frank, the expert on the history of IPRs, believed that the *Patent Act 1793* was drafted or at least influenced by Jefferson in its enactment.[135] The *Patent Act 1793* repealed the Patent Committee and canceled the invention examination procedure. The patent work became a pure writ work led by the Secretary of State. The *Patent Act 1793* actually transferred the work of patent examination from the former Patent Committee to the court, and the Council of State was responsible for nominal examinations. This reformation copied the British patent authorization pattern at that time. The patent practice in Britain since the seventeenth century was that the authorization required nominal examinations rather than substantial ones, and all substantial problems with the patent were left to the court. As was explained by Representative Williamson, who was responsible for the draft of the bill, the patent law imitated the British patent system to prevent excessive burdens on the officials responsible for it.[136] This improvement was seen as enormous progress in the reformation of the American patent system; for instance, William Thornton believed that this reformation deprived the discretion of the Council of State over approval or refusal of the patent authorization.[137]

However, this reformation failed to transform the United States into the paradigm of private rights of patents. The critical problem – whether the patent was a privilege or a private right – was not solved by depriving the Patent Committee of the discretion over patent examinations, which just transferred the government's power ex-ante to examine and clarify the patent's potency to the court with examinations ex-post. The influence of this reform was two-sided. On the one hand, an examination ex-post greatly increased the work of the court, therefore generating more complicated rules for the patent lawsuits established by the court.[138] On the other hand, given the lack of patent standards and rules, transferring the examination power to the judge could entitle the court to explain and apply the patent standards and give them the full discretion to construct patent rules. The court was deeply influenced by Jefferson's thought, considering the patent as a monopoly supposed to be strictly controlled, which could only be granted based on the need of the public interest. In law practice, the most popular explanation at that time was that the patent was a special right granted by the government to an individual; its utility was the positive application of public interests, and the authorization should help improve public interests. The court usually judged the feasibility of the patent based on explaining and applying the standard of utility. Because the law didn't define the content of utility, the court had full discretion over it. The judgment of utility mainly depended on considering special cases by judging whether the invention was beneficial to the public, which was a concept with quite a broad meaning, serving as the policy consideration. Therefore, the judge, who was somewhat akin to traditional sovereign organs, granted the patent privilege based on related policies. The judge became the subjective ruler of the patent's value.[139] As Judge Van Ness said, the Patent Committee set up in 1790 brought these officials the power to judge the utility and authorization of patents. In terms of the new system, he thought, considering convenience and public security, when all primary examinations were canceled, and monopoly and patents were granted to anyone with the identity of inventors or discoverers, some simple systems were required to examine the patent's value and decide its feasibility.[140] Scanning the responsibility and practice of the court at that time, he thought that the judge mastered the full supervision power over the feasibility of patents, which was the discretion. In other words, the court played the role of the former British royal family or the "Patent Committee" in the 1790 patent system, for instance, the decision-maker of the patent's value in public policies. According to Adam Mossoff, at least before 1800, the court reiterated in verdicts that the patent was a monopoly and a privilege supposed to be examined based on public interests.[141] For instance, in "Evans v. Eaton," judged by the Supreme Court, Joseph Ingersoll expressed the same opinion in the court that the judge replaced the Patent Committee and possessed the critical power to judge if an invention constituted a patent important and useful enough.[142]

Overall, the early American patent system was deeply influenced by Jefferson, reflecting the slowly developing values of the agrarian society. On behalf of the benefits of farmers and the Southern capitalists, Jefferson held a suspicious and cautious attitude toward patent monopoly. He emphasized the protection of civil rights and liberty and worried that a powerful central government would lead to despotism and tyranny, harming local and civil benefits. In terms of the patent, he was worried about its monopoly and took a conservative and strict stance on the authorization standard. Therefore, Jefferson, as the Secretary of State in the new federal government and with responsibility for patent authorization, insisted on the opinion that patent authorization served the public interest and took strict and high-level policies when examining patent applications and defining rules. His concept influenced citizens and the law practice at that time.

Formation of the American private right of patents at the beginning of the nineteenth century

Motivations for the institutional concept of the American private right of patents

TECHNOLOGY, ECONOMY, AND THE RISE OF INDUSTRIAL AND COMMERCIAL CAPITALISTS

All these transitions started very slowly. Having experienced the introduction of British and European technologies, creating American technologies entered a new stage. On the one hand, theories and treatises about scientific research became abundant, and great achievements were made in astrology, geography, geology, biology, meteorology, and oceanography.[143] On the other hand, the number of inventors and technical associations in the United States began to increase, and Americans gradually understood the importance of technology. For example, the American Philadelphian Association was an active center that encouraged other regions to organize similar groups and associations. Simultaneously, the industrial and commercial classes and technicians set up associations and libraries and encouraged research into new thoughts and technologies, promoting industrial crafts. An example was the "Association of Awarding Products and Useful Crafts in Pennsylvania," which began to provide awards for those who designed elegant potteries, ceramics, and other useful products at the end of the eighteenth century to promote the design talents of Americans. In addition, it provided awards for British mechanics who brought new blueprints and models of machines to the United States, which had already made Britain the factory of the world.[144] In terms of materials, the inventors and the industrial and commercial class played a leading role in innovation. They always concentrated on benefits and seldom thought about the future results brought by their efforts. Various machine inventions gradually transformed the United States into an industrial civilization. However, the critical parts were copied from Britain, Watt's steam engine, Stevenson's train, and Arkwright and Crompton's weaving machine – American inventors would always add many new designs. Fulton applied the steam engine to boats, starting a new era of navigation. Howe created the sewing machine, McCormick and Hershey created the harvester for farmers, making the sickles and scythes from the Tutankhamun age immediately old-fashioned. Morse invented the telegram that connected the continent, and the commerce and trade of the country could be operated on a table. Whitney's cotton gin destroyed the old economic activities. It challenged the exhausted spinning factories in New England, the lords of the cotton plantations, and the slave armies in Mississippi and Louisiana. Indeed, behind every inventor sat an industrial magnate who was prepared to seize machines from the factory, raise capital and labor forces to make them function, and pursue the market for continuous production from the machines. Society in the North was quite suitable for the career of businessmen, where there were no stubborn monks or aristocrats who looked down on their production and labor. Instead, it had abundant natural resources for the industry – wood, coal, iron, lead, and copper, as well as countless immigrants from Europe, which increased the labor force and compensated for the lack of children of American farmers. Factories, mines, and various other enterprises could all raise new hands from European laborers, and the capital was sufficient. As crops, cotton, and gold flowed into foreign countries, the credit of the United States also increased, and there was a large domestic market dominated by the American manufacturing industry.[145] Therefore, the Industrial Revolution broke out at the end of the nineteenth century, and the trend for the development of industry and commerce was defined.

In fact, another important factor that motivated the industrial development of the United States was that Jefferson's attitude toward industrial economic development altered. In 1801, Jefferson was elected the third president of the United States, who maintained the economic thought of agriculture first, commerce as a supplement, and with no industry at the beginning of his presidency. However, the embargo of the United States by Britain in 1807 considerably altered his economic thought,[146] which evolved from the "agrarian state" to "the simultaneous development of agriculture and commerce" that encouraged and supported the development of commerce and the manufacturing industry. After the 1812 Anglo–American War, the United States overcame a series of barriers to developing its industrial and commercial economies. Transportation was improved,[147] the process of urbanization was accelerated,[148] and the industrial and commercial economies increased at an astonishing speed. Therefore, since the beginning of the nineteenth century, the industrial and commercial class of the United States invested large amounts of private capital into the construction of factories and public transport with the support of the international situation, technology, and the protective tariff policies of the government. Private manufacturing factories were set up, and the power of the industrial and commercial classes began to be strengthened. For example, in 1800–1823, 557 companies participating in the manufacturing industry were set up in eight states in the east. The investment capital reached 72 million dollars, and 20 million of this was in Massachusetts, where the industrial and commercial foundation was developed. Processing industries, such as cotton and leather weaving, clothing, rubber, and iron smelting, all rapidly developed.[149] By the 1830s, the federal institution of the United States was increasingly stable, and the industrial economy gradually developed from factory handicrafts to production with large machines. The American economy rapidly developed from a colonial economy at the beginning of independence, which was dominated by agriculture and highly dependent on foreign markets and led to enormous revolutions in productivity and production relationships.

RISE OF INDIVIDUALISM AND LIBERALISM

In this technical and economic environment, the commercial trend was popular throughout the United States; the pursuit of individual private benefits was excessive, and the money worship was a prevalent social phenomenon. Social life was altered by industrialization and Enlightenment reasoning. Honorable ideas and internal depth were gradually lost, and superficialness and vulgarness reproduced and devoured their competitors. Materialism became an important standard used to judge whether someone was successful or not.[150] The thoughts of politicians were no longer praised as the creed, and Bentham's utilitarianism and Spenser's laissez-faire thoughts began to infiltrate the United States,[151] which evolved into the individualism and liberalism culture that was specific to the United States. In the 1840s, the Frenchman Tocqueville considered individualism and liberalism as the core of American cultures and their major values at that time. He believed the concept of American individualism and liberalism could be generalized as strong confidence in himself or his power. Wisdom and struggles were carried out by all citizens for their wealth and character as well as scorn to depend on other's will. Tocqueville noticed that it was the "individualism" that made the Americans at that time "isolated from the peers of the general public and shrink into small circles of families and friends; with these small societies constituted based on his interest, one happily neglected the big society."[152] All economic production and related activities belonged to the private management category; the control and decisions of democratic politics could not intervene in this private right. Republican thought in colonial times and at the end of the eighteenth century gradually faded. Americans began to ignore social obligations and had a dominant right over properties that were more liberal than before based on their will.[153] In all aspects, including using individual properties, managing enterprises, and selecting religious beliefs, people tried to exploit more liberal space free from the control of governmental power. Therefore, the situation that concentrated on individuals and on more severe competition emerged. More and more people believed that because governmental power was difficult to master, restrictions or the privatization of some power would be available. Individualism was like a greedy deep hole that absorbed people's desires and produced enormous energy to promote the development of society.[154]

The concept of property laws in the United States at this stage was mainly to cultivate one's enterprising spirit, reflecting the instrumentalism law outlook to guarantee individual liberty to the greatest extent,[155] and the main objective of the law was to protect one's property rights. The trend of individualism and liberalism profoundly developed Locker's individual absolute property theory. As said by Grand Justice Storey, the basic principle of a liberal government is supposed to be regarding private property rights as being sacred and inviolable.[156] Judge Kent also believed that the law should propose to protect the right to possess existing properties and concentrate on protecting the right to obtain properties.[157]

CONCLUSION

At the beginning of the nineteenth century, based on the introduction of British and European technologies, the technical level in the United States developed into a new stage. On the one hand, scientific theories became gradually more abundant; on the other hand, various industrial technologies continuously emerged. Handicrafts gradually developed into the production of large machines, and the inventions that saved the labor force and improved labor productivity played an increasingly apparent role in the value and function of economies. With the development of American industrial technologies, the United States stepped from an agricultural economy into an industrial one. At the same time, the expansion of the domestic market and the development of commerce and trade progressively stimulated the requirements for industrial products and technologies. Commerce and trade provided the capital accumulation for the industrial economy and technological creations. The industrial and commercial classes obtained new inventions by sponsoring inventors and became more and more dependent on technology. They used technology as a tool to develop industry and create wealth. At the same time, the thought of the American government represented by Jefferson tended to convert from concentrating on agriculture to supporting agriculture and commerce. It increasingly emphasized the development of the industrial and commercial economy. With the rise of the trend of individualism and liberalism, the outlook of Americans transformed from social rights to private rights, and Locker's individualism absolute property theory obtained profound development and gradually became mainstream. Therefore, in this technological, economic, and cultural environment, the concept of the private right of patents in America was born among the industrial and commercial classes and the general public at that time.

The Patent Act 1836 *and the formation of the American private rights system of patents*

Thomas Jefferson's presidency ended in 1809, he retired in Monticello and passed away in 1826. In the nineteenth century, Jefferson didn't intervene in the regulation of the rules of the patent system anymore. However, he was still attracting notice in the patent system when he passed away.[158] He could not resist the transition of people's opinions on the patent. The increasingly powerful industrial and commercial class and inventors constantly emphasized the natural rights they enjoyed from patents in applications and lawsuits, which required a loose authorization environment, effective patent protection, and affirmation and protection from the state. As Edward C. Walterscheid said, although these inventors and merchants were hardly familiar with the natural right theory, they were gradually aware of the distinction between "a privilege" and "a natural right." They reiterated in the applications and lawsuits that they had a natural coherent right to inventions, and the state was obliged to protect them.[159] The conservative patent policy applied by Jefferson previously annoyed the industrial and commercial classes like Fitch,[160] who believed that the current patent was a right and property. For instance, Joseph Barnes thought that every American citizen had the constitutional right to ask for the protection of their innovation result by the national power organs.[161] Distinct from the British patent privilege system, Rep. William Murray believed that they should be granted by the king's grace; American patents were the right possessed to one's invention result.[162] American lawyers at that time also played a role in promoting the private right of patents in America. For example, Dan Webster, the famous

American lawyer and jurist at that time, pointed out in a speech at the Congress in 1824: The patent was undoubtedly an individual property, as the invention was the intellectual result created by humans, and the development of American industrial economy was highly dependent on it, so the government should take all measures to motivate people to make technical creations to promote the chronic development of American industrial economy.[163]

Under the influence of the technical, economic, and cultural environment and the persuasion of the right owners and lawyers, the concepts of the patent system by American judges were also transforming. Since the nineteenth century, some judges began to use the natural right to prove the private property right of patents in judgments, and they believed that the patent should be authorized according to the related conditions defined by the law, which was similar to the immovable property.[164] The last barrier to destroying the patent privilege pattern was Judge Storey, who was a famous jurist at that time, nominated as the judge of the Federal Supreme Court in 1811–1845. When trying a series of patent cases, such as Lowell v. Lewis (1817), Bedford v. Hunt (1817), Kniss v. Schuylkill (1820), Elie v. Sawyer (1825), and Whitney v. Emmett (1831), he proposed his own opinion distinct from the traditional one that the patent authorization was regarded as the national public policy. The court was the judge of the value of public interests in the patent cases. Storey didn't deny that the judge was the ruler of the public interest and the social moral standard in patent cases. However, he thought the court was restricted to judging the utility of an invention from the perspective of whether it was harmful or dissatisfying instead of whether it was beneficial to the public interest or whether it was worthy for the government to grant the privilege. The utility and value of an invention had no relation to the public interest. Although Storey's explanations of utility were incomplete from today's perspective, he attacked the patent authorization pattern in at least two respects.

First, Storey thought the utility standard of the invention would not be harmful or immoral, which restricted the judge from using the standard of beneficial to the public to fully exercise his discretion. Second, he prophesied the importance to the market of an invention's value. Storey borrowed the market value theory popular in Britain in the late eighteenth century. If the actual use value of an invention was limited, the inventor could seldom and even impossibly benefit from it, so this invention would be valueless, neglected, and finally disappear from the market.[165] Therefore, the main duty of the judge was merely to apply for the patent after the authorization, according to the standard regulated by the patent law, rather than to judge the value of the patent in the name of public interest. The market was the real judge of the invention's value. After the 1830s, Storey's argument on the patent's value and the court's function in patent affairs became mainstream in the Supreme Court. It was regarded as the judgment basis of related cases and became the orthodox theory of the patent's value. The sole judger and distributor of the patent's value was the market, and the function of the court (of judging the potency of the patent right) was restricted to applying normal patent standards.[166]

At the same time, the structure of the American government was altered. In early times, it was dominated by the interest group constituted by the Southern capitalists.

With the rise of the industrial and commercial interest groups, they gradually became the dominant power, which facilitated the pursuits and benefits of the industrial and commercial class to be satisfied and responded better.[167] Based on this background, on 4 July 1836, Congress approved and signed the *Patent Act 1836*. Its drafter Lagos pointed out in the report on modification of the patent law that the patent system might be good enough in the agrarian society where it was enacted; however, it was not suitable for a manufacturing society developed by the creation and wisdom of Americans. The progressive spirit and creativity of citizens fulfilled achievements far beyond the expectations of those who enacted the institution at that time. Applying the newly invented boosting technology, a good harvest would be achieved without fertilized soils. With the help of creativity, a boundless kingdom was being explored, and countless treasures were being exploited. All natural secrets wouldn't naturally appear, and humans' steps to explore would never stop.[168] The United States embraced the most significant revolution in the history of patents. This law ultimately realized the fundamental transformation from the patent privilege pattern to the private patent correct pattern in the United States. On the one hand, it thoroughly altered the patent registration system established in the *Patent Act 1793*. It creatively constituted a patent authorization organ and a procedure system centered on the examination system, which established the earliest patent examination system in the world.[169] On the other hand, it regulated the normal standard of patent authorization. Because of the practical influence of Judge Storey's opinion that the utility of inventions was unharmful to the public interest and the real value of inventions was decided by the market, the utility examination standard of inventions became weaker, and the novelty standard became critical. Therefore, in 1836, the American patent law defined the concrete application rules on the novelty standard. Whether a patent was granted was examined according to the patent conditions defined by the law rather than subjective conditions judged by the examiners.

Therefore, the *Patent Act 1836* totally abandoned the former patent privilege pattern based on particular cases and public economic interests. It established a law that provided all citizens with equal and generalized opportunities.[170] Although the American patent law was not complete at that time, it shaped the basic model of the paradigm of modern private rights of patents. The patent is an exclusive individual property right defined by the law, and the law regulates the authorization standard. Anyone can obtain equal rights as long as their invention satisfies the authorization standard. The patent examination organization is the examiner of the authorization standard, which makes examinations according to the law, and the court is the imposer of patent rights and makes legal insurance on other's private rights. The framework of the American private right of patents also influenced other countries. Most countries that established the patent system, including Britain and Germany, inherited and adopted the American patent private pattern of substantial examinations.

Obstacles and explorations: Twists and turns in the development of the private right of patents

With the development of modern science and technology and the maturity of the patent system theory, more and more countries began to establish their own private rights system of patents. However, the establishment and dissemination of this system were never a smooth process. In the nineteenth century, an influential anti-patent movement broke out in Western Europe, and the patent system was abolished in some countries. What was the reason? What historical enlightenment could we obtain from the twists and turns in the development of the private right of patents?

Motivations for the anti-patent movement

The anti-patent movement in Western Europe was active mainly in the 1850s and at the beginning of the twentieth century. This movement involved several countries, including Britain, France, the Netherlands, Switzerland, and Germany. The groups like law experts, judges, economists, industrial and commercial classes, inventors, and lawyers participated in the widespread controversy about abolishing or maintaining the private rights system of patents. The causes of this movement are described as follows.

First, after the 1830s, Western Europe sank into the slow phase of the First Industrial Revolution. Technological innovation began to slow down, and the free trade economy became the focus of the economic development of all countries. The First Industrial Revolution lasted from 1760 to 1830, and this unprecedented technological revolution brought an enormous transformation in technology and the economy. Britain was usually regarded as the cradle of the First Industrial Revolution, followed by other Western European countries. The inventions of the First Industrial Revolution, regardless of their incredible quantity, could be classified into three categories. Machine production replaced handicraft skills and operations, making production more rapid, standardized, precise, and sustainable. Inanimate energy replaced animate energy, and the invention of steam machines, which converted heat energy into working energy, brought humans a brand-new and almost inexhaustible source of energy. New raw materials were applied, and minerals especially took the place of animals and plants as raw materials. Although there was a limited increase in average consumption and living standards, production technology changed significantly in many sectors and industries. When technical progress spread to the countries that weren't influenced before, the positive effects of technological and economic development began to diffuse and explode.[171] However, as Christopher Freeman and Francisco Lusan pointed out, technological revolutions always witnessed the alternation between high and low tides, which was called the Kondratieff cycle. After the high tide of the First Industrial Revolution from the mid-eighteenth century to the early nineteenth century, technological innovation began to decline in Western Europe.[172] At this time, the industrial productivity of European countries greatly increased, and industrial products were countless. They needed a broad market that allowed them to import cheaper raw materials and export industrial products. Therefore, they were eager to develop free trade. The rapid development of transportation technology like railways, steamboats, and shipping made the markets in European countries more unified and liberal. Britain was the champion of free trade and the first country to carry out free trade. Britain exported industrial products via overseas trade to vast markets, earned increasing profits, and continuously obtained new resources. Foreign trade created the world's requirements for new British products.[173] At that time, Germany was not politically unified. In the context of constant wars and economic decline, rapid economic development became a top concern. Therefore, the government motivated free trade and took measures to strengthen domestic industries. In 1806, Prussia initiated revolutions after being defeated by Napoleon. The industrial and commercial class, who grew up under the influence of Adam Smith's theory, began to seize power. The Prussian regime actively promoted free trade policies in Germany and abolished tariffs in Germany prior to 1862. France depended on textile products imported from Britain to develop its industry; therefore, France was a staunch supporter of Britain's free trade policy,[174] which marked the peak of the free trade movement in Western Europe.

Second, free trade theory began to rise against this economic backdrop. Influenced by Adam Smith and David Richardo's international trade freedom theories[175] and motivated by the British Manchester School represented by Richard Cobden, the thought that opposed protectionism in all forms and championed competition without any restriction was quite popular for a time.[176] Under the flag of trade and contract liberty, the phenomenon of some industrial and commercial enterprises being granted the patent right to receive protection and be exempt from competition aroused the concern of some economists. They believed that the patent law of the countries granted a monopoly right within a given term, and the monopoly right adversely affected domestic economic activities and hindered international trade and the free flow of goods in the same way as the tariff barrier did between countries. The supporters of international free trade activity associated patent protectionism with tariff protectionism and patent monopoly with monopoly privileges, which greatly influenced the general public, even the decision makers in the upper class.[177]

Finally, the problems of the patent system aroused people's growing dissatisfaction. The opinions and doctrines against the system never ceased to appear. For example, the patent system in France in 1791 had problems, such as excessive application fees, complicated legal proceedings, high litigation costs, distrust of foreign inventions, lack of systems to promote the disclosure of inventions, and the facilitation of rent-seeking activities. The British patent system was particularly annoying. Before the mid-nineteenth century, Britain insisted on its patent privilege system, which featured high costs, time-consuming and ambiguous authorization procedures, widespread vagueness concerning the theme of patents, and less effective guarantees for the status of the patent rights holders.[178] The patent lawsuit would even gradually erode the creativity of great technical brains and bankrupt the inventor.[179] Robinson said that a British judge normally had no sympathy for inventors, and the patent law was so vague that the result of a patent lawsuit was unpredictable.[180] As such, Charles Babbage wrote in 1829 that the British patent law was an evil, fraudulent legal system that deprived the patent owner of the natural right to obtain his results from intelligence.[181] By investigating the British Industrial Revolution, Mike Lauder finally concluded that 90% of patents came from industries that didn't experience many innovations. The patent system only provided inventors with fragile and unstable protection, and innovators in many fields could not apply for patents. The patent activity was closely related to commercialization and the pursuit of profits; however, the definite relationship between patent and technical progress remained vague.[182] To solve their problems with the patent system, Britain and France established the awarding, compensation, and priority systems for inventions, which actually motivated inventions and creations.[183]

Therefore, the appeal for reformation in the patent system became stronger and stronger. Although some related laws of the patent were issued in 1835–1851, they brought little changes to the original patent system. After the opening of the World Exposition in 1851, Britain issued the *Patent Law Amendment Act 1852*. This Act signaled the beginning of the modern patent law reformation in Britain and achieved great success. However, the reformation was incomplete, and many problems remained. For instance, the draft still considered the patent as a privilege granted by the royal family, and the patent right could not be fully ensured by the state, which made many people disappointed and unconfident with the British patent system. The modification of the French patent system in 1844 failed to substantially solve its existing problems.[184]

Under this technological, economic, and cultural environment, the institutional concept that opposed and even abolished patents gradually emerged among many Western Europeans. Some interest groups who couldn't benefit from the patent system even tried to put the concept into practice via legislation. Some members of the industrial and commercial class, which were under the influence of free trade theory, expected a more liberal environment for investment and even monopoly; therefore, commerce and trade would be expanded, and they would obtain huge wealth by selling goods to the colonies, but this was hindered by the existing patent system. As the potency of the patent law in developed countries failed to expand in their colonies, the producer in capitalist countries was likely to be disadvantaged in competition with colonial companies due to their free rides.[185] The patent system became a barrier for merchants to expand businesses and obtain wealth. Therefore, they lobbied to abolish the patent system. However, others were against abolishing patents, especially factory owners and entrepreneurs who had the advantage of technology. Britain was the most typical example of the class struggle in the industrial and commercial classes. The firmest supporter of the abolitionists in Britain was Robert Andrew McPhee, a sugar processor who was elected to the House of Commons. To defend the commercial benefits of the domestic sugar-making industry, he contended that the businessmen in this industry needed to pay high patent royalties for sugar-making facilities and processes. However, the patent system was not applied in the colonies, so the producers there could use these facilities and processes free of charge. Therefore, the producers in Britain had to endure higher production costs and a disadvantaged position in competition. He brought the bill to abolish the patent into the House and supported and promoted the patent-abolishing movement through his political influence. The reformationists of the patent system were represented by Hindmarch and Webster. They supported the patent system, advocated its reformation, and argued against any attempts to abolish the patent system. The controversy in Britain was more like a conflict between different interest groups with different objectives and finally. Finally, it became controversial concerning whether to abolish the patent system in Britain. That was also the case with the Netherlands. A great number of small and medium-sized enterprises without advantages lobbied and exerted pressure on the government, and they considered the patent as the barrier to industrial development and the economic prosperity of the country.[186]

The anti-patent movement

In Britain, disagreements between the abolitionists and supporters of the patent system were usually seen in various newspapers, magazines, brochures, and meetings. An influential and typical debate took place at the annual meeting of the National Association for the Promotion of Social Science, which was established in 1857. They had heated debates in all fields and at all levels, and their disagreements were centered on three aspects: justice and administration, right attribute and legitimacy in patents, and free trade. Due to the great pressure exerted by the anti-patent public opinion, the British Congress had to instruct a special committee in 1862–1865 and 1869–1872 to investigate the operation of the patent system. In 1871, parliament drafted a reformation act that significantly restricted the private right of patents according to the report of the committee.[187]

In the nineteenth century, Germany was divided into numerous states before the German Empire was founded in January 1871. Some, like Prussia, Austria, and Saxony, had already established the patent system, but some regions along the Rhine River applied the *Patent Act of 1791* of France; therefore, there was no unified patent law for all states. In response to the appeals of the industrial and commercial classes in all states, Germany began to enact a unified patent convention for all states. However, since the mid-nineteenth century, the anti-patent trend began to gain traction in Germany and throughout Europe. Therefore, in 1853 and 1863, some trade associations strongly asked for repealing the unified convention of the patent law. As Adam Smith's liberal economic institution and the free trade theory became the national economics of Germany, some scholars regarded it as a treasure and criticized the patent system on public occasions. For instance, John Prince Smith claimed in the German National Economists Assembly in 1863 that granting a patent was imposing a monopoly by law and hindered industrial and commercial activities. on his advice, the Assembly believed that giving protection to invention patents was harmful to the public interest and suggested canceling it. The Assembly also denied an inventor's right to their result because the invention was the result of civilization and was public property. Official scholars, such as the government's think tank, also strongly opposed the patent system, and they thought the awarding system would be a better substitute for it.[188] The liberal economic thought and the free trade theory had such a great influence on the administrators in Prussia that Rudolf von Delbrück, the Minister of State of Prussia, once restricted the granting of patents very strictly, leading to an enormous decrease in the rate of patent granting. In the 1750s and 1760s, almost 90% of patent applications were rejected.[189] In addition, some went further to suggest canceling patent protection. According to the results of opinion polls operated by chambers of commerce and the government in 1853, only a few people argued for canceling patent protection. However, 10 years later, two-thirds of the people (due to leading questions by the chamber of commerce) were supporters.[190] Otto Eduard Leopold von Bismarck, as the chancellor of the North German Confederation, even proposed a bill in 1868 that asked for examining whether patent protection should be granted in the range of the Confederation in the future and delayed the establishment of the Deutscher Zollverein (German Tariff Alliance).[191] Viktor Böhmert wrote in his *Die Erfindungspatente nach Volkswirtschaftlichen Grundsätzen und Industriellen Erfahrungen* that the patent system was too mature, and it increasingly became a rotten fruit on the tree of human civilization.[192]

In France, Renourd and OlinPicard, the acknowledged authority in patents and copyrights, also suspected the private right system of patents, because the idea of granting the writer and inventor rights within a given term went against the thoughts of property rights. The Frenchman Michel Chevalier may have been the one who opposed the tariff and patent most fiercely. He thought they were based on the same principle but were both abused. He claimed in an open declaration in November 1863 that the patent monopoly system should be replaced by a national awarding system, and he criticized the disadvantages of the patent system at the meeting of economists in 1869. In the same year, Boehmer also mentioned that it would be unnecessary to encourage an inventor by means of the patent system since the inventor had already gained sufficient benefits from free trade.[193] There was also a more radical opinion in France. For example, Sismondi believed the consequence of granting privileges to the inventor was to secure their monopoly in the market. As a result, consumers seldom benefited from the invention, but the inventor gained a lot. What's more, other producers suffered losses, and their workers suffered too. Sismondi hoped that all inventions would be immediately opened and imitated by competitors.[194] Influenced by the anti-patent thoughts, in terms of legislation, the *Patent Act 1791* declared the private rights property of patents, and the 1844 new French patent law avoided any comments on the property of the patent right. The French Supreme Court even declared that IPRs never existed without any reason in 1887.[195]

Although the movement against the patent system started slowly in the Netherlands, it elicited a strong response. Due to heated discussions and powerful lobbies by small and medium-sized enterprises in the Netherlands, many experts considered the patent law as infeasible and failed to find a reformation project that satisfied all parties. Once the patent was abolished, middle and small-sized commercial groups didn't need to pay patent royalties before they manufactured the same products as foreign ones at a low cost. Therefore, at the end of 1869, the government proposed to parliament the draft of abolishing the patent system, which was finally approved by the legislature, and the patent system in the Netherlands was abolished at the end of 1869.[196] In Switzerland, although the traditional patent privilege pattern was maintained, the unified patent law was not enacted across the country because there was no motivation from interest groups. Swiss companies could imitate others' inventions and products freely.[197] In Spain, a great number of invention patents and introduced patents that failed to be operated within a given time limit were abolished in 1849–1878, and 75% of introduced patents lost their monopoly within 3 years.[198]

Results and follow-up developments of the anti-patent movement

After the 1870s, the anti-patent movement finally faded away for several reasons, as follows.

First, after the 1870s, various technologies ushered the capitalist countries of Europe into the Second Industrial Revolution, whose dominant feature was the invention and wide application of electricity. All countries were trying to promote technological innovation and industrial production. The achievements gained by the United States during the Industrial Revolution dispelled the misgivings that the patent system would hinder the development of technology and the economy. In the mid- and late nineteenth century, technology and industry of the United States began to increase rapidly. After the end of the American Civil War in 1865, the Industrial Revolution began to accelerate. In 1870, the United States initiated the Second Industrial Revolution and occupied the leading position in the world. European countries noticed that the patent system was widely applied in the United States, and many inventions associated with the Industrial Revolution in the late nineteenth century were submitted to the patent office (e.g., Thomas Edison applied for over 1,000 patents in the American Patent Office). This dispelled their prior misgivings about the patent system.[199]

Second, in 1873, an economic crisis broke out in European countries, such as Britain, Germany, France, the Netherlands, and Sweden. Europe entered a period of economic depression. Eric Hobsbawm said the depression in the last 25 years of the nineteenth century altered everything; it weakened free trade in industry and agriculture and strengthened trade protectionism.

> Politically, the end of the liberal era meant literally what the words imply … [the Liberals]…were undermined not only by the defeat of their ideology of free trade and cheap (i.e., relatively inactive) government, but by the democratization of electoral politics…which destroyed the illusion that their policy represented the masses.[200]

Moreover, the competition to exploit the colonies for economic interests among countries was also an important reason for the decline of the free trade theory.[201] In essence, the free trade theory was merely an ideal situation at peace, which could not be applied when national benefits conflicted. Based on economic benefits,

Germany, France, Italy, Britain, and other countries approved the acts to increase the tariff to the greatest extent during these years.[202] While the monopoly was strengthened in all countries, the concept against monopoly and patents lost ground and was gradually forgotten. Trade protectionism revived, free trade thought was no longer treasured, and those who ever voiced their opinions about the patent system gradually understood that the patent system, although a monopoly right, was conducive to fostering domestic economic development and maintaining the public interest of the country.[203] For example, the economic crisis in Germany in 1873 led to an economic panic. Bismarck, who insisted on the free trade policy, immediately resorted to tariff protection and industry-supporting policies. Influenced by these policies, the opinion that patent protection was beneficial began to gain traction in Prussia.[204]

Third, ideology. The discussion on the patent system that was caused by the abolitionism movement helped people gain a deeper understanding of the patent system. The defenses for the legitimacy of the patent system facilitated people to accept that the patent system was a legal monopoly right.[205] In addition, after 1870, the economists who led the orientation of public opinions in the patent abolitionism movement seldom discussed problems with the patent system at expert meetings. The controversy of patent abolition disappeared from economic journals. The new generation of economists didn't care about the controversies of the precedents but wrote articles on economic theories and policies for the sake of patent protection. Most of them didn't study the controversies that used to be popular in brochures and magazines. Instead, they regarded the opinion of John Müller, who once argued for the patent system, as the authority and the starting point of their argumentation.[206]

Fourth, efforts of the interest groups and support for the patent system by governments in European countries. The supporters of the patent system, represented by industrial groups like technicians, inventors, and the industrial and commercial classes, took positive action. They proved the legitimacy of the patent system with various theories. In particular, they realized that people respected and admired scientists and inventors, so they treated inventors as the top beneficiaries of patent protection and kept beautifying and apotheosizing them.[207] They wrote books, elected speakers at meetings of professional or commercial groups, distributed a great number of brochures and leaflets, published articles in commercial journals and reprinted them in newspapers, paid awards for the best article that supported the patent system, offered applications to the government and legislatures, organized international conferences, and even reformed the institutional defects identified by the abolitionists, removing the basis of their opinions.[208] They submitted drafted agreements for the conference to the newspaper office and made compromises between organizations to support the patent reformation. For instance, in Britain, the Reformation Party reformed and modified all defects in the British patent system after 1852, according to the critique of abolitionists. In 1854, the most powerful supporter of the British abolitionists, McPhee, failed in his reelection, which symbolized the collapse of the most powerful political power behind the abolitionists. In Germany, in about 1860, many technical invention associations, including the Association of Engineers and the Association of Chemistry and Metallurgy, greatly supported the patent system. At that time, the German industrial and commercial magnate Siemens set up an organization arguing for the patent system in Europe, which was responsible for lobbies in foreign countries. The 1873 Exposition in Vienna, Austria, made the German government realize the importance and urgency of protecting patents. In 1874, the Patent Protection Academy headed by Siemens was established, which advocated the formulation of patent law. The agreement of the conference pointed out that all civilized countries should ensure the legislation could protect inventions, because justice demanded that intelligence labor be protected by law. This association drafted a draft law, which was offered to Bismarck together with the memorandum written by Siemens in 1876. The opening of the conference played a great role in the promotion of the establishment of a unified German patent law, which was finally enacted on 25 May 1877.

In the Netherlands, there were a few controversies about recovering the patent system among the public. Due to the strong request from the industrial group with technical advantages and urging by the Unified International Bureau of International Protection of Intellectual Property Rights, the pressure from other countries that asked the government to recover the patent system increased; therefore, the patent law was finally recovered by the Netherlands' government in 1910. As the only country in Europe that didn't enact a patent law, Switzerland was active in drafting the *Paris Convention* and signed it in 1883. The Swiss government worried that the lack of legislation on patents would make it lose the chance to speak in international politics or economics, and some domestic industrial groups also exerted pressure on the government. In July 1887, the Swiss *Patent Law* was issued; however, it was called the most incomplete and simple among modern patent laws. It only aimed at inventions in the form of machines, because the emerging Swiss chemical industry and the government thought it more beneficial to imitate Germany, its more advanced competitor in chemistry. However, the external pressure from critical interest groups, especially trade revenge and the threat from the German and American governments, forced the Swiss government to further modify the patent law in 1907 to protect the IPRs in the chemistry industry and expand its range of protection to the chemical production process (except product inventions, which was involved in legislation after the mid-twentieth century).[209]

Enlightenment of the history

The transition history of the patent system in the Industrial Age could offer some enlightenment as follows.

First, during different historical stages and countries, the technical, economic, and cultural differences contributed to the formation of different institutional concepts. This was the root cause of the gap in the concepts of private rights of patents in France and America. However, the establishment of the private rights system of patents in these two countries was attributed to the game and the compromise of benefits. In France, although the French Revolution caused the patent privilege system to be abolished, the new government intended to develop an industrial and commercial economy, and the emerging industrial and commercial capitalists hoped to monopolize technology and improve production. The shared benefits of the two sides helped the patent system revive under the new guise of private rights. In the United States, at the end of the eighteenth century, the industrial and commercial class was weak. Jefferson, on behalf of the peasant class, advocated the development of agriculture, proposed republicanism thought, called for the restriction of the patent monopoly, and exerted his political influence on the formation of the early patent system in America. In the early nineteenth century, the industrial and commercial classes grew stronger. The new government hoped to develop an industrial and commercial economy, and the capitalists pursued exclusive technical benefits. These two factors led to the enactment of the Patent Act of *1836*. In this process, concrete institutional designs, such as the natural right theory, inventor orientation, and registration system, were merely tools used to justify and actualize these benefits.

Second, Western Europe receded to the low ebb of the First Industrial Revolution after the 1830s. Technical innovation began to slow down, commerce and trade played a more significant role in economic development than technology, and the free trade economy became the focus of economic development in all countries. In this economic situation, free trade theory started to gain traction. Patent protectionism was associated with tariff protectionism; the defects of the patent system became apparent, and constant critiques and comments appeared about the patent system. Against such technological, economic, and cultural backgrounds, the institutional concept of opposing and even abolishing the patent system emerged in Western European countries. Some interest groups even attempted to put the institutional concept into practice. For example, the patent system in the Netherlands was abolished. However, at the end of the nineteenth century, several factors catalyzed the end of the anti-patent movement, including the Second Industrial Revolution and the rise of trade protectionism in the context of the economic crisis. People's deeper understanding of the patent system from the perspective of ideology in the abolition movement and economists' lost interest in critiquing the patent system, the efforts of interest groups, and governmental support for the patent system.

Third, the establishment of the patent system by the new governments in France and America initially aimed at developing industrial and commercial economies, and the patent system was designed to protect the public interest rather than the so-called rights of inventors. In France, the natural right was seen as the mask, and in the United States, it was gradually clarified in the constant struggles of the industrial and commercial classes. Considering people's respect and admiration for inventors, this class prioritized the inventors in the patent system and kept apotheosizing them. Because of the industrial and commercial classes' lobbies and efforts, the private rights system of patents in France and the United States was an inventors-centered system. However, in essence, many inventors were hired by the industrial and commercial classes, or they had to sell the patents to the latter for a slender income. Therefore, the industrial and commercial classes were ultimately the beneficiaries, and the protection of inventors was merely their excuse. If the inventors couldn't obtain the fruits of their work, the patent system could hardly achieve the motivation for inventions. The separation and possible conflict between benefits produced the result – the patent law apparently encouraged inventions and creations, but essentially stimulated investors.

Fourth, the patent law was the policy tool in the government's hand to control economic and technical development. Whether and how to protect the patent right was associated with the choice and arrangements made by the government after the development status and future development requirements were taken into consideration. This was featured as follows. 1. The French and American governments aimed at encouraging industrial and commercial development at the outset. 2. One of the reasons for the anti-patent movement in Western Europe in the mid-nineteenth century was the slowdown in technical innovation. The economic growth mainly depended on commercial expansion and free trade, and the government restricted patents for the sake of a free economy and trade growth. As a result, patent protection became weaker. Considering the economic structure of some industries, such as the railway, highway transportation, electricity, natural gas, and communications, the government regulated them to serve valuable social purposes. The industries involved in the patent system were essentially the same as these industries.

Fifth, it was a problem worth discussing whether the patent could encourage technological innovation and economic growth. On the one hand, the rapid development of industries in Britain and the United States and the existence of patent systems in these countries were considered by some interest groups as the sufficient condition for the causality between the patent and progress. Roger criticized all attempts at this historical evidence because of "false causality." As history revealed, the patent system played a limited role in the industrial revolutions in France and Britain and even had negative effects. Many times, the function of the patent system was exaggerated and justified by the interest groups, and its influence on technology and the economy had never been subject to rigorous argumentation. On the other hand, some German and Swiss economists attributed industrial progress in their countries to the lack of a patent system. Other scholars argued that patents might foster technological innovation during the early stages of industrial development, but patents became obstacles to technological innovation when industry reached an advanced level. In fact, in the late nineteenth century, although the patent system no longer existed in the Netherlands and Switzerland, the speed of technical progress almost remained intact.[210] As Eric Schiff pointed out, in a country like the Netherlands, without the patent system ... the whole progress in the industrial field would not be much different from today.[211]

Patent, whether it's named "privilege" or "private right," was not an inherent natural right of the inventor. Instead, a patent was an artificial construction and a monopoly on technology. That was also the reason why patents were always controversial. Western Europe and the United States used to suspect the function of the patent system, which indicated that the unfavorable effects of the patent monopoly on technical and economic development were never local. Moreover, the history of Venice, Britain, and France all demonstrated that the patent system was never the only mechanism to motivate technological innovation, and governmental awards, subsidies and compensations, and the priority system were all contributors to invention and creation in history.

Sixth, in the abolition movement in Western Europe, the economists' theories influenced people's opinions about the patent system. When faced with the complexity and mystery of the patent system and the complicated relationship among technology, patents, and the economy, people hoped to gain insights from the economists' comments and analyses. As was seen in the patent crisis of Western Europe, the discussions about the legitimacy and problems of the patent system by all related subjects in a country, including jurists, judges, economists, the industrial and commercial classes, inventors, and lawyers, could help dissolve the crisis in the patent system and promote its reform.

Notes

1 David S. Landes. The Unbound Prometheus. Xie Huaizhu. Beijing: Huaxia Publishing House, 2007:1.
2 Thomas Kuhn. *The Structure of Scientific Revolutions*. Jin Wulun, et al. Beijing: Peking University Press, 2012:47.
3 Han Ruibo. The Zero Marginal Cost Society in the Perspective of Generalized Political Theory-Another Review of the Zero Marginal Cost Society-A New Economic Era of Internet of Things and Win-Win Cooperation. *Journal of Sichuan Administrative College*, 2015 (3).
4 P. J. Federico. State Patents, 13 *Journal of the Patent and Trademark Office Society*, 1931, p. 166.
5 Xie Xiaoyao, Wu Chumin. The Paradigm of Transformation: Rethinking Intellectual Property Theory. *Intellectual Property Rights*, 2016 (7).
6 Xie Xiaoyao, Wu Chumin. Paradigm of Transformation.
7 N. R. Lamoreaux, K. L. Sokoloff. Long-term Change in the Organization of Inventive Activity. *Proceedings of the National Academy of Sciences*, 1996:12686–12692.
8 Lewis Mumford. *Technics and Civilization*. Chen Yunming, et al. Beijing: China Construction Industry Press, 2009:26.
9 Joel Mokyr. *The Gift of Athena: Historical Origins of the Knowledge Economy*. Duan, Yibing, Tang Le. Beijing: Science Beijing: Science Publishing House, 2011:108.
10 In addition, Laplace applied Newton's gravity doctrine in the research of the solar system in 1773 and discovered the acceleration of the moon and the eccentricity ratio of the Earth's orbit. In the late eighteenth century, mathematician Monge published *Descriptive Geometry* and *Application de L'analyse à la Géométrie,* establishing the algebra method of three-dimension geometry, revolutionizing the field of engineering designs. In the eighteenth century, naturalist Buffon wrote *Histoire Naturelle, Générale et Particulière*, which divided the history of geology and first proposed the theory that the planet was created by the collision between the sun and comets. In 1778, the famous evolutionist in France published the three-volume *Flore Françoise, ou, Description Succincte de Toutes les Plantes qui Croissent Naturellement en France*. Zhang Zeqian. *History of French Civilization*. Wuhan: Wuhan University Press, 1997:377–381.
11 Zhang Zeqian. *History of French Civilization*, 390.

12 In the eighteenth century, feudal despotism was increasingly corrupt: the royal court and aristocrats wallowed in luxurious lifestyles, frequent external wars wasted vast wealth, excessive taxes and levies on people decreased their purchasing abilities and hindered the expansion of the internal market, all of which seriously impeded the development of the productivity. Wang Zhanghui. A Comparison of the British and French Industrial Revolutions. *Studies in Historical Theory*, 1994 (2).
13 Wu Chunwu. *The Social and Economic History of France*. Beijing: The Commercial Press, 1937:46.
14 Wu Chunwu. *Social and Economic History of France*, 47.
15 Wu Chunwu. *Social and Economic History of France*, 47–50.
16 Lou Junxin. *The Industrial Modernization of France. Journal of Hangzhou University* (Philosophy and Social Sciences), 1991 (3).
17 Philippe Pinchemel. *La France*. Qi Zhusheng. Shanghai: Shanghai Translation Press, 1980:144.
18 But until the end of the British Industrial Revolution (in the mid-nineteenth century), Britain surpassed France in all main industrial sectors and transportation. In 1820, Britain's proportion of the world's industrial production was 50%, and France occupied only 15%–20%. In 1860, Britain fell to 36% and France to 6%. Wang Zhanghui. Comparison of the British and French Industrial Revolutions.
19 Wang Zhanghui. Comparison of the British and French Industrial Revolutions.
20 Mumford. *Technics and Civilization*, 321.
21 Wu Chunwu. *Social and Economic History of France*, 47, 50.
22 Chen Yan. *Ideological Enlightenment and Political Change: The Bicentennial of the French Revolution. French Studies*, 1989 (4).
23 Marquis de Condorcet. *Esquisse d'un tableau historique des progrès de l'esprit humain*. He Zhaowu. Nanjing: Jiangsu Education Press, 2006:45.
24 J. A. Hammerton. Outline of Great Books*: The Historical Part*. He Ning. Beijing: The Commercial Press, 1963:394.
25 In 1751, Diderot and D'Alembert organized a group of avantgardes who were dedicated to improving rationalism, nature theism, new science, belief liberty, and humanism, to write the French encyclopedia. Voltaire, Rousseau, Holbach, Rametli, Lavoisier, Condorcet, and others also participated in writing the work.
26 Zhang Zeqian. *History of French Civilization*, 384–389.
27 Roger Chartier. *Les Origines culturelles de la Révolution française*. Hong Qingming. Nanjing: Yilin Publishing House, 2015:43.
28 Chartier. *Les Origines culturelles de la Révolution française*, 45.
29 Chartier. *Les Origines culturelles de la Révolution française*, 50.
30 Chartier. *Les Origines culturelles de la Révolution française*, 50.
31 Tetsuo Tomita. *Intellectual Property Rights in Market Competition*. Liao Zhengheng, et al. Beijing: The Commercial Press, 2000:69.
32 Chartier. *Les Origines culturelles de la Révolution française*, 53.
33 Frank D. Prager. A History of Intellectual Property from 1545 to 1787, 26 *Journal of the Patent and Trademark Office Society*, 1944, p. 715.
34 Prager. History of Intellectual Property, p. 716.
35 Li Zonghui. *The Intellectual Property System in Historical Perspective*. Beijing: Intellectual Property Press, 2015:120.
36 Wu Chunwu. *Social and Economic History of France*, 56–57.
37 Wu Chunwu. *Social and Economic History of France*, 56–57.
38 Zhang Zeqian. *History of French Civilization*, 439–440.

39 François de Nafchado believes that one of the purposes of the French Revolution was to promote the mechanical arts, which was sadly neglected by the researchers of the old institution. He points out:

> The crafts neglected by the old institution are called mechanic crafts, and these crafts, which are abandoned and taken for granted for a long time, deserve to be further researched and completely developed .... Diderot hopes these crafts can have their own institutes, while the despotic government doesn't understand him! It only considers these crafts as the slave of luxury rather than the tool to bring welfare to society... These arts, which seem to be the most simple, most ordinary, will be splendid in the light of science, and mathematics, physic, chemistry, and practical design of craft arts should guide their method, improve the machine, simplify the form, increase the efficiency, and save the labor force.
>
> (Partice Higonnet, 2013)

Patrice Higonnet. *The Paris Myth: From the Enlightenment to Surrealism.* La Weiguo. Beijing: The Commercial Press, 2013:137.

40 Julia von Douthwaite. *The Frankenstein of 1790 and Other Lost Chapters from Revolutionary France.* Chicago, IL: The University of Chicago Press, 2012:267

41 Perovic. Frankenstein of 1790 and Other Lost Chapters, pp. 1612–1613.

42 Gabriel Galvez-Behar. Was the French Patent System Democratic? France, 19th Century, Working Papers France: HAL, 2008:234.

43 Galvez-Behar. Was the French Patent System Democratic, 234.

44 Ulf Anderfelt, *International Patent-legislation and Developing Countries.* Germany: Springer Science & Business Media, 2013:167.

45 Fritz Machlup, Edith Penrose. The Patent Controversy in the Nineteenth Century, 10 *The Journal of Economic History*, 1950, pp. 1–29.

46 Galvez-Behar. Was the French Patent System Democratic?, 237.

47 Machlup, Penrose. Patent Controversy in the Nineteenth Century, pp. 16–17.

48 Ulf Anderfelt, *International Patent-Legislation and Developing Countries*, The Hague: Martinus Nijhoff, 1971:16.

49 Rudolf Krasser. *German Patent and Utility Model Law, European and International Patent Law*, Zhang Taolve, et al. Beijing: Intellectual Property Press, 2016:251.

50 Anderfelt, *International Patent-Legislation and Developing Countries*, 145.

51 Galvez-Behar. Was the French Patent System Democratic?, 138.

52 Galvez-Bchar. Was the French Patent System Democratic?, 139.

53 Julia V. Douthwaite. *The Frankenstein of 1790 and Other Lost Chapters from Revolutionary France.* Chicago, IL: University of Chicago Press, 2012:267.

54 The *Patent Act 1791* also regulated that the applicant could request protection for 5, 10, and 15 years according to the level of the fee paid. This law demanded that the invention should have an operation limit of 2 years.

55 S. P. Ladas. *The International Protection of Industrial Property*, Cambridge: Harvard University Press, 1930:231–232.

56 Including problems like high application fees, excessive lawsuit procedures, distrust of foreign inventions, and lack of systems to encourage the opening of inventions.

57 B. Zorina Khan. *The Democratization of Invention: Patents and Copyright in American Development, 1790–1920*, Cambridge: Cambridge University Press, 2005:41–48.

58 Prager, *History of Intellectual Property*, p. 711.

59 Anderfelt, *International Patent-Legislation and Developing Countries*, 267.

60 Christine MacLeod. The 1690s Patents Boom: Invention or Stock-Jobbing? 39 *The Economic History Review*, 1986, pp. 549–571.

61 Huang Haifeng. *The Discourse and Reality of Intellectual Property Rights-A History of Copyright, Patent and Trademark*. Wuhan: Huazhong University of Science and Technology Press, 2011:136–137. Zhang Xinfeng. *The Property Right Attributes of Patent Rights-A Study on the Path of Privatization of Technology*. Wuhan: Huazhong University of Science and Technology Press, 2011:142.

62 Especially in the "Robert Mansell case," which happened shortly after the issue of the *Statute of Monopolies 1624*, the Council clearly declared: If patents granted by reasonable causes are examined by common courts, it will lead to excessive interference to the power of the monarch; therefore, it ordered to terminate all trials about the patent controversies in common courts. Edward C. Walterscheid. The Early Evolution of the United States Patent Law: Antecedents (Part 2), *Journal of the Patent and Trademark Office Society*, 1994, 78, p. 850.

63 In this case, Baker requested the Council to repeal a patent for a fever powder granted by British King James I, and the Council rejected this request. However, Baker believed a piece of proof offered by James I to the Council was faked, so he prosecuted James I in the common court for forgery and demanded the Council appear in the court to provide related materials. The law official thought, in this case, that the Council could follow no related precedent and had no reason to reject it; however, Baker was not entitled to ask the Council to disclose related materials. After trade-offs, the Council decided to give up the jurisdiction of patent controversies based on the constitution at that time. E.W. Hulme. Privy Council Law and Practice of Letters Patent for Invention From the Restoration to 1794 II, *Law Quarterly Review*, 1917, pp. 33–63.

64 In 1611, an applicant named Simon Sturtevant proposed actively to expose his application. His reasons included. 1. to prove his invention was not obtained by stealing. 2. His invention would not prevent other's inventions. 3. No one ever applied to the king for the same patent. 4. He would be restricted by the regulated content of the patent authorization in the future. (Ramon A. Klitzke. Historical Background of the English Patent Law, *Journal of the Patent Office Society*, September, 1959, p. 64.) Other scholars believed that the first existing patent application in the world was the patent applied by Rasburn and Boggis in 1617 "Engraving and Printing Maps, Plans." This five-page patent explanation introduced the protection range of the patent and clarified the operation project. Zhang Xinfeng. *Property Right Attributes of Patent Rights*, 145.

65 Since 1734, all patents had to apply the explanation; otherwise, the patent was likely to be judged as ineffective. The explanation became a kind of regulated behavior. Certainly, the function of the patent explanation was merely to facilitate the judge to explain the patent technology. Until the mid-eighteenth century, its function began to be similar to today's claims, which could be used to define the range of the protection of rights. In 1711, the applicant, John Nasmith, was worried that his invention would be publicly exposed before the authorization, so he took the initiative to request to offer a detailed explanation within some time after the authorization. His proposal and suggestion were accepted by the officials and gradually became a common procedure for patent authorization. Christine MacLeod. *Inventing the Industrial Revolution: The English Patent System 1660–1800*. Cambridge: Cambridge University Press, 2002:49.

66 In "Liardet v. Johnson," Judge Mansfield considered the patent explanation one of the necessary elements of the application of patents, and he made concrete and detailed demands on the publication of the patent explanation. It should be able to instruct other workers of the same industry to make the same production or manufacture. After that,

the patent explanation was an initiative request of the inventor and an obligation of the patent applicant. Boulton & Wattv. Bull, 1 carp. p.c.117, 126, 126 Eng. Rep. 651, 654 (C.p1795).

67 Huang Haifeng. *Discourse and Reality of Intellectual Property Rights*, 138.
68 John N. Adams, Gwen Averley. The Patent Specification the Role of Liardetv Johnson, 7 *The Journal of Legal History*, 1986, p. 161.
69 Yang Lihua. *A Study of the History of U.S. Patent Law*. Beijing: People's University of China Press, 2009:55.
70 Zhang Xinfeng. *The Property Right Attributes of Patents: A Study of the Path of Privatization of Technology*. Wuhan: Huazhong University of Science and Technology Press, 2011:176.
71 Zhang Xinfeng. *Property Right Attributes of Patents*, 148–149.
72 Adam Mossoff. Rethinking the Development of Patents: An Intellectual History, 1550–1800, 52 *Hastings Law Journal*, 2000, p. 1258.
73 Mossoff. Rethinking the Development of Patents, p. 1286.
74 Hulme. Privy Council Law and Practice of Letters, p. 194.
75 Hulme. Privy Council Law and Practice of Letters, pp. 72–73.
76 Hulme. Privy Council Law and Practice of Letters, pp. 191–193.
77 D. Seaborne Davies. Early History of the Patent Specification (pt. 1), 50 *Law Quarterly Review*, 1934, p. 103.
78 Davies. Early History of the Patent Specification, p. 22.
79 W. M. Hindmarch. *A Treatise on the Law Relative to Patent Privileges for the Sole Use of Inventions: And the Practice of Obtaining Letters Patents for Inventions*. London: Stevens & Norton & Benning, 1846:431.
80 Oren Bracha. The Commodification of Patents 1600–1836: How Patents Became Rights and Why We Should Care, 38 *Loyola of Los Angeles Law Review*, 2004, p. 177.
81 MacLeod. *Inventing the Industrial Revolution*, 198.
82 Adam Mossoff. Who Cares What Thomas Jefferson Thought about Patents? Reevaluating the Patent 'Privilege' in Historical Context, *Cornell Law Review*, 2006, p. 76.
83 MacLeod. *Inventing the Industrial Revolution*, 199.
84 MacLeod. *Inventing the Industrial* Revolution, 1256–1257.
85 Harold Irvin Dutton. *The Patent System and Inventive Activity During the Industrial Revolution*, 1750–1852. Dover, NH: Manchester University Press, 1984:18–21.
86 MacLeod. *Inventing the Industrial Revolution*, 199.
87 MacLeod. *Inventing the Industrial Revolution*, 196–199.
88 Bracha. Commodification of Patents, 177.
89 Edward C. Walterscheid. *The Nature of the Intellectual Property Clause: A Study in Historical Perspective*. New York: William S. Hein & Co., Inc., 2002:92.
90 Walterscheid. *Nature of the Intellectual Property Clause*, 92.
91 Richard Godson. *A Practical Treatise on the Law of Patents for Inventions and of Copyright*. London: Joseph Butterworth & Son, 1823:47.
92 Hindmarch. *Treatise on the Law Relative to Patent*, 431.
93 Thomas Green Fessenden. *An Essay on the Law of Patents for New Inventions*. Boston, MA: C. Ewer, 1822:64–65.
94 Wang Changya. *Fundamentals of Patent Science*. Wuhan: Hubei Science and Technology Press, 1985:5.
95 Jeremy Atack, Peter Passell. *A New Economic View of American History: From Colonial Times to 1940*. Luo Tao, et al. Beijing: China Social Science Press, 2000:42.
96 The governmental award was the most common motivation method in the colonies to promote large-scale production; the special award was mainly used to encourage

research of technology, which was shown in the form of cash awards offered by individuals, organizations, or the colonial government. Sometimes, the government proposed to provide some financial support to those that developed new industries; sometimes, it would impose some products by law. Bracha. Commodification of Patents, 177.

97 Li Jianming et al. *A General History of the United States: Volume 1*. Beijing: People's Publishing House, 2001:254.

98 Bracha. Commodification of Patents, 177.

99 Edward C. Walterscheid. To Promote the Progress of Science and Useful Arts: The Background and Origin of the Intellectual Property Clause of the United States Constitution, *Journal of Intellictual Property Law*, 1994, p. 1.

100 Tomita. *Intellectual Property Rights*, 269.

101 Li Jianming et al. *General History of the United States: Volume 1*, 254, 376.

102 Liu Xuyi, Yang Shengmao, Zhang Youlun, et al. *A General History of the United States: Volume 2: Independence and Initial Prosperity of the United States (1775–1860)*. Beijing: People's Publishing House, 2002:373.

103 Liu Xuyi, Yang Shengmao, Zhang Youlun, et al. *General History of the United States: Volume 2*, 373.

104 Liu Xuyi, Yang Shengmao, Zhang Youlun, et al. *General History of the United States: Volume 2*, 373.

105 Ralph de Bedts. *Recent American History, Vol. 1: 1933 Through World War II*. Department of History, Nanjing University, Department of British and American Foreign Relations, translation. Beijing: People's Publishing House, 1984:456.

106 De Bedts. *Recent American History, Vol. 1*, 53.

107 De Bedts. *Recent American History, Vol. 1*, 54.

108 De Bedts. *Recent American History, Vol. 1*, 54.

109 De Bedts. *Recent American History, Vol. 1*, 54.

110 Merrill D. Peterson. *Thomas Jefferson: Writings*. Liu Jochang, et al. Beijing: SDX Joint Publishing Company, 1993:311.

111 Peterson. *Thomas Jefferson*, 311–312.

112 He used to passionately say:

> I only wish to live in a homely farmhouse with my families, my books and some old friends. We will enjoy the morning and evening, eat simple foods, and forget the glories and shame in the world, instead of mastering great power as a dignitary.

113 Gui Yang. An Analysis of the Transformation of Jefferson's Economic Thought and its Continuity, *Journal of Suzhou Institute of Science and Technology* (Social Sciences), 2009 (3).

114 Liu Zuochang. *Jefferson's Biography*. Beijing: China Social Science Press, 1990:327.

115 Peterson. *Thomas Jefferson*, 343.

116 Edward C. Walterscheid. The Nature of the Intellectual Property Clause: A Study in Historical Perspective (Part 1), 83 *Journal of the Patent and Trademark Office Society*, 2001, p. 763.

117 Prager. History of Intellectual Property, p. 93.

118 *United States v. Ewell*, 383 U. S. 116 (1966).

119 It remains controversial why Madison absorbed this term into the Constitution in the Constitutional Convention because no evidence could indicate that the Constitution suggested that drafts of representatives from states included the pursuit of adding the intellectual right term at the beginning. Related documental records indicated that Madison and Charles Pinckney, the representative of South Carolina, commonly

proposed the bill that finally became the intellectual right term. Madison made no further explanation of this term in his notes, only to claim that this term was unanimously approved without any controversy. At present, there are several explanations for that. 1. The patent privilege pattern was chronically used in some colonial regions, which had path dependency on it. 2. At the beginning of the construction, the economy and finances of the United States were limited. The patent privilege pattern had a lower cost than awards or subventions to encourage the development of industry and commerce; and 3. During the Convention, John Fitch spent an afternoon exhibiting his newest invention, the steamboat, to representatives of states on the Delaware River, which created a perfect atmosphere for patent protection. Walterscheid. *Nature of the Intellectual Property Clause*, p. 763.

120 Siva Vaidyanathan. *Copyrights and Copywrongs: The Rise of Intellectual Property and How it Threatens Creativity*. New York: NYU Press, 2001:23–24.
121 Mossoff. Who Cares What Thomas Jefferson, p. 953.
122 Mossoff. Who Cares What Thomas Jefferson, p. 953.
123 Walterscheid. Nature of the Intellectual Property Clause: pp. 115–116, 763.
124 Walterscheid. Nature of the Intellectual Property Clause, p. 117.
125 *Grant v. Raymond*, 31 U.S. (6 Peters) 218, 241 (1832).
126 Edward C. Walterscheid. Patents and the Jeffersonian Mythology, *John Marshall Law Review*, 1995, p. 269.
127 Bracha. Commodification of Patents, 177.
128 Walterscheid. Patents and the Jeffersonian Mythology, *John Marshall Law Review*, 1995, p. 269.
129 Yang Lihua. *Study of the History of U.S. Patent Law*, 69.
130 Prager. History of Intellectual Property, pp. 711–758.
131 William Thornton. *Short Account of the Origin of Steam Boats*. Washington, DC: Rapine and Eliot, 1983:1314.
132 Thornton. *Short Account of the Origin of Steam Boats*, 1983.
133 Thornton. *Short Account of the Origin of Steam Boats*, 1983.
134 Yang Lihua. *Study of the History of U.S. Patent Law*, 75.
135 Prager. History of Intellectual Property, p. 711.
136 Annals of Congress 855 (1793).
137 William Thornton. Patents (1811), reprinted in 6 *Journal of the Patent and Trademark Office Society* 1923, p. 98.
138 W. I. Wyman. The Patent Act of 1836, *Journal of the Patent and Trademark Office Society*, 1918, p. 203.
139 William Callyhan Robinson. *The Law of Patents for Useful Inventions*. Vol. 2. Boston: Little, Brown, and Co. 1890:137.
140 *McGaw v. Bryan*, 16F. Cas. 96, 99 (s. d. n. y. 1821).
141 Mossoff. Who Cares What Thomas Jefferson, p. 953.
142 *Evans v. Eaton*, 16 U.S. (3 Wheat.) 454, 488 (1818).
143 In 1802, Nathaniel Bowditch, a mathematician in Massachusetts, published the *American Practical Navigator* and translated Laplace's *Traité de Mecanique Céleste* after a few years; In 1815, Constantine Rafinesque published the first part of his great work in botany in Philadelphia. Joseph Henry achieved new progress on electric currents after Franklin and discovered the principle of the self-conduction of electromagnetism. William Maclure, the father of American geology, completed the geological construction map of East America in 1817. Mossi Konrad published the *Tertiary Fossiliferous Stratum in North America* in 1832.

144 The National Science Academy and Columbia Science Improving Institute, established in the capital, Washington D.C., in 1816, and the later National Science Research Organization all played an important role in improving scientific research. The most distinguished were the American Science Promotion Association and the Smithson Institute. In fact, popular science speeches also became popular in the United States. In the beginning, some foreign visitors made these speeches; the famous Italian Signore Folkeni made speeches about natural philosophy and some experimental performances in New York and other cities. Then, some American scholars began to make frequent popular speeches, such as John Griscom, John Gorham, Benjamin Waterhouse, and others. Some universities and academic research centers, like Jeru gave great support to popular science speeches. The American Science Promotion Association also held a series of popular science speeches. At this time, someone set up technical night schools in some big cities; for instance, William Eliot set up a math night school in Washington D.C., in 1820, which taught algebra, geometry, and their applications in measurement, navigation, and astrology. Charles A. Beard, Mary R. Beard. *The Rise of American Civilization: Part I*. Xu Yafen, et al. Beijing: Commercial Press, 2010:354–356.

145 De Bedts. *Recent American History, Vol. 1*, 501.

146 In the Napoleonic Wars, the neutral trade of the United States suffered critical attacks from Britain and France, and the lives of people were rather painful. To protect the benefit of the United States as a neutral country, the Jefferson government issued the *Law of Embargo* in 1807. During the embargo, "the objective situation forces us (referring to the productors) to apply some of our organized capital and labor into domestic manufacturing industries and improvements" to solve the supply of daily necessities; At the same time, the decline of the shipping industry meant that a large amount of capital was applied in the manufacturing industry, which began to prosper as an emerging industry.

147 At the end of the eighteenth century, a new era of transportation was opened in the United States, where highways, canals, and railways were being built. After 1830, the situation became apparent: the railway became the major method of transporting goods. In 1830, 3,328 mi (approximately 5,355.9 km) of railways were laid by the state, approximately equal to the length of the canals that were dug up. As the average speed reached 10 mi/h (approximately 16.1 km/h), the railway was much faster than wagons, water transport, and steamboats. Distinct from water transport, the railway functioned in all seasons in a year. The revolution of transportation greatly decreased the cost of carrying goods to market and stimulated the development of agriculture and industry. Paved highways, canals, and railways accelerated commercial development and improved the relations between the East and West. At the same time, the speed of transmissions became faster. In 1790, there were 92 newspapers in the United States, and the annual circulation was less than 4 million; by 1820, the number of newspapers published increased to 512 with an annual circulation of 50 million. James Kirby Martin, Randy Roberts, et al. *American and Its Peoples: A Mosaic in the Making,* Volume I. Fan Daofeng, et al. Beijing: Commercial Beijing: The Commercial Press, 2012:351.

148 In 1820–1830, the development of American cities was rather rapid. The urban population increased by 60% every decade, and its increasing speed was five times the national population. In 1810, the population of New York was less than 100,000, and it surpassed 200,000 after 20 years. The development of Western cities was especially rapid. Martin, Roberts, et al. *American and Its Peoples*, 351.

149 In 1809–1815, the cotton weaving industry in the United States entered a time of rapid development. By the end of 1815, there were 170 weaving factories and 134,214 spindles in the country. The number of weaving factories reached 801 in 1831, 1,240 in 1840, and in 1835. The production value of the cotton weaving industry reached 4.7 million dollars. The cloth industry developed into an annual production value of 73,219,765 dollars. The annual production value of the rubber industries reached 3,039,735 dollars. The production of cast iron in the steel industry in 1830 reached 165,000 t. Liu Xuyi, Yang Shengmao, Zhang Youlun, et al. *General History of the United States: Volume*, 196–202.

150 Liu Senlin. *In Search of the Subject*. Beijing: Social Science Literature Press, 2008:58.

151 Bentham believes "Individual interest is the only real interest" and "The happiness or security of the individual that constitutes the community is the objective that the legislator should remember, and is the only objective." He emphasizes that the fundamental basis of morality is the maximization of happiness. (Jeremy Bentham. An Introduction to the Principles of Morality and Legislation. In: Shi Yinhong. Beijing: The Commercial Press, 2000:81). Spencer proposes the evolution theory that the community appears in the form of organics or quasi-organics; the process of social development is the history of getting rid of primitives and stepping from anarchic individualism to the complete community, in which the legislation will be almighty and all-including. He is also "an anarchic individualist" or "administrative nihilist." Fu Zheng. Spencer's "Social Organism" Theory and Statism in the Qing Dynasty: Centering on Zhang Taiyan and Yan Fu. *Studies in Modern History*, 2017 (2).

152 Alexis De Tocqueville. *Democracy in America*. Translated by G. Lawrence. New York: Anchor Book, 1969:250.

153 William E. Nelson. *Americanization of the Common Law: The Impact of Legal Change on Massachusetts Society, 1760–1830*. Cambridge, MA: Harvard University Press, 1975:122–143.

154 Li Xiaofen. The Historical Evolution of American Individualism before the 20th Century, *Journal of Xiamen University* (Philosophy and Social Sciences), 2003 (5), p. 127.

155 Morton J. Horwitz. *The Transformation of American Law, 1780–1860*. Xie Hongfei. Beijing: China University of Political Science and Law Publishing Beijing: China University of Political Science and Law Press, 2005:40–42.

156 Bernard Schwartz. *The Law in America: A History*. Beijing: China University of Political Science and Law Press, 1990:23.

157 Schwartz. *Law in America*, 98.

158 Walterscheid. Nature of the Intellectual Property Clause, p. 763.

159 Walterscheid. Nature of the Intellectual Property Clause, p. 763.

160 Especially in the steamboat case in 1790, many inventors, including Fitch, applied for the steamboat patent and conflicts emerged. At this time, Jefferson was worried that granting the steamboat patent to one person would lead to a monopoly; therefore, he granted patent rights to all four applicants without priority, making them continue the competition in the court. Fitch was extremely disappointed and annoyed, because the patent range he applied was the largest, but its value couldn't be shown because of the failure to monopolize the market of steamboats. In addition, Fitch requested the government to subsidize his invention activities, but the American government granted him no assistance. Christine MacLeod. The Paradoxes of Patenting: Invention and Its Diffusion in 18th- and 19th-Century Britain, France, and North America, 32 *Technology and Culture*, 1991, pp. 885–910.

161 Joseph Barnes. Treatise on the Justice, Policy, and Utility of Establishing an Effectual System for Promoting the Progress of Useful Arts, by Assuring Property in the Products of Genius (Phils, 1792).
162 Annals of Congress (1793), available at https://memory.loc.gov/ammem/amlaw/lwaclink.html#anchor2.
163 Yang Lihua. *Study of the History of U.S. Patent Law*, 280.
164 Mossoff. Who Cares What Thomas Jefferson, p. 953.
165 *Bedford v. Hunt*, 3F. Cas.37 (C.C.D.Mass.1817).
166 Bracha. Commodification of Patents, 177.
167 De Bedts. *Recent American History, Vol. 1*, 502.
168 Yang Lihua. *Study of the History of U.S. Patent Law*, 282.
169 At that time, many inventors and rights owners were dissatisfied with the patent application system because many used facilities lacking novelty to apply for a patent and made speculations like lawsuit threatening and racketeering; the quality of patents and the reputation of the patent system were damaged.
170 Richard Hofstadter. *The American Political Tradition: And the Men Who Made It*. New York: Vintage, 2011:214.
171 Joel Mokyr. *The Lever of Riches*. Chen Xiaobai. Beijing: Huaxia Publishing House, 2008:88–89.; Brad Sherman, Lionel Bently. *The Making of Modern Intellectual Property Law: The British Experience, 1760–1911*. Jin Haijun, Beijing: Beijing University Press, 2006.
172 Christopher Freeman, Francisco Louçã. *As Time Goes By: From the Industrial Revolutions to the Information Revolution*. Shen Hongliang, et al. Beijing: People's University of China Press, 2007:225.
173 Gao Debu. *The Industrial Revolution and Industrialization in Britain: Institutional Change and Labor Migration*. Beijing: Renmin University of China Press, 2006:191.
174 Tomita. *Intellectual Property Rights*, 280.
175 Adam Smith considered the monopoly inefficient and easy to lead to corruption. Therefore, he opposed the monopoly of the East India Company at that time.
176 Li Zonghui. *Intellectual Property System*, 118.
177 Susan Sell, Christopher May. Moments in Law: Contestation and Settlement in the History of Intellectual Property, 8 *Review of International Political Economy*, 2001, pp. 467–500.
178 Brad Sherman, Lionel Bently. *Making of Modern Intellectual Property Law*, 122.
179 John Kay (inventor of the flying shuttle), engineer Jonathan Hornblower, and Charles Goodyear (inventor of vulcanization) were among the inventors destroyed by the patent legislation. Avery Whitney fought a patent campaign on the cotton gin, which ended up in arrest and poverty. Afterward, he claimed that the loss from the cotton gin was more than the benefits from it. The Fourdrinier Brothers, who introduced the mechanical paper-making technology into Britain, went bankrupt in 1810. Most of their lives was spent on endless and expensive patent lawsuits. Hargreaves' patent right was denied by the court due to technical reasons, and he sold some "spinning jennies" before the patent. After a chronic and expensive lawsuit, Arkwright lost all his patents in 1785, the same year that Argand lost his patents. In addition, in terms of technology, Tennant lost his patent for bleaching fluid rather than bleaching powder.
180 Mokyr. *Lever of Riches*, 276–277.
181 Mokyr. *Lever of Riches*, 276.
182 Mokyr. *Gift of Athena*, 301.

183 For instance, the British Congress awarded special allowances to these inventors; Harison, the inventor of the precise clock for navigation; Thomas Rome, inventor of the throwing machine, whose patent extension was rejected; Edmund Cartwright, whose patent on the power loom was robbed by the creditor. The Swede John Ericsson made a significant contribution to the invention of the propeller and obtained a £4,000 award from the Ministerium of Navy. After experiencing a series of disasters, Henry Cott lost his patent but obtained a small amount of assistance. In addition, the priority system on inventions, technologies, or thoughts was established in Britain as the motivation for reputation. The controversy between Newton and Leibnitz on the priority right of "calculus" was a famous example in history. Before the Revolution, the French government granted assistance to inventors who were regarded as bringing social benefits and gave awards for particular items, such as the item attempting to produce the synthetic niter in 1775–1794. In 1740–1780, the French government paid 6.8 million livres to inventors in the form of allowances and interest-free loans.

184 Galvez-Behar. Was the French Patent System democratic?, 257–280.

185 Li Zonghui. *Intellectual Property System*, 118.

186 Erich Kaufer. *The Economics of the Patent System*. Ke Ruihao. Beijing: Peking University Press, 2005:271.

187 It mainly includes shortening the patent protection term to 7 years, strict examinations of the patent application, confiscating all patents that failed to be implemented within 2 years, and applying imposed approval to all patents. This reformation bill was even approved in the House of Lords but was repealed later. Devaiah V. *A History of Patent Law*. Alternative Law Forum, 1992, p. 2010.

188 Tomita. *Intellectual Property Rights*, 85.

189 Rudolf Krasser. *Patent Law – German Patent and Utility Model Law, European and International Patent Law*. 6th ed. Zhang Taolve, et al. Beijing: Intellectual Property Press, 2016:272.

190 Krasser. *Patent Law – German Patent and Utility Model Law*, 272

191 Kaufer. *Economics of the Patent System*, 76

192 Kaufer. *Economics of the Patent System*, 273.

193 Prager. History of Intellectual Property, 711–758.

194 Wang Jianfeng, Guo Qingcun. The Development of the Patent System: Monopoly and Anti-monopoly of Technology, *Technology and Law*, 2004 (2).

195 Prager. History of Intellectual Property, 711–758.

196 Josh Lerner. Patent Policy Innovations: A Clinical Examination, *Vanderbilt Law Review*, 2000 (53), p. 1841.

197 Christopher May, Susan K. Sell. *Intellectual Property Rights: A Critical History*. Boulder, CO: Lynne Rienner Publishers, 2006:112.

198 May, Sell. *Intellectual Property Rights*, 112.

199 May, Sell. *Intellectual Property Rights*, 112.

200 Freeman, Louçã. *As Time Goes By*, 222.

201 At that time, Britain deliberately made a colony policy for India to monopolize its cotton resources. France also colonized Southeast Asia and Africa. Germany fell behind in this aspect: Diken explored East Africa after 1860 and founded the German Colony Company in 1884. Because all countries were chasing Britain, it had to farewell the "Small Britain." In 1872, Disraeli made a speech in the Crystal Palace, claiming that Britain should also follow the path of monopoly imperialism. Tomita. *Intellectual Property Rights*, 86.

202 Gao Debu. *Industrial Revolution and Industrialization in Britain*, 275.

203 Gao Debu. *Industrial Revolution and Industrialization in Britain*, 275.
204 Krasser. *Patent Law – German Patent and Utility Model Law*, 287.
205 Machlup, Penrose. Patent Controversy in the Nineteenth Century, pp. 1–29.
206 Müller proposed that the compensation and reward of the inventors should not be rejected; the law that allowed anyone to use an investor's labor result freely without paying equivalents or the permission of the inventor was immoral. Machlup, Penrose. Patent Controversy in the Nineteenth Century, pp. 1–29.
207 Machlup, Penrose. Patent Controversy in the Nineteenth Century, pp. 1–29.
208 Machlup, Penrose. Patent Controversy in the Nineteenth Century, pp. 1–29.
209 Kaufer. *Economics of the Patent System*, 13.
210 Mokyr. *Gift of Athena*, 302.
211 Eric Schiff. *Industrialization Without National Patents: The Netherlands, 1869–1912, Switzerland, 1850–1907*. Princeton, NJ: Princeton University Press. 2015:451.

4 Post-industrial age

Internationalization and alienation of the private right system of patents

Despite all the obstacles, the private system of patents was gradually established worldwide in the nineteenth and twentieth centuries. The Third Technological Revolution in the mid and late twentieth century represented a new age of technological innovation in human history and a new economic form that was distinct from agricultural and industrial economies. The post-industrial economy was rising. The patent privilege system appeared in pre-industrial society. In contrast, the private rights system of patents emerged and developed in industrial society. Different social environments shaped different concepts of the patent system. As Nobuhiro Nakayama said, all institutions were defined by the age when they were established.[1] In the Post-industrial Age, the profound changes in technology, economy, culture and authority led to new changes in the private rights system of patents. As David Kairys and Susan K. Sell said, before the twentieth century, patent law was a marginalized and eccentric part of the area of law that was exclusive to technical experts.[2] However, in the Post-industrial Age, Intellectual Property (IPR) laws and policies, including the patent system, were suddenly regarded as something closely related to free trade, national economic growth, and international competition. They were placed on the agenda of laws worldwide, and they became the focus of controversy in all countries. The protection scope of the IPR was greatly expanded, and a trend of alienation was even shown. Modern IPR laws faced an unprecedented challenge, especially the never-seen criticisms and questioning of the patent system. How come? What led to these changes? This chapter attempts to answer these questions.

Evolutionary motivations for the private right system of patents in the Post-industrial Age

In the mid and late twentieth century, the world witnessed a new technological revolution, which was marked by the research, development, and application of information technology, especially computers, bioengineering, new energy, new materials, optical fiber, laser, ocean development, and space technology, as well as other emerging technologies.[3] People were increasingly aware of the importance of knowledge and technology in economic development, and they tried to

DOI: 10.4324/9781003462453-5

describe the form of technology and economy that appeared after the new technological revolution. For instance, as Daniel Bell pointed out in *The Coming of Post-Industrial Society*, one can divide societies into pre-industrial society, industrial society, and post-industrial society and see them in contrast along many different dimensions. Therefore, he tried to show in an accompanying schematic table how, along different dimensions, the three societies differed radically. These were, of course, ideal-type constructions; however, the purpose of these constructs was to illuminate essential differences. Therefore, the design of pre-industrial society was a game against nature: its resources were drawn from extractive industries, and it was subject to the laws of diminishing returns and low productivity; the design of industrial society was a game against fabricated nature, which was centered on man–machine relationships and used energy to transform the natural environment into a technical environment; the design of a post-industrial society was a game between people in which an intellectual technology, based on information, rose alongside machine technology.[4] Others call it the knowledge economy. For example, the Organization of Economic Cooperation and Development (OECD) published *The Knowledge-based Economy*, which was the first to clarify the connotation of knowledge economy. According to the report, the age of the knowledge economy has already come, and the "knowledge economy" is a new form of society and economy, which is predated by the agricultural and industrial economies. A knowledge-based economy is directly dependent on the production, distribution, communication, and application of knowledge and information, and its defining feature is that the economic function of knowledge is demonstrated to the greatest extent. In terms of product value, the knowledge-based value constitutes the most significant proportion. This differentiates the knowledge economy from the agricultural and industrial economies, where materials claim the biggest share of the product share.[5] Although the perspectives and concepts proposed in the previous literature differ, they all emphasize the importance of technology, information, and knowledge in social and economic development when the new social form prevails. The extensive and rapid growth of the knowledge economy contributes to the increasing importance of knowledge in the material basis and organizational forms of social life; therefore, changing social paradigms, specifically from the paradigm of industrial society in which the creation of material products dominates, to the new paradigm of a "knowledge society" in which the creation of knowledge dominates as an overarching purpose. Knowledge and information flow in the economic system and even in cultural and political systems in the form of power and discourse, implanting some distinct operational mechanism into the social environment, which demonstrates some particular features.[6] In this book, this social form is called "the post-industrial society."

Characteristics of technological innovation and economic development in the Post-industrial Age

Technological innovation and economic development in the Post-industrial Age exhibit a development trend that is distinct from that of the agricultural and industrial societies. New technologies and economic development are revolutionary. Generally speaking, it has the following features.

The explosive growth and diversification of the technological creation

Maurice Daumas, an expert in the history of technology, once said that the first technological progress by humans was marked by making sharp tools, controlling fire, and wheels, and every important discovery took thousands of years. Before the Middle Ages, the technological inventions of humans could be calculated in a thousand years. After the Middle Ages, it could be calculated in a century. Then, half of a century or a quarter of a century could be used to describe the time taken for technological progress. Since the late seventeenth and early eighteenth centuries, decades could be used as the time unit to measure technological progress.[7] After the First and Second Industrial Revolutions, in about 200 years, the total amount of technology in human society increased, evolved, and reproduced in a geometric progression. In the first 20 years of the twentieth century, technological progress surpassed that of the nineteenth century.[8] Since the Third Industrial Revolution, human technology entered an era of explosive expansion and improvement in quality and quantity, depth and width, connotation and denotation. It was estimated that 90% of knowledge and technology in human society was produced and created within the last 50 years. This period was dubbed the age of "knowledge explosion." Technological dissemination is the process by which an invention is adopted and recognized in society. In the Post-industrial Age, the knowledge and technology acquired by human society exponentially increased in quantity. They decreased unprecedentedly in the time of acquisition and are accessible in every corner of the world.[9] Technology that used to be monopolized by a few is now available to millions of people in a short time. The technological life cycle becomes increasingly short. According to Moore's Law, proposed by Gordon Moore in 1965, when the price remains unchanged, the number of transistors that could be placed on an integrated circuit will double every 18 months, and so will its function.[10] More than 40 years later, the speed of change shows no sign of slowdown. The life cycle of products in some technological fields is usually shorter than 2 years.[11] The rapid development of technology relies on the self-accumulation and evolution of useful knowledge and the contribution of science. In previous ages, technological innovation mainly depended on the accumulation of production experience and valuable knowledge rather than scientific knowledge. In the Post-industrial Age, the accumulation of practical knowledge was enormous, and science and technology were mutually dependent and reinforcing, which made them gradually integrated and transformed into a unified scientific and technological system.

Moreover, technological innovation has become more complicated and diverse. The primary basis of technology in agricultural and industrial societies was limited to mechanical technology. However, in the Post-industrial Age, technological innovation has been expanded to information, new materials, bioengineering, new energy, space, electronics, communication, and marine engineering. According to the statistics, complicated technology accounted for 43% of 30 kinds of primary exports worldwide in 1970; however, this proportion rose to 87% in 2005. A typical example of post-industrial technology is a knowledge-intensive high-technology with complicated features, such as high intensity, integration, and coordination. High intensity is the accumulation and intensity of technology and the high assembly and integration of science, technology, and industry. High integration means that the relationship among different technologies in high-technology can be defined as complicated integration rather than simple interdependence. High coordination implies that these technologies are connected, coordinated, and well-organized. This means that they are not self-contained, isolated and restricted; instead, they are interconnected in an organically organized system.

Closer connection between technology and economy

In the Post-industrial Age, because science and technology and economic development have surpassed a given boundary, the relationship between them is fundamentally reversed and altered, and their combination and connection have become unprecedentedly close. Technology dramatically increases social productivity, accelerates economic growth, and contributes to significant changes in the economic structure. On the one hand, the proportion of technology in traditional industries increases. The penetration of technology into the economy is usually achieved by influencing traditional factors of production. For example, in material production represented by the manufacturing industry, the lean production model is gradually replacing the scale production model, which significantly increases the importance of management knowledge of products. On the other hand, many emerging industries based on technology have rapidly risen. The wide application of microelectronic and photoelectric technology, computer technology, optical fibers, and satellite communication facilities and the rapid rise of the information industry, which focuses on information services, constitute the emerging industry featuring the most rapid development and the most enormous scale. The pace of technological innovation is accelerating. A company could soon produce many products and new sectors according to the market situation after a new technology is developed. New technologies keep generating new economic benefits and industries and constitute a growing share of the national economy. In developed countries, the contribution of technological progress to the growth of gross national product (GNP) becomes increasingly important. At the beginning of the twentieth century, the contribution of technological advancement to the growth in the GNP in developed countries was merely 5%–20%, and the figure rose to about 50% in the 1950s–1960s and 60%–80% in the 1980s. Technological progress exerts a stronger effect on economic growth than capital and labor.[12] In the United States, the hi-tech industry has been developing fast since the 1960s, and its contribution to the national economy also quickly increased: 7% in 1961–1965, 21% in 1976–1980, 24% in 1991–1995, 33% in 1996, and 40% in 1997. In the hi-tech industry, the information industry enjoyed more remarkable growth: its contribution was 4.5% in 1985, 6.1% in 1990, and 8.2% in 1998.[13]

Compared with traditional economic forms, the knowledge economy no longer attributes its prosperity to the direct investment of resources, capital, and hardware technology but to the accumulation and application of knowledge and technology. Knowledge and technology are regarded as the main factors of production that can push productivity to a new development stage, because knowledge and technology largely enhance the human ability to recognize and transform the world.[14] In addition. it is an economy that is more individual and can better demonstrate the law of value. Based on the ability to acquire, occupy, and apply technology, promoting the breakthroughs in industrial revolutions by technology consolidated in production tools or products and compensating for the lack of resources and capital by technical innovation abilities have radically altered the pattern in which the total quantity or increment of resources and capital determines the development of a traditional economy.[15]

Economic globalization and the growing share of knowledge products in global trade

Since the 1970s, economic globalization has become an irreversible historical trend. In essence, economic globalization is a process of economic growth that integrates more economies into a unified financial system to achieve the objective of intensifying international distribution.[16] It is also an integration process in the international market that is constituted of global goods, labor, and capital.[17] Economic globalization is mainly attributed to the progress of information technology, the convergence of the macroeconomic systems of different countries, and the global arbitrage by microeconomic agents represented by multinationals. First, the development of information technology, such as the internet and multimedia, helps build a unified global market. This market reduces the enterprises' costs of remote control and provides technical support for the rapid circulation of information, goods, and elements worldwide. Second, countries with a planned economy, like the Soviet Union and China, have started the economic transformation, pursued reform and opening up policies, and established a market economy. An increasing number of countries have accepted the free market system. The economic stagflation caused by the oil crisis in the 1970s and the crisis of the global currency system brought by the collapse of the Bretton Woods Institutions caused the Western developed countries to relax economic control, which aroused financial and economic liberalization. Last, thanks to exclusive intellectual property rights, technical know-how, management strategies, and capital strength, multinationals can use the cheap factories of production in developing countries to sell products in the markets with higher prices for product arbitrages and invest the enormous surplus capital in developing countries with scarce money and high investment rewards for capital arbitrages. This promotes the globalization of economic development.[18]

With economic globalization, high-technology and high-tech products become the object of transactions and play an increasingly important role in international trade. On the one hand, the global export of high-tech products in 1990 was 17.4% of the export of industrial products, which rose to 29% in 2014, according to the statistics of the World Bank.[19] The output value in the gross domestic product (GDP) worldwide is associated with the information industry and products.[20] On the other hand, technological innovation promotes the restructuring of global trade. The technology trade in all countries is constantly increasing. The international technology trade totaled 50 billion dollars in 1985, 120 billion dollars in 1990, and 260 billion dollars in 1995, jumping to 500 billion dollars in 2000 and nearing 1,000 billion dollars in 2002. In other words, these figures doubled every 5 years on average.[21] In developed countries like the United States, which have the advantage of technology and knowledge reserves, technology transactions and licensing have become an essential source of economic income. For example, in 1995, the royalties and license fees of the U.S. multinational manufacturing industries reached 27 billion dollars, and imports were no more than 6.3 billion dollars.[22]

Dominance of neoliberalism in the Post-industrial Age

In the mid-1970s, Keynesianism,[23] a popular economic theory after World War II that combined social welfare policy with multilateralism, began to decline because it failed to solve the problems of stagnation in economic development.[24] A neoliberalism trend of monetarists started to revive in academic and political circles. By the 1980s, this neoclassical theory of economic liberalism had spread worldwide. In capitalist society, as national monopoly is developing into international monopoly, neoliberalism begins to expand from theories and academia to politics, national ideologies, and paradigms to satisfy this requirement. It becomes an essential part of the theoretical system of globalization promoted by Anglo–American international monopoly capital. Its iconic event was the agreement of the "Washington Consensus,"[25] which symbolizes that neoliberalism became an ideology and the mainstream value in Europe and America. For example, Margaret Hilda Thatcher, the former Prime Minister of the United Kingdom, and Ronald Reagen, the former President of the United States, embraced the neoliberalism of the Chicago School after they took office in 1981. The new method is not just about the change in policies but also a deliberate effort to change the opinions about the government's best role, the function of private enterprises, and the advantage of the market.[26]

The opinions of neoliberalism about the economy and politics can be summarized as follows. First, it opposes the government's interference and advocates market and liberalization, including trade, market and financial liberalization, and the "invisible hand." Overall, everything enters the market, and the market determines everything. According to the French philosopher Jean Baudrillard, everything is transformed into exchange values that can be transacted and purchased. The process is ruthless because consistency is considered to be the theoretical state. During this process, any unique things and features, any special culture, and any value that fails to be represented by money will be canceled. Second, it promotes privatization on a large-scale to meet the requirements of the free market and launches a series of reforms, especially the property rights reform, which is actually the privatization of means of production. For example, the leading advocate of neoliberalism, Zhang Wuchang, believes that Ronald Harry Coase's theory of property makes the whole world realize the importance of private property rights. Private ownership can resolve all the problems of economic development. Private ownership is the only choice.[27] Third, in terms of strategies and policies, it advocates global capitalization. Neoliberalism greatly encourages globalization dominated by superpowers and emphasizes the globalization of the economy, politics, and culture dominated by superpowers, such as global capitalization.[28] Fourth, it exaggerates the value of technological innovation and knowledge resources.[29] Neoliberalists believe that capitalist society has become a consumption society or entered the post-industrial stage; however, it takes a more undecorated and developed form. In the late stages, capitalism expanded the power of commodities to almost every aspect of social and individual lives, including all knowledge and information. Information and knowledge become a resource or capital in the discourse of economics. In an information society, what makes a difference is not capital but information and knowledge in the hands of the majority.[30] In the new economic order, information, like automobiles, can be mass-produced and become a driving force of the economy. According to neoliberalism, the emergence of a knowledge society means that human society will evolve from a "capital society" based on capital, land, and the labor force into a society where knowledge will be the primary resource, and organizations will be the key structure. In a knowledge society, knowledge will replace capital and become the decisive "factor of production" that controls resources. Information gradually becomes property, commodity, and the most valuable goods in all industries. Then, the use of capital will no longer be the focus of the power struggle, and capitalism will be converted from money into information worship.[31] Theodore Roszak said in *The Cult of Information*:

> We can almost believe that we can soon eat plastic floppy disks and walk on the road paved with integrated circuit chips. It seems unnecessary to cultivate land, exploit minerals, and make heavy industry products. These daily necessities are seldom mentioned and will soon disappear in the buzzing of electronic energy that can easily satisfy all requirements of humans.[32]

Neoliberalism makes developed countries, like the United States, gradually relax control, wholly or partially, over industry and initiate a large-scale privatization process across all sectors. This orientation is also demonstrated in the government's relaxation of the antitrust environment. The antitrust rule that is used to strictly restrict patents is now significantly liberalized.[33] Free trade is stressed, and the property concept of effective IPR protection is also rising. It is the neoliberalism theory that motivates Europe and the United States to apply the protection logic of tangible properties to intangible ones, like knowledge. They are convinced that if the right owner's control over knowledge is so powerful and exclusive, the market benefits of knowledge as a commodity will be maximized.

Changes in technology, economy, and authority in the Post-industrial Age

Changes in the paradigm of technological innovation

In the nineteenth century and even in earlier periods, the knowledge that enabled technological inventions was neither complicated nor professional. Technicians or inventors could complete inventions by themselves, and they could obtain rewards through direct application or commercialization.[34] However, after the twentieth century, the paradigm of technological inventions begins to change. Technological development has become so diverse and complicated, and innovations have become so professional and specialized that inventors cannot afford the costs and risks of research independently. At the same time, more and more enterprises realize the significance of technology to their development. Competition among enterprises is increasingly dependent on product quality and cost, which are entirely determined by the scale and efficiency of scientific research. The research and development of new technology is not for the technology itself but for developing or improving new products. Research is regarded as an essential approach to protecting and developing companies; therefore, these companies begin to develop new technologies and products by organizing experiments. In addition, technical experts and inventors become dependent on enterprises and are controlled by them. Enterprises see technological research and investment as a management strategy and combine them with organized production and consumption organs with the same conditions. Therefore, the enterprise is responsible for everything from basic research to the development of products. Technological creation and commerce have formed a formal distribution of responsibility inside the enterprises, and independent inventors have become the minority.

In fact, the first industrial laboratory was set up by Thomas Edison in Monroe Park, New Jersey, in 1876, where many scientists and experimenters were hired to perform experiments. The production objective of the "invention factory" he established was to create a small invention every 10 days and a big invention about every 6 months.[35] This pattern was then inherited by large companies in Germany and the United States. German companies first realized its significance, and companies such as Bayer, BASF, Hurst, Casella, and Agfa all established industrial laboratories. After the twentieth century, industrial laboratories proliferated in the United States. Early examples included the large R&D departments established by General Motors, Westinghouse, AT&T, DuPont, Kodak, Goodyear, International Harvester, and Parker Davis. Establishing R&D laboratories in companies is one of the most significant institutional innovations in the twentieth century. Throughout the twentieth century, industrial laboratories worldwide increased from 300 to 13,500, and R&D costs in enterprises continuously increased, occupying 60%–70% of the total research cost in all countries. These laboratories hired over 70,000 employees, with an annual budget of 200 million dollars.[36] From 1953 to 1999, the GDP of the United States increased only several times; however, the expenses of enterprises increased a dozen times.[37] In 1975, 126 large enterprises in the United States made up around 75% of the total industrial R&D, and four companies were responsible for about 20%.[38]

In the Post-industrial Age, establishing an industrial research department has become the basic pattern in the organizational structure of an enterprise, which spawns the social, organizational system that supports inventions and creations and forms the social and technological process covering technological requirements, forecasting, planning, development, experiment, and industrial production.

Companies like Google, Microsoft, and Sony can attract the most outstanding technology talents. Enterprises have become synonymous with patents and technology and are the country's most powerful drivers for innovation. As Joseph Schumpeter said, technological innovations depend not only on progress in scientific theory but also on competition among entrepreneurs and their pursuit of market profits.[39] W•W. Rostow also believed that the pursuit of market profits by innovative entrepreneurs who keep forging ahead is the fundamental basis for the supply of inventors and technological creations,[40] and large enterprises are the most powerful machines in destructive innovations.[41]

Changes in the dominant force of the economy

In this trend, economic activities are highly concentrated in several large-scale enterprises. These enterprises with centralized regimes gradually grow in economic development and become the dominant power of economic growth. In the Post-industrial Age, the competitiveness of the market subjects depends on their ability to innovate, which is mainly demonstrated in their exploration and pursuit of new raw materials, production methods, products, and markets through technological innovations. In addition, because a technology platform requires enormous capital investments, a centralized and top-down model of vertical integration is the most effective and unique way to ensure the recovery of investment costs. However, this model would not function properly without a highly intensive means of production. As a result, the means of production will be increasingly controlled by several large enterprises. As Jeremy Rifkin said, Fortune Global 500 enterprises control global commerce. In 2011, their incomes totaled 22.5 trillion dollars, which was more than one-third of global GDP (62 trillion dollars).[42] The market subjects that emphasize and control technological innovations have become increasingly powerful, especially high-tech multinationals with a growing influence, such as Microsoft, Sony, and Apple.[43]

Some companies that control key technologies have actually formed a cartel that continuously introduces new products and monopolizes the market.[44] For example, according to the research findings disclosed by the United States in 2010, 5% of companies (38 out of 699) control 40% of national electricity, four automobile companies (General Motors, Ford, Chrysler, and Toyota) control 60% of the automobile market, and five new companies (News Corp, Google, Garrett, Yahoo, and Viacom) control 54% of the American news market. In home appliances, the top four companies (Whirlpool, Electrolux, General Electric, and LG Electric) control 90% of the market share. A similar pattern that large enterprises are intensive is prevalent in all industries worldwide.[45] John Kenneth Galbraith pointed out that this phenomenon is not unique in the United States. In Britain, the 100 largest manufacturers contributed 16% of the total net output in the manufacturing industry in 1909, 33% in 1958, and approximately 45% in the 1970s and 1980s, almost tripling the initial share. In an important thesis, Frederic L. Pryor stated that this phenomenon can be seen through regular observations, and from a practical perspective, the industrial concentration of technologies is the same in all mature industrial countries.[46] In the Post-industrial Age, high-technology and IPR-based industries, such as pharmaceutical, entertainment, and computer software, occupy a favorable position. They are at least big exporters enjoying a trade surplus. They are seen as the leading industries of the next tide. In contrast, powerful industries that were glorious during the Industrial Age, like steel and weaving, are gradually reduced to the "sunset industries."[47]

Changes in the authority structure

In the Post-industrial Age, as high-tech sectors and enterprises brought more and more economic benefits and competitive advantages to capitalist countries, and some multinationals could also provide useful foreign information for government officials, the governments in capitalist countries gradually preferred these enterprises. They manifest a natural "paternalism" toward these large enterprises and put high-tech participants above commercial rules. As J.H. Reichman said: "The growing capacity of manufacturers in developing countries to penetrate distant markets for traditional industrial products had forced the developed countries to rely more heavily on their comparative advantage in the production of intellectual goods than in the past.."[48]

These knowledge and technology-intensive enterprises (e.g., pharmaceutical, entertainment, and computer software) have resources, motivations, and abilities to search for chances worldwide to guarantee rewards and profits. They seek all chances for benefits and profit-seeking and rely on their status in domestic economies, pursuing to actualize their benefit via deliberate political activities. As Palan and Albert pointed out, capitalist enterprises require the country to provide political and social conditions for their intensity.[49] These multinationals with strong economic power and key technologies convert the preferences helpful to their benefits into policies and institutions in various ways, such as alliances, lobbying, and elections. They form partnerships in industry, even among industries, to lobby the government to maintain and expand their technological and beneficial advantages. The government also arranges for these private sectors to participate in legislation and offers them chances to contact decision makers. The state provides them with the right to choose so that the interest groups can prevent and influence the making and operating of policies. In making legal institutions and decisions, large enterprises are associated with national governments more closely than ever before.[50] Therefore, the power structure that the state monopolizes the legislative power and controls the majority of law enforcement forces is broken. As governments reduced plans, promoted privatization, and relaxed controls in the Post-industrial Age, profound changes happened to the social authorities. Enterprises with strong technological and economic power began to participate and became essential. These social control powers share dominance with the state. As the former president of the Harvard Business and Government Center, Ella Jackson, said, companies and their leaders have already "replaced politics and politicians ... to become the new leaders and dominant oligarchs in our institution." Some large technological multinationals influence and infiltrate the country's political situation depending on their solid technical and economic power, and their function and influence even gradually eclipse some political parties. Some political parties and politicians also become the "spokesmen" of these companies.[51]

As some scholars have said, politics in Western countries has already descended to speculation controlled by money, just like the National Football League or the National Basketball Association in the United States. As a speculator, the word "politician" suggests nothing but shame.[52] Another important reason why these enterprises can frequently obtain chances for institutional arrangements is that public interests are too separated to have a representative selected, which means the absence of owners. According to Mancur Olsen's theory, the expenses paid by an individual to organize a large group are usually higher than the benefits obtained by the individual to join the group, so it is hardly possible to find a representative when public interests remain separated.[53] G.M. Grossman and E. Helpman also pointed out that organized interest groups have advantages in two aspects. On the one hand, an interest group finds it easier to obtain professional knowledge about policies that are related to its industry, profession, and hobby. On the other hand, an interested group could accumulate resources to obtain enough information capable of producing collective benefits, and the information-related expenses will be shared by all members.[54]

Conclusion

In the Post-industrial Age, technology became more complicated and diverse. With the technology's infiltration into and influence on economic activities, new technologies continuously generated new products and economic interests. Apart from that, technology-intensive products and technologies in the context of economic globalization contribute to structural changes in international trade and investments and play an increasingly significant role in international trade. Economic globalization also makes enterprises realize that their products have a much larger overseas market and that technologies and IPRs are progressively important. Coupled with rapid technological development, others can replicate these expensive and advanced IPR products more quickly and cheaply. Anyone with the necessary copying conditions and facilities can copy software, videos, and CDs. The copying of diverse products and technical processes threatens the competitive advantages of these technology and knowledge-intensive companies. Moreover, new technologies developed by these companies, such as semiconductors, software codes, and biological technologies, can't be protected by being listed in traditional IPR classifications. Therefore, they are gradually copied and imitated by other competitors. However, enterprises' cost of innovation and development increases significantly, and enterprises have to make more investments if they are to continuously develop new products in the intensely competitive market.[55] These elements reflect the fundamental contradictions between the original IPR system and the emerging market based on technologies and IPRs. The original IPR system is no longer adapted to the changes in the technological system, and a danger has appeared that an innovative enterprise has to, at its own cost, grant some new actors (imitators) the rights and reduce the benefits that they "steal" from the existing system. Neoliberalism makes the government relax control over these innovative enterprises, which are aware of the feasibility and necessity of monopolizing technologies more widely. Accordingly, in this technological, economic, and cultural environment, the ideas of reforming the original IPR systems begin to emerge in these enterprises. They hope to build a new institutional system that could prevent replication by others, keep expanding the IPR protection to new innovations, and occupy a larger overseas market.

The shared benefits make some high-tech industries side with these innovative enterprises. They become active in promoting IPR protection and attempt to convert their concepts, benefits, and proposals into policies and institutions by all means, including alliances, lobbying, and elections. They use their economic and political advantages to fabricate enticing words. On the one hand, these private interest groups influence legislation through domestic lobbies; on the other hand, they play an active and dominant role in the government's enactment of international trade and IPR policies. As the paradigm of innovations and inventions is centered on these large enterprises, which are the dominant force in economic development, the government's legislation and policies gradually change to their advantage. In addition, society widely accepts an institution in which these large enterprises are dominant in economic life and benefit fundamentally from this dominance. This acceptance is demonstrated by the political influence of commercial groups' opinions, and the economic influence of their market performance is taken into consideration.[56] Therefore, we could witness this phenomenon in the Post-industrial Age, where the government, which is the only representative of the public interest in Western societies, is unprecedentedly consistent with personal benefits,[57] and the IPR becomes the "club of the rich." No wonder some scholars uttered a sigh that IPR is designed by dreamers and entrepreneurs who are at the center of world power.[58] In this technological, economic, and cultural scenario, the IPR system, including the patent system, tends to be international and alienated.

Internationalization of the private right system of patents in the Post-industrial Age

Actually, at the end of the nineteenth century, the rapidly expanding international commerce exerted growing pressure over separated IPR protection systems in all countries. To tackle this situation, two international IPR conventions were approved –the *1883 Paris Convention* and the *1886 Bern Convention*, which established national treatment, nondiscrimination, and priority rights. However, these conventions established neither new substantive laws nor set new legal standards for their participants. Instead, they just converted the consensus achieved by countries into written law, and the governments had strong autonomy in enacting the laws. In 1994, the *Agreement on Trade-Related Aspects of Intellectual Property Rights* (TRIPS Agreement) implemented by the World Trade Organization (WTO) was approved unanimously. The TRIPS Agreement initiated a mature and binding global IPR system, which infiltrates into the supervision environments of all countries, fosters consistency in IPR protection, and unifies the basic standard of IPR protection in all countries. The leading role in enacting this agreement was a special Intellectual Property Committee (IPC) consisting of 12 large knowledge-intensive enterprises in the U.S. software, pharmaceutical, and entertainment.[59] These enterprise groups successfully gained international support and obtained most of what they wanted from a global IPR convention, opening up a new prospect of international IPR protection.

Domestic background of the strong IPR protection in the United States in the 1980s

In the 1980s, due to technological, economic, and cultural elements, the United States began to execute a series of strong patent protection systems. There are three primary reasons for this. First, the technological advantage of the United States began to be threatened. It suddenly realized that its technological leadership worldwide was challenged, especially by Japan and Europe, in areas such as fibers, automobiles, and semiconductors.[60] It is believed that it was too easy for companies in other countries to acquire and imitate American technologies.[61] Second, the economic development of traditional industry in the United States was at a low tide. In contrast, high-tech industries, especially software, pharmaceutical, and entertainment industries that maintained an absolute export surplus, began to prosper.[62] The United States government realized that the tide of technological innovations began to revive, which provided economic value for information and biological technologies. The arrival of the information society made the United States adjust its policy by highlighting owner-centered patent policy.[63] Finally, the Chicago School began to secure discourse power in American ideologies after 1980 and started to influence American society. The Chicago School thought it necessary to strengthen governmental investment and encourage technological research. The stronger the stimulation to technological research was, the faster the technological innovation progressed.[64] The Prime Minister of the United Kingdom, Mrs. Thatcher, and the President of the United States, Reagan, favored the Chicago School's opinion after they took office in 1981. Moreover, some economists and theorists advocated that the value of technological innovations and knowledge resources (including IPRs) should be more emphasized,[65] and the recognition of IPRs in the antitrust law was also altered. Previously, the antitrust law always considered the IPR a monopoly; therefore, the IPR and antitrust law were contradictory. However, in the 1980s, the antitrust law gradually realized that the IPRs, including the patent right, were not necessarily to generate a monopoly or any power over the market. The American Department of Justice emphasized the following opinion. The market power or monopoly is the result of superior efforts. Acuity, observation, or fortune don't violate the antitrust law. Therefore, all economic subjects, including the owners of IPRs, are entitled to share the market power brought by their just properties.[66] The antitrust law shouldn't be used to hinder competition that is frequently emphasized.[67]

Therefore, in the age of Reagen, the American government generated the concept of a strong IPR protection system and began to formulate the famous "Propertent" strong IPR protection system, which primarily included the following aspects. 1. The United States approved a series of laws strengthening patent protection, the most typical of which was the *Federal Court Reform Act* to establish particular Federal Circuit Courts. The patent judicial system centered on the Federal Circuit Courts took shape. 2. The United States issued definite regulations on the patents generated by universities and governmental laboratories in R&D activities. The iconic regulation was the *Bayh-Dole Act* in 1980, which admitted that universities and governmental laboratories could acquire patent rights and exclusive privileges for items they invented. 3. In the judiciary, the Federal Supreme Court pointed out via the trial of Dawson v. Rohm that if the free trade policy has an essential position in our laws, the position of the patent system aimed at encouraging innovations should never be inferior to it. The Federal Circuit Court also played a role in reducing the proportion of patents rejected by the court from ⅔ to ⅓, which made a patent easier to acquire.[68] These judicial practices effectively ended the age when the antimonopoly law suppressed the patent law in the judicial field.[69]

Preliminary results of lobbies by American enterprise groups

In the technological, economic, and cultural environment and due to the government's strong IPR protection in the 1970s and 1980s, enterprises were faced with a shortage of capital regarding IPR protection. Producers of agricultural chemicals, book publishers, software makers, video and entertainment suppliers, and trademark-free medicine producers experienced discordance with the original IPR system. Seeking new economic interests, they began to make lobbies. Initially, the industries suffering negative influences made lobbies, respectively, and the patent and copyright interest groups initiated parallel but unassociated political movements. With time, these groups were promoted by several key people (Edmund Pratt, John Opel, and Jacques Gorin) and realized they were pursuing a common objective: strengthening IPR protection. Therefore, they began to make common lobbies; the patent interest groups helped the copyright ones and vice versa. They achieved some primary progress in the 1970s and 1980s.

At the end of the 1970s, private sectors, including Pfizer, Formosa (FMC), International Business Machines Corp. (IBM), and DuPont, motivated the United States government to make bilateral negotiations with Hungary on agricultural chemical industries.[70] Their acts gained support from the International Anti-Counterfeiting Alliance for the Agrochemical Industry and the Copyright Alliance. They pressured the United States to change its trade policy. They asked Hungary to strengthen the IPR protection according to laws and handle the counterfeiting problems in agricultural chemical products in the bilateral negotiation. In the 1980s, motivated and persuaded by many knowledge-intensive enterprise groups, the United States initiated bilateral negotiations with South Korea, Singapore, Mexico, Hungary, and Chinese Taiwan about IPR issues (including copyrights, patents, and trademarks). Finally, these countries and regions proclaimed that they would take stronger measures on IPR protection, and the American government believed that its bilateral measures had already achieved tangible results. Moreover, the private sector and the American government realized that the association between trade and IPR protection could lead to unexpected results. As Enyart, the president of international affairs of the Monsanto Agricultural Company, pointed out, the success of early bilateral negotiations made the U.S. high-tech enterprises believe that the combination of IPR and trade would bring them numerous rewards.[71]

Lobby and design skills of American enterprise groups for constructing the international IPR protection framework

After success in some legislation, these enterprise groups gained the impetus for further movements, and they initiated a more active and prudent mobilization in 1983–1984. They assembled and set up the International Intelligence Property Alliance in 1984. The enterprise groups were gradually aware of the substantial benefits they wanted and defined the suitable, normal, and legal understanding. Therefore, they began to lobby and design skills for the construction of international IPR protection, which proved to be successful, and the clues to their success could be concluded in several points.

First, when authority is transferred from the state to the market, the enterprises' dominance in the structure of production and knowledge gives them more discourse power. The government acknowledges the economic rights of these high-tech enterprises. It grants them the right to participate in the enactment of legal policies, and the enterprises also depend on the government's cooperation and support in ideology. Second, the government relies on enterprises to offer information that could provide potentially helpful foreign details for government officials. They use private policy networks established in foreign countries, like law offices and subsidiary corporations, to collect detailed information about foreign IPR legislation and the practice, as well as the observation of bilateral negotiations with the United States. In fact, these enterprises offer an incredible amount of information and materials about the offense against American IPRs by other countries to the American government.[72] Third, another resource the enterprise could provide for the government is expert opinions about relatively mysterious topics. To a certain extent, the IPR law is as obscure as the Bibles written in Arabic and reminiscent of the Catholic Church. The IPR lawyers are providers of privileged expert opinions akin to writers of Arabic. The IPR laws are pretty professional, complicated, and obscure to many lawyers, and most IPR lawyers have some technological background in science, engineering, chemistry, or biology. They are able to convert complicated terms into political terms and clarify the relationship between the IPR and international trade.[73]

Moreover, another point is quite significant. When these private sectors require the government to improve their benefits, they will make large-scale lobbies and attempt to create some conceptual attractions to persuade the government to enact domestic policies and even to conclude bilateral negotiations, which plays a significant role in converting private benefits to public ones. For example, the enterprise groups knew that the American government was worried about the increasing trade deficit and the improvement in international competition abilities. Hence, they "whitewashed" measures beneficial to them as measures that were beneficial for the American government to solve the trade crisis and improve international competitiveness. These high-tech enterprise groups reiterated that they were the main driving force of the United States' economic growth and international trade in this century and the next. They will provide numerous employment opportunities for the United States, and IPR protection is significant for their development and international trade. They try all means to promote their situation to Congress and the authorities, emphasizing the relationship between concepts and information, seeking the government's help to establish a fairer international trade order, and successfully making the American government redefine its benefits in IPRs.[74] In addition, the private sector reiterates that IPRs are "property rights" that are undoubted and natural. That they can talk about rights is partly attributed to the environment of respecting property rights in the United States, especially the transformation of the domestic attitude toward patent rights. They call the so-called offenders "bandits," reflecting their anger toward those who offend their "rights." This aggressive language emphasizes illegal behaviors, but many behaviors condemned as "bandits" are entirely legal under national and international laws.[75]

Therefore, when the private sector reaches an agreement with the government, they apply professional knowledge (defining the problem, providing information, and evaluating losses), design skills (converting obscure IPR problems into new trade policy tools), and propose solutions to cognitive problems. Moreover, another reason for their success is that they have acquired the solution from the Advisory Committee on Trade Negotiation (ACTN), which is composed of administrative organs and provides opinions about trade policies to the private sector. As the supreme supervision committee responsible for multilateral trade negotiations, ACTN is managed by the American Trade Negotiation Representative, and its members are nominated by the President, who are usually high-tech enterprises with considerable influence.[76] The ACTN proves to be significant when designing IPR strategies based on trade, and it is an essential tool for the globalization of the private benefits of its enterprise members.

The IPC and the TRIPS Agreement

Consensus between the government and enterprises and Goering's article

In 1984, the ACTN, represented by Opel and Pratt, the two large enterprises, persuaded the American government to include the IPR issues in the round negotiation of the General Agreement on Tariff and Trade (GATT). Distinct from patent benefits, some enterprises related to copyrights didn't initially emphasize the GATT negotiations. Computer software enterprises represented by IBM preferred the modification of the Bern Convention to protect computer software, and the music, book, and movie industries were keen on solving copyright problems through bilateral negotiations, which was also seen as a better path to quick results by the International Intellectual Property Alliance (IIPA). Indeed, another significant reason was that the GATT round negotiation was so complicated and lengthy that it was not the best choice for enterprises eager to achieve beneficial results quickly. However, these interest groups finally achieved consensus and aimed at multilateral negotiations via substantial guarantees by high-tech enterprises and encouraging discussions hosted by the American trade representative.[77]

These interest groups entrusted their counselor, the famous economist Jacques Goering, to provide reports at that time. 1985 witnessed the turning point in which private sectors pursued protecting the globalization of the IPR concepts based on trade. Goering's contribution was that he justified and expanded enterprises' beneficial requests by writing reports and files. For example, he offered Congress a legislation file on behalf of related enterprise groups, similar to the *Protecting International Copyrights of Computer Software Based on Trade* he published before. He described a new concept to put IPR protection as the background of international trade.[78] Goering believed that combining IPR protection and international trade could provide a platform for communication among different countries, help the government to solve the increasingly rampant infringement lawsuits and enforcement, and help improve IPR legislation that did not match the standards in some countries. To develop this mechanism, Goering thought it was necessary to insist on multilateral negotiations in the OECD and GATT. Goering's suggestions were widely accepted by enterprise groups and the IPR particular group in ACTN, which entirely adopted his suggestions in the report offered to ACTN in October 1985.[79]

Transnational association mobilized by the IPC and reaching consensus

In February and March 1986, the American trade representative Clayton required the IPR issues to be put on the agenda of the Uruguay Round Negotiations. However, he knew that although the ACTN had already realized the urgency and necessity of developing the IPR industries, Europe, Japan, and Canada were quite likely not. Without the support of these three countries, it would be hopeless to achieve the goal mentioned previously. Therefore, the support of the governments of the United States and other important countries should be ensured, and the participation of more high-tech enterprises with international relations and the ability to involve the enactment of policies would be required.[80] In March 1986, Opel and Prada contacted their advocates and persuaded the members to establish the IPC. To avoid disagreements in the negotiation and achieve consensus as quickly as possible, the IPC deliberately restricted the number of its members and insisted that its members should be the companies with top technological or financial resources in the United States. These companies contained those in the top ranks of different industries, such as electronics, heavy and light industries, chemicals, pharmaceutical, computer, and creative arts. The IPC was far stronger than any other trade group or association.[81]

After its establishment, the IPC was active in the international protection of IPRs. It first contacted chambers of commerce and industrial associations in the United States and convinced them of the necessity and urgency of solving the IPR problem based on international trade. They accepted the IPC's suggestion and agreed to its multilateral strategy. Then, IPC members immediately contacted chambers and associations in Europe and Japan. For example, the IPC contacted the Confederation of British Industry, the Confederation of German Industry, and the French Employers' Association, and contacted the Union of Industrial and Employers' Confederations of Europe via them. In July, the IPC held a conference with the Confederation of Japan Economic Groups.[82] In the beginning, some enterprise groups didn't advocate their strategy, because they were worried that the IPR problem was too new to be widely accepted and considered in the GATT. It might be inappropriate to discuss the IPR issues during the Uruguay Round Negotiations. They were also concerned that developing countries would oppose it.[83] Therefore, the IPC once again demonstrated its strong lobby skills.

First, they reiterated that IPR was quite important to trade and investments, but they couldn't entirely depend on the government. Instead, they should archive a general agreement before informing the government what to do. The IPC's initiator, Enyart, said, "If war is much too important a subject to leave up to generals, as Bismarck said, the rules of international commerce are far too important to leave up to government bureaucrats." They also believed that the World Intellectual Property Organization (WIPO) excessively emphasized the benefits of developing countries but ignored IPR piracies in developed countries. However, IPRs were related to trade and investment and should be negotiated in the GATT. Second, the IPC tried to persuade Europe and Japan of the advantages of using trade methods to solve IPR problems. The IPC used data and reports to prove the extent of piracies and infringements in IPRs and the high costs of fighting against infringements by the enterprises alone. It also demonstrated the threats and dangers of the infringements and abuse of IPRs to the future development of industrial countries and some accomplishments achieved by the American government via bilateral trade negotiations.[84] Last, the IPC explained the plan for constructing the lowest standard of IPR protection, compulsory enforcement, and dispute settlement mechanisms in the framework of the GATT based on Goering's blueprint. The IPC believed that the measure against the offense in IPR based on the GATT would be more transparent, which involved direct measures, adjustment procedures against the infringement of IPRs, and the completion of existing WIPO arrangements by providing enforcement mechanisms.[85]

The IPC soon achieved a beneficial consensus with commercial groups in Japan and Europe. The joint actions of these interest groups exhibited an interesting breakthrough achieved by international commercial groups in trade negotiations. Industrial groups in Japan and Europe managed to persuade domestic governments within a short time and opened a 9-month new trade negotiation. Therefore, commonly motivated by the United States, Japan, and Europe, the IPR problem was finally involved in the GATT.

The blueprint painted by enterprise groups and its achievement

In September and October 1986, private sectors in the United States, Japan, and Europe held a conference where they drafted a suggestion of consensus that reflected the benefit of the three parties that was derived from developed industrial countries' laws. Its contents were similar to Goering's previous suggestion and finally became the foundation of the TRIPS Agreement. It advocated minimal standards, national enforcement measures, boundary measures to confiscate fake commodities and dispute settlement mechanisms. As a consensus, it also contained some compromises. For instance, the American pharmaceutical industry was not entirely satisfied with the compulsory license. However, the United States ensured a united front with Europe and Japan via a compromise. The European commercial groups also asked to offer preferential treatment, technical assistance, and transition provisions to developing countries to ensure that the IPR convention was suitable for the majority of them.[86] The three private groups began to promote the agreement widely; the American government asked for 100–150 copies of the three-party suggestion in 1988 and distributed them as a file reflecting its opinions.

From 1986 to April 1989, the IPR issues stagnated during the Uruguay Round Negotiations because India and other developing countries strongly hindered them.[87] Then, these countries gradually participated in the TRIPS Agreement for multiple reasons.

First, the United States continuously pressured other countries based on the newly modified trade law. In 1998, the American Congress approved protecting IPRs in the trade and modified the domestic trade law motivated by related interest groups. At the same time, the American Congress demanded that the administrative organs apply Section 301 of the *Trade Act of 1974* more actively. The private sector urged the American government to pressure new industrial and developing countries to pursue their benefits and construct the international IPR protection system. For instance, the American government pressured Brazil, South Korea, and India based on Section 301 and the Generalized Scheme of Preferences (GSP) movements. These countries hoped that the pressure from Section 301 and GSP movements would be relieved in the cooperation framework of the TRIPS Agreement. The agrarian products of some developing countries received pressure from the market permission proposed by the United States and other countries; therefore, they hoped to offset this pressure by agreeing to more IPR protection.[88] Moreover, the American government signed the North American Free Trade Agreement (NAFTA) with Canada and Mexico, which contained strict IPR Section 301s.[89] Second, American industries, especially the IPC, strongly allied with the ACTN in the Uruguay Round Negotiations. Because the IPC member companies were the representatives of the ACTN or formal advisers on IPR problems (high officials in The Pharmaceutical Research and Manufacturers of America (PHRMA)), Dow, Johnson's, Merck, DuPont, Monsanto, and Procter & Gamble),[90] there were always close relations between the ACTN and IPC. Although the private sector had no formal positions in GATT, Prada, as a member of the IPC, could be nominated as the official representative of the United States in the negotiations in the name of the president of the ACTN. Therefore, these enterprise groups could make lobbies via the ACTN. Finally, due to the professionalism of IPRs, developing countries like India were all amateurs in terms of IPRs and lacked experience and knowledge. In contrast, developed countries like the United States had rich experience in IPRs and licenses, and they were so well-prepared that they rejected various projects and opinions issued by developing countries.[91] Through negotiations for many years, the TRIPS Agreement finally achieved consensus on 15 April 1994.

Influence of the TRIPS Agreement

The TRIPS Agreement involved all IPR-related patents, copyrights, trademarks, and commercial secrets and significantly expanded the rights of IPR owners. For instance, the patent right was expanded into almost all fields, including medicines, chemicals, pesticides, and plant breeds, and the protection term was extended to 20 years. It also mainly regulated the clauses to protect semiconductor chips and integrated circuit layouts. It constructed a consistent IPR protection system and expanded the content and range of the IPR protection standard that all countries should implement. It listed these standards and associated the principle of national treatment with a series of higher IPR standards. At the same time, it established the WTO Dispute Settlement Body (DSB), responsible for handling IPR lawsuits. This meant all members should strictly fulfill the obligations set forth in the TRIPS Agreement. Otherwise, it would be judged by the DSB. The WTO was authorized to supervise the operational situation of all members to ensure that the prosecuted party performed its duties within given restrictions. If the charged party refused to act, the WTO could entitle the prosecutor to initiate trade sanctions when necessary, which guaranteed the compulsory execution ability of the TRIPS Agreement.[92] In its enactment, most developing countries had no awareness of IPR protection, because their related industries failed to form interest groups strong enough, and they were primarily importers rather than exporters of IPR products. When signing the TRIPS Agreement, they were not entirely aware of the influences it would bring to them. As mentioned previously, they were restricted to the economic stress of developed countries, hoping to compromise the TRIPS Agreement in exchange for short-term promises on the economies of developed countries, which would undoubtedly contribute to resources flying from consumers and companies in developing countries to companies in industrially developed countries.[93] More importantly, the TRIPS Agreement set a precedent for developed countries to use international agreements to improve economic trade and grant solid property rights to companies with high-tech resources worldwide. It was their advanced technological and economic power that led to their final success; their professional knowledge, thoughts, information, and design skills about the IPR also made a difference.

However, the TRIPS Agreement was never an end. Instead, it was merely a new beginning. Companies represented by the IPC accomplished most of the objectives they wanted in the Agreement. As Goering said, the IPC fulfilled 95% of its wishes except for the lengthened restriction of developing countries.[94] However, many other industries in the United States were still dissatisfied with the Agreement, considering it weaker and less comprehensive than NAFTA. The associations of industries were discontented with the transition in developing countries, the lack of protection obligations against parallel imports, the lack of "public orders," and the boundary operation clause was lower than their expectations. They were required to seek stronger protection, and the TRIPS Agreement undoubtedly set a precedent that made them aware that they could infiltrate national and international politics, national legislation, and international trade. They could also acquire the benefits they wanted via multilateral IPR negotiations. Therefore, these enterprises united again later and persuaded the government to establish a protection standard that was higher than the TRIPS Agreement. For example, the American government and enterprises were disappointed and discontented that many existing multilateral international organizations, such as the WIPO and WTO, always fell into lengthy debates and could not fully function. Therefore, they hoped to establish a new platform. Superpowers in the IPR issue, including the United States, European Union (EU), and Japan, ignored developing countries and found the *Anti-Counterfeiting Trade Agreement* (ACTA) beyond the framework of the WIPO and WTO to handle so-called commercial counterfeiting and piracy problems. It was signed on 1 May 2011. This agreement regarded developing countries, including China, as the target of attack, and its protection standard for IPRs was far higher than the TRIPS Agreement. In addition, the United States and other countries attempted to establish a higher protection standard for IPRs that was "in the face of the twenty-first century" "high-standard and comprehensive" through the Trans-Pacific Partnership Agreement (TPP). They even tried constructing a worldwide unified Substantive Patent Law Treaty (SPLT).[95] These multilateral negotiations would undoubtedly have a significant influence on IPR protection.

Alienation of the private rights system of patents in the Post-industrial Age

In the Post-industrial Age, private enterprises fostered the internationalization of the private patent system through international legislation and influenced domestic legislation and patent practices for their interests. As a result, the private rights system of patents was gradually alienated.

Concept of the alienation

Alienation is a concept in philosophy and sociology, and the use of this concept is gradually transformed. In the seventeenth and eighteenth centuries, Jean-Jacques Rousseau and Thomas Hobbes mentioned alienation when they talked about the transfer of rights and properties. Then, Georg Wilhelm Friedrich Hegel first discussed the meaning of alienation from the perspective of philosophy, and he thought that alienation was based on absolute consciousness. Any living thing must be gradually alienated to different existences to achieve completeness and overcome this alienation by continuous withstanding. Therefore, he spiritually explained alienation. In contrast, the great philosopher Ludwig Andreas Feuerbach believed that alienation emerges when humans lose their species' nature and act freely and spontaneously. He called God an alienation of human nature, essentially a critique of religions. Influenced by these thoughts, Karl Marx thought that alienation means the detachment of human objects from the human body. To be specific, a human is in existence as an object and makes their power externalized and objectified in the development process. In contrast, these objectified existences are converted into external foreign power that is not controlled by humans but controls humans.[96]

Today, "alienation" is widely used as a generalized philosophical concept in various fields. In the Post-industrial Age, when patents were gradually developing into dominant property rights,[97] the alienation of private rights of patents was also unavoidable. As mentioned previously, as technologies become more complicated and diverse and the trend of economic globalization prevails, the awareness of the private right of patents becomes more noticeable. Governments and enterprises in developed countries interfere in and even construct the private rights of patents to maximize their benefits, and many unreasonable regulations appear. Meanwhile, when the private right of patents is applied and practiced, its essence is alienated, and the power that contradicts the purpose of protecting rights is generated. This leads to the alienation trend of the private rights system of patents. In the Pre-industrial Age, the government constructed the patent privilege system to encourage industrial development and improve social welfare, mainly for the public interest. In the Industrial Age, because of the compromise and game between the industrial and commercial classes and the government, the patent system, on the one hand, gradually became the private right and property of inventors; on the other hand, the government claimed to encourage creations and technological innovations. The industrial and commercial classes and the government tried to seek a balance between public and private interests. In the Post-industrial Age, enterprises and the government sided with each other due to the neoliberalism trend to encourage technological and economic development. Enterprises propagandized that the patent was a private right, and in this situation, the patent was contradictory to promoting innovations and technological progress that it proclaimed in institutional construction and patent practices. The patent system hindered the diffusion of knowledge, new technologies, and innovation activities.[98] It restricted, restrained, and suppressed vulnerable groups of the private rights of patents and occupied public interests.[99]

Forms of alienation

Achilles' Heel:[100] Patents as the competition strategy and tool of enterprises

As mentioned previously, as technological development becomes diverse and complicated and technological innovations become specialized, the invention paradigm of technology has changed, and enterprises have already become subjects of technological innovation. In the United States, 12% of patents were granted to enterprises in 1885, and only 12.5% were granted to individual inventors in 1998.[101] As enterprises increasingly emphasized technologies and patents and controlled more abundant technological resources, they continuously influenced legislation and judicature through interest groups and converted preferences that could accomplish their benefits into policies and regulations.

On the one hand, they gradually transferred patent rights from the invention employees to enterprises. For example, in the United States, patent law in the nineteenth century focused on individual inventors. The rules at that time acknowledged an employee's rights related to their inventions: whoever invented them would apply it, and the invention ownership had nothing to do with the inventor's employment status. It mainly inherited the conventions in the Industrial Age, when inventions were made primarily by craftsmen enlightened by the production process. When hiring craftsmen, employers concentrated on the level of technologies they mastered instead of expecting them to create inventions, and they made no extra investments in R&D activities. Therefore, the creation of new technologies became the by-product of employment relations. Employers didn't possess the invention results of employees, and the craftsmen were responsible for patent application and possessed the patent right.[102]

By the end of the nineteenth century, as enterprises' power grew stronger and their investment and development expense became higher, inventors were gradually controlled by enterprises, which appealed for applying the rights of employees' inventions in judicial practice. Courts also began to favor enterprises. In the case of Blauvelt v. Interior Conduit & Insulation in 1897, the court first introduced the shop right that as long as the employee's inventions used resources provided by the employer, the employer was entitled to use this invention without the employee's permission.[103] After the twentieth century, more and more enterprises established R&D departments, and enterprises became the subject of technological innovations. The American courts increasingly preferred enterprises. In 1924, the United States Supreme Court denied that the patent right belonged to employees in the case of Standard Parts Co. v. Peck. The Supreme Court believed that before Peck was hired to improve the functions of automobile components, his employer, the Ford Motor Company, had regulated in the employment contract signed with him that the enterprise possessed the patent right. On this occasion, the patent right was owned by the employer. Then, the following conventions were formed in the United States: if employers signed contracts with employees, then the configuration of patent rights shall be governed by the contract; without the contract, if the employee used the employer's resources, the patent right belonged to the employee but could be applied by the employer.[104] In 1952, the United States converted this convention into a written law. In 2011, the patent law was modified again, and the procedure for the employer to own an employee's inventions was simplified in the *Invention Clause*. The employer could appeal for patent applications directly as an applicant rather than appealing on behalf of inventors; the employer could possess the patent after authorization. This legal modification solved the problem of the postponement in operating patent protection when the employee didn't support the patent application. Therefore, many countries have gained inspiration from American legislation, and enterprises have become the center of patent law.

On the other hand, as enterprises gradually seized patent rights, patents became their core resources. Patents existed as an exclusive legal right and became a competition tool in enterprises. As a strategic resource and competition weapon, patents played a powerful new role. According to the survey of the Content Management

System implemented in the United States, the leading causes of applying patents for enterprises were (in descending order of importance) preventing replication, shielding competitors, and acquiring liberties of applications (e.g., freedom of threats or lawsuits of others based on their patents). However, acquiring reputation and permission profits were rarely mentioned. Surveys by European companies offered the same ranking. When confronting more intense competition, enterprises tended to apply for more invention patents.[105] In practice, especially in the IPR management of many enterprises and multinationals, patents were merely commercial and competition tools, and they even lost the noble purpose granted by law and the moral threshold set by society. Specifically, they have the following features. 1. Enterprises sought patent "enclosure movements" and brought many questionable patents. If enterprises used their strong R&D abilities to create many inventions and applied for patents, which was normal, some enterprises applied for many low-quality questionable patents or nonsense patents that were widely distributed in all industries to demonstrate development capacity and gain more bargaining power in cross-licensing.[106] Harhoff and Scherer investigated patents and discovered that the value distribution of patents was already severely twisted. Most were valueless, and only the minority had considerable value. 2. Some enterprises applied for or purchased patents, not for commercial purposes but to seize market advantages and prevent competitors from entering the same market. An example was the case of McDonald v. Johnson & Johson in 1983. Johnson & Johson purchased many of McDonald's patents but didn't put them into commercial applications. Instead, Johnson & Johson used them to restrict its competitors from entering the same market. In addition, in the case of Alling Co. v. Global Co. in 1991, after Global Co. purchased the new patents of Alling Co., it didn't use them and left them unused for several years.[107] 3. They use patent lawsuits to oppress and attack competitors. A typical example was the patent war between Samsung and Apple from 2010 to 2014. The fundamental purpose of Apple's prosecution against Samsung was to suppress Samsung using the patent lawsuit.[108] 4. Patents could be used to control technological and industrial development. In the Post-industrial Age, enterprises used "patent alliances"[109] and "patent standards"[110] to control technological development and, therefore, industrial development or to tighten their control over technologies and industries.

Consequently, in the Post-industrial Age, the function of patents has been largely altered. Patents are not merely a legal concept; they have become a management concept[111] in the eyes of greedy entrepreneurs who keep "alienating" the patent system. This system has gotten rid of its original position and seemed to leave the assigned role of encouraging inventions and motivating the commercial development of new products.[112] The existing patent system is already alienated as the commercial tool for enterprises to grasp economic benefits at their will, which hinders knowledge diffusion, postpones the spread of new technologies, restricts innovations, and wastes precious resources in the economy and time of the rights owners and the third person. In addition, it sets barriers to prevent competitors from entering the market, which makes the majority of the market controlled by some large enterprises with numerous patents, which will have less motivation for innovation. After all, these enterprises are in a commercial environment with less competition. They can secure monopoly profits from early innovations that have already become patents.[113]

Irrational expansions of the private right of patents

With the development of technology, enterprises and developed countries continuously advance the all-around and multilayered expansion of the private rights of patents to gain more profits. In the Industrial Age, the object of the patent system was still mainly mechanical procedures and facilities. As Robert P. Merges described, in the first century of the United States, "if you put technology in a bag and shook it, it would make some noise."[114] In the Post-industrial Age, the rapid development of high technologies, like biotechnology and information technology, poses new questions and challenges to the traditional patent system. Many objects that challenge traditional theories are granted patents and protected in developed countries because of their significant economic benefits. Therefore, the results of knowledge innovations in many high technologies become the theme of patents, and the range and field of knowledge innovations protected by patents also expand quickly. As the superpower of technologies and knowledge innovations worldwide, the United States was the first, because of its comprehensive and extensive reality of knowledge innovations, to have strong, substantial requirements for the expansion of the subjects of patent protection. In 1952, the United States extended the patent themes with corresponding regulations to everything created by humans. This tendency of patent expansion has been further strengthened since the 1980s. The American Federal Supreme Court set a precedent for gene technologies, including microorganisms, multicellular plants, seeds, and even multicellular animals, to be granted the patent right in the case of Dimond v. Chakrabarty and the case of ex parte Hibber (1980). In the case of State Street Bank (1998), the American Federal Circuit Court decided that the computer system in the management of stocks and funds constituted the theme of patents, which extended the patent theme to knowledge innovation such as commercial methods. In the case of AT&T v. Excel Communication, the case of Amazon v. Barnes & Noble, and the Bilski case (2009), the court further defined the patent of commercial methods and removed the ban that commercial methods shouldn't be granted a patent in the United States. Especially in the Amazon case, the Primary Court of West Washington D.C. even believed that Amazon's "One-Click" method could also be granted a patent.[115] Today, the range of patent objects in the United States is becoming wider and wider and becoming so close to the commercial world that any method or product with commercial value is likely to gain patent protection. One can see various invention applications or judicial lawsuits in the American Patent Office and courts, such as artistic methods, athlete's motions, building styles, and economic theories.[116]

Japan and the EU pay close attention and respond actively to the continuous expansion of American patents. They also continue to expand the patent themes. The Board of Appeal of the European Patent Office widely explains the patent standards (technology standards) via related precedents, which protect plants and animals, computer software, commercial methods, and others. Japan also "applies natural rules" to patent standards and involves genes, computer software, and commercial methods in patent protection.[117] Oppressed by developed countries, many developing countries expanded their patent objects to a certain extent. Moreover, the 1994 TRIPS Agreement was dominated by large American enterprises, the ACTA was established with the participation of developing countries and beyond the WIPO and WTO frameworks, and the TPP Agreement set a higher standard "in the face of the high-quality development in the twentieth century," all improve standards for expanding protection of patent objects, extending the term of protection, and rejecting parallel import.

The irrational expansion of private rights of patents arouses wide critiques of people. First, putting medicines under the protection of patent rights leads to public health crises in some regions. For example, as patent rights protect medicines, they become too expensive, especially those used for rare diseases like AIDS. Patients in Africa and America, where AIDS is rampant, can't afford the high expense of these medicines, lose the chance of treatment, and encounter fatal threats. Second, putting research tools like genes under the protection of patent rights will significantly increase the cost of related scientific research. For example, there are a lot of related technologies in biological technologies. If these technologies apply for patents, once someone attempts to develop and apply some biological technology, they have to obtain permission for numerous upstream patents, which hinders later research and applications and leads to the so-called "anti-public tragedies." Third, putting plants, animals, and human genes under the protection of patent rights triggers widespread controversies over ethics. For example, religious groups and the Green Peace Organization strongly oppose involving creatures and genetic materials in patent objects, considering it an offense against the destiny of life.[118] Grassroots activists, farmer organizations, environmental groups, development groups, human rights organizations, and consumer organizations launched a global "Living Things No Patent" movement.[119] They stated that transnational seed and medicine companies continuously rob developing countries of biological diversity and traditional knowledge. They alter these discoveries by science, apply for patents, and sell them to people at high prices. The condition of granting patents to seeds and plants goes like this. The top ten seed companies currently control 30% of the world's USD 23 billion commercial seed market. These enterprises control the food supply with all efforts and impose increasingly complicated authentication and application expenses on farmers and local residents.[120] Finally, as the life cycle of technologies accelerates, the application and maintenance restrictions of patents are increasingly shortened. However, the average protection cycle of patents today is 40% longer than in the nineteenth century. The justification for the extension of the patent protection term by ACTA and TPP deserves to be discussed.

The all-powerful patent system: One size fits all?

In the Pre-industrial and Industrial Ages, technology merely took the form of mechanical technologies, and industries were not very distributed. Although the problem of homogeneity was already exposed, it was tolerant. In the Post-industrial Age, technologies have become diverse and complicated, and inventions and creations have corresponding formation mechanisms according to their respective industries. However, when constructing the patent system, enterprises and governments still follow the single patent system that was initiated in Venice, regardless of type, features, development costs, difficulty in development, and social influences.

First, the development expenses vary significantly in industry and invention. Some inventions emerge from pure occasionality and require no research investments. At the same time, other industries, such as pharmaceutical enterprises, are likely to pay enormous research expenses due to the complexity of the development of related technologies and excessive waiting times for administrative approvals. For instance, an American pharmaceutical company proclaimed that its average cost to develop a new medicine was 802 million dollars.[121] Akin to the pharmaceutical industry, the semiconductor industry is also a field that requires significant effort. The development of microprocessors requires strenuous efforts in line designing and, an investment of millions of dollars and the establishment of brand-new production facilities and procedures. The requirement for senior technicians and professional technological facilities makes microprocessor development a highly money-intensive industry. Generally speaking, the expense used to develop the new generation of microprocessors is likely to be higher than 4 billion dollars. In contrast, other industries, like computer software, have a much smaller requirement for research investments. Two programmers could develop a commercial software program in a garage. Although in these years, the expenses of programming codes have increased, in most cases, it is still possible to complete a set of application programs with expenses of fewer than 1 million dollars. The R&D expenses vary from industry to industry, leading to various requirements for protecting the patent system. The industries with higher R&D costs in money and time have a higher and more urgent requirement for the patent system to recover investments.[122]

Second, the difficulty of imitation in different industries varies due to the related technological features. In some industries, like product invention, imitation is cheaper and faster because product consumption reveals technological clues and valuable information. In contrast, imitation in some industries is more expensive and time-consuming. For example, method inventions are usually difficult to imitate, because competitors have no chance of observing them. Therefore, in terms of method inventions, commercial secrets could provide sufficient protection (e.g., the recipe of Coca-Cola) compared with patents. Some studies indicate that as the chemical industries pay more attention to method innovations, they depend more on commercial secrets rather than patent protection.[123]

Third, there are differences between discrete and accumulative innovations. Discrete innovations, including those in the pharmaceutical and chemical industries, can be separated into pieces. Innovative inventions can be improved, but they usually adopt small-ranged subsequent inventions. In contrast, accumulative innovations are progressively improved based on existing products. A product of accumulative innovation may contain numerous components. The most typical examples are the semiconductor and computer software industries. The meaning of patent protection differs between discrete innovations and accumulative ones. In the former case, the robust protection of patents won't hinder subsequent technological innovations, and in the latter case, it may hinder subsequent technological innovations.

Fourth, different industries have different significance in society. For example, luxurious products are unnecessary for society, and people have smaller requirements for them. However, medicines are related to human health and life and have great significance in society. Strong protection of patented medicines might greatly influence public health and lives. In developing countries, people can't afford high prices for medicines, leading to patents and public health crises in developing countries. For instance, one in eight in South Africa is infected with HIV, but the prices make the infected unable to afford medicines. Even in the United States, some patented medicines are so expensive that they betray the purpose of the R&D investments in medicines, which arouses dissatisfaction among American citizens. For instance, the selling price of an EpiPen, an American allergy medicine, has risen to USD 608.61, which has increased by 500% in almost one decade. So many citizens with allergies can't afford such an expensive medicine.[124]

Empirical studies by European scholars also indicate that the influence of patents on different industries is various. They are only effective in chemistry, biological sciences, medicines, and new products when protecting medical facilities. They are relatively effective in machines, computers, radio, TV, and automobiles. They are only effective in innovative methods in glass and oil. They are considered ineffective in the following industries, including some high-technology sectors, such as electronic components, instruments, and aerospace.[125] Therefore, the proportion of products that are granted patents in Europe is relatively high in pharmaceutical (80%), chemistry, machines, offices, computer facilities, and precise instruments (50%) and relatively low (20%) in transport, communication, other traffic facilities, basic metal, weaving, and cloth.[126] Patents are more effective for product innovations than method innovations. According to a survey in 1990–1993, 36% of the product innovations by large European companies were granted patents; however, only 22% of method innovations were patented. Compared with products, methods are difficult to acquire by the competition. Therefore, their secrets could be kept more effectively, and they would suffer more losses via disclosure in patent files.[127]

The contradictions are apparent because technologies and industries differ in their requirements for the patent system. The patent system is like a "master key," in which large enterprises and developed countries make efforts to construct, which is actually a method that suits all technologies. The operation of this system has become increasingly expensive. Although the train hasn't gone off the track yet, it gradually loses control. Worse still, the problems with the patent system increase the uncertainty of innovation investments, which harms various encouraging measures designed by the patent system.[128] Mueller believes it might never be possible to provide a thorough solution that determines rewards and encouragement; the most probable project is to give different answers to different types of technologies.[129] Dan L. Burk and Mark. A. Lemley gave a more concrete answer. They thought that the court could apply various patent rules and flexible standards on particular cases based on industrial features. These standards could be called the policy levers used by the court in patent cases. When the court distinguishes different inventions, it won't clearly mention the industries they are situated to, but the influence of the method it applies on different industries is disproportionate. Although the court doesn't clearly demonstrate the technological distinctions, it becomes possible for the patent law to establish industrial distinguishment rules in particular cases by applying some policy levers.[130]

Explosive increase in patent applications and lawsuits

In the Post-industrial Age, the increase in the knowledge of society, the shortening cycle of technological innovation, and the rapid technological innovation and diffusion contributed to an explosive increase in patent applications worldwide. However, Peter Drahos and John Braithwaite have proposed a disturbing reason. The policy committee behind the American Patent Office inevitably includes the representatives of the private sector rather than consumers and other nongovernmental organizations. Therefore, the motto of the American Patent Office is to satisfy their clients of multinationals, which makes the Bureau's patent authorization more unbridled.[131] As the strongest patent power worldwide, patent applications in the United States were 151,491 in 1988, 260,889 in 1998, and 485,312 in 2008, which increased by 72.2% from 1988 to 1998 and 86% from 1998 to 2008. By September 2013, the American Patent Trademark Bureau's patent application reached 601,317.[132] In the EU, the patent applications of the European Patent Office increased by 150% from 1995–to 2006, from 800,000 to 2 million. The annual increase rate of applications was more than 9%, and the increase rate in GDP was less than 2.5%. On the one hand, the explosive increase in patent applications leads to unprecedented patent overstock in all countries, even in the United States, which has the first-ranked professional patent examination teams.[133] The most fundamental cause is that the examination ability of the patent examination organ doesn't match patent and technology development. On the other hand, numerous patent applications lead to a reduction in patent authorization quality and an increase in uncertainty.[134] According to surveys by these scholars, more than half of patent rights are finally proclaimed ineffective in prosecutions. These phenomena indicate from various perspectives that the patent quality in the current patent system has decreased, which wastes many administrative costs and hinders the progress of science and useful technologies. Lemley believed,

> As long as the Patent Office (PTO) is beset with a flood of applications and little time to review them, and as long as the incentives are to grant rather than deny patents, the PTO as the will continue to issue bad patents.[135]

In addition, since 1980, patent lawsuits have become more frequent, which is mainly due to the deterioration in patent reports, an increase in special industrial elements and prosecution rewards, enterprises' growing lawsuit tendencies, an increase in patent trolls, and a decrease in patent examinations.[136] In the United States, patent lawsuits tend to increase much more quickly than ordinary civil prosecutions. Patent prosecutions increased by 122% from 1988–2005, and civil prosecutions increased by 5%.[137] Excessive patent lawsuits waste social resources and unsettle the stability of the patent's private rights. De Soto believed that if the patent could effectively function as a property, it would provide enough stimulation for investments and trade. However, if the patent system is not implemented effectively, a large number of controversies and expenses will appear.[138] When the effectiveness of patent rights becomes uncertain, the property right is also likely to be ineffective.[139]

Enlightenment of the history

The transition history of the patent system in the Post-industrial Age could offer some enlightenment as follows.

First, in the Post-industrial Age, changes in the technological, economic, and cultural environments made knowledge-intensive enterprise groups generate the institutional concept of expanding the scope of IPRs continuously and constructing the global IPR protection framework. Therefore, they made all efforts to convert their concepts, benefits, and proposals into policies and institutions, including alliances, lobbies, and elections. The government's policies and legislation gradually prefer these enterprises because they are the dominant force in technological innovations and economic development. Therefore, in the Post-industrial Age, the government, as the only representative of the public interests in Western society, is unprecedentedly consistent with private enterprises in terms of benefits. The IPR system, including the patent system, gradually becomes international and even continuously tends to be alienated.

> The patent law does not live in the seclusion and silence of a Trappist monastery … . Once you segregate the patent law from the natural environment in which it now has its being, you contract the area of its exposure to the self-correcting forces of the law. In time, such a body of law, secluded from the rest, develops a jargon of its own, thought patterns that are unique, internal policies that it subserves and which are different from and sometimes at odds with the policies pursued by the general law.[140]

In the Post-industrial Age, the private rights mechanism of patents acts like a wild horse that gallops beyond the path of purposive rationality. The private rights system of patents has degenerated into a tool used by enterprises to fulfill their benefits and an institution designed to encourage enterprise investments. In other words, the private rights system of patents goes further and further from the rational purpose of encouraging technological innovations that it claims.

Second, the patent system is still the policy tool used by the government to develop the economy and technology. It was gradually upgraded in the Post-industrial Age to the weapon of the developed countries, like the United States, to initiate trade sanctions and wars. In the Pre-industrial and Industrial Ages, the patent system was no more than a regulatory measure for developing domestic technology, industry, and commerce. However, in the Post-industrial Age, with the globalization of technology and the economy and the continuous lobbies of enterprise groups, the American government gradually associated the IPR system with foreign trade and modified trade acts in 1979, 1984, and 1988 to strengthen the connection between IPR protection and trade. Today, international treaties, including Section 301 and the TRIPS Agreement, have become a weapon in the hands of the American government to initiate trade sanctions and trade wars worldwide. For instance, in history, the United States made special Section 301 investigations on Chinese IPRs in April 1991, June 1994, April 1996, and October 2010. On 23 March 2018, the United States again used Section 301 to initiate a trade war against China.

Third, in the Post-industrial Age, technology has an increasingly important influence on the transition of the patent system. The most fundamental reason is that the function and value of technology in the economy become increasingly apparent, and their influence on authority figures becomes larger. Technological innovation has reached an unprecedented height, becoming more rapid, complicated, and diverse. Technology has developed closer connections with economic activities than ever and fundamentally altered the paradigm of technological innovation and the dominant driver of economic development. This makes the enterprises the most significant authority figures that shape the rules of the patent system. Galbraith pointed out in *The New Industrial State* that in society, authority obviously migrates among the factors of production, and in different historical stages, different factors of production become the most precious, the most difficult to replace, and the most significant because of the gap in technological development levels. Whoever controls the supply of the factor of production will possess the authority. In the Pre-industrial Age, land was the most significant factor of production. Due to the scarcity of land, authority was associated with land, and the feudal government that controlled land was the primary authority figure in shaping institutional rules. In the Industrial Age, people reclaimed wastelands, made expansions, and continued to acquire new lands. In addition, with the increase in mechanical inventions and knowledge about metallurgy and engineering, the chances for the application of capital also increased at an astonishing speed. Therefore, people invested more capital in more advanced technologies, production was expanded, and income and deposits also increased. For example, during the First Industrial Revolution, the proportion of industrial sectors, such as coal, iron and steel, railways, and automobiles, in state-made products kept increasing. At the same time, the share of agriculture in production kept shrinking. To manufacture these products, the industrial and commercial classes needed land, which was easy to acquire, and a labor force, which was exceptionally abundant. What counted most was capital. Therefore, capital replaced land and became the most essential factor in production, and the prestige and authority of the state were increasingly controlled by industrial and commercial capitalists.[141]

In the Post-industrial Age, on the one hand, the development of industry made the supply of capital increasingly abundant; therefore, the tendency of "excessive deposits" appeared, and capital was no longer the scarce factor of production. On the other hand, the professional knowledge required for industrial and technological development becomes more complicated. Professional knowledge becomes the decisive factor in production for an enterprise's success. Large enterprises with advanced R&D departments and organizations gradually control the authority, and the people who dominate the production are those who control capital and technology. There is a decreasing number of capital and technology giants who seize and monopolize the benefits of this reform.[142] Price and salary are regulated based on their collective benefits. They dominate society, define the moral principle of society, and control the state, and the state has become an executive committee that serves the will and benefits of the large industrial and commercial classes. The market power that is granted to corporate giants on a large-scale, whether absolutely or relatively, is the foundation of economic power and the foundation of political and social power.[143]

Fourth, the TRIPS Agreement is not as brilliant as people expected, and its influence on the international community is not as positive. In reality, it has led to many problems. The United States, as the firmest advocate of the TRIPS Agreement, also believes that it will pay an enormous economic price for the agreement. As Reichman said, neither all the developed countries nor the United States should expect to achieve success easily from the execution of the TRIPS Agreement. Although some developed countries might benefit more than others, all countries will feel the heavy burden in some economic sectors in the age of the social costs of IPR protection. This movement contradicts the global trade liberalization promised widely and has the residual odor of mercantilism.[144] The TRIPS Agreement implies such an assumption that what the developing countries benefit from applying foreign technologies without permission is equal to the illegal losses of the enterprises in the developed countries.[145] This assumption reflects merchants' opinions, which weakens the free competition regulation and a regime based on better performance, lower prices of products, and more efficient production procedures, and it takes the protection of license owners into consideration. Vulnerable IPR protection laws allow someone to access the market again who could provide cheaper and better products through imitation and additional innovations.[146] Therefore, strengthening these laws might counteract competition. Other analysts also advocated that the current IPR rules are incompatible with economic innovation. D. Foray believed that innovations are not motivated by technological breakthroughs but by the conventional development of existing technologies.[147] The property rights system that serves as protection and exclusion in the TRIPS Agreement significantly influences innovation, because it hinders the spread of existing knowledge. To some extent, research and discovery are mainly recreations based on precedent inventions. Excessive patent protection will lead to monopoly prices that are of low efficiency in society and discourage competitors from developing a new generation of products.[148]

Fifth, because the global economy and technology are related to trade, the relationship between the patent systems in all countries becomes closer and closer. However, as the profit-seeking activities of interest groups become more apparent, the patent system of capitalist countries has no natural justice in the least. In addition, these interest groups are not satisfied with the beneficial framework of the TRIPS Agreement and try to seek a broader and more diverse international institutional protection. The ACTA and TPP are the best examples. They attempted to construct a unified SPLT worldwide. The globalization of the patent system has significant value in the coordination of national laws; however, it might incur larger coordination expenses. Moreover, the history of patent law indicates that patent law is derived from diversity rather than similarity between national laws, and IPR protection measures are to be taken according to different economic and social development stages.[149] Countries and regions, such as Venice, France, Germany, Britain, and the United States, have different laws and practices that improve and enhance the patent practice, and experiments in diversity and laws have continued until today. Therefore, the international community shouldn't be urged to define a uniform legal responsibility for IPR protection. Instead, the diversity of the patent systems should be maintained. As Professor Dufy pointed out, if domestic and international patent policymakers realize the importance of diversity, patent law in the twenty-first century will develop in more diverse forms.[150] Developing countries should enact their patent systems when their economic and technological development status is taken into account. Based on their national reality, they should keep autonomy intact when signing bilateral or international treaties, propose their own requirements, try to build the interest balance mechanism within the international IPRs, and resolutely oppose the abuse of international private rights of patents by developed countries.

Notes

1 Nobuhiro Nakayama. *Multimedia and Copyright*. Zhang Yurui. Beijing: Patent Literature Press, 1997:3.
2 David Kairys. *The Politics in Law: A Progressive Critique*. Xin Chunying. Beijing: China University of Political Science and Law, 2008:185; Susan K. Sell. *Private Power, Public Law: The Globalization of Intellectual Property Rights*. Dong Gang, Zhou Chao. Beijing: China Renmin University Press, 2008:178.
3 Zhang Zhuoyuan. *Dictionary of Political Economy*. Beijing: New Economic Science Press, 1999:201.
4 Daniel Bell. *The Coming of Post-Industrial Society: A Venture in Social Forecasting*. Beijing: Xinhua Publishing House, 1997:128–129.
5 Organization for Economic Co-operation and Development, ed. *The Knowledge-Based Economy*. Yang Hongjin, Xue Lan. Beijing: Machinery Industry Press, 1997:17–26.
6 Zhang Wenxian. *Knowledge Economy and Legal System Innovation*. Beijing: Peking University Press, 2012:4–10.
7 Maurice Daumas. *A History of Technology and Invention. Progress through the Ages, Vol. I, The Origins of Technological Civilization; Vol. II, The First Stages of Mechanization*. New York: Crown, 1969:1–2.

8 European Patent Office. *Scenarios for the Future: How Might IP Regimes Evolve by 2025?*. Guo Minsheng. Beijing: Patent Literature Press, 2008:141.
9 Gao Hongshen, Yang Hongzhi. *Tutorial on the Economics of Knowledge*. Beijing: China Renmin University Press, 2002:8.
10 Peercy Paul S. The Drive to Miniaturization, 406 *Nature*, 2000, p. 1023.
11 Paul S. The Drive to miniaturization, p. 143.
12 Zhao Yulin. *Economics of Innovation*. Beijing: China Economic Press, 2006:32.
13 Zhao Yulin. *Economics of Innovation*, 32.
14 Chen Baosen. Talking about the "New Economy" and "Knowledge Economy" in the United States, *Contemporary World*, 1998 (9).
15 Gao Hongshen, Yang Hongzhi. *Tutorial on the Economics of Knowledge*, 148.
16 Hua Min. Economic Globalization and China's Opening to the Outside World, *Academic Monthly*, 2007 (7).
17 Liang Youcai. World Economic Outlook 1997, *New Century Leader*, 1997 (3).
18 Hua Min, Sun Feng. The Causes, Characteristics, Effects of Economic Globalization and China's Response, *Fudan Journal* (Social Science Edition), 2000 (5).
19 He Fei. *Who Is the Best in Global Knowledge and Technology-Intensive Industries?*. http://china.caixin.com/2016 01 31/100905592.html.
20 He Fei. *Who Is the Best in Global Knowledge and Technology-Intensive Industries?*.
21 Yu Tao, Weng Lingjun. The Development Trend of International Technology Trade and China's Countermeasure Options, *Economist*, 2008 (11).
22 Sell. *Private Power, Public Law*, 36.
23 Keynesianism (also called Keynesian economics) is an economic theory based on the thoughts in Keynes' *The General Theory of Employment, Interest and Money*. It proposes that the country should apply expansive economic policies and encourage economic growth by increasing demands; in other words, the macro control should be enhanced, the government spending should be increased, and deficit financing should be applied to stimulate the economy and maintain prosperity.
24 Wei Zhimin. The Evolution of Industrial Organization Theory in the Last 70 Years, *Economic Review*, 2003 (1).
25 In 1990, the American International Economy Institute held a seminar discussing the adjustment and reform in Latin America since the mid and late 1980s in Washington, D.C. In the seminar, John Williamson, the former president of the Institute, said the participants reached a consensus to a certain extent in terms of the ten policy tools used or to be used in Latin American countries. Since the headquarters of the international organization and the U.S. Department of Finance are in Washington, D.C., the seminar was also held there. This consensus is called "The Washington Consensus." This consensus argues that Latin American countries should reduce governmental interference and promote trade and financial liberalization, which are proposed and form a series of policies.
26 G. Sen. Comment on Gill and Law, 16 *Millennium: Journal of International Studies*, 1987, pp. 87–88.
27 Zhou Zhaoguang. How to View Western Neoliberalism and Its International Impact, *Fujian Forum* (Humanities and Social Sciences Edition), 2007 (3).
28 Zhou Zhaoguang. How to View Western Neoliberalism.
29 Susan Sell, Christopher May. Moments in Law: Contestation and Settlement in the History of Intellectual Property, 8 *Review of International Political Economy*, 2001, pp. 467–500.

30 John Naisbitt. *Megatrends: Ten New Directions Transforming Our Lives*. Mei Yan. Beijing: China Social Science Press, 1984:15.
31 Yang Lixiong. Commodity or Gift: Neoliberalism versus New Left in Cyberspace, *Studies in Natural Dialectics*, 2004 (1).
32 Chen Yekui. A Rational Critique of the "Cult of Information", *Intelligence Data Work*, 1999 (6).
33 David Silverstein. Patents, Science and Innovation: Historical Linkages and Implications for Global Technological Competitiveness, 17 *Rutgers Computer & Technology Law Journal*, 1991, pp. 313–314.
34 N. R. Lamoreaux, K. L. Sokoloff. Long-Term Change in the Organization of Inventive Activity, 93 *Proceedings of the National Academy of Sciences*, 1996, pp. 12686–12692.
35 Peter Drahos, John Braithwaite. *Information Feudalism: Who Owns the Knowledge Economy*. Liu Xuetao. Beijing: Intellectual Property Press, 2005:44.
36 Suzanne Scotchmer. *Innovation and Incentives*. Liu Yong. Shanghai: Gezhi Publishing House, 2010:13.
37 Scotchmer. *Innovation and Incentives*, 13–23.
38 John Kenneth Galbraith. *The New Industrial State*. Ji Fei. Shanghai: Shanghai People's Publishing House, 2012:73.
39 Joseph Schumpeter. *Capitalism, Socialism, and Democracy*. Wu Liangjian. Beijing: The Commercial Press, 1999:64–68, 182.
40 W.W. Rostow. *How It All Began: Origins of the Modern Economy*. Huang Qixiang, et al. Beijing: The Commercial Press, 2014:122–175.
41 Rostow. *How It All Began*, 177.
42 Jeremy Rifkin. *The Zero Marginal Cost Society: The Internet of Things, the Collaborative Commons, and the Eclipse of Capitalism*. Beijing: CITIC Press, 2014:22.
43 Susan Strange. The Westfailure System, 25 *Review of International Studies*, 1999, pp. 345–354.
44 Liu Shixin. How Much More China Has to Lose on Intellectual Property Rights?. *Science and Technology Information*, 2003 (9).
45 Rifkin. *The Zero Marginal Cost Society*, 22.
46 Galbraith. *The New Industrial State*, 74.
47 Sell. *Private Power, Public Law*, 183.
48 Sell. *Private Power, Public Law*, 34.
49 Ngaire Woods. Economic Ideas and International Relations: Beyond Rational Neglect, 39 *International Studies Quarterly*, 1995, p. 170.
50 Geoffrey R. D. Underhill. Global Issues in Historical Perspective, in R. Stubbs and G. R. D. Underhill (eds.), *Political Economy and the Changing Global Order* Oxford, UK: Oxford University Press, 1994 pp. 145–161.
51 Ma Ye. On the Three Basic Principles of Neoliberalism, *Marxist Studies*, 2006 (2).
52 Kairys. *The Politics in Law*, 183.
53 Drahos, Braithwaite. *Information Feudalism*, 251.
54 Gene M. Grossman, Elhanan Helpman. *Interest Groups and Trade Policy*. Li Zenggang. Beijing: China Renmin University Press, 2005:3–4.
55 Sell. *Private Power, Public Law*, 183.
56 Stephen Wilks. Comparative Capitalism and the Political Power of Business, *Globalization and Capitalist Diversity: Experience on the Asian Madomestic*, conference proceedings, 1996, p. 45.
57 Kairys. *The Politics in Law*, 190.
58 Drahos, Braithwaite. *Information Feudalism*, 2.

59 In 1986, members of the IPC were Bristol, CBS, DuPont, General Motors, Hewlett-Packard, IBM, Johnson & Johnson, Merck, Monsanto, and Pfizer.
60 In 1959, the U.S. manufacturing industry of high-technology products occupied 79% of the global market, but its proportion fell to 47% in the 1970s–1980s. At the same time, Japan and Western European countries represented by West Germany began to share the global market of high-technology products. Tetsuo Tomita. *Intellectual Property Rights in Market Competition*. Liao Zhengheng, et al. Beijing: The Commercial Press, 2000:158.
61 Dominique Guellec, Bruno van Pottelsberghe. *The Economics of the European Patent System: IP Policy for Innovation and Competition*. Zhang Nan. Beijing: Intellectual Property Press, 2016:27.
62 According to a survey of the American government in 1981, the profit increase rate of high-tech enterprises with high R&D investments was three times higher than those with low R&D investments; its productivity was doubled, the employment growth rate was nine times, and the price increase was only one-sixth. Bao Haibo, Sheng Shihao. Innovation and Performance of the U.S. Patent System Since the 1980s, *Technology and Law*, 2002 (4).
63 Sell, May. Moments in Law, pp. 467–500.
64 According to the economic theory of the Chicago School, the larger the scale was, the higher the efficiency would be. Therefore, it naturally emphasized free competition, commodity competition (including technology competition) in the market, and the choice right of consumers as the basis of capitalism. Tomita. *Intellectual Property Rights in Market Competition*, 169.
65 Ibid.
66 US Department of Justice, 1988:16.
67 Paul S. Hoff. *Inventions in the Marketplace: Patent Licensing and the US Antitrust Laws*. Washington, DC: American Enterprise Institute, 1986:19.
68 Many courts believed "the existence of the patent system proved the legality of the patent right." They asked any accuser to offer "precise, detailed, and convincing" proofs when prosecuting the court. Wang Bingyin, Wang Jianfeng. The Development of Patent System: Monopoly and Anti-monopoly of Technology, *Guangxi Social Science*, 2004 (3).
69 L. G. Kastriner. The Revival of Confidence in the Patent System, 73 *Journal of the Patent & Trademark Office Society*, 1991, p. 20.
70 J. Enyart. A GATT Intellectual Property Code, *Les Nouvelles*, June 1990, 25, p. 54.
71 Enyart. A GATT Intellectual Property Code, p. 54.
72 Sell. *Private Power, Public Law*, 96.
73 IPR's "technological knowledge is closely related to improving its protection promises. Compared with countries and other actors, the large companies in the Committee have a decisive advantage in the Uruguay Round Negotiations." Sell. *Private Power, Public Law*, 97.
74 According to the comment of Jacques Goering, the counsellor of the IPC, "without the close cooperation between the American government and private sectors, it will never appear that the IPR is converted to a trade problem, and IPR protection is improved via trade." Sell. *Private Power, Public Law*, 97–98.
75 Sell. *Private Power, Public Law*, 96.
76 Sylvia Ostry. *Governments and Corporations in a Shrinking World: Trade and Innovation Policies in the United States, Europe and Japan*. New York: Council on Foreign Relations, 1990:21–22.
77 M. P. Ryan. Function-Specific and Linkage-Bargain Diplomacy of. International Intellectual Property Lawmaking, 19 *University of Pennsylvania Journal of International Economic Law*, 1998, p. 562.

78 Goering issued a series of strategies in the legislation file, including motivating economic movements in this aspect by IPR experts; participating in the Bern Convention; discussing IPR conventions in the framework of OECD or GATT multilateral negotiations with industrial countries with the same thought as "a strategy to prevent obstacles from least developed countries"; being aware of the necessity to negotiate with World Intellectual Property Organization (WIPO) to establish IPR principles in GATT; maintaining unilateral and bilateral measures to fight against piracy and failure of operations in foreign countries. Sell. *Private Power, Public Law*, 99–100.
79 Sell. *Private Power, Public Law*, 96.
80 Enyart, A GATT Intellectual Property Code, p. 54.
81 Enyart, A GATT Intellectual Property Code, p. 54.
82 Sell. *Private Power, Public Law*, 102.
83 Ostry. *Governments and Corporations in a Shrinking World*, 21–22.
84 Sell. *Private Power, Public Law*, 96.
85 Sell. *Private Power, Public Law*, 103.
86 The Intellectual Property Committee, Keidanren, UNICE, *Basic Framework of GATT Provisions on Intellectual Property: Statement of Views of the European, Japanese and United States Business Communities (June)*, 1998, p. 27.
87 This included Argentina, Brazil, Cuba, Egypt, India, Nicaragua, Nigeria, Peru, Tanzania, and Yugoslavia.
88 Sell. *Private Power, Public Law*, 96.
89 Peter Drahos. Global Property Rights in Information: The Story of TRIPS at the GATT, *Prometheus*, 1995, pp. 6–19.
90 R. Weissman. Long, Strange Trips: The Pharmaceutical Industry Drive to Harmonize Global Intellectual Property Rules, and the Remaining WTO Legal Alternatives Available to Third World Countries, *University of Pennsylvania Journal of International Economic Law*, 1996, p. 1076.
91 Peter Drahos. Thinking Strategically about Intellectual Property Rights, 21 *Telecommunications Policy*, 1997, pp. 202–203.
92 Drahos. Thinking Strategically about Intellectual Property Rights, pp. 202–203.
93 Denise Eby Rodrik. Comments on Maskus and Eby-Konan, in A. V. Deardoff and R. M. Stern (eds.), *Analytical and Negotiating Issues in the Global Trading System*. Ann Arbor, MI: University of Michigan Press, 1994, p. 449.
94 Sell. *Private Power, Public Law*, 96.
95 Liang Zhiwen. On the Patent Crisis and Its Solution. *Political Law Series*, 2011 (3).
96 Marx said in *Economic and Philosophical Manuscripts 1844*, "Alienation ... is the contradiction between freedom and consciousness, between consciousness and self-consciousness, between objects and subjects. In other words, it is the contradiction between abstract thoughts and perceptual realities or real sensibilities in the range of thoughts." Karl Marx. *Economic and Philosophic Manuscripts of 1844*. 3 ed. Marx, Engels, Lenin, and Stalin, Compilation Bureau of the Central Committee of the Communist Party of China. Beijing: People's Publishing House, 2000:99.
97 In 1982, the proportion of tangible and intangible properties (mainly IPRs) in the market value of 500 typical listed companies in the United States was 62% of the former and 38% of the latter, which was reversed in 1992 to 38% former and 62% latter. In 2002, the proportion of tangible properties was reduced to 13%, and intangible properties occupied 87%. Therefore, 87% of the market value of the stocks of American large enterprises was constituted of intangible properties. The value of IPRs, as an essential part of intangible properties, rose from year to year. Zhang Yurui, Zhou Yan, Gu Boxing, Cha Zhiqi. *How*

Do Foreign Companies Realize the Patent Value in China? Wielding the Two Weapons of Licensing and Litigation. www.sipo.govvcn/sipo/zscqb/guancha/t20040622_30329.htm.

98 Fang Xingdong. *Alert to Intellectual Property Degeneration.* www.cas.cn/Html/Dir0/02/79/68.htm.

99 Famous American economists, Adam B. Jaffe and Josh Lerner, criticized the obstacle function of the existing patent system on technologies and economies. They believed that the existing patent system became sand rather than lube in the wheels of development. Adam B. Jaffe, Josh Lerner. *Innovation and Its Discontents: How Our Broken Patent System Is Endangering Innovation and Progress, and What to Do about It.* Luo Jianping, Lan Hua. Beijing: China Renmin University Press, 2007:102.

100 Achilles is a nearly perfect and independent hero in Greek mythology whose only fatal defect was his heel. It is said that he was grasped at the heel by his mother the Goddess of Marine and put into the Styx after his birth. Therefore, he became invulnerable all around his body, and his only weakness was the heel, which was not soaked in the Styx. During the War of Troy, the invincible Achilles was finally shot by an arrow of Apolo at his heel and lost his life. After that, "Achilles' Heel" was used to describe a fatal weakness.

101 Robert P. Merges. One Hundred Years of Solicitude: Intellectual Property Law, 1900—2000, 88 *California Law Review*, 2000, p. 2187.

102 Wu Xinwang. *Innovative Markets and the Rise and Fall of Nations.* Beijing: Social Science Literature Press, 2012:46.

103 Wang Chongyuan. The Evolution of the American Job Invention System and Its Implications for China, *Journal of Anhui University* (Philosophy and Social Science Edition), 2012 (1).

104 Wang Chongyuan. The Evolution of the American Job Invention System.

105 Anthony Arundel, Isabelle Kabla. What Percentage of Innovations Are Patented? Empirical Estimates for European Firms, 27 *Research Policy*, 1998, p. 127.

106 Yuan Zhenfu. Intellectual Property Alienation: The Prisoner's Dilemma: The Purpose of Intellectual Property Legislation as a Reference, *Research on Intellectual Property Law*, 2006 (1).

107 Yee Wah Chin. Unilateral Technology Suppression: Appropriate Antitrust and Patent Law Remedies, *Antitrust Law Journal*, 66, 1998, pp. 441–447. Lv Wei. *Strengthening Antitrust Measures in Intellectual Property Protection.* www.blogchina.com/new/display/?id=14552.

108 Wang Taiping. *Study on the Reform of Patent System in the Era of Knowledge Economy.* Beijing: Law Press, 2016:84.

109 The patent alliance is the protocol in that the patent owner grants their patents to another party or a third party. Due to its essence (cooperative behavior of multiple enterprises) and other restriction clauses in the external authorization contract, patent alliances will inevitably form a monopoly and restrict competition. (1) Patent alliances are used to monopolize prices, restrict production, and distribute the market. (2) Without contracts, the members of the alliance will become competitors or potential competitors, and their alliance is quite likely to restrict competition. (3) If the patent alliance rejects other enterprises' participation on some occasions, it will be regarded as influencing normal market competition. For example, enterprises excluded by the alliance will lose the ability to make effective competition in the related product market. The patent alliance has a monopoly in the market, and the restriction to participate has no necessary relation to technological development in the alliance; and (4) It is likely to hinder the

development and innovation of alliance members. Li Yujian, Xuan Guoliang. Patent Alliance: A New Field of Strategic Alliance Research. *China Industrial Economics*, 2004 (2).

110 A technological standard is social and public. In essence, it is the condition necessary to be satisfyingly established for one or several production technologies. In traditional industries, standards and patent rights seem to be unrelated. Technological standards are concerned with technologies in the field of public knowledge, and patents care more about technologies in exclusive fields. However, this situation has fundamentally altered in the age of the knowledge economy. On the one hand, patent problems in technological projects selected in the enactment of standards in some fields cannot be avoided; however, on the other hand, more and more patent owners actively pursue the combination of technological projects with patents and signs to perform the patent strategy and consolidate their market advantage. When technologies protected by patents are involved in standards, the public standard is, at least partly, privately controlled by patent owners to a certain extent. Li Chuntian. *Introduction to Standardization*. Beijing: China Renmin University Press,2005:143.

111 Wang Jinguang, Zhang Tiejun. *Patenting for Survival: The Patent Blade and the Survival Dilemma of Chinese Enterprises*. Beijing: Intellectual Property Press, 2005: Preface VII.

112 Jaffe, Lerner. *Innovation and Its Discontents*, 68.

113 Stephan Kinsella. *Do Business without Intellectual Property*, available at www.stephankinsella.com/2014/10/do-business-without-intellectual-property.

114 Robert P. Merges. As Many as Six Impossible Patents Before Breakfast: Property Rights for Business Concepts and Patent System Reform, 14 *Berkeley Technology Law Journal*, 1999, p. 2.

115 *Amazon. com, Inc. v. Barnes and noble. com, Inc.*, 73F. Supp.2d 1228, 1249 (W.D. Wash. 1999).

116 Rick Feinberg. *Peculiar Patents: A Collection of Unusual and Interesting Inventions from the Files of the US Patent Office*. Secaucus, NJ: Carol Publishing Group, 1994, p. 154.

117 Wang Taiping. *Research on Patent Eligibility Criteria in the Era of Knowledge Economy*. Beijing: Intellectual Property Press, 2015:49–71.

118 For example, on 18 May 1995, about 200 religious leaders made a statement in Washington, D.C., that declared to stop granting patent rights for genes and genetically modified animals.

> We, the religious leaders signing in the following article, oppose any patents based on the life forms of humans and animals. We are extremely astonished by the act that the American Patent Office granted patents to human body parts and several genetically modified animals. We firmly believe that humans and animals are all created by God rather than humans; therefore, they shouldn't be granted patents as humans' inventions.

The Green Peace Organization believes that patents of living things and life materials are "modern slavery." Hu Bo. *The Ethical Basis of Patent Law*. Wuhan: Huazhong University of Science and Technology Press, 2011:193.

119 In 1995, an alliance "constituted of 255 agricultural, scientific, and trade organizations and more than 100,000 farmers and led by Economic Trend Foundation" made an appeal. It asked the American Patent and Trademark Bureau to repeal the plant patent granted to Grace Company in 1992, as it "lacks novelty and violates morality."

120 Sell. *Private Power, Public Law*, 96.

121 Dan L. Burk, Mark A. Lemley. *The Patent Crisis and How the Court Can Solve It*. Ma Ning, Yu Jun. Beijing: China University of Political Science and Law Press, 2013:52.
122 Burk, Lemley. *The Patent Crisis*, 55.
123 Wang Taiping. *Research on the Change of Patent System in the Era of Knowledge Economy*. Beijing: Law Press, 2016:30.
124 Scott Alexander. *Reverse Voxsplaining-Drugs vs. Chairs*, available at https://news.cnyes.com/news/id/2169438.
125 W. M. Cohen, D. A. Levinthal. Absorptive Capacity: A New Perspective on Learning and Innovation, in R. L. Cross, Jr. and S. B. Israelit (eds.), *Strategic Learning in a Knowledge Economy*. Boston, MA: Butterworth-Heinemann, 2000, pp. 39–67.
126 Arundel, Kabla. What Percentage of Innovations Are Patented?, p. 127.
127 Arundel, Kabla. What Percentage of Innovations Are Patented?, p. 127. Moreover, Mansfield's survey reveals that without patent protection, 60% of medical inventions won't be researched, and 65% won't be applied; 38% of chemical inventions won't be researched, and 30% won't be applied. However, except for the medicine and chemical industries, the lack of patent protection has little or even no influence on many industries. (E. Mansfield. Patents and Innovation: An Empirical Study, 32 *Management Science*, 1986, pp. 173–181.) Levin and others' surveys also indicate that the patent is not the most important method except in the chemical and pharmaceutical industries. In terms of process innovations, patents are the least effective; in terms of product innovations, the function of patents is inferior to the advanced time and learning curve. (Richard C. Levin, et al. Appropriating the Returns from Industrial Research and Development, 18 *Brookings Papers on Economic Activity*, 1987, pp. 783–831.)
128 The law adopts the one-size-fits-all approach that is usually explained as: The unified continuing time can help avoiding having to judge the cost of "deciding one by one," ensure the predictability of rights, and get rid of potential political conflicts led by different settings. However, this explanation is not persuasive. In terms of the legislative purpose, maintaining the positive correlation between intellectual contribution and effective time can demonstrate the encouragement level of the law. In terms of investments, the market, developing expenses, industrialization difficulty, and profit rates are distinct in different technological industries, and patent protection should correspond to expenses and profits. Jaffe, Lerner. *Innovation and its Discontents*, 156.
129 J. M. Mueller. *Patent Law*. 3 ed. Shen Chao, et al. Beijing: Intellectual Property Press, 2013:24–25.
130 Dan L. Burk and Mark A. Lemley summarized the judicial practice and proposed three types of policy levers in five technological fields, including chemistry, pharmaceutical, biotechnology, semiconductors, and software, which are levers of whether the inventor gets the patent, whether the patent is effective, levers applied to patent protection range, and levers influencing the relief measures of patent infringements. First, in terms of the acquirement and effectiveness of patent rights, policy levers, such as utility, experimental appliance, levels of the ordinary technicians in the technological field it belongs to, indirect supplementary investigations, and written descriptions, are used based on distinct industrial features. Second, in terms of the patent range, for control, one can use lever policies, such as abstract creativities, reasonable irreplaceability, separated analysis of elements, groundbreaking patents, the reverse doctrine of equivalents, and relief-reasonable patent fees. Third, in terms of

relief-reasonable patent fees, the court can refer to all situations of the related industries to determine the profit rate the company expects and the ordinary patent permission fee in this industry. The patent license expenses vary in different industries. Burk, Lemley. *Patent Crisis*, 170–264.

131 Drahos, Braithwaite. *Information Feudalism*, 188–190.

132 Taiping. *Research on the Change of Patent System*, 24–25.

133 The patent overstock in the United States is unprecedented and accelerated more quickly during these 25 years than at any other time. In 1986–1996, the patent overstock increased by more than 70%, and it increased by approximately 500% in the last decade and reached 700,000 pieces today. Wang Taiping. On the Patent Reward System—Also on China's Invention Reward System and its Reconstruction. 2009 Annual Meeting of the Intellectual Property Law Research Society of the Chinese Law Society and Seminar on Intellectual Property Protection in the Context of Economic Globalization.

134 A qualified patent should satisfy novelty, creativity, and utility, and the invention should be completely open. However, a large number of authorized patents don't fit these demands. As the OECD estimated, the patent authorization rate in the EU was 50%–60% and 80%–90% in the United States in the 1980s–1990s. Quillen and Webster also point out that in 1993–1998, the authorization rate in the United States was 85%–97%. Yang Cheng. *Global Patent Application Overheating. Patent Quality Needs To Be Improved.* http://ip.people.com.cn/GB/11458442.html.

135 Burk, Lemley. *The Patent Crisis*, 33.

136 Burk, Lemley. *The Patent Crisis*, 17.

137 Taiping. *Research on the Change of Patent System*, 104.

138 James Bessen, Michael J. Meurer. *Patent Failure: How Judges, Bureaucrats, and Lawyers Put Innovators at Risk.* Princeton, NJ: Princeton University Press, 2008:45.

139 Bessen, Meurer. *Patent Failure*, 7.

140 Jaffe, Lerner. *Innovation and Its Discontents*, 94.

141 For example, the leading figure in British politics was Joseph Chamberlain, a significant entrepreneur from Bermingham and the avant-garde of screw production. The American government was also controlled by the industrial and commercial classes with a large amount of capital and money. Galbraith. *The New Industrial State*, 52.

142 Karl Max. *Capital.* New York: Modern Library, 1936, chapter 32:836.

143 Galbraith. *The New Industrial State*, 52.

144 J. H. Reichman. The TRIPS Component of the GATT's Uruguay Round: Competitive Prospects for Intellectual Property Owners in an Integrated World Market, 4 *Fordham Intellectual Property, Media & Entertainment Law Journal*, 1993, p. 175; Porter T. Hegemony and the Private Governance of International Industries, in *Private Authority and International Affairs*. Albany, NY : State University of New York Press, pp. 257–281.

145 Reichman. The TRIPS Component of the GATT's Uruguay Round, p. 175.

146 Reichman. The TRIPS Component of the GATT's Uruguay Round.

147 Dominique Foray. *Knowledge Distribution and the Institutional Infrastructure: The Role of Intellectual Property Rights*, in Albach H. and Rosenkrantz S. (eds.), Intellectual Propert Rights and Global Competition. Germany: WZB Publication, 1995:112.

148 Suzanne Scotchmer. Standing on the Shoulders of Giants: Cumulative Research and the Patent Law, *Journal of Economic Perspectives*, 1991, pp. 29, 31, 34.

149 In the history of IPR development, Western developed countries, including the United States, have experienced a process from "selective protection" to "comprehensive

protection," from "weak protection" to "strong protection." If the IPR protection level of a country is higher than its technological and economic abilities and the supportive ability of the related public policy system, this system can't stimulate inventions, creations, technological investments, or introduce and absorb foreign technologies, and it will increase the learning and diffusion expenses of knowledge, oppress domestic imitation behaviors, and hinder the increase in autonomous innovation abilities. W. Lesser. *The Effects of TRIPs-Mandated Intellectual Property Rights on Economic Activities in Developing Countries*. WIPO, available at www.wipo.int/about-ip/en/studies/pdf/ssa_lesser_tnps.Pdf.

150 John F. Duffy. Harmony and Diversity in Global Patent Law, *Berkeley Technology Law Journal*, 2007, 17, p. 685.

5 Technological age

Resurrection or decline of the private right system of patents

Throughout history, the evolution of human society has experienced three forms: pre-industrial society, industrial society, and post-industrial society, and every evolution of social forms can be regarded as a huge leap in history. The private rights system of patents is continuously developing as the social forms change. This long historical evolutionary process, as Benjamin N. Cardozo said, is a process from vague, uncertain, and homogeneous to clear, certain, and heterogeneous.[1] In this volatile world, the only sure thing is change, which can be either a radical revolution or a gradual transition against the macro background. Either form of change will undoubtedly lead to further changes in the social form and patent system.

In the face of changes in future social forms, people will naturally feel puzzled and have doubts about the prospect of the private rights system of patents. Although scholars are not prophets, and neither are they good at foreseeing the future nor should they,[2] we have to make choices when confronting continuous changes: responding to actual conditions or making plans for possible results in the future. The only problem about the future is not what will take place but how to respond when something really happens.[3] For the private rights system of patents, the prediction of its future pattern is not divination arts based on tarot cards and crystal balls but made by reviewing its development history and offering reasonable explanations of various phenomena. This is what this chapter is mainly about.

Evolution of the private rights system of patents in the technological age

Our perception of the world provides us with the foundation on which to imagine the future social form. This perception is derived from our summary of the historical development principles and is established on the social development status. As mentioned previously, the primary element of institutional evolution is the change in new institutional concepts and authority subjects, which is attributed to the interaction among technology, economy, and culture. Through the systematic thinking of the four elements, we can better understand the institutional forms that continue to evolve. Insight comes from the systematic combination of the four parts and is also based on explorations and discoveries of the contents of every part. Overall,

DOI: 10.4324/9781003462453-6

they highlight the primary impetus that will probably affect the future development of the patent system and the framework that can be examined. Technological revolutions are always the beginning of revolutions in all cultures. Approximately 80 years ago, Keynes described the blueprint of the future world as follows. Robots would liberate humans from heavy labor in the market economy system; people would devote themselves to cultural activities in a cooperative and sharing way and pursue noble goals beyond worldly concerns.[4] The future, in the eyes of Keynes, is not entirely a castle in the air. More signs and proofs indicate that the arrival of the new technological era will promote the improvement in productivity and the abundance of materials, and influence the economic, cultural, and authority structures and bring considerable changes to society.

Technological and economic landscapes in the future

The self-accumulation of useful knowledge, the motivation of science, and the technological system's adaptation to other environments through self-organized processes make technological innovations and diffusion more rapid, more diverse, and more complicated than in the age of the knowledge economy. Brian Arthur, an expert on the history of technology, pointed out that with the self-generation and the combined evolution of technologies, their number will reach a critical point where the combination opportunities will increase explosively, and some technologies will increase exponentially. These technologies, which are distributed in different fields and locations, will be constructed into a dense network system akin to a complete organ or a more advanced, functional, and purposeful organism that can self-construct, self-optimize, perceive the surroundings, and make reactions. When they evolve into something that can self-assemble, self-constitute, self-repair, and "recognize," they become more similar to a creature.[5] In fact, many experts on the history of technology and philosophers are worried about the development trend in future technologies. They are afraid that the alienization of future technology will threaten humanity's survival. For example, Mumford believes that rapid development has infiltrated different fields, such as the economy, politics, and culture, and transformed it into an autonomous power.[6] Martin Heidegger said in *The Pursuit of Technology* that technology is not a tool of humans at all; instead, it is a phenomenon or an exhibition, the governance of which derives from the existence of technology itself. This is especially demonstrated in the history of the West.[7] Jacques Ellul also believed that technological development follows this path and becomes increasingly independent of humans. The more advanced technologies are, the more dependent on technologies humans are. Technological progress is irreversible. It has become an environment essential to humanity's survival, and human lives are guided by it and have to surrender and adjust to it. Opposing or abandoning technology is as if primitive men had burned the forest and their hometown. The autonomy of technology is that it creates an all-mighty world with its own rules and excludes all old traditions.[8]

Technology experts predict that future technological development seems to be distant and vague; however, the revolution in several new technologies mentioned in the following sections will seem quite close. The internet-led revolution in digital content is already widely acknowledged; however, few people know that big data, the Internet of Things (IoT), and three-dimensional (3D) printing and artificial intelligence (AI) technologies are provoking a new revolution, which will change products and services as the internet changes the content. Innovations in these key technologies mentioned previously will significantly change the innovation paradigm of technology and have a sweeping impact on the commodity economy, even the service economy. The famous technologists and economists Jeremy Rifkin, Klaus Schwab, and Wu Jun even predict that these key technologies will be the power that leads to the transformation in the Fourth Technological Revolution.[9] Some of these technologies are still in the primary stages, and there are numerous obstacles in the way to success. Nonetheless, they are likely to alter the economic field significantly in the next decades or centuries.

Key technological forces in the technological age

BIG DATA

Big data refers to large-scale, rapidly varying, and/or numerous varieties of information properties that require new processing methods to improve people's abilities in making decisions, expanding horizons, and optimizing processes.[10] In other words, big data is a cutting-edge technology for data analysis that enables people to acquire valuable information from various data. Generally speaking, big data involves all data in nature and human society and connections among them. Network broadband, global digitalization, and the internet's application in all industries contributed to big data's rise, and the accumulated data has become increasingly larger. More and more enterprises, industries, and countries realize that similar technologies can better serve clients, discover new business opportunities, break into new markets, and increase efficiency. Surveys also indicate that the data generated in the last 2 years occupied 90% of all data in history. More than 250 MB of data are generated in the world every day, and in the next decade, the global amount will increase by 40% per year.[11] The world-famous McCarthy Consulting was the first to propose the arrival of the big data age. It claims that data have infiltrated every industry and business field and become one of the essential components. People's mining and use of numerous data imply a new wave of increased productivity and consumption surplus. Professor Garegin at Harvard University also thinks that it is a great revolution in which enormous data resources initiate the quantitative processes in all fields, which will start in the academic world, the commercial world, and the government.[12]

INTERNET OF THINGS

The IoT refers to using intelligence, network communication, and data combination technologies to make information programs for items in a certain unit (region or sector) and insert them into the global internet system so as to achieve the information connection and associations between all related items. It is the important information input port of things and is connected with the cloud computing platform.[13] The IoT connects all people and things in the integrated world network. The sensors and software in this platform connect people, devices, natural resources, production lines, logistics networks, habits of consumption, and recycling streams with all aspects of economic and social lives and continuously provide real-time big data for all nodes (commerce, families, and vehicles). In return, big data receives timely analyses, converts them into predictive algorithms, and programs them into an autonomous system, which improves thermodynamic efficiency and productivity. Therefore, the marginal cost of producing and distributing commodities or services in the economy will be reduced to zero.[14] The Research Center of European IoT pointed out that the IoT has connected the world into an extensive network in thousands of ways.[15]

About 37 million digital intelligent electric meters in the United States are improving real-time information on electricity consumption. In the next decade, every building in the United States, Europe, and other countries will be equipped with intelligent electric meters. Every facility (including constant temperature controllers, assembly production lines, storage facilities, TVs, washing machines, and computers) will be equipped with sensors that can be connected to intelligent electric meters and platforms of the IoT. In 2007, about 10 million sensors connected all types of human inventions to the IoT. The number of sensors surpassed 3.5 billion in 2013, and more astonishingly, there will be 1 million sensors connected to the IoT by 2030, including air sensing technologies, software logs, Radio Frequency Identification (RFID) readers, and wireless sensor networks. These sensor facilities will help to collect broader big data, such as the changeable electricity prices in the electricity network, the logistic vehicle currency in the supply line, the production procedure in the assembly production line, the front and back-office services, and the real-time tracing of consumption behaviors. For instance, in the aerospace industry, the IoT and big data analysis technologies are used to project transport lines, monitor facilities, and repair projects. Although fuel efficiency increases only by 1%, it will save 30 billion dollars in 15 years. In terms of health, the IoT, big data analysis response, advanced analysis methods, prediction algorithms, and autonomous systems can save 25% of expenses in the global medical market, which is equal to 100 billion dollars per year.[16]

3D PRINTING TECHNOLOGY

Since the first commercial 3D printer emerged in the 1980s, this technology has become widely used by laboratories and families, gradually entering and changing our production and lives. The 3D printing technology is still in its infancy but has demonstrated great potential to win the market. The procedures in 3D printing technology are not complicated. People don't require any operation except for constructing the software, and the software is responsible for the production process.[17] Today, only dozens of materials are applied in commercial 3D printing, most of which are made of metal and plastic. Now, people are experimenting with more materials. Researchers are now testing new materials, such as wood pulp and carbon nanotubes, and expanding their application range. Some 3D printers can print electric circuits and make complicated electronic products from nothing; others can print sugar coats on cupcakes and spray liquid food like melted chocolate. For large-scale products, 3D printers can already "print" multistage buildings made of concrete. Besides, researchers have also tried to progress in the opposite direction: to use 3D printing at the molecular level. There are already "biological printers" that can 3D print cells of patients on "braces" made of inert materials, and bladders, kidneys, and stem cells have already been created in laboratories.[18] More importantly, 3D printers can even print components of new 3D printers, which means 3D printers can gradually improve their levels.[19]

Existing 3D printing technology was akin to the computer industry in 1976: a set of large and expensive machines were applied commercially, while a small part of cheap household computers was used by amateurs. [20] However, in 1980, the improvement in production technology and the decrease in the size and expense of computers made computers rapidly grow in popularity, and individuals could afford computers.[21] Therefore, we could expect that 3D printers would embrace the same development trend. In 2002, the 3D printing company Stratasys put the first "low-cost" 3D printer into the market at 30,000 dollars. Today, technological development has decreased the cost of 3D printers, and the average selling price is 1,500 dollars. Sector analysts estimate that 3D printers will produce more cutting-edge products with an unprecedentedly low cost in the next 30 years, making the information production process almost zero-cost.[22] The publisher of *Forbes*, Rich Karlgaard, believed that 3D printing was the revolutionary technology in 2015–2025 and that 3D printers could be used to reshape the manufacturing economy from large-scale industries to the former retail shop pattern of individual craftsmen.[23]

AI TECHNOLOGY

The concept of AI was first proposed by John McCarthy at the Computer Conference in Dartmouth, U.S., in 1956. AI soon gained popularity among scientific research organizations and set off a wave of AI research.[24] Intelligence, the unique feature of humans, refers to human's ability to recognize objective things and use knowledge and thought to solve problems. AI technology aims to study the laws of human intelligence activities and construct artificial systems or hardware with specific intelligence.[25] The AI system mainly contains symbolic knowledge expressions (calculation rules, models, and algorithms) and nonsymbolic knowledge expressions (to imitate the human neuron model's functions). The AI systems now in wide use are mainly symbolic knowledge expressions,[26] and their operation mechanism goes as follows. First, the designer or user of the computer programs inputs data and designs algorithms in AI robots in advance. Then, AI robots make deep learning based on numerous data and make precise operations by extracting and analyzing data. Regarding technological development status and industrial situations, AI is widely distributed in 13 countries, relating to a dozen industrial fields, such as commercial intelligence, electronic business, and medical health.[27] Especially in culture and art, including painting, music, games, and news, AI has been widely used in creative activities, such as the AI news-writing platform "Wordsmith" operated by the Associated Press together with AI companies,[28] the painting AI "Deep Dream,"[29] and music score composition AI "Plan Magenta"[30] developed by Google, the poem collection *Sunshine Without Glass Windows* written by the Microsoft AI "Xiaoice,"[31] and the AI Recurrent Neural Network (RNN) designed by American engineer Zach Toot that continues to write the world-famous novel *A Song of Ice and Fire*.[32] In addition to literature and art creation, AI robots have been used in many fields to make valuable inventions. For example, John Cozza developed AI to make creative inventions, and most of its inventions fit the authorization condition for patents, such as the American patent with authorization number 851.[33] The IBM Company developed a Watson robot in 2016. Praised as one of the six coolest AIs, it can make creations never seen in the world. It has excellent functions in diagnosis, medicine, and food and has become the new-generation AI with a worldwide reputation.[34] Hitachi has developed an AI robot that can design bullet train components to reduce noise.[35] Similarly, someone has designed AI specialized in creating new piston structures to reduce energy consumption in diesel engines.[36] Others have also invented robots specialized in designing medical formulas.[37] Cloem even invented a robot to make thousands of inventions independently.[38] It is reasonable to believe that with the deep research of AI technologies and nonsymbolic knowledge expressions and the support of big data and IoT, AI robots could conduct independent research and create more and more inventions. An engineer in Silicon Valley, Anthony Levandowski, set up an organization named "Road of Future" in 2015, aimed at using AI to develop and create the brain of God. More and more developed countries, including Japan and the United States, are trying to analyze the neural circuit of humans to create an AI system that imitates human brains (generally called whole brain emulation).[39]

Influence of key technological forces on technological innovation and economic development

As experts in technology and economy, Klaus Schwab, Jeremy Rifkin, and Wu Jun, said, every one of the four technological forces mentioned previously is likely to have a limited influence. However, once the four technological forces are combined, they will fundamentally alter the paradigm of technological innovation and become the transformative force in technological and economic development in the future. Once technological developments in such fields as big data, the IoT, 3D printing, and AI are combined, the cost of production and diffusion of products will be radically reduced. The information and content (design) contained in items are separated from manufacturing, and most things people need can be downloaded and produced on-site at little cost (mainly the expenses of raw materials). This technology-based society was named a non-scarce world by M.A. Lemley but a "zero marginal cost society" by Jeremy Rifkin. It has the following features.

CHANGES IN THE PARADIGM OF TECHNOLOGICAL INNOVATION: THE RISE OF "MAKERS" AND THE LOW COST OF CREATIONS

In the Post-industrial Age, technological development would be impossible without enormous investment. Technological application and innovation are full of risks, and enterprises have sufficient means of production and strong financial resources. Therefore, the traditional paradigm of invention and innovation is enterprise-centered, and a small number of enterprises, especially large enterprises, are synonymous with technology and innovation. In the future technological age, the development and popularity of 3D printing and AI will gradually lead to the formation of an innovation paradigm that is highly separated, democratic, and user-centered.[40] Chris Anderson believed that the industrial structure in the technological age was necessarily different from that in the current world. Technological innovations no longer depend on large enterprises, which are motivated by the top-down centralized methods, but on bottom-up autonomous innovations by separated groups, such as countless professionals, entrepreneurs, and amateurs, which Anderson calls, the rise of the "maker movement."[41] Rifkin and Lemley also described such a scenario as follows. In the technological age, people use the IoT and big data technology to acquire any design and invention information they need, and they can use AI robots to help invent and design information and 3D printers to convert digital designs or inventions into substantial objects. In addition, some services requiring unique technologies in shops and factories will gradually be provided by household robots and robots in small enterprises. The marginal costs of applying these designs will be reduced to zero, because many services only require the internet's data on existing robots to operate. At the same time, the development of the IoT will lead to a significant reduction in the costs of these products.[42]

In fact, according to the surveys by Eric von Hippel, Rosenberg, Freeman, and Saw, amateur users once outshone professional researchers in terms of the number of innovations, even before the emergence of the internet. For example, Eric Hippel believed that in fields including computer-aided design (CAD) software in electric circuit printing, pipe bridge metal products, shell operation facilities, and the information systems in libraries, the frequency with which users and individual consumers develop and improve products for their own sake varies from 10% to 40%. Users have developed 80% of the most important innovations in scientific instruments and significant innovations in semiconductor processing.[43] He also believed that the gradual increase in the software and hardware quality contributes to breakthroughs and enhancement in users' innovation abilities, technological development will undoubtedly make users become an increasingly important source of innovation, and innovation will be gradually generalized.[44] Keith Saw also called the users' innovation "trans-organizational innovations," which means innovation does not come from enterprises or is not linear; instead, it comes from the cooperation network, a widely separated social network. In the environment of a cooperation network, all processes for products, including creative inspiration, selection, and development, are spontaneous and simultaneous, and many people make significant contributions via the internet.[45]

Nonetheless, the combination of big data, the IoT, 3D printing, and AI technologies will construct a technological paradigm of users' innovations, which facilitates the mass innovation and the separation of creation, production, and commercialization of technology and makes them no longer scarce. First, any user can use the internet and data mining technology to search for concepts and designs they want in the open-source communities and connect to the AI robots on the internet to help them create new inventions. Therefore, the expenses of creation are eliminated. Once the big data and AI technologies are developed enough in the future, such a paradigm of technological creations will be formed. Big data inputs the knowledge and data available by searching into AI machines, which process these data and knowledge and make autonomous creations intelligently. In this way, the technological creation achieves a sequential and mechanical production process. Second, users can use 3D printing technology to print inventions and designs into substantial objects with 3D printing technology. It can achieve individualization flexibly and make single or small-scale products at minimum costs (the only cost is the raw material and electricity, and the raw material used by 3D printing is relatively cheap). When everyone uses 3D printers at home or in public facilities, products in the manufacturing industry no longer require large-scale production and are no longer scarce. Finally, the development and popularization of the IoT enables any user to use the internet and IoT to distribute their products. Therefore, the logistic expenses in the supply chain and the delivery of finished products will significantly decrease. Deven Desai and Gerard Magliocca described this result as the "Napsterization" of technological invention.[46] Therefore, in this new paradigm of technological innovation, big data and AI technologies greatly reduce the expenses of technological creation, 3D printing significantly decreases the costs of substantializing and production, and the internet and IoT reduce commercialization costs.

CHANGES IN THE ECONOMIC STRUCTURE AND DOMINANT FORCE

As Chapter 4 mentioned, large enterprises control most of the means of production, including technology and capital; therefore, they are the dominant power in economic development in the traditional economic structure. The rise of the "maker movement" corresponds to the personal computer revolution in 1985 – inventions that emerged in garages began to challenge the economic order disruptively.[47] The change in the paradigm of technological innovation and the rise of the "maker movement" means the coming of the society of "prosumers." Large enterprises begin to decline, and economic subjects in the future form are converted from vertically integrated large enterprises to small and medium-sized enterprises that are distributed, decentralized, cooperative, and adjustable; the sharing economy is gradually rising.

Toffler was the first to propose the term "prosumer" in the *Third Tide*, which refers to consumers who participate in production activities and are both producers and consumers.[48] Rifkin described such a future scenario in the *Zero-Cost Community* that in the coming technological age after 3D printers are embedded in the infrastructure of the IoT, anyone in the world can become a prosumer who can make products with open-source software to use or share. However, the material required for the production process is only one-tenth of traditional production, requiring very little labor force. First, one can use big data, AI, and other technologies to collect information from the site or locally and make inventions and designs, the marginal cost of which is close to zero. Second, when 3D printing technology is used to make substantial inventions, the main cost is incurred by buying materials for 3D printing, and it will become extremely low with the development of 3D printing technology. Finally, the marginal cost of marketing through global marketing websites is close to zero. Users obtain products via electronic payment, and the transmission of products is driven by the developed IoT technologies; therefore, the marginal cost is also close to zero.

This book believes that even if Rifkin's prediction about the zero-cost society will not be wholly realized, he at least identified a new trend in the future economic order: the decentralization of large enterprises and the rise of small and medium-sized enterprises and consumers. On the one hand, the development of new technology enables individuals to start a business from the bottom up and make separate innovations, realizing democratization in manufacturing industries. This means that creating new products is a chance for the majority rather than a profession for the minority, and anyone is entitled to obtain the means of production. Therefore, the owner and controller of the means of production are no longer important, and the means of production are redistributed between the monopoly groups of large enterprises and ordinary residents. On the other hand, with the rise of prosumer society, the centralized enterprise pattern formed by vertical integration has no more advantages, while small informative makers have an absolute advantage. Centralization requires a capital-intensive economy of scale, which means constructing fixed production lines with high expenses that can make large-scale production; however, this method is inflexible and costly. However, as the IoT has features like distributions, cooperation, and horizontal expansions, small informative producers can make production with simple 3D printers. They can also be connected to local infrastructures in the IoT and provide power for vehicles with extremely limited renewable energy sources. Therefore, the logistic expenses in the supply chain and delivery of finished products will be greatly reduced. For example, some small and medium-sized enterprises in Europe and other regions have begun to cooperate with green energies in the area to acquire the advantage of horizontal expansion.[49]

As Rifkin pointed out,

> What's becoming apparent is that a growing number of giant capitalist enterprises across a range of commercial sectors that are already facing plummeting profit margins will not be able to survive for very long against the rising tide of near zero marginal costs in the production and delivery of goods and services. Although the thousand or so highly integrated, vertically scaled mega corporations that currently account for much of the world's commerce are imposing and seemingly invincible, they are, in fact, highly vulnerable to a collaborative economy that is quickly eating away at their already precariously low profit margins. At the very least, we can say that conventional capitalist markets

will increasingly lose their dominant hold over global commerce and trade as near zero marginal costs push an ever greater share of economic activity onto the Collaborative Commons in the years ahead.[50]

Only small and medium-sized enterprises can adjust the IoT's open, separated, and cooperative structure in the future technological age. Rifkin stated that the only feasible economic pattern in the zero marginal cost society is the divided cooperative pattern of middle and small-sized enterprises, which aim to share resources. Only by uniting together and using a separate, cooperative, and horizontally integrated network rather than the vertically integrated commercial pattern in the capitalist market economy can small and medium-sized enterprises fully exploit their potential and achieve mutual benefits.[51] The future forms of companies exhibit features, including separation, decentralization, cooperation, and adjustment, and companies will be continuously networked and transformed into real information factories.[52] In fact, studies already indicate that the tendency of decentralization and the decline in large enterprises already emerged in this age.[53] Many real-life examples have also fully demonstrated this point. For example, offshore outsourcing in the IT sectors of Microsoft, IBM, and GE has already become a global phenomenon, and 35% of Procter & Gamble Co.'s new products come from external scientific networks. In 2015, the international competition for untied office space initiated by the Smart Resort Industry Council was the typical demonstration of collective wisdom. It integrated the industry chain, and the downstream and upstream enterprises could provide the required services and bring mutual benefits.[54]

With the coming of the prosumer society and the change in economic subjects, the sharing economy will gradually rise. The mature application of big data technology achieves the virtualization of substantial resources and high efficiency in data processing. This provides empirical tools and lays a solid foundation for the platform-based economic structure with enormous sharing spaces and all-directional data analysis. The iteration updates of the internet and communication technologies can collect various participants in the market, fulfill the rapid matching of suppliers and demanders, promote the appearance of prosumers, eliminate the intermediaries in the vertical value chain in the traditional economy via repeated games, and reduce extra costs and friction costs in transactions. The development and evolution of the IoT and the energy revolution bring distributed, cooperative, and horizontally equivalent ways of production and trade. This achieves a scaled expansion effect, the production impetus of which is renewable energies, and creates new channels and pathways for the all-element, transindustry, and green production for society, which are the communication, medium, energy, and transport channels that a successful economic paradigm has to possess. Based on this, the sharing economy appears, and human economic development enters a new stage because of features like separation, horizontalization, cooperation, and zero marginal cost.[55] Rifkin said,

While the Communications Internet is an enabler, as it merges with the Energy Internet and the Logistics Internet in the years ahead, establishing an integrated

> and sharable communication, energy, and logistics infrastructure—an Internet of Things—that can operate at near zero marginal cost, it dramatically boosts the potential of the other sharable sectors, including rentals, redistribution networks, cultural exchanges, and exchanges of professional and technical skills. When that happens, collaborative production and exchange will scaleup from a niche sector to the dominant paradigm.[56]

Through a networked sharing mechanism, thousands of people can share automobiles and bicycles, houses, clothes, toys, and skills, which are common in today's world. First, shared automobiles and bicycles have come into reality. In 2012, 900,000 people in the United States and 2 million in 30 countries worldwide enjoyed the service of sharing automobiles. According to Frost & Sullivan Co. surveys, there will be more than 300 service stations sharing automobiles in the European Union (EU) and shared automobiles are estimated to increase from 30,000 to about 300,000 by 2030. In China, the market scale of Chinese sharing bicycle brands, like Mobike and Ofo, rose by 736% to 10.28 billion yuan in 2017;[57] by 2020, it had already reached 3.38 trillion yuan.[58] Second, sharing spaces like houses is possible. A typical example is Airbnb, an enterprise specializing in sharing houses. It was set up in 2008, and its business covered over 30,000 cities worldwide by the end of 2012. It had 21 branch companies and provided short-rent services for more than 40 million users. By the end of 2016, its estimated value reached 30 billion dollars.[59] Moreover, toy and clothing-sharing is achieved. BabyPlays, Rent That Toy, and SparkBox Toys are famous sharing companies. Tie Society, Rent the Runway, I-Ella, MakeupAlley, Avelle, TFN, and ThredUP are all world-famous clothing-sharing enterprises. Even backyards, agrarian land, and scientific laboratories are involved in the sharing system; for example, the ShareEarth company provides sharing backyards and agrarian lands for farmers. The Weblab established by Massachusetts Institute of Technology (MIT) in the 1980s, the "Xport Item" proposed by the U.S. in 2000, and the "Mig-laboratory" in China in 2016 commonly create a scientific research platform that "crowdsources" idled. Low-efficient facilities in scientific research institutes improve the application efficiency of facilities and solve the scarcity of research resources for users with scientific requirements.[60] Sharing studies, vehicles, medicines, and genes have also come into existence.

With technological development, all resources, substantial and human, tangible and intangible, idle and low-efficient, can be shared and tend to thrive. Portman grasps the internal mechanism of the new economic pattern that grows near us. She wrote,

> Every day people are using Collaborative Consumption—traditional sharing, bartering, lending, trading, renting, gifting, and swapping, redefined through technology and peer communities. Collaborative Consumption is enabling people to realize the enormous benefits of access to products and services over ownership, and at the same time save money, space, and time; make new friends; and become active citizens once again… . These systems provide significant

environmental benefits by increasing use efficiency, reducing waste, encouraging the development of better products, and mopping up the surplus created by over-production and consumption.[61]

Semiotic democracy:[62] Surge of knowledge-sharing and participatory culture

Advanced knowledge and culture were originally the privileges of the elite class, including aristocrats and royal families in the Middle Ages and large enterprises and politicians later. In the twentieth century, most Western countries were increasingly concerned about cultural dominance. Images, sounds, and signs are becoming richer and richer, but they are also increasingly controlled by disk companies, film distributors, TV stations, advertisers, and other large enterprises and politicians. Semiotic power is always seized by minorities, and the elite and bureaucratic classes control the production and diffusion of culture. However, increasingly "cultural populists" believe that ordinary consumers are not passive adopters with no ability to criticize. If people have a chance to express more opinions when constructing the cultural environment, they will participate rather than be alienated. When the centralization of semiotic power is broken, the cultural background will become more abundant and encouraging. Long before, John Stuart Mill proposed the "utopian" ideal of the semiotic democratic culture. In a society, the more diverse the living methods, thoughts, and arts of public performance, the society members are required to make judgments about beliefs and behaviors, which is beneficial to developing members' mental and moral abilities and creates the entire social culture that is richer, more diverse and more active. That is called the cultural accumulative effect.[63]

With the development of technologies and the rise of the sharing economy, knowledge-sharing and citizens' participatory culture gradually become a new trend. On the one hand, technological development enables ordinary citizens to own knowledge's means of production and no longer be prevented from cultural innovations and circulations. Citizens are knowledge receivers and participate in and recreate cultural products via comprehension, evaluation, modification, edition, and improvements. The development of big data and network technologies makes everyone a well-equipped "knowledge factory." Their electronic devices are actually mobile printing factories, broadcast stations, community centers, markets, schools, and books containing knowledge.[64] 3D printing makes innovations in the narratives of ordinary people's daily lives. On the other hand, the rise of network communities provides pathways for ordinary people's knowledge-sharing and cultural participation.[65] The progress of technologies and the popularization of the network facilitate communities to break the restriction of practice and space. Therefore, communities really fulfill the free integration and interpersonal knowledge-sharing, greatly liberating the energy and value created by the ordinary civil culture.[66] Network communities provide the stage for the revival of amateurs, and the "people's age" of "large-scale amateur" has become a trend; open storing,[67] free software,[68] creation sharing,[69] "gene sharing,"[70] Wikipedia, "examination of public patents," and other knowledge communities have become common. Some enterprises also invest millions of dollars in cracking genomes and pushing the extensive DNA database into the public field to prevent other enterprises from seizing them.[71] The culture of knowledge-sharing and participation emphasizes collective wisdom. Tom Standish believes that humans are born to be cooperative and selfless, and sharing belongs to human nature and is regarded as the "central feature" in social relations. Internet and network communities liberate such natures.[72] Professor Shirky at New York University also proposes the "recognition surplus" theory, which refers to those who are well-educated (a rich knowledge background in some aspects) and have free time and strong sharing desires. These people assemble their free time and share knowledge with others on some platforms, creating a strong social effect. In essence, the recognition surplus is that the explosion of educated people enables us to consider people's time and intelligent resources as the collection of social resources, consumed mainly by entertainment, after investing in people's daily lives and learning. In the age of network technologies, the rapid development of media facilitates resources like rest time and intelligence to become a public social resource via writing and people's other behaviors, creating the results of civilizations, such as Wikipedia, open storing, and free software. Sharing free time can create more recognition surpluses and effectively achieve cooperation and mutual benefit among participants.[73]

With the further development of technology and the sharing economy, citizens' moving abilities and intellectual creations will embrace a more revolutionary leap in the age of future technology. In addition, knowledge-sharing and cultural participation will become more popular. As Fisher says, new technologies will provide newer creation patterns, more cooperation and interest, and less individualism and bureaucracy. In the future, sharing will contain more creation … . Collective creation is beneficial for us to become a more collective living.[74] The future society will be an age when creativity and information are significantly liberated, and anyone can share.[75] Rifkin also believes,

> A sense of shared community and an ethical belief in the value of collaboration was over proprietorship and access over ownership.[76] The democratization of innovation and creativity on the emerging Collaborative Commons is spawning a new kind of incentive, based less on the expectation of financial reward and more on the desire to advance the social well-being of humanity. And it's succeeding.[77]

Changes in the authority structure

Jürgen Habermas proposed in his *Structure Transformation in Public Fields* that there is a public field where every individual participates in the public interest equally. He said, "In the fully developed Greek city-state the sphere of the polis, which was common(koine) to the free citizens, was strictly separated from the sphere of the oikos."[78] The public field refers to an area collected by individuals in social life where something akin to public opinion can be formed.[79] According to Habermas, it is the reason instead of position or tradition that becomes the final winner through contacts in the public field.[80] In essence, he thought that inequality and inference by authority could be excluded, and Hannah Arendt's public field theory shares this opinion.[81] Rifkin believed that the economic paradigm of zero marginal cost would fundamentally alter the traditional class structure in the future technological age and would help fulfill the social form described by Habermas and Arendt. In that age, the old paradigm constituted of owners, workers, sellers, and consumers will be broken. The emergence of prosumers reflects that new social power expects to acquire room to express their political appeals via institutional pathways. Suppose the political paradigm corresponding to the market economy mechanism dominated by vertically integrated enterprises is power politics featuring authority obedience. In that case, it will be the right politics featuring equality in a horizontal and cooperative society with zero marginal costs.[82] The former concentrates on organization and power, and the latter focuses on cooperation and sharing. In societies with zero marginal cost, hierarchy will gradually fade away, and people will realize that the accomplishment of self-awareness is the precondition for the achievement of others' value. The value concern of "right politics" is to respect the power and rights of every political subject and to guarantee the political subject position of humans. The keynote of human-based politics is that the political subjects in every class have equal positions and chances to acquire benefits,[83] similar to one of Rawls' principles of justice: vocations and positions are open to anyone on the condition of opportunity equality and justice.[84] If the traditional economic society is motivated by utility and based on private benefits, the zero-cost society will be gradually motivated by collective profits and the sharing spirit. The former advocates ownership, self-cautiousness, and self-governance of consumers. In contrast, the latter advocates open-source innovations, transparency, and the pursuit of community construction.[85]

This book believes that even the ideal society described by Habermas, Arendt, and Rifkin cannot wholly be achieved in the future technological age, and struggles for benefit and hierarchy will last for a long time. However, one thing is for sure: as the economic power of large enterprises declines, the power of prosumers and small and medium-sized enterprises will rise, and "a collaborative future will greatly expand human participation and creativity across society."[86]

Conclusion: Decline of the private right system of patents in the technological age

According to the discussion in Chapter 2, the Intellectual Property Rights (IPR) institution did not exist in most parts of human innovation history. However, the patent system began to emerge by the end of the Middle Ages. The patent system originated from a scarce world, and it artificially made technologies scarcer by appointing the patent's owner to motivate others' creations and investments. The historical development in the later period indicated that inventors, the industrial and commercial classes, and enterprises increasingly depended on the patent system as the "amulet" for production and competition. Especially in the Post-industrial Age, technology played an increasingly significant role in economic development. Large enterprises that own technological and economic advantages continue to use public selections to shape the discourse power of the patent system. They continuously expand the range of patent rights, converting the patent system into their competitive strategy and tool via coemption and lawsuits; the system gradually becomes alienized. During the evolution of the patent system, the government always considers the patent system as a tool of macro regulation to control technological and economic development. However, in the gaming process against private rights subjects, it sometimes acts as the spokesman of the public interests, and sometimes it becomes the guardian of private rights subjects. Consumers and public power remain spectators on the historical stage. Since the essence of the patent system is to promote inventions and creations, it played a significant role in promoting technological development in the special historical age when useful knowledge and technologies were relatively scarce. However, it doesn't mean that it will always play a role. In the future post-scarce age, great changes will occur in technology, economy, culture, and authority subjects, and so will the position and function of the patent system.

First, if the content on the thread of technological development discussed in this book is correct, the amount of useful knowledge will gradually increase. The accumulation will be richer, and knowledge will be more popular. Knowledge follows the rule of increasing abundance rather than gradual exhaustion.[87] With the self-accumulation of useful knowledge and the promotion of science, the technological system adjusts to other environments via self-organized processes. The speed of technological innovations and diffusion in the future will be more rapid, diverse, and complicated than in the Post-industrial Age. When big data, the IoT, 3D printing, and AI technologies are matured and developed to a certain stage, the technological combination they formed is likely to fundamentally change the paradigm of technological innovations, which, in addition to the rise of "makers' power," means that the creation, production, and commercialization of inventions will no longer become scarce. Big data and AI greatly decrease the cost of technological creation, 3D printing significantly reduces the cost of technological substantializing and production, and the internet and IoT reduce the commercializing costs of technologies. Indeed, the development of these technologies won't eliminate all scarcities. However, in the post-scarce age, products with high expenses will gradually become an exception instead of common, mainly when society develops into the "zero marginal cost society" described by Rifkin.

Second, in the future post-scarce age, due to the prosumer society brought by technological innovation paradigms and the transformation of economic subjects, the sharing economy will gradually rise, and technological development will facilitate the achievement of the sharing economy. In addition, citizens' acting ability and intellectual creation will bring a more revolutionary leap, and knowledge-sharing and participatory culture will become more popular. With the coupling effect of technology, economy, and culture, the deep-rooted concept of knowledge monopoly will gradually be altered, and the idea of knowledge monopoly and exclusive rights will decline progressively.[88] Compared with exclusiveness, inclusiveness becomes increasingly essential, and future society will accomplish the transition from private knowledge to sharing knowledge.[89] Rifkin believes that the IoT technology, sharing economy, and culture mean that knowledge ownership will gradually be converted into application and involvement rights.[90]

Finally, the discourse power of the construction of the patent system is always dominated by related interest groups and the government. Separate public interests and the rights of consumers are incohesive and even insignificant. The development of new technologies and the rise of "maker's activity" means the coming of the "prosumer" society; large enterprises will gradually decline, while small and middle-sized enterprises will rise progressively. With the transformation of the economic paradigm, diverse civil power could negotiate with the government and enterprises to equally construct a more just and reasonable private rights system of patents. In fact, although private interest groups still dominated institutional arrangements in the Post-industrial Age, diverse civil power began to rise gradually. For example, social, nongovernmental, international, and other organizations have begun to participate in and try to influence the construction of the IPR system. Sometimes, some of the public will organize and unite spontaneously to revolt and resist the negative effects brought by it. For instance, in 1991, the Indian population resisted the American Grace Company's acquiring European patents by extracting insecticide components from *Azadirachta indica*. In 2000, anti-AIDS activists and humanistic organizations managed to participate in the medicine-acquiring movement in South Africa, and these nongovernmental organizations (NGOs) provided practical technological authority analyses.[91] Then, some organizations and social groups established for given purposes gradually emerged, such as the Free Software Foundation (FSF)_ advocating free software, the Open-Source Initiative (OSI) promoting open-source software, and the Creative Commons Organization (CCO). These civil powers use active campaigns to resist the restriction of the IPR system to technological innovations and the market of cultural industries and to restrain the trend in the expansion of IPRs.[92] As Susan K. Sayre said, TRIPS promotes the increasingly powerful organizations of civil society's activities to coordinate the industry-dominated IPR agendas that failed to be mentioned previously. At least, the post-TRIPS trend indicates that the new arena has appeared.[93] Based on worries about the protection in the public field, they will become more united to prevent the excessive expansion of IPRs. Although they still face obstacles to enterprise groups' power, these NGOs and public powers skillfully use political chances in HIV/AIDS, public health, and bioterrorism threats to gradually alter the concepts of groups, departments, and governments, challenging the standards of high protectionists. On this background, there is no reason to believe that these social groups that actively respond to new opinions … always occupy the obedience position in the system.[94]

When technological innovations in the future become no longer scarce, the sharing economy and culture become the mainstream awareness, and the gradual coherence of public power will gradually lead the patent private system to decline. Indeed, it doesn't mean the patent system will disappear overnight, because we are still quite a distance from the post-scarce age. In addition, the interplay between technology, economy, culture, and authority will be quite long. More importantly, the large enterprises mastering technological and economic power will continue to fight against the death of scarcity. They are likely to control the origin of technologies because the patent system provides them with the best weapon. Historical experience tells us that in the Post-industrial Age, knowledge innovation results, such as microorganisms, genes, cells, organs, embryos, commercial methods, and rules, gradually became the patent object of developed countries and transnational enterprises. They solidly control the most advanced high technologies. In fact, some companies have already appealed to enhance the patent system, requests to prohibit 3D printers are already quite common, and some are even trying to prevent the distribution of patent products of the designs of 3D printers. Large biotechnological companies try to resist the current transformation to patterned and open-sourced synthesized biology.[95] So is the field of copyright laws: content owners used to hinder digital content development; they used to attempt to avoid this technology and prosecute its users and anyone related to them. In fact, the 1980 Sony case will enlighten us that the film industry attempted to use the copyright law to eliminate a probable new technology – video cassette recording (VCR). Jack Valenti, the primary lobbyer for the film industry, used to analog the VCR technologies to the "Boston Killer" in a hearing of Congress, which was quite impressive. Valenti further indicated that the VCR would destroy Hollywood:

> Now, we cannot live in a marketplace, Mr. Chairman—you simply cannot live in a marketplace, where there is one unleashed animal in that marketplace, unlicensed. It would no longer be a marketplace; it would be a kind of a jungle, where this one unlicensed instrument is capable of devouring all that people had invested in and labored over and brought forth as a film or a television program, and, in short, laying waste to the orderly distribution of this product.[96]

This request originated from the film industry's fear that people would record films and TV programs, which was almost successful. The Supreme Court judged the VCRs legal with a 5:4 vote. Then, they also tried all means to suppress the development of peer-to-peer (P2P) sharing technologies, like Napster and even tried to use the extremely strict *Stop Online Piracy Act* (SOPA) Act to close pirate websites. We should foresee that in the future age, large enterprises will continue to use IPR laws and lawsuits to control these new technologies and play games with the public and the government. This also means that the patent system will remain for some time in the future; however, when the four impetuses mentioned previously make a difference, its importance on technological innovations will gradually decrease and finally exit the stage of history.[97]

As Lamley says in the *Non-Scarce World*, in a post-scarce age, especially in the "zero marginal cost society" described by Rifkin, science and technology have shaped a world where more things can be created at lower costs, the lowering cost of technologies and economic development will weaken the importance of IPRs. Even without IPR, making and publishing content will become easier and easier, and more and more content can be provided. At the same time, if the meaning of

IPRs is to encourage the creation or the distribution of content, technologies with lower costs actually mean that our requirements for IPRs will decrease rather than increase. Therefore, the varying technological and economic features are likely to break the theoretical basis of IPRs, weaken and alter the traditional logic that considers the IPR as a commercially encouraging tool, and destroy the classical theory that the IPR is a tool to encourage creativity. Once creating becomes cheap enough, any motivations from IPR will probably be unnecessary. In the future, due to the continuous struggle and rebellion by interest groups like large enterprises against the "death of scarcity," the patent system will still exist for some time. However, its importance as the motivator of innovations might decrease. Creations depending on the patent system might play an increasingly unessential role in the post-scarce age. When production and publication costs finally reach a certain point, IPR protection will be useless. Therefore, we should pay more attention to alternative tools to encourage creation rather than assume that the IPR system is somehow superior.[98]

God is dead? A world without patent systems

Humans are the history that continues to call the end. Nietzsche once shouted, "*Gott ist tot!.*"[99] From his perspective, "*Gott ist tot*" is a crucial and brave criticism of God and the loss of supreme values. Its meaning is enriched after that. Some believed it symbolized the rise of science and technology and the decline of religious beliefs.[100] From the historical perspective, in the history before the Middle Ages, technological innovations were all performed without the encouragement of the patent system; it was accumulated by countless precedents based on learning and imitating from each other, and the progress was slow but irreversible.[101] It was not until the fifteenth century that the patent system appeared and until the late eighteenth century that it was solidly established. Moreover, the patent system was merely a legal tool to motivate technological innovations, and subsidies for public research and awards provided reward choices for inventors. When it comes to the opinion that the private patent system will be abolished in the future technological age, these interest groups try all means to remind us that it is related to enormous economic benefits. Without the patent system, these large enterprises might not continue researching new products, and the world would stagnate and have no energy.[102] However, is that really the fact? For the majority, their panic about the disappearance of the patent system is attributed to the fact that they are accustomed to it. They think a patent system with a history of hundreds of years has become a part of our private property system. The patent system might contribute to the prosperity of culture and technologies. Therefore, although they know that the patent system is already out of control or ineffective, they do nothing but continue to advocate reforms rather than make considerable revolutions to this system. People are always eager for stability and panicked by severe transformations.[103] In the future post-scarce age, what will society be like if people return to a world without patent systems?

Technological innovation and human self-need

First, if the technological essence and technology history are taken into account, technological innovations are essentially an empirical activity to satisfy social needs. Human needs are multidimensional: reputation, survival, entertainment, culture, wars, and the economy. Economic needs include acquiring rewards, commerce, investments, and industrial development. Chapter 1 of this book states that social elements, including institutions, economy, culture (value outlooks, religions, and technological outlooks), population, and the military, will all stimulate people's needs and affect their creations. Privileges or properties are merely the factors to boost creation needs. As a British scientist said, properties or privileges are unnecessary for motivating inventions. Seeds of invention have existed since long ago and will develop under the right environments and seasons. Therefore, it is unessential to enact laws to interfere with its growth.[104] The American experts on the history of technology, George Basara, Gilfillan, and Merton, all reveal through historical proof how other social elements stimulate human needs to affect technological creations (see "Relations among technology, economy, and culture" in Chapter 1).

Second, more substantial proof in the literature about innovations and psychology proves that the motives of innovations are usually endogenous or problem-motivated.[105] People make creations because of their inspiration, because they are motivated, or because they hope to solve problems.[106] As Rosemary Coombe emphasizes, the nature of humanity is the ability to create, reform, and suspect. Therefore, she comes to a quite significant conclusion that abusing IPRs and continuously expanding their protection range will deprive us of humanity.[107] George Basalla, an expert on technology history, also pointed out that the technological dream of inventors is an important source of their creations.[108] In fact, some pieces of evidence even prove that financial rewards will reduce creativity. Things made for needs or money promises are less creative than those made for other objectives, because creating for money seems to harm internal motives.[109] In 2007, Andy Oram, the editor of the O'Reilly Media Company, carried out a 1-year survey to reveal the motives behind people's creations in Internet sharing, and the survey result showed that the top reason was "community." People consider themselves community members and hope to devote themselves to its activeness and development. The second was "individual development," namely self-accomplishment, which returns to the highest level of the "pyramid model" in Abraham Maslow's hierarchy of needs. The third was mutual assistance or willingness to share. Interestingly, according to Oram's survey, reputation and money motivations ranked relatively lower in all motivating elements.[110]

In the technological age, big data and IoT technologies will make information and resources no longer insufficient and technology and materials will be highly abundant. As Neal Stephenson imagined in the *Diamond Age*, if a "material coding machine" motivated by nanotechnology is invented, which could produce anything from air cushions to foods, the only thing that humans should do is to offer designs to the machine to make new things, and machines are responsible for all work. At that time, will people continue to make innovations? What will motivate our further development? Collison Anderson gave us the answer. He held that the best analog for us is the Athens and Sparta cultures. The two *poleis* were at their peak, supported by many slaves. Slaves provided all life necessities, and the aristocratic class had little need to work for survival, which is similar to the robot society. However, these two societies did not stagnate due to their lack of purpose. In contrast, Athenians became artists and philosophers who tried to explore the meaning of the abstract world, and Spartans devoted themselves to pursuing military power and authority. In other words, abundant money and materials won't affect the meaning of people's lives or innovations. Athenians and Spartans went up along Maslow's pyramid of needs, exploring the great creativity and the value of self-accomplishment.[111]

Enterprises' way to innovation driven by other factors than laws

Suppose the hypothesis that humans' other needs, besides properties, motivate innovation is correct. In that case, it doesn't mean that the patent system has never played a role in the creation or that it won't continue to function in some aspects. It might be because the primitive motive of enterprises' creations is money, although that of individual inventors is not. Enterprises pay rewards for inventors' creations or obtain their inventions and pay prices to expose them to the public, aiming to acquire the economic value of products. However, it doesn't necessarily indicate that the patent system is necessary for enterprises. On the one hand, as mentioned in Chapter 5, in the Post-industrial Age, enterprises mostly applied for patents based on market competition strategy. The operation of the patent system in modern society has already caused social resources to be wasted and the innovation process to slow down. It hinders rather than promotes the commercialization of products. Gans and Stern believed that new small companies would be more competitive without the protection of the patent system. Korn, Nelson, and Walsh's studies also demonstrated that the most fundamental reason that hinders small rather than large companies from seeking IPR protection is the excessive protection cost of the patent system.[112] On the other hand, many facts and proofs indicate that elements motivating innovation are also multidimensional. Enterprises usually use multiple ways instead of the patent system alone to protect their products and innovations and to ensure their competitive advantages. Their methods mainly include the market, social principles, technological means, and human resources. These diverse mechanisms could provide enough motivation for the company's innovation. As Lawrence Lessig, professor at Stanford University, U.S., said, in the real world, four rules regulate people's behaviors: law, code of conduct, market, and structure (technology), which cooperate and influence our behaviors.[113]

Market power

When it comes to the market's power, it induces and promotes innovation to a great extent. The "induced innovation" theory believes that when one resource element is scarcer than others, the method to save more expensive elements will be induced, and the market's choice to pursue profits induces innovations and inventions.[114] As Johannes Huth once said, someone advocates a free market not because of his moral mottos but because humans cannot distribute knowledge in local conditions or effectively organize the economic relations among thousands of individuals. When we have a free market, we will likely describe its image … . Compared with the state monopoly, the free market can better provide what people want because it allows many unrestricted providers to do so. Consumers can determine the most effective means by subsidizing those who can satisfy their special needs more effectively and preventing them from losing efficacy.[115] Economic proof indicates that the market, rather than the temptation to monopolize rights, usually motivates enterprises to make innovations.[116]

Professor Yoshiyuki Tamura defines the IPR law as "the supportive, encouraging mechanism." When market powers like the first-mover advantage are enough to motivate innovation, the interference of IPRs will be quite unessential. If necessary, market encouragement should be superior to law, and the "support" of laws is only available on the exceptional occasion that the substantial encouraging mechanisms cannot play the self-discipline function.[117] Professor Li Chen also said that the law and the market should make positive interactions: legal protection should promote market innovations rather than lead to an inert; it should improve the market efficiency rather than transaction expenses.[118] In fact, the regulation of the radio industry in the United States is the most typical example. In the early twentieth century, the United States made a compulsory macro regulation on the radio industry based on considerations about public benefits to solve the band interference in the industry. *Radio Act 1927* and *Communication Act 1934* were issued to stipulate that the federal government provided the free right to use rather than own radio bands. However, any enterprises using bands for radio broadcasts should be approved and authorized by the government. However, the government's legal control made little difference in practice. As Coase said, land, labor force, and capital are all scarce, which doesn't need the interference of governmental control. Scarce items are distributed by the market instead of the government because consumers' free choices can bring higher satisfaction. In the American economic system, the solution is usually the price mechanism. With this problem, the best choice for the government is to sell broadcast rights by auction at the beginning instead of compulsory interference. The government adopted Coase's suggestions in the 1990s and finally achieved the desired outcome.[119]

Market powers contain the first-mover advantage, public praise, trends and tides, price discrimination, product differentiation, the complexity of designs, and barriers to access (entrance barriers and replication costs).[120] Among them, the first-mover advantage, public praise, trends, and tides are usually used by enterprises. The first-mover advantage refers to the exclusive time enterprises enjoy before others become able to replicate their innovative products. In other words, it takes replicators some time to replicate an innovative work or product successfully, and during this time, the innovator has the first-mover advantage. Suppose enterprises could use this time to lock their advantage in the market or at least make others find it hard to threaten them, which is the best first-mover advantage. In some cases, this advantage is enough to motivate enterprises to continue to explore profound innovations. Gallié and Legros use many pieces of evidence to indicate that the first-mover advantage is the way small-scale companies prefer.[121] Levin and others believe the motivating effect brought by the first-mover advantage is usually more effective than patent protection in industrial fields like computer software.[122]

The essence of public praise is the commercial reputation of an enterprise. It affects consumers' willingness to consume, enables enterprises to maintain a high price, gives them a larger market share, and ensures their more active market performance. The function of public praise in encouraging innovations is that if the innovators can raise their products to the height of a successful brand, they could own the ability to set a high price after their products are imitated. For example, Advil's patent protection only won a 2-year exclusive control for its reputation; however, it still dominates the market for Ibuprofens after many years. Therefore, no matter how short the exclusive time is, as long as the innovator manages to set up a brand, they can continue to win benefits on an enormous scale. Imitated products are unlikely to influence their market positions, although the imitations are almost the same.[123] Trends and tides mean that enterprises follow the trend of the industry to make innovations. Trends inform consumers of essential information about what product is the most popular at present, and it facilitates them to know the probable best-sellers more easily and make corresponding innovations. Trends lead to the emergence of a product tide, and when the scale of this tide reaches a certain extent, similar imitations begin to appear. The overflow of imitations accelerates the spread of trends and tides and promotes enterprises to develop new types. Therefore, trends and tides play a significant role in encouraging innovation in such industries as food, fashion, and font.

Social principles

Social principles are the conventions established in related industries, which can better reflect their specialty and the advantages and disadvantages of competition and replication. Although these conventions have no legally compelling force, they can restrain the industry members to a certain extent and control replicating and copying in this industry, therefore, reducing the damages from imitations to innovators and providing compensations in addition to the law. Social principles are pretty effective in some creative industries by reducing the damage caused by replication. Many surveys indicate that regulations have played a significant role in supervising social lives, specifically in the market, providing a general order with no need for laws.[124] For instance, an insightful survey published by Emmanuelle Fauchard and Eric von Hippel proved that an informal and regulation-based quasi-IPR system existing in the elite group of French cooks had regulated the application of the others' original recipes, which explains the profound influence of anticopy principles and regulations with apparent origins in the French cooking world.[125] Christopher Buccafusco's survey also indicates the existence of an informal IPR system based on regulations.[126] Fauchard and von Hippel believe this informal IPR system excludes the need to use law-based IPRs to protect recipes.[127] Aram Sinnreich and Marissa Gluck believe a similar regulation-based quasi-IPR system exists in the industry.[128] In addition, this proves that there are highly consistent conventions of the principles' contents in the magic and comedy industries and clear regulations regarding behaviors out of bounds. The operation of these principles is secular and free from legal restrictions – sometimes even illegal or violated. However, the critical thing is that people in these fields universally acknowledge the principle-based system, which is beneficial to maintaining innovations and self-discipline in these industries.

Technological means

Technological means are also a form of non-IPR innovation protection used by enterprises. In terms of technological means, Lawrence Lessing, a professor at Stanford University, U.S., believed that the effect of technologies (codes) is far more powerful and comprehensive than that of law. Technology can provide almost perfect and all-mighty control, much better than the legal institution that has many defects.[129] Richard Spinello said that technological means are a powerful regulation force that uses decentralized management projects and technologies to reduce social harm. It is a noninvasive, simple, cheap, and bottom-up method, which could save the high expenses of governmental infrastructure brought by operating regulation plans.[130] The legal consultant of the Copyright Council of the International Publishers Association, Charles Clark, made a public speech at the IPR academic conference held in Amsterdam in June 1995, *The Answer to the Machine is in the Machine*. In Clark's opinion, the problem was not how to prevent people from acquiring, using, and enjoying knowledge products but how to monitor these acquisitions and applications. His answer was to enlist the digital systems used for spreading creations freely. Clark described several items worldwide to construct his so-called "recording charge" system that could trace the operating status of a single creation and prepare for charging. The technology protection measure is the key element of this structure, which uses computer codes to exclude free riders. A problem that remains unsolved by Clark is the lack of dominant legislation emphasizing technology protection.[131] Copyright protection and technological means are also quite common in the practice of patent protection. As López says, there are many means to protect technologies in practice, such as passwords, electronic handprints, and protection mechanisms to avoid replications.[132]

In addition to the law, these mechanisms are usually combined with IPR laws by enterprises, and they are highly dependent on some selective nonlegal mechanisms. Much empirical evidence proves that the effect of the previous powers might be distinguished from the level of industrial and economic development. As Pisano said, the protection mechanism of enterprise innovations is a multidimensional concept containing patents and other available means, which are influenced by the features of companies and industries as well as market strategies.[133] For instance, Laursen and Salter's surveys have found that the first-mover advantage is the method used by British enterprises most frequently, and it occupies the second position in product inventions. Sattler's survey indicated that German enterprises consider the efficiency of these mechanisms as follows: chronic employment relationship, first-mover advantage, the complexity of designs, commercial secrets, and patent and appearance designs. In Spanish manufacturing companies, the most preferred mechanism is the first-mover advantage; others are the practice and expense of imitation (complexity of designs), commercial secrets, and patents. The ranking preferred by Finnish manufacturing companies is the first-mover advantage, technological or empirical means (including commercial secrets, passwords, and restriction measures), silent knowledge, contracts, IPR laws, labor legislations, and human resource management. Those who depend on and even advocate these nonlegal mechanisms are mainly new developing countries. Related surveys also indicate that the restriction measure of first-mover advantage and technology is the critical way companies gain profits from product and method innovations, followed by brand construction.[134]

Negative space of IPRs: Paradigms of some industries

The patent system was established in a scarce world, and in the technological age if the content about the trace of technological development discussed previously is correct, technology will make the production and distribution of products no longer scarce, and the IPR protection will gradually become unnecessary in more and more industries. Many people could hardly imagine a world without patent systems. However, there are many industries that are free from the protection of the patent system and other IPRs in the current world. These industries and creative fields are regarded as the "negative space" of IPRs, which includes those fields that should be theoretically regulated by the IPR law (e.g., the fashion industry that will be mentioned in the following part). However, due to occasional or unsubstantial reasons, IPRs fail to interfere in these fields, or the IPR protection is weak.[135] The fundamental reason may be the enactment of IPR policies, and stakeholders might be too separated or not united enough, or they fail to secure a superior position when pursuing positive changes in the law due to objections from other benefits. For example, C. Scott Hemphill and Jeannie Suk pointed out that American copyrights don't protect fashion designs because designers are not powerful enough and are resisted by retailers and producers.[136]

However, when there is no IPR protection or the protection is weak, non-IPR protection mechanisms, such as market power, social principles, and technological means, are still active in the innovations in these industries. The negative space of IPR exhibits the relationship between the collection based on individuals and the production chain and the consumption of creative works. The interplay between individualism and collectivism constructs the eternal tension between innovation and regulation. Innovations embodied in explanations, adaptations, recombination, and sharing will benefit from them rather than be damaged by the absence or weakness in legal protection.[137] However, the scenarios exhibited in these fields are likely to be the situation in industrial development without mechanisms of patent protection in the future technological age. The industries with gaps in IPR include fashion, food, comedy, tattoos, databases, microprocessors, hairstyles, font, academic science, "amateur band," and perfume. This book will examine fashion and databases in detail.

Fashion industry

The fashion industry is one of the most important creative industries in the world, much larger than movies, books, music, and other innovative industries.[138] However, unlike these, the fashion industry has its primary element – fashion design – mainly uncovered by IPR laws. The IPR protection of fashion designs in the United States is always controversial. First, two-dimensional fashion designs can be seen as pictures; however, 3D clothes have useful functions and, therefore, cannot be protected by the *Copyright Law of the United States*. Second, although new fashion designs can apply for appearance design patents to avoid replications, the design patent provides 14-year protection for "novel, original, decorative" samples.[139] However, the clause on appearance design patents fails to protect fashion designs for two reasons. First, design patents are unsuitable for those new designs produced by reconstructing the existing ones. Most fashion designs don't fit the "novel" patent and fail to obtain patent protection. Second, the expenses when applying for patents are too high, and the waiting time is too long. However, the possibility of finally acquiring patent protection is hard to determine (the Bureau of American Patents and Trademarks will reject almost half of the applications for design patents.) The life expectancy of most fashion designs is no more than one or two seasons; acquiring design patents is too delayed and difficult to make a difference. Surveys indicate that the application for design patents takes the form of bags, luggage, and shoe manufacturing, and most fashion designs can't acquire adequate protection from appearance design patents.[140] Third, trademarks play a significant role in the fashion industry, because they help brands maintain their reputation and commodity premium. However, trademark protection of fashion designs is almost zero. Although the *Trademark Law of the United States* protects the "appearance of the commodity," which was proposed initially to protect unique package patterns and applied in product designs later, it is limited to the design elements without practical functions. It has to possess the function of identifying the source of the commodity. In other words, when consumers see this design, they have to be able to recognize that the given manufacturer produces it. Fashion designs can hardly satisfy this standard.[141]

Although the American fashion industry lacks the protection of IPRs, the large, energetic, and competitive fashion industry continues to make innovations rapidly and develops various clothes and accessories designs. On the one hand, designers don't lose the motivation for creation because of replications and piracies; instead, they imitate, share, and obtain creativity and enlightenment from others' products. Designers will always "furnish" popular commodities to a certain extent without copying the original one. For example, they will resort to "explanation" and "reference." They will quote, comment, or refer to creations of precedents – Monsieur Schwartz of the fashionable brand A.B.S. (Allen B. Schwartz) suggests that the new designers should stop complaining. "When discussing fashions, ask those young designers where their inspirations come from. Others also inspire them. That's quite normal. You can't always just stay at the window and wait for inspiration to turn into reality by itself." In an interview show in the United States, the compere Oprah Winfrey interviews the famous fashion designer: "How do you keep reinventing?" Ralph Lauren answered: "You copy. Forty-five years of copying; that's why I'm here."[142]

On the other hand, the various nonlegal mechanisms in the fashion industry have motivated this industry to maintain an enduring innovative life. First, the cycle of the trends and tides in the fashion industry is relatively quick. New fashion designs are first popular among fashion followers and then accepted by a larger number of customers. As these designs are replicated and copied and become popular in the market, they are no longer attractive to the original customer group. Imitations and sharing accelerate the changes in popular elements, encouraging entrepreneurs to abandon existing designs more quickly and pursue new designs to attract consumers' attention and replace the old products in the competitive market. Second, the fashion industry can confront the rampant copies and continue to make innovations, possibly because "the first-mover advantage" brings enough benefits to support innovations. If entrepreneurs can sell enough genuine clothes before imitations appear in the market, their profit will be quite considerable; therefore, continuous innovation becomes profitable.[143] Finally, social principles might play a role in the innovations of the fashion industry. Evidence proves a principle-based system in the American fashion industry, which imposes severe punishment on violators, such as bad comments from the fashion circle or being forced out by fashion media, will finally damage the brand image and decrease profits. In haute couture, plagiarizing too apparently might sometimes arouse controversies. if an ambitious designer is commented as "mirroring" others excessively, their career development might be harmed.[144]

Database industry

As the development of information technology enables much data to be constructed in digital forms or converted into digital forms, scanners and other devices make the digital conversion of data available, therefore promoting the emergence of the database. The database industry creates a series of products that collect and process information, and people can use computers to search for related information.[145] The database is an enormous commercial system. The turnover of online data and real-time information services worldwide in 1989 was about 8.5 billion European currency units. Europe's estimated scale of the electronic information supply market was GBP 5.138 billion.[146] Due to the considerable commercial benefits of the database, interest groups try to use legal mechanisms to restrain copying and replicating behaviors.

In the United States, what people first think of is to use the copyright law to protect databases, which the American court advocated for some time in the name of collective works. However, in the 1991 "Feist Case," the Supreme Court reversed a series of former verdicts that databases could own the copyright even if they were completely constituted of facts. The court believed that even though it takes great effort to assemble data in the telephone book according to the alphabetical order, it doesn't satisfy the novelty as defined in the copyright laws. Therefore, it can't acquire the protection of copyright law.[147] After this case, the American law world initiated a campaign aimed at changing the law and granting databases some legal protection against copying. The interest groups of data protection proposed that if we grant no copyrights to facts, people can plagiarize them freely; the free and legal copy will damage people's impetus to collect real information. These people even believed that the verdict of the Supreme Court would lead to the decline of the American database industry, and the development of European databases soon offered proof that advocated them. Soon after the "Feist Case," activists for database protection in the EU warned that the weak copyright law would lead the EU to a "helpless" situation for ownership protection similar to the "Feist Case" in the United States. Influenced by lobbies from interest groups in the database industry, the EU established a pan-European special IPR since the 1996 Database Order. It set a special right for makers of databases in case all or a substantial part of the data was extracted or reused for commercial purposes without permission. This right was an exclusive property right with a broad content, almost equal to acquiring a property right of immovable property. It was applied to databases of any form, regardless of being electronic or nonelectronic, and no matter whether the data's content has copyright, its protection term was 15 years. The European Database Order only protected databases made by Europeans or citizens of the third country that took "corresponding protection."[148] After the enactment of new laws in the EU, the interest groups of American databases warned that the European database industry would be superior to the United States with the help of new protection measures.

However, the actual case is astonishing. The database industry developed rapidly in the United States while stagnating on the other side of the Atlantic. The freedom to copy data failed to smother the American database industry; in contrast, it seemed to improve its development. In 2005, the European Commission completed a report to analyze the influence of the 1996 Database Order on computer databases in the EU.[149] This report found that the Database Order played no role in inducing the improvement in databases in the EU. The economic influence of "special" rights on database production is not yet proven. Although it was introduced as a stimulant to European databases, this new method has brought no empirical influence on its production.[150] In fact, the situation in the European database industry was much worse than those exposed in the survey in 2005. The production of databases in the EU in 2004 was half the level before the final enactment of the new law in 1998, and the proportion of the global database market of the EU also fell into stagnation. In 1992, 26% of online data was made by European companies, and about 60% by companies in North America. In 2005, the production in North America exploded to about 70% of the global market, and the market proportion of the EU had almost no change and even slightly reduced, according to some surveys.[151] The American database industry operated in relatively weaker IPR environments and grew even faster than those in the EU. The American database industry became increasingly superior to that of the

EU. The number of American database companies increased, as did the investments in these enterprises. For example, the database of Dun & Bradstreet, one of the top 500 companies, contains detailed information on over 150 million companies worldwide, with an investment of hundreds of millions of dollars. At the same time, the form and type of American databases became increasingly varied. When visiting the website of Dow Jones, the magnate of the information industry, one can find dozens of databases based on facts, which provide data about energy and commodities, real-time market index, foreign exchange rates, company reports including revenues, key company officials, and investors, price information on the auction of the American Department of Finance, and a series of common data including the government's anticorruption and anti-money laundering sanction lists.[152]

The reason why the American data industry can maintain strong innovation impetus and development momentum can be described as follows. First, although American courts provided no copyright protection on databases after the "Feist Case," some states applied the principle of misappropriation to using data without permission, which is unique anti-unfair competition protection in American law. It demands that the design methods of the database should be so original and valuable that competitors can't plagiarize this method. They also used the policy in contract law to connect users and usages to prohibit and restrict copies. The traditional property right was also applied. For instance, the magnate of the online auction, eBay, won the infringement lawsuits against Bidder's Edge, which was an auction "collection" website that used to acquire auction information from the eBay server. Compared with copyrights and special database rights with apparent property rights features, the principle of misappropriation and other legal means are merely counted as one of the weakest property rights.[153] However, an absolutely secure strategy doesn't exist. More critically, the American data industry uses nonlegal mechanisms to protect its data. For instance, database makers use classified measures and technological measures, like digital copyright management tools. They also continue to actively explore innovative commercial patterns and learn from each other, exploring new functions based on existing data, making users' lives increasingly manageable. A good example is that the *Los Angeles Times* made a micro innovation in the database maintained by the Los Angeles Unified School District.[154] Measures in the EU enable individual database makers to enjoy higher profits. However, it smothers the space for micro innovations and mutual improvements between different database enterprises, which is harmful to the development of the industry. In contrast, the "free copy" allowed in American law reduces the expenses when creating new databases. The failure to provide large-scale protection for databases means that competitors can reuse the existing database in innovative ways.

Conclusion

We were accompanied by scarcity for so long that it is difficult to imagine the transformation to the post-scarce economy. The patent system makes us strictly stick to scarcity, which is a general principle that can't be lost in our world.[155] But it won't prevent the appearance of transformations. If the post-scarce age comes, technological creation will no longer be scarce in a world where most of what we produce is cheap or even free of charge. People praise the knowledge-sharing culture, and the coming of a prosumer society means the rise of consumers' power. In such a post-scarce age, the patent system will gradually decline. The patent system was created by history and will probably be ended by history.

How will enterprises and industries develop without the patent system in the technological age? Creative industries, such as fashion and databases, provide us with the situation of their development without the guarantees of the patent system. Creative industries are not limited to fashion and databases; therefore, we can reasonably believe that more similar industries will appear with the development of technology. Unlike today's mainstream opinion that replicating and sharing will pose severe, even fatal, threats to creativity, these examples demonstrate a world where creativity grows stubbornly without or with little IPR protection, and imitation, sharing, and innovation can indeed coexist. The development of Silicon Valley also shows a similar scenario. The extraordinary performance of Silicon Valley in the innovation market worldwide is mainly attributed to its openness, mobility, and shareability because it usually ignores the operation of the law.[156]

The history of the patent system has told us that the patent system was originally a policy tool used by the government to develop technology and the economy. The government has conducted appropriate controls for valuable social purposes, such as supervising market access or controlling prices. The government still used this regulatory tool in the Industrial and Post-industrial Ages. The government previously supervised various industries, such as the railway, highway delivery, electricity, natural gas, and telephones. Considering the economic structure of these industries, the government can't predict how a free market can bring the best results to society. However, in numerous practical cases, we find that the market and other nonlegal controls can find a way to provide items that we thought were only available under government surveillance once the supervision over these industries was relaxed.[157] In this aspect, the patent system is no different from any other form of supervision. We often exaggerate the influence and function of monopoly rights on enterprise innovation. Therefore, monopoly rights have become the safe haven for companies in market competition. However, replications and piracy have existed long and can never be eliminated. Knowledge-sharing will become a trend in the technological age. At the same time, the rapid development of high technology will make the production and distribution of products no longer scarce. The expenses used to prevent knowledge and technology from being copied will increase, and the patent system will gradually lose its potency in the post-scarce age.

In a free society without a patent system, the companies that used to be protected by the patent system (e.g., manufacturing, chemistry, pharmacy, biotechnology, semiconductors, and software) will be faced with competition together with industries with IPR negative spaces (e.g., fashion and databases). These enterprises must be aware that their products are easily imitated or copied by others when the government's regulation is absent; therefore, it is their responsibility to tackle this problem. Every enterprise and producer is confronted with harsh competition in this free market. When supervision is absent, enterprises will explore new commercial patterns or cultural products to pursue exclusive profits and continue searching for better ways to entertain consumers. In different industries, enterprises will adopt different strategies according to the industry features. Accordingly, how to explore better ways for innovations and competition should be left to the enterprises. Respecting innovations that go beyond laws and abandoning the concept of all-mighty laws can make enterprises return to the diversity of institutions and search for more efficient choices.[158]

Notes

1 Benjamin N. Cardozo. *The Growth of the Law*; *The Paradoxes of Legal Science*. Dong Jiong, et al. Beijing: China Legal Publishing House, 2002:141

2 Hu Bo. Sharing Model and the Future Development of Intellectual Property – Addressing the "Alternative Model of Intellectual Property", *Legal and Social Development*, 2013 (4).

3 European Patent Office. *A Vision of the Future Intellectual Property System*. Guo Minsheng. Beijing: Intellectual Property Publishing House, 2008:186.

4 European Patent Office. *Vision of the Future Intellectual Property System*,186.

5 Brian Arthur. *The Nature of Technology: What It Is and How It Evolves*. Cao Dongming, Wang Jianyi, Translated. Hangzhou: Zhejiang People's Publishing House, 2014:231, 232.

6 Autonomous programs have generated imprisoned spirits. Due to the abused power of "enormous machines," humans deviate from the original life purpose and gradually become part of the machine. Humans are converted into machines with no awareness of the prospect. Technics and machines become the true rulers of the world, dominating the world and its residents. Lewis Mumford. *Technics and Civilizations*. Chen Yunming, et al. Beijing: China Architecture & Building Press, 2009:192.

7 Heidegger believed that the essence of technology is never technological. Technology is a truth or exhibition that reveals and fights with nature to produce a sort of energy that can be independently stored and transferred. Jiang Zhenhuan. *Introduction to the Philosophy of Technology*. Beijing: People's Publishing House, 2009:49.

8 Jacques Ellul. The Technological Society. *Science and Philosophy* (Research Material). 1 *Journal of Natural Dialectics Newsletter of the Chinese Academy of Sciences*, 1983, pp. 41–61.

9 Jeremy Rifkin. *The Zero Marginal Cost Society: The Internet of Things, the Collaborative Commons, and the Eclipse of Capitalism*. China Center for Information Industry Development. Beijing: CITIC Press, 2014; Klaus Schwab. *The Fourth Industrial Revolution: The Power of Transformation*. Hu Jun. Beijing: China Industry and Information Technology Publishing & Media Group, 2016; Wu Jun. *The Age of Intelligence: Big Data and the Intelligent Revolution Redefine the Future*. Beijing: China Industry and Information Technology Publishing & Media Group, 2016.

10 Xie Wen. *Big Data Economics*. Beijing: Beijing United Publishing Co., Ltd, 2017:10.

11 Xu Jin. *Big Data Economics*. Shanghai: Shanghai Jiao Tong University Press Co., Ltd., 2014:1.

12 Zhang Qijin. *The Industrial Revolution in the Era of Big Data*. Beijing: China Commercial Publishing House, 2016:3.

13 Hong Zhisheng, Xue Lan, Zhou Yuan. Driving Industrial Innovation and Economic Transformation with the Concept of "Sharing". *Guangming Daily*, 2016-05-11.

14 Rifkin. *Zero Marginal Cost Society*, 11.

15 The IoT is getting involved in industrial and commercial fields. Companies set sensors in all commercial steps to trace the flow of goods. Sensors in retail shops can help the sales and marketing departments to learn customers' behaviors and acquire related information. It is also used in the construction of intelligent cities, because sensors can monitor the material waves and states of buildings, bridges, roads, and other infrastructures and analyze the construction situation of the building environment to make repairs in time. It is also rapidly used in the natural environment to manage the ecological system of the Earth. For example, sensors in the forest can alarm potentially dangerous factors for a fire to firemen, and sensors on wild animals can help to evaluate their living environment. The IoT is also changing the way of producing and transporting foods; for instance, farmers are using sensors to predict weather and monitor the soil moisture to ensure that the environment remains the most suitable for plant growth. It can also be applied to vegetables and fruits to judge whether they are rotten by analyzing their smell. Doctors even implant sensors into the human body to examine body functions, including heart rates, pulse, temperature, and skin colors, so that they can notice changes in important body features. Rifkin. *Zero Marginal Cost Society*, 88–90

16 Rifkin. *Zero Marginal Cost Society*, 88–90.

17 The traditional laser (or inkjet) printers are two-dimensional (2D) printers: they acquire pixels from the screen and convert them into ink dots or toner dots on 2D mediums (usually paper). 3D printers acquire blueprints of products by Internet downloading, CAD software, or 3D scanning and make products by layer-by-layer crafts based on digital model files and adhesive materials, including metal, plastic, or high polymer materials. It totally changes the current production pattern of substantial products. Liu Qiang, Luo Kaizhong. Study on the Change of Patent System in the Context of 3D Printing, *Journal of Central South University (Social Scienc*e), 2015 (5)

18 Chris Anderson. *Makers: The New Industrial Revolution*. Xiao Xiao. Beijing: CITIC Press, 2015:113 114.

19 3D Printer Parts, Makerbot Thingiverse, available at www.thingiverse.com/explore/newest/3d-printing/3d-printer-parts.

20 N. V., Difference Engine: The PC All Over Again?, *Economist*, available at www.economist.com/blogs/babbage/2012/09/3d-printing.

21 History of Personal Computers, Wikipedia, available at http://en.wikipedia.org/wiki/History_of_personal_computers.

22 The cost curve of 3D printers reduces as fast as computers, mobile phones, wind, and solar energy. Rifkin. *Zero Marginal Cost Society*, 89.

23 Mark Hatch. *The Maker Movement Manifesto: Rules for Innovation in the New World of Crafters, Hackers, and Tinkerers*. Beijing: China Machine Press, Yang Ning. 2015:115.

24 Stuart Russell, Peter Norvig. *Artificial Intelligence: A Modern Approach*. Yin Jianping, et al. Beijing: Tsinghua University Press, 2006:21.

25 Research Media Consulting. 2017 China Artificial Intelligence Industry Special Research Report. https://baijia.baidu.com/s?old_id=816979.

26 Cao Yuan. The Reasonableness of Copyright Protection for Artificial Intelligence Creations. *Journal of Law and Technology*,2016 (3).

27 Deep Interest in AI, New High in Deals To Artificial Intelligence Startups In Q4'15, available at www.cbinsights.com/blog/artificial-intelligence-startup-funding-trends.

28 Xu Man. *The Development and Reflection of Foreign Robot News Writers*, China Newspaper Industry, 2015 (23).

29 IFONG. *Art in Danger? Google's New Technology Deep Dream May Become "a Machine That Can Automatically Paint" in the future.* http://arti.feng.com/2016/0331/2819902.shtml.

30 Sohu. *Google's Home Artificial Intelligence Can Already Compose Music!* https://m.sohu.com/n/453537300/.

31 Liu Entong. *Xiaoice Published a Poetry Collection: Sunlight Without Glass Windows: 100% AI Creation.* www.sohu.com/a/142577676_356153.

32 Tencent Technology. *An Interview with American Engineer: How I Renewed the Sixth Novel of<Game of Thrones>with AI.* http://tech. qq.com/a/20170906/074791.

33 Certainly, during this stage, the application of this AI depends on human intelligence, and the parameters of the research objective and the standard of accomplishment are artificially set in advance. Ryan Abbott, *I Think, Therefore I Invent: Creative Computers and the Future of Patent Law*, Social Science Electronic Publishing, 2016:57.

34 Abbott. *I Think, Therefore I Invent*, 57.

35 Robert Plotkin. *The Genie in the Machine: How Computer-Automated Inventing Is Revolutionizing Law and Business*. Redwood City, CA: Stanford University Press, 2009:125.

36 Plotkin. *Genie in the Machine*, 3.

37 A system named "Eva Robot" was developed for the research of malaria treatments. The Eva Robot selects the most effective ones among the given 5,000 molecules. Finally, it discovered a medicine for cancer treatment that has the best treatment effects for malaria. Plotkin. *Genie in the Machine*, 126.

38 *Official Records-Cloem, Register of Commerce and Companies*, available at www.infogreffe.fr/societes/entreprise-societe/792987836-cloem-060213B005530000.html?typeProduitOnglet=EXTRAIT&afficherretour=true.

39 For example, in November 2017, an AI thesis was published on the cover of the magazine *Science* and marked a significant breakthrough in the field of AI. Three researchers from MIT, New York University, and Toronto University developed an AI system that "can write at a glance." The AI system they created could rapidly learn how to write strange words, which meant to a certain extent that it understood the basic features of characters (e.g., the whole structure of characters) and could recognize its unessential features (e.g., these slight variations led by writing). Brenden M. Lake, Ruslan Salakhutdinov, Joshua B. Tenenbaum. Human-level Concept Learning through Probabilistic Program Induction, *Science*, 2015, pp. 1332–1338.

40 Erik von Hippel. *Democratizing Innovation: How User Innovation Improves the Innovation Efficiency of Firms.* Chen, Jin, et al. Beijing: Intellectual Property Publishing House, 2007:2–3

41 Chris Anderson believes that the "maker movement" contains three revolutionary features. 1. People use digital desktop tools to design new products and make models "Digital DIY." 2. Sharing design results and making cooperations in open-source network communities have become a cultural regulation. 3. If necessary, anyone can transfer their design to commercial producers based on the general standard of designing files and make designed products at any amount, or they can make products with desktop tools. These two methods are the same and convenient and greatly shorten the distance between creativity and entrepreneurs; their influence is no less than innovation brought by the internet to software, information, and content. Anderson. *Makers*, 30.

42 Rifkin. *Zero Marginal Cost Society*, 88–101.

43 Moreover, Rosenberg's quantitative research indicates that some of the most important and newest products and crafts are developed by companies and individual users. An

Enos report pointed out that almost all of the most significant innovations in the oil refining industry are developed by company users. Freeman found out that most chemical production crafts widely approved are also developed by them. Saw discovered that most of the significant facilities in the four movement fields are developed by individual users. von Hippel. *Democratizing Innovation*, 19–22.

44 von Hippel. *Democratizing Innovation*, 14–15.

45 Sawyer K. The Collaborative Nature of Innovation, *Washington University Journal of Law and Policy,* 2009, p. 293.

46 Mark A. Lemley. IP in a World without Scarcity, *New York University Law Review,* 2015, p. 460

47 Anderson. *Makers*, 30.

48 Alvin Toffler first proposes the term "prosumer" in his book *The Third Wave*, and names those who create products, services, and experiences for self-appliance or self-satisfaction rather than consumption or exchange "prosumers." Alvin Toffler. *The Third Wave*. Huang Mingjian. Beijing: CITIC Press, 2006:150–151.

49 Rifkin. *Zero Marginal Cost Society*, 91.

50 Rifkin. *Zero Marginal Cost Society*, 265

51 Rifkin. *Zero Marginal Cost Society*, 105–109

52 Kevin Kelly. *Out of Control: The New Biology of Machines, Social Systems, and the Economic World.* East West & Library, Beijing: New Star Press, 2010:286.

53 Rajesh Narula pointed out at the end of the twentieth century that, enterprises began to transform from large scale and high amounts to small scale and high price. Most of the value chains, even core businesses are gradually outsourced. Enterprises have realized that depending on global thought and human resources is still better than limited internal resources. In the last twenty years, enterprises no longer preferred vertical integration; their dependence on internal research accelerated to decrease, while that on external ones increasingly grew. Rajneesh Narula. *Globalization and Technology: Interdependence, Innovation Systems and Industrial Policy.* Leng Min. Beijing: Intellectual Property Publishing House, 2011:134–135.

54 Zhang Yuming. *Sharing Economics*. Beijing: Science Press, 2017:162.

55 Zhang Yuming. *Sharing Economics*, Introduction.

56 Rachel Botsman believes that the social network has experienced three developing stages. In the first stage, programmers can share network rules with each other. Facebook and Twitter belong to the second stage, which enables people to share their lives. The third stage is YouTube and Flickr, which enables people to share the results they create. "Now we're entering the fourth stage, where people can use technology to share all offline properties in the real world with others." Rifkin. *Zero Marginal Cost Society*, 243–244, 250.

57 AskCI. Data Analysis of the Bicycle Sharing Industry in 2017 and 2018 Forecast: The Market Size Will Exceed 17 Billion Yuan in 2018. http://news.cnfol.com/chanyejingji/20180126/25956729.shtml.

58 Qianzhan. Analysis of the Current Market Situation and Development Trends of China's Shared Travel Industry in 2021, www.qjanzhan.comanalgst/detail1220/210412-4602ccc/.htm.

59 Zhang Yuming. *Sharing Economics*, pp. 11–12.

60 Zhang Yuming. *Sharing Economics*, pp. 13–14.

61 Rifkin. *The Internet of Things*, 267.

62 Cassirer, the famous German cultural philosopher, believed that humans don't simply live in the physical universe; instead, they live in a symbolic universe. Languages, mythologies, arts, and religions construct the symbolic web, and human's thoughts, behaviors,

and experiences make it more delicate and solid. Ernst Cassirer. *An Essay on Man*. Gan Yang. Shanghai: Shanghai Translation Publishing House, 2004:34.

63 John Stuart Mill. *On Liberty, A Selection of His Works*. London: Palgrave, 1966:252–257.

64 Jeff Howe. *Crowdsourcing: Why the Power of the Crowd Is Driving the Future of Business*. Niu, Wenjing. Beijing: CITIC Press, 2011:142.

65 A sociologist, Rheingold, calls the internet community the "virtual community." He thought that a virtual community is constituted of

> a group of people connected by the computer network and breaks the limit of regions, who communicate with each other via the Internet, share information and knowledge, and form a network of special relations with similar hobbies and interests. They finally form a common community awareness and emotions.

Rheingold H. *The Virtual Community: Home Steading on the Electronic Frontier*. Cambridge, MA: MIT Press, 2000: 243.

66 Xu Yuanzhong. *Social Economy: The Philosophy of Survival in the Mobile Internet Era*. Beijing: CITIC Press, 2015:12–13.

67 In 1998, the American programmers Raymonde and Prince set up the "Open Source Initiative Association" that motivated the "Open Source Initiative" in California, the U.S. The open-source software was essentially a beneficial balance pattern in which the software's right owner opened his commercial secrets of the source code and clearly abandoned the rights of modification, license, and rewards in copyrights. In return, the software users later also opened the commercial secrets and abandoned the same rights in the copyrights.

68 In 1984, supported by some enterprises, Richard Stallman, a programmer at MIT, U.S., established the Free Software Foundation out of dissatisfaction with the monopoly of software development technologies. Therefore, he opened his large "Free Software Alliance Project" and initiated the engineering of free software. To date, the development of free software has achieved great success and has been acknowledged in many countries. There were thousands of free software in the American Free Software Alliance alone, and the typical representative was the GNU/Linux OS and GNU/C++ language systems. By 1998, the increase rate of the Linux OS was 212%, occupying 27.6% of the global Internet servers, while the market proportion of Microsoft Windows OS in this field was merely 23.6%.

69 The concept of "creation sharing" was first proposed by a nonprofit organization established at Stanford University, the headquarters of which lies in San Fransisco. It uses the concepts of software developers and motivates open resources. Today, there are more than 60 countries worldwide that participate in the basic creation-sharing agreements or authorization systems.

70 In 2002, the Foundation on Economic Trends put this theory into practice. About 250 organizations from about 50 countries gathered at the Global Social Forum in Porto Alegre, Brazil, which advocated the *Treaty to Share the Genetic Commons*. Since then, many groups and organizations have been established to promote global gene sharing and prevent it from being "monopolized."

71 Michael Heller. *The Gridlock Economy*. Lv Jia. Beijing: China Machine Press, 2009:1; Robert P. Merges. New Energy in the Public-owning Field, Du Ying, et al. *Private Law Review*, 2012, 10 (1), p. 40; Xie Xiaoyao, Wu Chumin, The Transformed Paradigm: Rethinking Intellectual Property Theory. *Intellectual Property,* 2016 (7).

72 Tom Standage. *Writing on the Wall: Social Media – The First 2,000 Years*. Lin Hua. Beijing: CITIC Press, 2015:22.

73 Clay Shirky. *Cognitive Surplus: Creativity and Generosity in a Connected Age*. Hu, Yong, et al. Beijing: China Renmin University Press, 2011:72–73.

74 William W. Fisher III. *Promises to Keep: Technology, Law, and the Future of Entertainment*. Li Xu. Shanghai: Shanghai SDX Joint Publishing House, 2008:20–21.
75 Kal Raustiala, et al. *Knockoff Economy: How Imitation Sparks Innovation*. Lao Ka, et al. Beijing: Publishing House of Electronic Industry, 2015:16.
76 Rifkin. *Zero Marginal Cost Society*, 101.
77 Rifkin. *Zero Marginal Cost Society*, 21.
78 Jürgen Habermas. *The Structural Transformation of the Public Sphere: An Inquiry into a Category of Bourgeois Society*. Cao Weidong, et al. Shanghai: Academia Press, 1999:3.
79 Habermas. *Structural Transformation*, 2
80 When citizens make negotiations using unrestricted methods, they act as a public group. In this middle area, people can make liberal, equal, and rational discussions about problems they are concerned with and continuously make criticisms regardless of restraints of political power, conventions, and traditions. Citizens must make an agreement through public debates. Every citizen makes comments on public affairs based on their benefits, values, beliefs, and conscience and forms the ultimate public opinion via debates. Habermas. *Structural Transformation*, 113.
81 Arendt believes the public field is the field where people act, and it is commonly maintained and possessed by liberal and equal citizens. Distinct from private fields, which are concealed spaces for negotiating private benefits or exhibiting personal emotions, it is an open field completely demonstrated to the public and the field or situation for public affairs. In this process, citizens discuss freely and express themselves openly. The value of this activity is not aimed at practical results. Instead, it highlights that the subjective characteristics of citizen's activities are unrestricted. It is neither demonstrated as governing nor as being governed. Zeng Xianggeng. Thinking Between Public Life and Private Life: An Analysis of Arendt's Theory of Human Activity Field, *Journal of Hainan Normal University (Social Science Edition)*, 2017 (5).
82 Rifkin. *Zero Marginal Cost Society*, 25–30.
83 Han Ruibo. The Zero Marginal Cost Society in the Perspective of Generalized Political Theory – A Review of "The Zero Marginal Cost Society – A New Economic Era of Internet of Things, Cooperation and Win-Win", *Journal of Sichuan Administrative College*, 2015 (3).
84 John Rawls. *The Theory of Justice*. He Huaihong, et al. Beijing: China Social Sciences Press, 2009:4.
85 Rifkin. *The Zero Marginal Cost Society*, 18.
86 Rifkin. *The Zero Marginal Cost Society*, 21
87 Peter Drahos. *A Philosophy of Intellectual Property*. Zhou Lin. Beijing: The Commercial Press, 2008: Preface to the Chinese edition, 2–3
88 Rifkin. *Zero Marginal Cost Society*, 234–240
89 Jeremy Rifkin. *The Empathic Civilization: The Race to Global Consciousness in a World in Crisis Jiang*, Zongqiang. Beijing: CITIC Press, 2015:396–397.
90 Abandoning market and property right transaction, promoting interpersonal relationship from concepts to achieve structural transformations are the conversion from property rights to sharing concepts. When it comes to many people at present, this transformation is quite unbelievable. For instance, 500 years ago, people were difficult to believe that enclosure movements, land privatization, and labor would become the interpersonal property relation. In the future, in terms of more and more enterprises and consumers, the concept of knowledge ownership will be apparently restricted and even seem to be inappropriate.[90] Jeremy Rifkin. *The Age of Access: The New Culture of Cybercapitalism Where All of Life is a Paid-for Experience*. New York: Tarcher-Putman Books, 2000:228.

91 In addition, during the early stage of the enactment of the *Doha Declaration*, an article published in the *Journal of the American Medical Association* believes the level of poverty and medical expenses contrary to the patent right is the main obstacle to solving the acquisition problem of AIDS medicines in Africa. This conclusion is used by The Pharmaceutical Research and Manufacturers of America (PHRMA) and regarded as powerful proof to oppose the enactment and adjustment of the *Amendments of TRIPS Agreement*. Some NGOs, like the Médecins Sans Frontières (MSF), soon responded and believed that the patent system had a large negative influence on the medicine acquisition problem, which promoted the birth of the *Doha Declaration*. Susan K. Sell. *Private Power, Public Law: The Globalization of Intellectual Property*. Cambridge, UK: Cambridge University Press, 2003:27.

92 Civil power rose with the beginning of the Trans-Pacific Partnership Agreement (TPP) and Anti-Counterfeiting Trade Agreement (ACTA) negotiations. At this time, the general public, except civil groups, NGOs, and stakeholders, began to participate in movements to resist the strengthening of IPR protection. For instance, in 2012, 7,000 websites were closed to resist the approval of SOPA, and Google received about 7 million signatures to resist the approval on its website. Since 2012, the civil protesting movement to resist ACTA has swept across Europe, which directly facilitated Germany, Poland, Lithuania, Czech, and Slovakia to postpone the approval procedures in ACTA. Du Ying. New Developments in the International Protection System of Intellectual Property Rights and China's Path Choice. *Jurist*, 2016 (3).

93 Sell. *Private Power, Public Law*, p. 278

94 Margaret Archer. *Realist Social Theory: The Morphogenetic Approach*. New York: Cambridge University Press, 1995:317.

95 Nicole Syzdek. Five Stages of Patent Grief to Achieve 3D-Printing Acceptance, *University of San Francisco Law Review*, 2015, p. 335.

96 Kal Raustiala, et al. *Knockoff Economy*, 28–29.

97 Michael Abramowicz. Perfecting Patent Prizes, *Vanderbilt Law Review*, 2003, 56, pp. 115–122.

98 Lemley. IP in a World without Scarcity, p. 460.

99 Xie Xiaoyao, Wu Chumin. The Paradigm of Transformation: Rethinking Intellectual Property Theory. *Intellectual Property*, 2016 (7).

100 Yu Wujin. How Exactly to Understand Nietzsche's Words "God Is Dead", *Philosophical Research*, 2006 (9); Xie Xiaoyao, Wu Chumin. Paradigm of Transformation.

101 Joel Mokyr. *The Lever of Riches: Technological Creativity and Economic Progress*. Chen, Xiaobai. Beijing: Huaxia Publishing House, 2008:60.

102 Stephan Kinsella. There's No Such Thing As a Free Patent, *Mises Daily*, 2012, p. 7.

103 Stephan Kinsella. Do Business WITHOUT Intellectual Property, available at www.stephankinsella.com/2014/10/do-business-without-intellectual-property.

104 Mokyr. *Lever of Riches*, 325–326.

105 Oshin Vartanian, Adam S. Bristol and James C. Kaufman, eds, *Neuroscience of Creativity*. Cambridge, MA: MIT Press, 2013; Erez Reuveni. Copyright, Neuroscience, and Creativity, *Alabama Law Review*, 64, 2013, p. 735.

106 Henry Biggs. Towards a More Comprehensive Approach to the Promotion of Creativity, *University of Dayton Law Review*, 38, 2013, p. 401; Julie E. Cohen. Creativity and Culture in Copyright Theory, *U.C. Davis Law Review*, 2007, 40, pp. 1151, 1178, 1183, 1190; Jeanne C. Fromer. A Psychology of Intellectual Property, *North Western University Law Review*, 2010, 104, pp.1441, 1443, 1144; Eric E. Johnson. Intellectual Property and the Incentive Fallacy, *Florida State University Law Review*, 2012, 39, pp. 623, 627.

107 Joost Smiers et al. Abandoning Copyright: A Blessing for Artists, Art, and Society. Liu Jinhai. Beijing: Intellectual Property Publishing Intellectual Property Publishing House, 2010:3.

108 George Basalla pointed out that they solve the problems they meet, triumph over challenges in front of them, make all efforts to conquer nature and human competitors to win the game and get great satisfaction in psychology and social benefits. Therefore, humans are likely to make creations when making things at any time, any place, and anyway. George Basalla. *The Evolution of Technology Development.* Zhou Guangfa. Shanghai: Fudan University Press, 2000:146.

109 Teresa M. Amabile. *Creativity in Context: Update to the Social Psychology of Creativity.* London: Hachette UK, 1996:171; Beth A. Hennessey, Teresa M. Amabile. Reward, Intrinsic Motivation, and Creativity, American *Psychologist*, 1998, 53, pp. 674–675; John Quiggin, Dan Hunter. Money Ruins Everything, *Hastings Communication and Entertainment Law Journal*, 2008, 30, pp. 203, 214–215.

110 Chris Anderson. *Free: The Future of a Radical Price.* Jiang Xufeng, et al. Beijing: CITIC Press, 2009:229.

111 Anderson. *Free*, 229.

112 Anderson. *Free*, 250–252.

113 Lawrence Lessig. *Code: And Other Laws of* Cyberspace, Version 2.0. Li Xu, et al. Beijing: Tsinghua University Press, 2009: 111.

114 Yujiro Hayami et al. *Development Economics: From the Poverty to the Wealth of Nations.* Li, Zhou. Beijing: Social Sciences Academic Press, 2009:4–12.

115 John Hasnas. 1995 The Myth of the Rule of Law, *Wisconsin Law Review*, 1995, p. 199.

116 Arrow Kenneth. Economic Welfare and the Allocation of Resources for Invention, in *The Rate and Direction of Inventive Activity: Economic and social Factors.* Princeton, NJ: Princeton University Press, 1962:619–620.

117 Yujiro Hayami et al. *Development Economics*, 4–12.

118 Professor Li Chen believed that when evaluating the IPR law's response methods and degrees for a certain problem, the first of all is to judge. Is the crux of the problem the market environment or the legal environment? What influence will the level of legal interference have on the development of the market? Legal transaction chances depend on the protection of rights and admitting the market's function instead of denying the effect of laws. However, when designing the protection degree of laws, its influence on the market should be taken into consideration. The law should first introduce and offer legal content. On the occasion when legal content online is insufficient, the copyright law should be especially cautious when determining whether to improve the existing punishment strength, especially considering its influence on commercial innovation impetus. Certainly, existing rights rules should be respected, and the innovations of commercial patterns should only be introduced rather than forced by law. If the protection of copyright rights is not powerful enough, right owners will also be unavailable to transaction chances. The commercial pattern to reduce transaction expenses is primarily explored by the industrial world, and the law cannot interfere excessively. Overall, because the industrial transformation is incomplete, it seems wiser for the law to maintain a laissez-faire attitude instead of abusing severe regulations. Li Chen. *A Critique of the Basic Theory of Copyright.* Beijing: Intellectual Property Publishing House, 2013:48–56

119 Stuart Banner. *American Property: A History of How, Why, and What We Own.* Chen Xiankai, Xu Ke, Beijing: China University of Political Science and Law Press, 2017:310–337.

120 Xie Xiaoyao, Wu Chumin. *Paradigm of Transformation.*
121 Richard C. Levin, et al. Appropriating the Returns from Industrial Research and Development, No.862. New Haven, CT: Cowles Foundation for Research in Economics, Yale University, 1988:125.
122 Levin, et al., 127.
123 Kal Raustiala, et al. *Knockoff Economy*, 292.
124 Kal Raustiala, et al. *Knockoff Economy*, 264.
125 Emmanuelle Fauchard, Eric von Hippel. *Norm-Based Intellectual Property Systems: The Case of French Chefs*, available at http://papers.ssrn.com/sol3/papers.cfm?abstract_id=881781.
126 Christopher J. Buccafusco. *On the Legal Consequences of Sauces: Should Thomas Keller's Recipes Be Per Se Copyrightable?*, available at http://papers.ssrn.com/sol3/papers.cfm?abstract_id=923712
127 Emmanuelle Fauchard, Eric von Hippel. *Norm-Based Intellectual Property Systems: The Case of French Chefs*, available at http://papers.ssrn.com/sol3/papers.cfm?abstract_id=881781.
128 Aram Sinnreich, Marissa Gluck. *Music & Fashion: The Balancing Act Between Creativity and Control,* available at http://learcenter.org/pdf/RTSSinnreichGluck.pdf.
129 Lessig. *Code*, 78.
130 Richard Spinello. *CyberEthics: Morality and Law in Cyberspace.* Li Lun. Beijing: Peking University Press, 2007:40–44.
131 Paul Goldstein. *Copyright's Highway: From Gutenberg to the Celestial Jukebox.* Beijing: Peking University Press, 2008:170.
132 Eden Sarid. *Fostering Innovation without IP – What Enables Informal Creativity?* available at www.epip2016.org/book-of-abstracts/sarid.
133 Sarid. *Fostering Innovation without IP.*
134 Sarid. *Fostering Innovation without IP.*
135 Kal Raustiala, Christopher Jon Sprigman. Duan Yunlei. Response: The Piracy Paradox Revisited, *Private Law*, 2014, 24 (2), pp. 1201–1225.
136 C. Scott Hemphill, Jeannie Suk. The Law, Culture, and Economics of Fashion, *Standford Law Review*, 2009, 61, p. 1147.
137 C. Scott Hemphill, Jeannie Suk. The Law, Culture, and Economics of Fashion, Cai Yuanzhen. *Private Law Review*, 2014 (2).
138 As a primary product of commercial globalization, its annual consumption in the United States is more than 200 billion dollars; the global fashion industry sells clothes for over 750 billion dollars per year. Safia A. Nurbhai. Style Piracy Revisited, *Journal of Law and Policy*, 2002, 10, p. 489.
139 Kal Raustiala, et al. *Knockoff Economy*, 264.
140 Kal Raustiala, et al. *Knockoff Economy*, 264, fn. 1.
141 As the court said in "Knitwaves Case," consumers might appreciate a fashion design, but they hardly realize that special design elements are connected with brands. Little fashion design elements can reach the extent that can stimulate the recognition source in the brains of the public to enhance commercial protection. The final result is that commercial appearance protection isn't suitable for most fashion designs. Laustia, Sprigman. Piracy Paradox.
142 Kal Raustiala, et al. *Knockoff Economy*, 264.
143 Kal Raustiala, et al. *Knockoff Economy*, 180.
144 Kal Raustiala, et al. *Knockoff Economy*, 177–178.

145 As an industry, it is constituted of three elements: the database, producers, and providers. The database is made by producers, and providers publish them or offer searching. At the same time, many database producers become providers by offering online searching in their databases or publishing their CD-ROM editions. Xie Xinzhou Yifan. The Development of Database Industry in Europe and America. *Journal of the China Society for Scientific and Technical Information*, 1997 (6).

146 Mark Davidson. *The Legal Protection of Databases*. Zhu Li, Beijing: Peking University Press, 2007:1.

147 *Feist Publications, Inc. v. Rural Telephone Service Co.*, 499 U.S. 340(1991).

148 Davidson. *The Legal Protection of Databases*, 1.

149 Commission of the European Communities. *DG Internal Market and Services Working Paper, First Evaluation of Directive 96/9/EC on the Legal Protection of Databases 1.4*, available at http://ec.europa.eu/internal_market/copyright/docs/databases/evaluation_report_en.pdf.

150 Commission of the European Communities. *DG Internal Market and Services Working Paper*.

151 Kal Raustiala, et al. *Knockoff Economy*, 241–242.

152 Kal Raustiala, et al. *Knockoff Economy*, 240–241.

153 Li Qian. How the Law Deals with Data Property – From Databases to Big Data. *Law and Social Sciences*, 2016, 15 (1)

154 Li Qian. How the Law Deals with Data Property, pp. 243–244.

155 Lemley. IP in a World without Scarcity, p. 460.

156 Ronald Gilson believed that a relatively weaker IPR protection achieved Silicon Valley. One of the reasons is that the legislation in California prohibits the business strife limitation clause, which is harmful to innovation companies. However, the entire industry benefits from the knowledge overflow in job-hopping. Ronald J. Gilson. The Legal Infrastructure of High Technology Industrial Districts: Silicon Valley, Route 128, and Covenants Not to Compete, 575 *New York University Law Review*, 1999, pp. 74, 195.

157 Gilson, Legal Infrastructure of High Technology, p. 480

158 Stephan Kinsella. Law and Intellectual Property in a Stateless Society, *Libertarian Papers*, 2013, p. 5.

References

I. Books Translated into Chinese

Anderson, Chris. *Free: The Future of Business*. Jiang Xufeng, et al. Beijing: CITIC Press, 2009.

Anderson, Chris. *Long Tail Theory*. Qiao Jiangtao. Beijing: CITIC Press, 2012.

Anderson, Chris. *Creators: The New Industrial Revolution*. Xiao Xiao. Beijing: CITIC Publishing House, 2015.

Aoki, Masahiko, Masakuan Okuno, et al. *Comparative Institutional Analysis of Economic Systems*. Beijing: China Development Press, 1999.

Aristotle. *Nicomachean Ethics*. Liao Shenbai. Beijing: The Commercial Press, 2003.

Arthur, Brian. *The Nature of Technology: What It Is and How It Evolves*. Cao Dongming, Wang Jian. Hangzhou: Zhejiang People's Publishing House, 2014.

Atack, Jeremy, Peter Purcell. *The New American Economic History: From the Colonial Period to 1940*. Luo Tao, et al. Beijing: China Social Science Press, 2000.

Banner, Stuart. *The Story of Property*. Chen Xiankai, Xu Ke. Beijing: China University of Political Science and Law Press, 2017.

Basara, George. *A Brief History of Technology Development*. Zhou Guangfa. Shanghai: Fudan University Press, 2000.

Baudrillard, Jean. *Consumer Society*. Liu Chengfu, Quan Zhigang. Nanjing: Nanjing University Press, 2001.

Beard, Charles A., Mary R. Beard. *The Rise of American Civilization*. Xu Yafen, et al. Beijing: The Commercial Press, 2011.

Berner, J. D. *The Social Function of Science*. Chen Tifang. Beijing: The Commercial Press, 1982.

Bianchin, Jimmy. *An Introduction to the Principles of Morality and Legislation*. Shi Yinhong. Beijing: The Commercial Press, 2000.

Bodenheimer, Edgar. *Jurisprudence: Philosophy of Law and its Methods*. Deng Zhenglai. Beijing: China University of Political Science and Law Press, 1998.

Bozeman, Rachel, et al. *The Era of Sharing Economy: Collaborative Consumption Business Model under the Internet Thinking*. Tang Chaowen, et al. Shanghai: Shanghai Jiaotong University Press, 2015.

Brodeur, Fernand. *Material Civilization, Economy and Capitalism in the 15th to 18th Centuries*. Gu Liang, Shi Kangqiang. Beijing: Life, Reading, New Knowledge, 1992.

Burke, Dan L., Mark A. Lemley. *Patent Crisis and the Way to Cope*. Ma Ning, Yu Jun. Beijing: China University of Political Science and Law Press, 2013.

Cardozo, Benjamin N. *The Growth of Law, the Paradox of Legal Science.* Dong Jiong, et al. Beijing: China Legal Publishing House, 2002.

Carter, Thomas Francis. *The Invention of Printing in China and Its Transmission to the West.* Wu Zeyan. Beijing: The Commercial Press, 1957.

Chartier, Roger. *The Cultural Origins of the French Revolution.* Hong Qingming. Nanjing: Yilin Publishing House, 2015.

Coase, R., A. Alchian, D. North, et al. *Property Rights and Institutional Change: A Collection of Translations from the School of Property Rights and the New Institutional School.* Liu Shouying, et al. Shanghai: Gezhi Publishing House, Shanghai People's Publishing House, Shanghai Sanlian Bookstore, 2014.

Cole, Harbhajan. *Outsourcing and Offshoring in the 21st Century: A Socio- Economic Analysis.* Jiang Rongchun. Shanghai: Gezi Publishing House, 2012.

Commons, John. *Institutional Economics.* Zhao Rui. Beijing: Huaxia Publishing House, 2017.

Condorcet. *Outline of the History of Human Spiritual Progress.* He Zhaowu. Nanjing: Jiangsu Education Publishing House, 2006.

Crowley, Roger. *The City of Wealth: Venice's Maritime Hegemony.* Lu Dapeng, Zhang Zhan. Beijing: Social Science Literature Publishing House, 2015.

Dampier, William Cecil. *The History of Science and its Relation to Philosophy and Religion.* Li Heng. Guilin: Guangxi Normal University Press, 2001.

Davidson, Mark. *Legal Protection of Databases.* Zhu Li. Beijing: Beijing University Press, 2007.

de Betz, Ralph. *History of the United States: The First Book.* Department of History, Nanjing University. Beijing: People's Publishing House, 1984.

Dehousse, Peter. *The Philosophy of Intellectual Property Law.* Zhou Lin. Beijing: The Commercial Press, 2008.

Devereaux, Peter, John Braithwaite. *Information Feudalism.* Liu Xuetao. Beijing: Intellectual Property Publishing House, 2005.

Dube, George, ed. *History of France.* Lv Yimin. Beijing: The Commercial Press, 2010.

Dugger, William M., Howard J. Sherman. *Back to Evolution: A Dialogue between Marxism and Institutionalism on Social Change.* Zhang Lin, et al. Beijing: China Renmin University Press, 2007.

Ehrman. *Comparative Legal Culture.* He Weifang, Gao Hongjun. Beijing: Life, Books, New Knowledge, 1990.

European Patent Office. *A Vision of the Future Intellectual Property System.* Beijing: Intellectual Property Press, 2008.

Fetter, Gilbert C., Jim E. Rees. *Economic History of the United States.* Situ Chun, et al. Shenyang: Liaoning People's Publishing House, 1981.

Fisher, William W. *Talking Counts: Technology, Law, and the Future of Entertainment.* Li Xu. Shanghai: Shanghai Sanlian Publishing House, 2008.

Freeman, Chris, Francesco Luzan. *From the Industrial Revolution to the Information Revolution.* Shen Hongliang, et al. Beijing: China Renmin University Press, 2007.

Galbraith, John Kenneth. *The New Industrial State.* Ji Fei. Shanghai: Shanghai People's Publishing House, 2012.

Geertz, Clifford *The Interpretation of Culture.* Han Li. Nanjing: Yilin Publishing House, 2008.

Giddens, Anthony. *The Composition of Society: An Outline of Structured Theory.* Li Kang, et al. Beijing: Life, Reading, New Knowledge, 1998.

Gleick, Dominic, Bruno van Portersburg. *The Economics of the European Patent System: Innovation and Competition in Intellectual Property Policy*. Zhang Nan. Beijing: Intellectual Property Publishing, 2016.
Goffey, Jean-Yves. *Philosophy of Technology*. Dong Maoyong. Beijing: The Commercial Press, 2000.
Gordon, Scott. *Control the State – A History of Western Constitutionalism*. Ying Qi, et al. Nanjing: Jiangsu People's Publishing House, 2001.
Gostin, Paul. *The Way of Copyright: From Gutenberg to the Digital On Demand Machine*. Jin Haijun. Beijing: Peking University Press, 2008.
Goudelier, Maurice. *The Mystery of the Gift*. Wang Yi. Shanghai: Shanghai People's Publishing House, 2007.
Habermas, Jürgen. *The Structural Transformation of the Public Sphere*. Cao Weidong, et al. Shanghai: Xue Lin Publishing House, 1999.
Haigh, Dennis. *The Historical Background of the Italian Renaissance*. Li Yucheng. Beijing: Life, Reading, New Knowledge, 1988.
Hamilton, Edith. *The Greek Way: Source of Western Civilization*. Xu Qiping. Hangzhou: Zhejiang People's Publishing House, 1988.
Hammerton. *Synopsis of Western Masterpieces: History Section*. He Ning. Beijing: The Commercial Press, 1959.
Harvey, David. *The Postmodern Condition*. Yan Jia. Beijing: The Commercial Press, 2003.
Heller, Michael. *The Economics of Distress*. Lu Jia. Beijing: China Machine Press, 2009.
Hershleifer, Jack, et al. *Uncertainty and Information Analysis*. Liu Guangling, et al. Beijing: China Social Science Press, 2000.
Hinsley, F. H.. *The New Cambridge Modern History: Material Progress and World- Wide Problems (1870-1898)*. Institute of World History, Chinese Academy of Social Sciences. Beijing: Chinese Social Science Press, 1987.
Hodgson, Geoffrey M. *Evolution and Institutions: On Evolutionary Economics and the Evolution of Economics*. Ren Ronghua, et al. Beijing: China Renmin University Press, 2007.
Hoover, Toby. *Why Modern Science Was Born in the West*. Yu Xia. Beijing: Peking University Press, 2010.
Horwitz, Morton J. *The Transformation of American law (1780-1860)*. Xie Hongfei. Beijing: China University of Political Science and Law Press, 2004.
Howe, Jeff. *Crowdsourcing: The Future of Business Driven by Group Power*. Niu Wenjing. Beijing: CITIC Press, 2011.
Huraly, Yuval. *A Brief History of Mankind: from Animals to God*. Beijing: CITIC Press, 2014.
Hyde, Lewis. *The Gift: How the Spirit of Innovation Changes the World*. Sun Tian. Beijing: Publishing House of Electronics Industry, 2015.
Igoné, Patrice. *Paris Mythology: From Enlightenment to Surrealism*. La Weiguo. Beijing: The Commercial Press, 2013.
Jaffe, Adam, Josh Lerner. *Innovation and Its Discontents: The Harmful Effects of the Patent System on Innovation and Progress*. Luo Jianping, Lan Hua. Beijing: China Renmin University Press, 2007.
Jenkins, Henry. *Convergence Culture: The Conflict Zone between New and Old Media*. Du Yongming. Beijing: The Commercial Press, 2012.
Jones, Erik. *The European Miracle: Environment, Economy, and Geopolitics in Eurasian History*. Chen Xiaobai. Beijing: Huaxia Publishing House, 2015.
Kairys, David. *Politics in Law: A Progressive Critique*. Xin Chunying. Beijing: China University of Political Science and Law Press, 2008.

Kassir, Ernst. *Humanism*. Gan Yang. Shanghai: Shanghai Translation Press, 2004.
Kato, Masanobu. *The Birth of "Ownership"*. Zheng Furong. Beijing: Law Press, 2012.
Kauf, Ilyich. *The Economics of the Patent System*. Ke Ruihao Beijing: Peking University Press, 2005.
Kelly, Kevin. *Out of Control: The Ultimate Fate and End of All Mankind*. East West Library. Beijing: New Star Press, 2010.
Kelly, Kevin. *New Rules for the New Economy: Ten Strategies for the Network Economy*. Liu Zhongtao. Beijing: Publishing House of Electronics Industry, 2014.
Kelly, Kevin. *What Technology Wants*. Yan Lijuan. Beijing: Publishing House of Electronics Industry, 2016.
Kerr, Robert. *A Weekend of German History*. Ouyang Lin, et al. Shanghai: Shanghai Jiaotong University Press, 2012.
Kirby, James, Randy Roberts, et al. *History of the United States: The first book*. Fan Daofeng, et al. Beijing: The Commercial Press, 2012.
Krasser, Rudolf. *German Patent and Utility Model Law, European and International Patent Law*. Shan Xiaoguang, Zhang Taolve, et al. Beijing: Intellectual Property Publishing House, 2016.
Kuhn, Thomas. *The Structure of Scientific Revolutions*. Jin Wulun, et al. Beijing: Beijing University Press, 2012.
Landers, William M., et al. *The Economic Structure of Intellectual Property Law*. Beijing: Peking University Press, 2005.
Landes, David. *The Unbound Prometheus*. Xie Huaizhu. Beijing: Huaxia Publishing House, 2007.
Lapp, F. *Introduction to the Philosophy of Technology*. Liu Wu. Shenyang: Liaoning Science and Technology Press, 1986.
Lausdia, Carl, et al. *CopyRight! How Imitation Inspires Innovation*. Lao Ka, et al. Beijing: Publishing House of Electronics Industry, 2015.
Lenin, Vladimir. *Selected Works of Lenin: Volume 2*. The Bureau of Compilation and Translation of the Works of Marx, Engels, Lenin and Stalin of the Central Committee of the Communist Party of China. Beijing: People's Publishing House, 1995.
Lesger, Lawrence. *The Future of Ideas: A Cautionary Tale for the Public Knowledge Sphere in the Internet Age*. Li Xu. Beijing: CITIC Press, 2004.
Lesger, Laurence. *Code 2.0: Law in Cyberspace*. Li X., et al. Beijing: Tsinghua University Press, 2009.
Lintner, Valerio. *Italian History in a Weekend*. Guo Shangxing, Liu Yajie, et al. Shanghai: Shanghai Jiaotong University Press, 2009.
Marx, Karl. *Philosophical Manuscripts on Economics of 1844*. Bureau of Compilation of the Works of Marx, Engels, Lenin and Stalin of the Central Committee of the Communist Party of China. Beijing: People's Publishing House, 2002.
Marx, Karl, Friedrich Engels. *The Complete Works of Marx and Engels: Volume 3*. Bureau of Compilation of the Works of Marx, Engels, Lenin and Stalin of the Central Committee of the Communist Party of China. Beijing: People's Publishing House, 1995.
Mauss, Marcel. *The Gift: Forms and Reasons for Exchange in Archaic Societies*. Ji Zhe. Shanghai: Shanghai People's Publishing House, 2005.
Mauveley, Rosenberg. *The Road to Innovation: Technological Innovation in the United States in the 20th Century*. Wang Hongyu. Chengdu: Sichuan People's Publishing House, 2002.

McClellan III, James E., Harold Dorn. *A General History of Science and Technology in the World*. Wang Ming Yang. Shanghai: Shanghai Science and Technology Education Press, 2007.

McIlwain, Charles Howard. *Constitutionalism, Ancient and Modern*. Zhai Xiaobo. Guiyang: Guizhou Publishing House, 2004.

Merges, Robert M. et al. *Intellectual Property Law in the Age of New Technology*. Qi Yun. Beijing: China University of Political Science and Law Press, 2003.

Merriam, Charles. *American Political Thought*. Zhu Zengwen. Beijing: The Commercial Press, 1984.

Merryman, John Henry. *Continental Law System*. Gu Peidong, Lu Zhengping. Beijing: Law Press, 2004.

Merton, Robert King. *Science, Technology, and Society in Seventeenth- Century England*. Fan Dainian, et al. Beijing: The Commercial Press, 2000.

Mitchum, Karl. *Thinking through Technology – The Road between Engineering and Philosophy*. Chen Fan, Qin Shusheng. Shenyang: Liaoning People's Publishing House, 2008.

Mogil, Joel. *The Gift of Athena: The Historical Origins of the Knowledge Economy*. Duan Yibing, Tang Le. Beijing: Science Press, 2011.

Mokyr, Joel. *The Lever of Affluence: Technological Innovation and Economic Progress*. Chen Xiaobai. Beijing: Huaxia Publishing House, 2008.

Mueller, J. M.. *Patent Law*. 3rd ed. Shen Chao, et al. Beijing: Intellectual Property Press, 2013.

Mumford, Lewis. *Technology and Civilization*. Chen Yunming, et al. Beijing: China Architecture & Building Press, 2009.

Naisbitt, John. *Megatrends: Ten New Directions that Will Change our Lives*. Mei Yan. Beijing: China Social Science Press, 1984.

Nakayama, Nobuhiro. *Multimedia and Copyright*. Zhang Yurui. Beijing: Patent Literature Press, 1997.

Narela, Rajesh. *Globalization and Technology: Interdependence, Innovation Systems and Industrial Policy*. Leng Min. Beijing: Intellectual Property Publishing House, 2011.

North, Douglas C. *Institutions, Institutional Change and Economic Performance*. Hang Xing. Shanghai: Gezhi Press, Shanghai Sanlian Bookstore, Shanghai People's Publishing House, 2014.

North, Douglas C. *Structure and Change in Economic History*. Chen Yu, et al. Shanghai: Shanghai Sanlian Bookstore, 1994.

North, Douglas C. *Understanding the Process of Economic Change*. Zhong Zhengsheng, et al. Beijing: China Renmin University Press, 2013.

Organization for World Economic Cooperation and Development, ed. *The Knowledge-Based Economy*. Yang Hongjin, Xue Lan. Beijing: China Machine Press, 1997.

Panshmael, Philippe. *France*. Qi Zhusheng. Shanghai: Shanghai Translation Publishing House, 1980.

Peterson, Merrill D. *Jefferson's Collection*. Liu Zuochang, et al. Shanghai: Shanghai Sanlian Bookstore, 1993.

Piron, Henry. *The Economic and Social History of Medieval Europe*. Le Wen. Shanghai: Shanghai People's Publishing House, 2001.

Popper, Karl. *Historical Determinism of Poverty*. Du Ruji, et al. Beijing: Huaxia Publishing House, 1987.

Postan, Micheal M. et al., eds. *The Cambridge Economic History of Europe: Volume 4 The expanding European economy in the 16th and 17th centuries*. Wang Chunfa, et al. Beijing: Economic Science Press, 2003.
Postan, Michael M. et al., eds. *The Cambridge Economic History of Europe: Volume 5: European Economic Organization in the Early Modern Period*. Wang Chunfa, et al. Beijing: Economic Science Press, 2003.
Rapp, F. *The Structure of Thinking in Technical Science*. Liu Wu, et al. Changchun: Jilin University Press, 1988.
Rawls, John. *The Theory of Justice*. He Huaihong, et al. Beijing: China Social Science Press, 2009.
Reisig, Lawrence. *REMIX: Remixing Other People's Work into a Money- Making Business*. Ye Xinlan. Taipei: Dashi Culture Co, 2011.
Rheingold, Howard. *Network Literacy: Digital Citizenship, Collective Intelligence, and the Power of Networking*. Zhang Ziling, et al. Beijing: Electronic Industrial Property Publishing House, 2013.
Ricardo, David. *Political Economy and the Principles of Taxation*. Guo Dali, Wang Yanan. Beijing: The Commercial Press, 1962.
Rifkin, Jeremy. *The Zero Marginal Cost Society: A New Economic Era of Internet of Things and Win- Win Cooperation*. CCID. Beijing: CITIC Press, 2014.
Rifkin, Jeremy. *Empathetic Civilization: Building Global Consciousness in a Crisis- ridden World*. Jiang Zongqiang. Beijing: CITIC Publishing House, 2015.
Rostow, W. W. *How It All Began: The Origins of the Modern Economy*. Huang Qixiang, et al. Beijing: The Commercial Press, 2014.
Sachsenin, Annalie. *The Silicon Valley Advantage*. Cao Peng, et al. Shanghai: Shanghai Far Eastern Publishing House, 2000.
Scheckey, Clay. *Cognitive Surplus: The Power of Free Time*. Hu Yong, et al. Beijing: China Renmin University Press, 2011.
Schumpeter, Joseph. *Capitalism, Socialism and Democracy*. Wu Liangjian. Beijing: The Commercial Press, 1999.
Schwartz, Bernard. *The History of American Law*. Wang Jun. Beijing: China University of Political Science and Law Press, 1990.
Sell, Susan K. *Private Rights, Public Law: The Globalization of Intellectual Property Rights*. Dong Gang. Beijing: China Renmin University Press, 2008.
Sherman, Brad, Lionel Bentley. *The Evolution of Modern Intellectual Property Law: The History of England (1760-1911)*. Haijun, Jin. Beijing: Beijing University Press, 2006.
Simon, Herbert. *The Cornerstone of Modern Decision Theory*. Yang Li, Xu Li. Beijing: Beijing Institute of Economics Press, 1989.
Skochim, Suzanne. *Innovation and Motivation*. Liu Yong. Shanghai: Gezi Publishing House, 2010.
Smiters, Joost, et al. *Abandoning Copyright – The Future of the Cultural Industry*. Liu Jin. Beijing: Intellectual Property Publishing House, 2010.
Smith, Adam. *The Wealth of Nations*. Yang Jingnian. Xi'an: Shaanxi People's Publishing House, 2006.
Spinello, Richard. *Iron Cage, or Utopia: Morality and Law in Cyberspace*. Li Lun. Beijing: Peking University Press, 2007.
Standage, Tom. *From Sagebrush to the Internet: Social Media 2000*. Lin Hua. Beijing: CITIC Press, 2015.
Stavrianos, L. S. *Global History: From Prehistory to the 21st Century*. Wu Xiangying. Beijing: Peking University Press, 2005.

Tamura, Yoshiyuki. *Japanese Intellectual Property Law*. 4th ed. Zhou Chao, et al. Beijing: Intellectual Property Publishing House, 2011.
Tamura, Yoshiyuki. *Yoshiyuki Tamura on Intellectual Property*. Li Yang, et al. Beijing: China People's University Press, 2013.
Thomas, Pratip N., et al, eds. *Intellectual Property Rights and Communication in Asia*. Gao Rui. Beijing: Tsinghua University Press, 2009.
Thompson, James W. *The Economic and Social History of the Middle Ages*. Geng Yanru. Beijing: The Commercial Press, 1984.
Thompson, James W. *Economic and Social History of Late Medieval Europe*. Xu Jialing, et al. Beijing: The Commercial Press, 1992.
Toffler, Alvin. *The Third Wave*. Huang Mingjian. Beijing: CITIC Press, 2006.
Tomita, Tetsuo. *Intellectual Property Rights in Market Competition*. Liao Zhengheng, et al. Beijing: The Commercial Press, 2000.
Van Buren, Thorstein. *The Place of Science in Modern Civilization*. Zhang Lin, Zhang Tianlong. Beijing: The Commercial Press, 2012.
Van Buren, Thorstein. *The Theory of the Leisure Class: An Economic Study of Institutions*. Gan Ping. Wuhan: Wuhan University Press, 2014.
von Hippel, Erik. *Democratizing Innovation: How User Innovation Improves a Company's Innovation Efficiency*. Chen Jin. Beijing: Intellectual Property Publishing House, 2007.
Wolff, Y. *A History of Science, Technology, and Philosophy in the Sixteenth and Seventeenth Centuries*. Zhou Changzhong. Beijing: The Commercial Press, 1985.
Xenophon. *Economic Theory: Income in Athens*. Zhang Bojian, et al. Beijing: Commercial Press, 1981.
Yujiro Sugimizu, et al. *Development Economics – From Poverty to Wealth*. Li Zhou, et al. Beijing: Social Science Literature Press, 2009.

II. Publications in Chinese

Beijing Continental Bridge Times Publications Co. *Italian Past*. Chongqing: Chongqing Publishing House, 2007.
Chen Wenhai. *History of France*. Beijing: People's Publishing House, 2014.
Cheng Xun. *Historical Jurisprudence*. Beijing: Law Press, 2005.
Gao Hongshen, Yang Hongzhi. *The Economics of Knowledge*. Beijing: China Renmin University Press, 2002.
Han Yi. *The Historical Process of Industrial Modernization in the United States: 1607-1988*. Beijing: Economic Science Press, 2007.
Huang Haifeng. *The Discourse and Reality of Intellectual Property Rights: A History of Copyright, Patent and Trademark*. Wuhan: Huazhong University of Science and Technology Press, 2011.
Huang Renyu. *Capitalism and the 21st century*. Beijing: Life, Reading, New Knowledge, 1997.
Huang Xinrong. *Modern Western Philosophy of Technology*. Nanchang: Jiangxi People's Publishing House, 2011.
Hu Shi. *Hu Shih's Collected Works*. Beijing: Peking University Press, 1998.
Hu Shi. *Outline of the History of Chinese Philosophy*. Beijing: China Book Bureau, 2012.
Jin Haijun. *The Theory of Private Rights of Intellectual Property*. Beijing: China Renmin University Press, 2004.
Li Chen. *Critique of the Basic Theory of Copyright*. Beijing: Intellectual Property Publishing House, 2013.

Li Jianming. *General History of the United States: Volume 1*. Beijing: People's Publishing House, 2002.
Li Zonghui. *The Intellectual Property System in Historical Perspective*. Beijing: Intellectual Property Publishing House, 2015.
Liu Cheng, Liu Jinyuan, Wu Qinghong. *Britain – From World Domination to Return to Europe*. Xi'an: Sanqin Publishing House, 2005.
Liu Senlin. *In Search of the Subject*. Beijing: Social Science Literature Publishing House, 2008.
Liu Xuyi, Yang Shengmao, Zhang Youlun, et al. *A General History of the United States: The Independence and Initial Prosperity of the United States (1775-1860)*. Beijing: People's Publishing House, 2002.
Liu Yejin. *Economic Evolution: Exploring the General Evolutionary Paradigm*. Beijing: China Social Science Press, 2015.
Liu Zuochang. *Jefferson's Biography*. Beijing: China Social Science Press, 1990.
Luo Ruilin, Liu Baimao. *The History of Chinese Silk*. Beijing: Beijing Textile Industry Publishing House, 1986.
Organization for World Economic Cooperation and Development, ed. *The Knowledge-based Economy*. Beijing: Machinery Industrial Press, 1997.
Qin Hai. *Institutions, Evolution and Path Dependence – A Theoretical Attempt at Institutional Analysis Synthesis*. Beijing: China Financial and Economic Press, 2004.
Ren Li. *The Mechanism of Technological Progress in Economic Growth: A Study Based on Theory Change*. Shanghai: Shanghai Academy of Social Sciences Press, 2014.
Sun Dapeng. *Nature, Technology and History*. Shanghai: Fudan University Press, 2009.
Shang Jie. *A Study of Venetian Aristocracy in the Late Medieval and Early Modern Period*. Wuhan: Wuhan University Press, 2013.
Tang Shiping. *A Broad Theory of Institutional Change*. Beijing: Peking University Press, 2016.
The History of Foreign Philosophy, Department of Philosophy, Peking University, Beijing, China. *Selected Works of Western Philosophy*: The first volume. Beijing: Commercial Press, 1981.
Wang Bolu. *Technological Dilemma and its Transcendence*. Beijing: China Social Science Press, 2011.
Wang Changya. *Fundamentals of Patent Science*. Wuhan: Hubei Science and Technology Press, 1985.
Wang Jingang, Zhang Tiejun. *Patenting Survival*. Beijing: Intellectual Property Publishing House, 2005.
Wang Hongsheng. *World History of Science and Technology*. Beijing: China Renmin University Press, 2008.
Wang Jingchuan, Hu Kaizhong. *Study on the Modernization of Intellectual Property System*. Beijing: Beijing University Press, 2010.
Wang Na. *The Transformation of Trademark Legal System in Modern China – From Parasitism to Autonomy*. Shanghai: Shanghai People's Publishing House, 2016.
Wang Taiping. *Research on Patent Eligibility in the Era of Knowledge Economy*. Beijing: Intellectual Property Publishing, 2015.
Wang Taiping. *Research on the Change of Patent System in the Era of Knowledge Economy*. Beijing: Law Press, 2016.
Wu Chunwu. *French Social and Economic History*. Beijing: The Commercial Press, 1937.
Wu Handong. *Research on Copyright Fair Use System*. Beijing: China University of Political Science and Law, 1996.

Wu Xinwang. *Patent Economics*. Beijing: Social Science Literature Press, 2005.

Wu, Xinwang, Zhu, Quantao. *Innovation Market and the Rise and Fall of Nations*. Beijing: Social Science Literature Press, 2012.

Xu Jin. *The Economics of Big Data*. Shanghai: Shanghai Jiaotong University Press, 2014.

Xu Liang. *Philosophy of Technology*. Shanghai: Fudan University Press, 2004.

Xu Yuanzhong. *Community Economics*. Beijing: CITIC Press, 2015.

Yang Lihua. *A Study on the History of U.S. Patent Law*. Beijing: China University of Political Science and Law Press, 2012.

Yang Wu. *Patent Technology Innovation—An Analysis of Law and Economics*. Beijing: Science Publishing, 2013.

Yang Yonghua. *Technological Innovation Mechanisms and Policies in the Perspective of Evolutionary Economics*. Beijing: Social Science Literature Press, 2015.

Yu Jun. *The Evolution of Trademark Law*. Wuhan: Huazhong University of Science and Technology Press, 2011.

Zhang Fujun. *Research on the Theory of Technology and Institutional Co-Evolution*. Beijing: Economic Science Publishing House, 2013.

Zhang Gongyao. *The History and Philosophy of Science and Technology*. Changsha: Zhongnan University Press, 2007.

Zhang Xinfeng. *The Property Right Attributes of Patent Rights: A Study on the Path of Privatization of Technology*. Wuhan: Huazhong University of Science and Technology Press, 2011.

Zhang Wenxian. *Knowledge Economy and Legal System Innovation*. Beijing: Peking University Press, 2012.

Zhang Xukun. *Introduction to Institutional Evolutionary Analysis*. Hangzhou: Zhejiang University Press, 2007.

Zhang Weiliang. *The Commercialization of British Society: 1500-1750*. Beijing: People's Publishing House, 2004.

Zhang Y. M., et al. *Sharing Economics*. Beijing: Science Press, 2017.

Zhang Zeqian. *History of French Civilization*. Wuhan: Wuhan University Press, 1997.

Zhang Zhuoyuan. *The Dictionary of Political Economy*. Beijing: Economic Science Publishing House, 1998.

Zhao Wenhong. *The Development of Private Property Rights System: A Study of the Origin of Western Market Economy and Capitalism*. Beijing: China Social Science Press, 1998.

Zhao Yulin. *Economics of Innovation*. Beijing: China Economic Press, 2006.

III. Chinese Papers

Cao Yuan. The Reasonableness of Copyright Protection for Artificial Intelligence Creations. *Technology and Law*, 2016 (3).

Chen Huiping. Dialectical Development of Marxist Theory of Consciousness. *Journal of Shandong University of Science and Technology: Social Science Edition*, 2018 (1).

Chen Yekui. A Rational Critique of the "Cult of Information". *Information Work*, 1999 (6).

C. Scott Hemphill, Jenny Sook. Law, Culture and Economics in Fashion. Cai Yuanzhen. *Private Law*, 2014 (2).

Du Ying. New Developments in the International Protection System of Intellectual Property Rights and the Choice of China's Path. *Jurist*, 2016 (3).

E. A. Bogatayh, B. H. Levchenko. The Origin and Class Substance of the Bourgeois Patent System. *Chinese and Foreign Jurisprudence*, 1979 (6).

Fu Zheng. Spencer's "Social Organism" Theory and Qing Dynasty Statism. *Studies in Modern History*, 2017 (2).

Haibo Bao, Shihao Sheng. Innovation and Performance of the U.S. Patent System since the 1980s. *Science, Technology and Law*, 2002 (4).

Han Ruibo. The Zero Marginal Cost Society in the Perspective of Generalized Political Theory – A Review of "The Zero Marginal Cost Society – A New Economic Era of Cooperation and Win-win in the Internet of Things". *Journal of Sichuan Administrative College*, 2015 (3).

Hong Zhisheng, Xue Lan, Zhou Yuan. Driving Industrial Innovation and Economic Transformation with the Concept of "Sharing". *Party Politics Vision*, 2016 (7).

Hu Bo. The Future Development of the Sharing Model and Intellectual Property Rights—Addressing the "Alternative Model of Intellectual Property Rights". *Legal and Social Development*, 2013 (4).

Hua Min, Sun Feng. The Causes, Characteristics and Effects of Economic Globalization and China's Response. *Fudan Journal (Social Science Edition)*, 2000 (5).

Hua Min. Economic Globalization and China's Opening to the World. *Academic Monthly*, 2007 (7).

Jiang Zhe'an. On the Causes of Economic Prosperity in Medieval Venice. *Journal of Anhui University (Philosophy and Social Science Edition)*, 1998 (4).

Karl Laustia, Christopher Sprigman. Response: The Piracy Paradox Revisited. Duan Yunlei. *Private Law*, 2014 (2).

Karl Laustia, Christopher Sprigman. The Piracy Paradox: Innovation and Intellectual Property in Fashion Design. Duan Yunlei. *Private Law*, 2015, 12 (2).

Li Qian. How the Law Deals with Data Property–From Database to Big Data. *Law and Social Scienc*e, 2016 (1).

Li Qian. How the Law Deals with Data Property–From Database to Big Data. *Law and Social Scienc*e, 2016 (1).

Li Xiaofen. The Historical Evolution of American Individualism before the 20th Century. *Journal of Xiamen University,* 2003 (5).

Li Yang. Some Special Problems of the Relationship between Intellectual Property and Antitrust Law: Next. *Study Forum*, 2008 (1).

Liang Youcai. 1997 World Economic Outlook. *Economy and Information*, 1997 (1).

Liang Zhiwen. On the Patent Crisis and its Solution. *Political Law Series*, 2011 (3).

Liang Zhiwen. On National Autonomy under the TRIPS Agreement: A Perspective of Intellectual Property Justice Theory. *Rule of Law Research*, 2009 (5).

Liu Qiang., Luo Kaizhong. Study on the Change of Patent System in the Context of 3D Printing. *Journal of Central South University (Social Science Edition)*, 2015 (5).

Liu Youhua. The Future Model of Patent System: Alternative, Innovation or Globalization. J*ournal of South China Normal University (Social Science Edition)*, 2011 (4).

Lou Junxin. An Experiment on the Industrial Modernization of France. *Journal of Hangzhou University (Philosophy and Social Science Edition)*, 1991 (3).

Ma Yeh. On the Three Basic Principles of Neoliberalism. *Marxist Studies*, 2006 (2).

Paul A. David. Intellectual Property Systems and the Panda's Thumb: Patents, Copyrights, and Trade Secrets in Economic Theory and History. Gu Yanfang. *Technology and Law*, 1998 (4).

Shi Bisheng. The Judicial Changes of the U.S. Patent Creativity System. *Comparative Law Research*, 2012 (5).

Sheng Guorong. Science, Technology and Society: The Historical Evolution of the Relationship between the Three. *Journal of Northeastern University (Social Science Edition)*, 2006 (3).

Shen Han. The Position of Germany in the History of the Occurrence of Capitalism in the 15th-16th Centuries. *Guizhou Social Science*, 2016 (1).

Tang Jian. System, Time and Social Evolution: A Review of Tang Shiping's Social Evolution of International Politics. *International Political Science*, 2015 (2).

Tang Shiping. The Foundational Paradigm of Social Science. *International Journal of Social Sciences*, 2010 (1).

Xiao Yudan. Cultural Transformation of Copyright and Micro-Historical Research Methods. *Northern Jurisprudence*, 2009 (4).

Xie Xiaoyao, Wu Chumin. The Transformed Paradigm: Rethinking Intellectual Property Theory. *Intellectual Property Rights*, 2016 (7).

Xie Xinshou, Yi Fan. The Development Status of Database Industry in Europe and America. *Journal of Intelligence*, 1997 (6).

Wang Jianfeng. The Development History of Patent System: Monopoly and Anti-Monopoly of Technology. *Science, Technology and Law*, 2014 (2).

Wang Yuanming. A Comparative Study of the Industrial Policies of the British and French Governments in the 16th and 17th Centuries. *Journal of Hangzhou University*, 1992 (1).

Wang Zhanghui. A Comparison of the Industrial Revolution in Britain and France. *Studies in Historical Theory*, 1994 (2).

Yang Lihua. From "Privilege" to "Property Right": An Exploration of the Origin of Patent Right. *Journal of Xiangtan University (Philosophy and Social Science Edition)*, 2009 (1).

Yang Lixiong. Commodity or Gift: Neoliberalism and New Leftism in Cyberspace. *Studies in Natural Dialectics*, 2004 (1).

Yu Saito. The International Political Economy of the Intellectual Property Regime: Shifting the Basis of Hegemony from Capital to Science and Technology. Li Xueying. *World Science and Technology Research and Development*, 1991 (2).

Yu Tao, Weng Lingjun. The Development Trend of International Technology Trade and China's Countermeasure Options. *Economist*, 2008 (11).

Yuan Zhenfu. Intellectual Property Alienation: The Prisoner's Dilemma: The Purpose of Intellectual Property Legislation as a Reference. R*esearch on Intellectual Property Law*, 2006 (1).

Zhou Guanxiong. Newton's Mechanistic and Metaphysical Worldview and Its Representation in Differentialism – Notes on Studying Marx's Mathematical Manuscripts. *Journal of Huazhong University of Science and Technology (Natural Science Edition)*, 1975 (1).

Zhou Zhaoguang. How to View Western Neoliberalism and Its International Impact. *Fujian Forum (Humanities and Social Sciences Edition)*, 2007 (3).

IV. Foreign Books and Papers

Adams, John N., Gwen Averley. The Patent Specification the Role of Liardet v Johnson. 7 *The Journal of Legal History*, 1986. J. J. Pollitt. *Art and Experience in Classical Greece*. Cambridge, 1972.

Anderfelt, U. *International Patent-Legislation and Developing Countries*. Germany: Springer Science & Business Media, 2013.

Arundel, A., I. Kabla. What Percentage of Innovations are Patented? Empirical Estimates for European Firms. 27 *Research Policy*, 1998.

Bessen, J., M. J. Meurer. *Patent Failure: How Judges, Bureaucrats, and Lawyers Put Innovators at Risk*. Princeton, NJ: Princeton University Press, 2008.

Bracha, Oren. The Commodification of Patents 1600–1836: How Patents Became Rights and Why We Should Care, Loy. 38 *Loyola of Los Angeles Law Review*, 2004.

Braudel, F. *The Structures of Everyday Life. The Limits of the Possible*. London: Collins, 1981.

Bugbee, B. W. *Genesis of American Patent and Copyright Law*. Washington: Public Affairs Press, 1967.

Cohen, W. M., D. A. Levinthal. Absorptive Capacity: A New Perspective on Learning and Innovation, in *Strategic Learning in a Knowledge Economy*. Boston, MA: Butterworth-Heinemann, 2000.

Collier, J. D. *An Essay on the Law of Patents for New Inventions, at v, xiv*. London: A. Wilson, 1803.

Drahos, P. Global Property Rights in Information: The Story of TRIPS at the GATT. *Prometheus*, 1995.

Drahos, P. Thinking Strategically about Intellectual Property Rights 21 *Telecommunications Policy*, 1997.

Eisenhardt, Kathleen M. D., Charles Galunic. Coevolving: At Last, a Way to Make Synergies Work. 72 *Harvard Business Review*, 2000.

Enyart, J. *AGAT Intellectual Property Code*, Les Nouvelles, 1990.

Epstein, S. R. Property Rights to Technical Knowledge in Pre-Modern Europe, 1300–1800. *American Economic Review*, 2004.

Federico, P. J. State Patents. 13 *Journal of the Patent Office Society*, 1931.

Feinberg, R.. *Peculiar Patents: A Collection of Unusual and Interesting Inventions from the Files of the US Patent Office*. Secaucus, NJ: Carol Publishing Group, 1994.

Fink, Z. S. Venice and English Political Thought in the Seventeenth Century. *Modern Philology*, 38, November 1940.

Foray, D. Knowledge Distribution and the Institutional Infrastructure: The Role of Intellectual Property Rights, in Albach H. and Rosenkrantz S. (eds.), *Intellectual Propert Rights and Global Competition*. Germany: WZB Publication, 1995.

Frumkin, M. The Origin of Patents. 27 *Journal of the Patent Office Society,* 143, 1945.

Frumkin, M. Early History of Patents for Invention. 26 *Transactions of the Newcomen Society*, 1947.

Galvez-Behar, G. Was the French Patent System democratic? France, 19th Century. *Working Papers*. France: HAL, 2008.

Godson, R. *A Practical Treatise on the Law of Patents for Inventions and of Copyright*. London: Joseph Butterworth & Son, 1823.

Goldstein, Judith, Robert Owen Keohane, eds. *Ideas and Foreign Policy: Beliefs, Institutions, and Political Change*. New York: Cornell University Press, 1993.

Hasnas, John. 1995 The Myth of the Rule of Law. *Wisconsin Law Review*, 1995.

Hindmarch, W. M. *A Treatise on the Law Relative to Patent Privileges for the Sole Use of Inventions: And the Practice of Obtaining Letters Patents for Inventions, 431*. London: Stevens & Norton & Benning, 1846.

Hoff, P. *Inventions in the Marketplace: Patent Licensing and the US Antitrust Laws*. Washington, DC: American Enterprise Institute, 1986.

Hofstadter, R. *The American Political Tradition: And the Men Who Made It*. New York: Vintage, 2011.

Holdsworth, William S. *A History of English Law*, 3rd ed., vol. 4. London: Methuen, 1945.

Hollabaugh, M. A., R. Wright. Compulsory Licensing under Antitrust Judgments. Staff Report, Subcommittee on Patents, Trademarks, and Copyrights, US Senate Committee on the Judiciary. Washington, 1960.

Hulme, E. W. On the Consideration of the Patent Grant, Past and Present. 13 *LAW Quarterly Review,* 313, 315, 1897.

Hulme, E. Wyndham. Privy Council Law and Practice of Letters Patent for Invention from the Restoration to 1794 (pt. 2). 33 *Laws Quarterly Review*, 1917.

Janzen, Daniel H. When Is it Coevolution 34 *Evolution*, 611–612, May, 1980.

Kastriner, L. G.. The Revival of Confidence in the Patent System. 73 *Journal of Patent. & Trademark offical Society*, 1991.

Khan, B. Zorina. *The Democratization of Invention: Patents and Copyright in American Development, 1790–1920.* New York: Cambridge University Press, 2005.

Kinsella, S. *There's No Such Thing as a Free Patent*, Mises Daily, 2012.

Klitzke, Ramon A., Historical Background of the English Patent Law. 41 *Journal of the Patent office Society*, September, 1959.

Kramer, Larry D. When Lawyers Do History. 72 *George Washington Law Review*, 2003.

Ladas, S. P. *The International Protection of Industrial Property*. Cambridge: Harvard University Press, 1930.

Lamoreaux, N. R., K. L. Sokoloff. Long- Term Change in the Organization of Inventive Activity. 93 *Proceedings of the National Academy of Sciences*, 1996.

Lemley, M. A. IP in a World Without Scarcity. *NYUL Review*, 2015.

Long, P. O. Invention, Authorship, "Intellectual Property," and the Origin of Patents: Notes Toward a Conceptual History. *Technology and Culture*, 1991.

Long, Weissman R. Strange Trips: the Pharmaceutical Industry Drive to Harmonize Global Intellectual Property Rules, and the Remaining WTO Legal Alternatives Available to Third World Countries. *University of Pennsylvania Journal of International Economic La*, 1996.

Machlup, F., E. Penrose. The Patent Controversy in the Nineteenth Century. 10 *The Journal of Economic History*, 1950.

Mackenney, Richard. *Tradesmen and Traders: The World of the Guilds in Venice and Europe, c.1250 – c.1650.* Totowa, NJ: Barnes and Noble Books, 1987.

MacLeod, C. The1690s Patents Boom: Invention or Stock- Jobbing?, 39 *The Economic History Review*, 1986.

MacLeod, C. The Paradoxes of Patenting: Invention and Its Diffusion in 18th- and 19th century Britain, France, and North America. 32 *Technology and Culture*, 1991.

MacLeod, C. *Inventing the Industrial Revolution*. New York: Cambridge Books, 2002.

Mandich, G. Venetian Origins of Inventors' Rights. *Journal of the Patent Office Society*, 1960.

Mandich, Giulio. Venetian Patents (1450— 1550). 30 *Journal of the Patent Office Society*, 1948.

May, C. The Venetian Moment: New Technologies, Legal Innovation and the Institutional Origins of Intellectual Property. *Prometheus*, 2002.

May, C., S. K. Sell. *Intellectual Property Rights: A Critical History*. Boulder, CO: Lynne Rienner Publishers, 2006.

May, C. The Hypocrisy of Forgetfulness: The Contemporary Significance of Early Innovations in Intellectual Property. 14 *Review of International Political Economy*, 2007.

Merges, R. P. As Many as Six Impossible Patents Before Breakfast: Property Rights for Business Concepts and Patent System Reform. *Berkeley Technology Law Journal*, 1999.

Merges, R. P. One Hundred Years of Solicitude: Intellectual Property Law, 1900–2000. 88 *California Law Review*, 2000.

Mossoff, A. Rethinking the Development of Patents: An Intellectual History, 1550–1800. 52 *Hastings Law Journal*, 2000.

Mossoff, A. Who Cares What Thomas Jefferson thought about Patents- Reevaluating the Patent Privilege in Historical Context. *Cornelll. Review*, 2006.

Nicholas of Cusa. Opera omnia, ed. *L. Bauer*, Leipzig, 1937.

Ostry, S. Governments & Corporations in a Shrinking World: Trade & Innovation Policies in the United States, Europe & Japan. New York: *Council on Foreign Relations*, 1990.

Perovic, S. The Frankenstein of 1790 and Other Lost Chapters from Revolutionary France. *American Historical Review*, 2013.

Plant, Arnold. The Economics Theory Concerning Patents for Innovation, 1 *Economica*, 30–51, 1934.

Pohlmann, H. The Inventor's Right in Early German Law. 43 *Journal of the Patent Office Society*, 1961.

Prager, F. D. The Early Growth and Influence of Intellectual Property. *Journal of the Patent Office Society*, 1952.

Prager, Frank D. A History of Intellectual Property from 1545 to 1787. 26 *Journal of the Patent Office Society*, 711, 1944.

Reichman, J. H. The TRIPS Component of the GATT's Uruguay Round: Competitive Prospects for Intellectual Property Owners in an Integrated World Market. 4 *Fordham Intell. Prop. Media & Ent. LJ*, 1993.

Rodrik, D. Comments on Maskus and Eby-Konan, in *Analytical and Negotiating Issues in the Global Trading System*. Ann Arbor, MI: University of Michigan Press, 1994.

Ryan, M. P. The Function-Specific and Linkage- Bargain Diplomacy of International Intellectual Property Law-Making. 19 *University of Pennsylvania Journal of International Economic Law*, 1998.

Sawyer, K. The Collaborative Nature of Innovation. *Washington University Journal of Law and Policy*, 2009.

Schiff, E. *Industrialization without National Patents: The Netherlands, 1869—912; Switzerland, 1850—1907*. Princeton, NJ: Princeton University Press, 2015.

Scotchmer, S. Standing on the Shoulders of Giants: Cumulative Research and the Patent Law. *Journal of Economic Perspectives*, 1991.

Scotchmer, S. *Innovation and Incentives*. MIT Press, 2004.

Sen, G. Comment on Gill and Law. 16 *Millennium-Journal of International Studies*, 1987.

Sherwood, R. M. *Intellectual Property and Economic Development*. Boulder, CO: Westview Press, 1990.

Stapleton, D. H., D. H. Stapleton. The Origin of American Railroad Technology, 1825—1840. *Railroad History*, 1978.

Strange, S. The Persistent Myth of "Lost" Hegemony. *International Organization*, 1987.

Syzdek, N. A. Five Stages of Patent Grief to Achieve 3D- Printing Acceptance. *USFL Review*, 2015.

Thornton, W. *Short Account of the Origin of Steamboats*. Washington, DC: Rapine and Eliot, 1983.

Uchitele, Louis. In a Productivity Surge, No Proof of A "New Economy". *New York Times*, 10 August 2008.

Vaidyanathan, S. *Copyrights and Copywrongs*. New York: NYU Press, 2001.

Walterscheid, E. C. The Early Evolution of the United States Patent Law: Antecedents (Part1). *Journal of Patent & Trademark Offical Society*, 1994.

Walterscheid, E. C. To Promote the Progress of Science and Useful Arts: The Background and Origin of the Intellectual Property Clause of the United States Constitution. *Journal of Intellectual Property Law*, 1994.

Walterscheid, E. C. Patents and the Jeffersonian Mythology. *Journal of Marshall Laws Review*, 1995.

Walterscheid, E. C. *The Nature of the Intellectual Property Clause: A Study in Historical Perspective*. New York: William S. Hein & Co., Inc., 2002.

Walterscheid, Edward C. The Early Evolution of the United States Patent Law: Antecedents (part2). *Journal of Patent & Trademark Offical Society*, 1994.

Webster, Thomas. *Reports and Notes of Cases on Letters Patent for Inventions*, Vol. 1. London: T. Blenkarn, 1844.

Weiss, Pia. *Patent Policy: Legal- Economic Effects in a National and International France-Work*. London and New York: Routlege Taylor and Francis Group, 2010.

Wilks, Stephen. Comparative Capitalism and the Political Power of Business, in *Globalization and Capitalist Diversity: Experience on the Asian Mainland*. Florence: European University Institute, 1996.

Woods, N. Economic Ideas and International Relations: Beyond Rational Neglect. 39 *International Studies Quarterly*, 1995.

Wyman, W. I. The Patent Act of 1836. *Journal of the Patent Office Society*, 1918.

Index

abolitionism movement 148
accumulative innovations 190–1
Acontius, Jacobus 83
Act of Subsidizing Arts and Science 125
Act on Derived Rights of the Patent (1762) 75–6, 88
actors/participants 16; artificial selection mechanism 25–6; bounded rationality 19; heterogeneous 19, 20, 28; self-interested 19, 26
Adams, John 129
Advisory Committee on Trade Negotiation (ACTN) 179, 180
agrarian state 129–30, 137
Agreement on Trade-Related Aspects of Intellectual Property Rights (TRIPS Agreement) 8, 11, 175, 179–84, 189, 195, 196
Agricultural Book of Chen Fu 44
agricultural economy 25, 42, 44, 48, 75, 87, 128, 130, 139
Agrippa, Marcus Vipsanius 41
Alchian, Armen 17
alienation, Post-industrial Age 184–93; Achilles' Heel 185–8; all-powerful patent system 189–92; competition strategy 185–8; concept of 184–5; forms of 185–93; irrational expansions, private right of patents 188–9; one size fits all approach 189–92; patent alliances/patent standards 187; patent applications 192–3; patent lawsuits 192–3; tool of enterprises 185–8; transfer of rights and properties 184
all-powerful patent system 189–92
American Civil War 147
American enterprise groups 177–9, 181–3; international IPR protection framework 178–9; lobby and design skills 178–9; property rights 179
American fashion industry 230–1
American patent privilege system, eighteenth century 127–36; agrarian state 129–30; Constitution (1787) 131; intellectual rights clause 131–2; Jefferson's influence, early patent system 131–6; modern patent system 131–2; monopoly privilege 131; motivations 127–31; *Patent Act (1790)* 132–4; *Patent Act (1793)* 134–6; republican thoughts 129–31; technological/economic/capitalist structure 127–8
American patent privilege system, nineteenth century 136–41; agrarian state 137; economic thoughts 136–7; individualism 137–8; industrial and commercial capitalists 136–7; liberalism 137–8; motivations 136–9; *Patent Act (1836)* 139–41; republican thoughts 138; technologies 136–7
American Property (Banner) 29
ancient Egypt 38, 39, 45, 47
ancient Greece *see* Greece
Anderson, Chris 212
Anderson, Collison 225
Anglo–American law system 8
Anti-Counterfeiting Trade Agreement (ACTA) 184, 189, 196
anti-patent movement 2, 10, 142–9; abolitionism movement 148; economic crisis/depression 147–8; failures 147–9; free trade theory 143–7, 150; interest groups and support 148–9; international trade freedom theories 143; motivations 142–5; technological innovation/industrial production 147; trade protectionism 147, 148, 150
anti-public tragedies 189
Aoki, Masahiko 17, 30

Apollonius 39
Archimedes 39, 40
Arendt, Hannah 219
Aristarchus 39
Aristotle 39, 41
Arnold, William 1
Arthur, Brian 22, 207
artificial intelligence (AI) technologies 210–1
artificial selection mechanism 25–7; bottom-up institutional arrangement 26; compulsory institutional change 27; top-down institutional arrangement 27; zero-sum game 26
Art of Craft (Senini) 53

Babbage, Charles 144
Bacon, Francis 54, 86
Banner, Stuart 29
bargaining 27
Barnes, Joseph 139
Basalla, George 23, 224
The Battle for Patent Abolition in England in the 19th Century (Zong) 5
Baudrillard, Jean 169
Bauer, Georg 77
Bayh-Dole Act (1980) 177
Bell, Daniel 165
Bern Convention (1886) 175
Berty, Florentine 83
Besson, Jacques 71
big data 208
biological evolution 4, 18, 19
biological metaphors 19
Bi, Sheng 44, 51
Bismarck, Otto Eduard Leopold von 146
Blackstone, William 46
Böhmert, Viktor 146
bold assumptions 3, 15
bottom-up institutional arrangement 26
Boufflers 117–8
bounded rationality theory 18
Bracha, Oren 6
Braithwaite, John 192
Bramah, Joseph 124
Braudel, Fernand 68
Bretton Woods Institutions 168
British Glorious Revolution 120
British Industrial Revolution 50, 70, 107, 111, 112, 116, 127, 128, 144
British patent privilege system 80–7; Dacey Case 86; House of Tutors 81–2; Ipswich Weaver Case 86; liberal tradition 85; motivations 80–2; operation terms 83; power struggle 85–7; principle of common law 86; *Statute of Monopolies (1623)* 85–7; succession 82–5
Buccafusco, Christopher 227
bureaucracy-centered thoughts 45
Burgon, Andrew 68
Burk, Dan L. 192
Byzantine Empire 63

Caesar, Tiberius 42
cameralism 58–60
Campbell, Donald 21
capital society 170
Caractere civilite 73
Cardozo, Benjamin N. 206
cautious confirmation 3, 15
Charles V 78, 82
Chen, Hefang 5
Chen, Yinke 44
Chevalier, Michel 146
China 44–5
Christianity 42, 43, 49, 52, 53, 55
civil law system, private right of patents 109–19
civil society organizations 221
Clark, Charles 228
Cline, Benjamin Fullan 129
Coase, Ronald Harry 169
Cobden, Richard 143
Colbert, Jean-Baptiste 57, 110
Collaborative Commons 218
collaborative consumption 216–7
combinatorial evolution 22
The Coming of Post-Industrial Society (Bell) 165
common law system, private right of patents: controversies 119–21; investigations/clarifications 122–7; laissez-faire approach 122; Privy Council 120, 123; textual law *vs.* law in practice 122
Commons, John R. 15, 17, 19
Communication Act (1934) 226
comparative research method 9
compulsory institutional change 27
Condorcet 112
Confucianism 45
consciousness 20–1
Coombe, Rosemary 224
copyright protection 228
Coulomb, Charles Augustin de 110
Cozza, John 211

Creative Commons Organization (CCO) 221
creative industries 234
Cromwell, Thomas 82
Ctesibius 39
The Cult of Information (Roszak) 170
cultural accumulative effect 217
cultural populists 217

d'Alembert, Jean le Rond 110
Dalmaticu, Blasius 78
Daumas, Maurice 166
David, Paul 7
Declaration of Independence 130
deity–humanity relationship 37
Delbrück, von Rudolf 146
Democritus 39, 41
De Natura Fossilium (Bauer) 77
De re Metallica (Bauer) 77
Desai, Deven 213
diachronic interpretation 1–2
Diamond Age (Stephenson) 224
Diderot, Denis 113
The Discourse and Reality of Intellectual Property Rights: A Treatise on the History of Copyright, Patents, and Trademarks (Huang) 5, 6
discrete innovations 190–1
disenchantment 52–4
Drahos, Peter 192
Durkheim, Emile 15

Edison, Thomas 147, 171
Elizabeth I, Queen 80, 82, 86
Ellul, Jacques 207
Enlightenment 112–3, 115, 129, 138
Eratosthenes 39
Euclid 39
Euripides 41
European Database Order 232
Evans, Oliver 128
evolutionary epistemology 21
evolutionary motivations, Post-industrial Age 164–75; authority structure changes 173–4; capital society 170; diversification 166–7; dominant force of economy 172–3; economic globalization 168–9; explosive growth 166–7; global trade knowledge products 168–9; knowledge-based economy 165; knowledge-based value 165; knowledge explosion 166; knowledge-intensive high-technology 167; neoliberalism 169–70; organized interest groups 174; paternalism 173; private ownership 169; technological dissemination 166; technological innovation/economic development 165–9; technological innovation paradigm 170–2; Washington Consensus 169
evolutionary theory model 4–5, 7, 9

Fauchard, Emmanuelle 227
Fay, Charles-Francois du 110
Federal Court Reform Act 177
feudal privilege system 112, 113
Feuerbach, Ludwig Andreas 184
First Industrial Revolution 37, 107, 142, 150, 194
first-mover advantage 226, 228, 231
Fitch, John 133
Fitch, Samuel 127
Foray, D. 195
Fourth Technological Revolution 208
Francis I, King 73
Freeman, Christopher 142
Free Software Foundation (FSF) 221
free trade theory 143–7, 150
French Industrial Revolution 10, 110, 111, 116
French patent privilege system 70–7; *Act on Derived Rights of the Patent* (1762) 75–6, 88; early practices 72–5; evolution 72–5; motivations 70–2; physiocratic power 75–6
French private right system of patents 110–9; associations of scientific inventions 116–7; Boufflers 117–8; eighteenth century 110–6; Enlightenment 112–3, 115; feudal privilege system 112, 113; handicraft industry 110–1; industrial/commercial capitalism 111, 115; *Lettre sur le Commerce de la Librairie* (Diderot) 112–5, 117; mercantilism policy 111; national commercial policy 111; *Patent Act* (1790) 118–9; rigid guild system 111; technological inventions 110
Frumkin, Maximilian 6
Fullon, Abel 73

Galbraith, John Kenneth 172
Galen 40
Gallas, Louis 127
Geertz, Clifford 22
General Agreement on Tariff and Trade (GATT) 179, 180

General Introduction on Tools (Besson) 71
Generalized Scheme of Preferences (GSP) movements 182
German Empire 145
German patent privilege system 77–80; evolution 78–80; motivations 77–8
Gibbon, Edward 42
global trade knowledge products 168–9
Gluck, Marissa 228
Godson, Richard 125
Goering, Jacques 180
Gorin, Jacques 177
Greece/Greeks 37, 39–43, 45–50, 52–4, 63, 118, 218
Green Peace Organization 189
gross domestic product (GDP) 168, 171, 172, 192
Grossman, G.M. 174
gross national product (GNP) 167
Guidotti, Antonio Sir 82

Habermas, Jürgen 218
Hamilton 129
Hayek, Friedrich 17
Hedler, Hans 78
Hegel, Georg Wilhelm Friedrich 42, 184
Heidegger, Martin 207
Helpman, E. 174
Hemphill, C. Scott 229
Henry II, King 73
Henry IV, King 72
Henry VIII, King 82
heterogeneous actors 19, 20, 28
hierarchy of needs 224–5
high coordination 167
high integration 167
high intensity 167
Hindmarch, W.M. 123
Hipparchus 39
Hippel, Eric von 212, 227
Hippocrates 39
The Historical Development of the U.S. Patent System (Sun) 5
historical evolutionary process 206
historical investigation methods 8
historical materials 8
historical research methods 3–4
The History and Inspiration of the U.S. Patent System (Chen) 5
A History of Intellectual Property from 1545 to 1787 (Prager) 6
Hobbes, Thomas 184
Hobsbawm, Eric 147
Holmes, Oliver Wendell Jr. 1
Holy Roman Empire 42, 49, 59, 77, 78, 82
House of Commons 86, 144
House of Tutors 81–2
Huang, Haifeng 5, 6
Hulmes, E.W. 123
human capital 24
human intelligence 19
humanism 52, 54, 55, 77
human self-needs 224–5
Hu, Shi 3, 15
Huth, Johannes 226

Independence War 121, 127–41
individual absolute property theory 138, 139
individualism 137–8
induced innovation theory 225–6
Industrial Age 10–1, 107–52; American patent privilege system 127–41; anti-patent movement 142–9; civil law system, private right of patents 109–19; common law system, private right of patents 119–41; enlightenment 149–52; French private right system of patents 110–9 *see also* private right of patents
Industrial Revolution 37, 50, 70, 107, 110–2, 116, 127, 128, 137, 142, 144, 147, 150, 166, 194
industrial society 165
Ingersoll, Joseph 135
institutional evolution model 4, 8, 9, 11, 15–31; applications 28–31; artificial selection mechanism 25–7; background 17–9; institutions 16–7; mutation mechanism 20–5; organization 17; physical environment 16; regulated concepts 17; replication mechanism 27–8; significance 17–9; society 16; structure 16
institutional transition 15, 17, 20
Intellectual Property Committee (IPC) 176, 179–81
The Intellectual Property from Historical Perspective (Li) 6
intellectual property rights (IPRs): database industry 231–3; fashion industry 230–1; "Feist Case" 231–3; institutions 1, 3, 6, 7, 11, 12, 30; negative space 229–33; protection 8, 170, 175–84, 193–6, 223, 225, 229–30, 234
Intellectual Property Rights: A Critical History (Christopher and Susan) 7

intellectual rights clause 131–2
International Intellectual Property Alliance (IIPA) 179
internationalization, Post-industrial Age 175–84; American enterprise groups 177–9, 181–3; IPC 179–81; IPR protection 175–84; transnational association 180–1; TRIPS Agreement 175, 179–84
international trade freedom theories 143
Internet of Things (IoTs) 208–9
Inventor Bylaws (1474) 61, 63–5
Islamic world 43–4

Jackson, Ella 173
James I, King 85, 86
Jefferson, Thomas 129, 139
Justinian I 42

Kairys, David 2, 30, 164
Kelly, Kevin 22
Keynesianism 169
Khan, Zorina 119
knowledge: explosion 166; society 165; for technologies 21
knowledge-based economy 165
knowledge-based value 165
knowledge factory 217
knowledge-intensive high-technology 167
knowledge-sharing culture 217–8
Kondratieff cycle 142
Kramer, Larry 29
Kuhn, Thomas Samuel 107

La Fontaine 113
Lauder, Mike 144
Lauren, Ralph 231
Lavoisier, Antoine-Laurent de 110
Law of Rewarding Inventions (1453) 64
Lemley, Mark. A. 192, 211
Lessig, Lawrence 225, 228
Lettre sur le Commerce de la Librairie (Diderot) 112–5, 117
Leucippus 39
Levandowski, Anthony 211
Levy, Jack 28
liberal economic theory 129
liberalism 137–8
Li, Chen 30, 226
Lin, Yifu 17, 26
literature reviews 5–7
"Living Things No Patent" movement 189
Li, Zonghui 6
Louis XI, King 72
Louis XIV, King 57, 71, 74, 110
Lucas, Robert 24
Lucretius 41
Lusan, Francisco 142
Luther, Martin 77

Machlup, Fritz 117
MacLeod, Christine 122
Madison, James 129
Magliocca, Gerard 213
Magna Carta 86
Mandich, Giulio 61
Manutius, Aldus 68, 73
Marini, Antonio 63, 67
market power 225–7
Marshall, Alfred 17
Marxist historical materialism 4
Marx, Karl 15, 17, 184
Maslow, Abraham 224
material coding machine 224
McCarthy, John 210
McPhee, Robert Andrew 144
Menger, Carl 17
mercantilism policy 58–63, 75; *1474 Inventor Bylaws* 61, 63–5; cameralism 58–60; French private right system of patents 111; industrial/commercial policies 60–3; product of balance of interests 63–5; Venice myth 58–60
Merges, Robert P. 188
Metallography (Agricola) 53
Middle Ages 9, 29, 37; China 44–5; cultural environment 48–9; economic form 48; economic values 49; Islamic world 43–4; technological development 47–8; Western Europe 42–3
Mill, John Stuart 217
model analysis method 8
Mokyr, Joel 23, 54
Moore, Gordon 166
Moore's Law 166
Mossoff, Adam 135
motivations 45–9; American patent privilege system 127–31, 136–9; British patent privilege system 80–2; French patent privilege system 70–2; Venetian patent privilege system 50–6 *see also* evolutionary motivations, Post-industrial Age
Müller, John 148
Mumford, Lewis 112
Murray, William 139
mutation mechanism 20–5; agricultural economy 25; cultural activity 22;

economic activity 22, 23; institutional concepts 20–1; material force 21; symbol control mechanism 22; technological advances/influences/innovations 24–5; technology/economy/culture concepts 21–2; technology/economy/culture relationships 22–5
Mutio, Theses 73, 74

Nakayama, Nobuhiro 164
Napsterization 213
narrative interpretation 1–2
National Association for the Promotion of Social Science 145
natural evolution 17
natural right theory 119, 139
neoliberalism 169–70
Neolithic Age 38
The New Industrial State (Galbraith) 194
New Machinery (Verentius) 53
nongovernmental organizations (NGOs) 221
non-IPR protection mechanisms: market power 225–7; social principles 227–8; technological means 228–9
Non-Scarce World (Lamley) 222
No Right to Request the Patent (Godson) 125
North American Free Trade Agreement (NAFTA) 182, 183
North, Douglass C. 15

Oeconomicus (Xenophon) 40
Olsen, Mancur 174
one-size-fits-all patent system 11, 189–92
On Floating Bodies (Archimedes) 39
On Inventors (Virgil) 53
On Minerals (Bauer) 77
Opel, John 177
Open- Source Initiative (OSI) 221
Oram, Andy 224
Organization of Economic Cooperation and Development (OECD) 165
organizations, institutional evolution model 17
organized interest groups 174
The Origin of Patents (Frumkin) 6
Ottoman Empire 69, 89
Owen, George 29

Paleolithic Age 38
Pareto Optimality 26
Paris Convention 149, 175
Parisian Congress 72–5
participatory culture 217–8
Patent Act (1790) 118–9, 121, 132–4
Patent Act (1791) 145, 146
Patent Act (1793) 134–6
Patent Act (1836) 139–41
Patent Committee 121, 126, 132–5
Patent Law Amendment Act (1852) 144
patent privatization 2
patent privilege system 6, 7, 9–12, 49–87; America 127–41; Britain 80–7; France 70–7; Germany 77–80; paradigm 107–9; Venice 49–70
Patent Protection Academy 149
patent system: evolutionary theory model 4–5, 7, 9; historical research methods 3–4; historical thinking 2–3; institutional evolution model 4, 8, 9, 11, 15–31; literature reviews 5–7; Marxist historical materialism 4; research methods 8–9; research subjects 7–8; scientific/reasonable perspectives 4, 15*see also* Industrial Age; patent privilege system; Post-industrial Age; Pre-industrial Age; private right of patents; technological age
paternalism 173
Petri, Franciscus 63
Philebus (Plato) 41
physical environment 16
physiocratic power 75–6
The Place of Science in Modern Civilization (Veblen) 46
Plato 40–2
Plutarch 40
Poems and Painting on Farming and Weaving 44
Pollard, William 133
Popper, Karl 21, 29
Post-industrial Age 11, 164–96; alienation 184–93; enlightenment 193–6; evolutionary motivations 164–75; internationalization 175–84
post-industrial society 165
Prager, Frank D. 6
Pratt, Edmund 177
Pre-industrial Age 9–10, 37–89, 108; ancient world 39–42; British patent privilege system 80–7; China 44–5; enlightenment 87–9; French patent privilege system 70–7; German patent privilege system 77–80; Islamic world 43–4; Middle Ages *see* Middle Ages; social development 42–5; Venetian patent privilege system 49–70; Western Europe 42–3
pre-industrial society 165

private ownership 169
private right of patents 7, 10, 11; anti-patent movement 142–9; enlightenment 149–52; irrational expansions of 188–9; origin in civil law system 109–19; origin in common law system 119–41; paradigm 107–9 *see also* American patent privilege system, eighteenth century; American patent privilege system, nineteenth century; French private right system of patents; Post-industrial Age
Privy Council 83, 120, 123
product of balance of interests 63–5
The Property Right Attributes of Patent Rights: A Study on the Path of Privatization of Technology (Zhang) 5
The Protestant Ethic and the Spirit of Capitalism (Weber) 54
Pryor, Frederic L. 172
Ptolemy 40, 49
public field theory 218–9
public praise 227
Pullan, Henry 54
punctuated equilibrium 18
The Pursuit of Technology (Heidegger) 207
pyramid model 224

Radio Act (1927) 226
Rawls' principles of justice 219
Reagen, Ronald 169
recognition surplus theory 218
recording charge system 228
Recurrent Neural Network (RNN) 211
Reformation 74, 77, 81, 87, 148
Reichman, J.H. 173
Renaissance movement 52, 54, 55, 71, 77, 78, 87
replication mechanism 27–8; bargaining 27; private property 27; public property 27; stabilize/legalize rules 27–8
republican thoughts 129–31, 138
research methods 8–9; comparative method 9; historical investigation methods 8; historical materials 8; model analysis method 8
research subjects 7–8
Ricardo, David 23, 143
Rifkin, Jeremy 172, 208, 211
Rome/Romans 37, 40–3, 45–7, 48–50, 52, 70, 77, 78, 80
Romer, Paul 24
Rostow, W.W. 172
Roszak, Theodore 170
Rousseau, Jean-Jacques 113, 184
Royal French Academy of Science 74

Saw, Keith 212
Sayre, Susan K. 221
scale effect 24
scenario analysis 8
Schiff, Eric 151
Schumpeter, Joseph 17, 172
Schwab, Klaus 208, 211
Science, Technology & Society in Seventeenth Century Britain (Merton) 54
scientific and reasonable model *see* institutional evolution model
scientific methods 3
Second Industrial Revolution 147, 150, 166
selection mechanism *see* artificial selection mechanism
self-centralism 19
self-interested actors 19, 26
Sell, Susan K. 2, 30, 164
semiotic democracy 217–8
Seneca 41
Sinnreich, Aram 228
Slater, Samuel 128
Smith, Adam 23, 75, 116, 124, 129, 143, 145
Smith Growth 24
Smith, Henry 83
Smith, John Prince 145
Social Contract (Rousseau) 113
social development: Islamic world 43–4; Song Dynasty 44–5; in Western Europe 42–3
social knowledge 21
social principles 227–8
society 16
socioeconomic evolution 4, 17
Socrates 40
Solow Growth Phenomenon 23
Solow, Robert 23
Song Dynasty 44, 45
Sophocles 41
Spannaus, Nancy 59
Spencer, Herbert 17
Spinello, Richard 228
Statute of Monopolies (1623) 85–7
Statute of Monopolies (1624) 5, 37, 88, 120, 122, 131
Stephenson, Neal 224
Stop Online Piracy Act (SOPA) 222
structure, institutional evolution model 16
Structure Transformation in Public Fields (Habermas) 218

Studies on the History of Patent Law in the United States (Yang) 5
"studying at work" 24
A Study of China's Modern Patent System (1859–1949) [Xu] 5
A Study of the Development of the British Patent System (Zou) 5
Substantive Patent Law Treaty (SPLT) 184, 196
Suk, Jeannie 229
Sun, Xuhua 5
Su, Song 44
Swiss Patent Law 149
symbol control mechanism 22
symbolic environment 22
systematical dynamics 16
system theory 22

Tang Dynasty 44
Taoism 45
technological age 206–35; artificial intelligence (AI) technologies 210–1; big data 208; collaborative consumption 216–7; copyright protection 228; cultural accumulative effect 217; economic structure/dominant force 213–7; enterprise groups 225–9; hierarchy of needs 224–5; human self-needs 224–5; innovation/economic development 211–7; Internet of Things 208–9; knowledge-sharing and participatory culture 217–8; paradigm 212–3; public field theory 218–9; recognition surplus theory 218; rise of makers/low cost creations 212–3; semiotic democracy 217–8; three-dimensional (3D) printing 209–10; trans-organizational innovations 212; zero marginal cost society 211, 214–6, 219–20, 222
technological dissemination 166
technological means 228–9
Technology of Thermal Processing (Billinguccio) 53
Thatcher, Margaret Hilda 169
Theodoros 41
A Theory of Human Motivation (Maslow) 23
theory of natural rights 119, 139
Third Industrial Revolution 166
Third Technological Revolution 164
Thornton, William 134
three-dimensional (3D) printing 209–10
Toot, Zach 211
top-down institutional arrangement 27
Trade Act (1974) 182
trademarks 230
trade protectionism 147, 148, 150
Traité de Dynamique (d'Alembert) 110
Traité élémentaire de chimie (Lavoisier) 110
trans-organizational innovations 212
Trans-Pacific Partnership (TPP) Agreement 184, 189, 196
trends and tides 227
Turkish Empire 64
Turquetti, Edini 72
Tusnikas, Johns 62

Unified International Bureau of International Protection of Intellectual Property Rights 149
Uruguay Round Negotiations 180–2

Valenti, Jack 222
Various Artificial Machines (Rammerli) 71
Varro 40
Veblen, Thorstein Bunde 15, 17
Venetian patent privilege system 49–70; Athena's gift 52–4; authorization and practice 66–9; disenchantment 52–4; industrial and commercial economy 50–2; industrial premature development 50–2; mercantilism policy 58–63; motivation aspects 50–6; Renaissance innovation 52–4; technology protections 56–8
Venetian Patents (Mandich) 6
video cassette recording (VCR) 222
virtual order 16
Vitruvius 40, 46–7

Walterscheid, Edward C. 139
Washington Consensus 169
Weber, Max 15, 22, 54, 81
Webster, Dan 139
White, Christopher 59
Whitney, Eli 128
whole brain emulation 211
Wilkins, John 81
Wonderful Machines (Ramilli) 53
World Bank 168
World Intellectual Property Organization (WIPO) 181, 184, 189
World Trade Organization (WTO) 175, 183, 184, 189
Wu, Jun 208, 211

Xenophon 40
Xu, Haiyan 5

Yang, Lihua 5
Yoshiyuki, Tamura 226

zero marginal cost society 211, 214–6, 219–20, 222
zero-sum game 26
Zhang, Xinfeng 5
Zong, Hua 5
Zou, Lin 5
Zuang, Wuchang 169

Kolibri 360 GmbH
Ferdinand-Jühlke-Straße 7
99095 Erfurt, Deutschland
produktsicherheit@kolibri360.de